This is the first of a subseries of specially commissioned collaborative volumes on key topics at the heart of contemporary philosophy of law that will be appearing regularly within *Cambridge Studies in Philosophy and Law*.

Five preeminent legal theorists tackle a range of fundamental questions on the nature of the philosophy of criminal law. Their essays explore the extent to which and the ways in which our systems of criminal law can be seen as rational and principled. The essays discuss some of the principles by which, it is often thought, a system of law should be structured, and they ask whether our own systems are genuinely principled or riven by basic contradictions, reflecting deeper political and social conflicts.

The volume as a whole shows how lively and exciting contemporary legal theory can be.

PHILOSOPHY AND THE CRIMINAL LAW

Cambridge Studies in Philosophy and Law

Other books in the series:

Jeffrie G. Murphy and Jean Hampton: *Forgiveness and Mercy*
Stephen R. Munzer: *A Theory of Property*
R. G. Frey and Christopher W. Morris (eds.): *Liability and Responsibility: Essays in Law and Morals*
Robert F. Schopp: *Automatism, Insanity, and the Psychology of Criminal Responsibility*
Steven J. Burton: *Judging in Good Faith*
Jules Coleman: *Risks and Wrongs*
Suzanne Uniacke: *Permissible Killing: The Self-Defense Justification of Homicide*
Jules Coleman and Allen Buchanan (eds.): *In Harm's Way: Essays in Honor of Joel Feinberg*
Warren F. Schwartz (ed.): *Justice in Immigration*
John Fischer and Mark Revizza: *Responsibility and Control*

Philosophy and the Criminal Law

Principle and Critique

Edited by

ANTONY DUFF

University of Stirling

CAMBRIDGE
UNIVERSITY PRESS

PUBLISHED BY THE PRESS SYNDICATE OF THE UNIVERSITY OF CAMBRIDGE
The Pitt Building, Trumpington Street, Cambridge CB2 1RP, United Kingdom

CAMBRIDGE UNIVERSITY PRESS
The Edinburgh Building, Cambridge CB2 2RU, United Kingdom
40 West 20th Street, New York, NY 10011-4211, USA
10 Stamford Road, Oakleigh, Melbourne 3166, Australia

First published 1998

Printed in the United States of America

Typeset in Times Roman

Library of Congress Cataloging-in-Publication Data

Philosophy and the criminal law : principle and critique / edited by
Antony Duff.
p. cm. – (Cambridge studies in philosophy and law)
ISBN 0-521-55044-0 (hc)
1. Criminal law – Philosophy. I. Duff, Antony. II. Series.
K5018.Z9P48 1998
345′.001 – dc21 97-25899
CIP

*A catalog record for this book is available from
the British Library.*

ISBN 0 521 55044 0 hardback

Contents

Contributors

ANTONY DUFF teaches philosophy at the University of Stirling.

JOHN GARDNER teaches law at King's College, University of London.

DOUGLAS HUSAK teaches philosophy and law at Rutgers University.

NICOLA LACEY teaches law at the London School of Economics.

ALAN NORRIE teaches law at King's College, University of London.

Introduction

ANTONY DUFF

The invitation to edit a collection of new essays on philosophy and the criminal law aroused both excitement and anxiety. The past three decades have seen an upsurge of interest among both philosophers and lawyers in philosophical issues connected with the criminal law – perhaps more in Britain than in the United States. This was clearly related, within academic philosophy, to the revival of political and social philosophy; and, among lawyers, to the strengthening of more theoretical perspectives on the criminal law informed by a range of other disciplines, including philosophy. Against this background, the prospect of editing such a volume was exciting, but it also aroused anxiety about how such a volume should be focused, given the wealth of possible topics that could plausibly be included.

I made three editorial decisions that helped to determine the shape and contents of this collection. The first was to interpret 'philosophy' in a generously inclusive sense. I would look for essays that would take a theoretical and critical – as opposed to, for instance, a purely empirical or doctrinal – perspective on the criminal law, without worrying too much about whether the writers or their essays would count as 'philosophical' in a narrow professional sense. But as well as considering substantive theoretical issues connected to the criminal law, the essays should also have something to say about the very enterprise of theorising, or philosophising, about the criminal law. For in this as in other philosophical contexts, we must face questions not only about the particular substantive topics under philosophical discussion but also about the philosophical activity in which we are trying to engage. Just what should its aims and methods be? What kinds of result should it seek? What is its relationship to, and what kind of impact (if any) should it have on, its subject matter? Of the five essays in this volume, Nicola Lacey's, and the early parts of Douglas Husak's and Alan Norrie's, address this issue most directly; but in different ways, each of the essays has something to say about it.

The second decision was to ask the contributors to focus their essays on the 'general part' of the criminal law, in order to give the volume a reasonably determinate – although still very broad – focus. The 'general part' of a system of criminal law is meant to contain those general principles of criminal liability that apply, if not to *all* particular offences, at least to most of them (section 2 of John Gardner's essay offers a useful classification of the various elements of the general part). Modern textbooks that deal with the general part thus typically include under that heading such items as the 'act requirement' (the main focus of Husak's essay); a general *mens rea,* or 'fault', requirement, together with definitions of the standard species of *mens rea* (intention, knowledge, recklessness, and negligence); causation; such general defences as insanity, infancy, automatism, mistake, duress, and necessity; and the general inchoate crimes of attempt, conspiracy, and incitement (see Articles 2–5 of the *Model Penal Code;* Part I of the English Law Commission's Draft Criminal Code Bill).

Each of the items in that list has been the focus of controversy amongst legal theorists, and some of those controversies figure in the essays in this book (for example, in Husak's critique of the 'act requirement' and in Alan Norrie's discussion of intention). But the orthodox conception of the general part (a conception expressed in such standard textbooks as Williams's *Criminal Law: The General Part,* Smith and Hogan's *Criminal Law,* and Ashworth's *Principles of Criminal Law*)[1] has recently come under attack from two different directions.

On the orthodox view, a system of criminal law can claim to be coherent, rational, and principled only insofar as it is structured by an extensive general part. For it can count as a *system* of law at all (as distinct from a set of discrete and disconnected rules), let alone as a rational and principled system of law, only insofar as its definitions of particular offences (forming the 'special part') are governed and structured by certain general principles; and the role of the general part is precisely to lay down such principles. Of course, the offences defined in the special part will differ from one another in their material or substantive character, dealing as they do with different kinds of harm or wrong. But their definitions should display a common form or structure, provided by the general part. For instance, they should respect the 'act requirement' by specifying the particular kind of 'act' that constitutes the *actus reus* of the offence. They should respect the general requirement of 'fault' or *mens rea* and specify the particular *mens rea* requirement in terms of the concepts defined in the general part. Furthermore, only a system of law structured by such a general part can satisfy the 'rule of law' requirements of certainty and consistency.

Now this conception of a 'rational and principled' criminal law is, of course, an ideal – an ideal that any existing system of law no doubt falls well short of actualising.[2] But on the orthodox view, it is an ideal towards which the law can properly aspire, and one that is at least implicit in our existing systems. They do not merely purport to be rational and principled; that could be mere rhetoric or, in a pejorative sense, rationalisation. They are (although imperfectly) actually structured by such general rationality-ensuring principles. In criticising aspects of the existing law as being irrational or unprincipled (a kind of criticism that such orthodox theorists are very ready to offer), we are thus criticising it in terms of its own internal values and aspirations. Despite the admitted and manifold defects in our existing criminal law, we can therefore engage, with reasonable hope of some success, in a process of 'rational reconstruction'[3]: a process of trying to render the law more consistent, rational, and principled, in terms of the values and principles that are already internal to it.

One kind of attack on this conception of the criminal law as being (in genuine aspiration, and to some degree in actual achievement) rational and principled has come from those associated with or sympathetic to the Critical Legal Studies movement. These critics argue that the criminal law (or at least those existing systems of criminal law, particularly the English and the American, on which discussion tends to focus) is not and cannot hope to become a system coherently structured by rational principles. For the law, and the 'liberal' ideology that informs the contemporary enterprise of 'rational reconstruction', is 'simultaneously beset by internal *contradictions* . . . and by systematic *repression* of the presence of these contradictions.'[4] The point is not merely (as even the most optimistic of rational reconstructers would admit) that the criminal law involves *conflicting* principles and values, between which some compromise or balance must be struck. It is, rather, that no such (rational, principled, or stable) compromise is possible. We should understand the law not (even in its aspirations) as a system of rational principles but rather as the site of various political and social conflicts – conflicts that are concealed rather than resolved by the attempt to identify or reconstruct the 'rational principles' of criminal law. What is required, such critics argue, is a process not of 'rational reconstruction' but of radical deconstruction. Norrie's essay offers a version of this kind of critique, though he prefers to talk of 'antinomies' rather than of 'contradictions.' But he rejects the purely destructive 'trashing' typical of some proponents of Critical Legal Studies[5] in favour of a more constructive attempt to identify and to make better sense of what is genuinely valuable in the 'liberal' tradition that he criticises. Lacey also emphasises one theme that is central to much of this kind of critical writing: the importance of understanding legal doctrines and principles, not as ahistorical expressions of supposedly timeless values or truths but as rooted in, and taking their meaning and significance from, specific historical contexts (from which it follows, of course, that 'contradictions' must also be understood as contingent conflicts). Both Husak's and Gardner's essays implicitly reject this kind of radical critique in identifying certain general principles by which, they claim, the law is (or could and should be) structured. My essay offers a direct response to the charge of 'contradiction' that Norrie has argued in his *Crime, Reason and History:* a response which seeks to rebut that charge, but also to show that it points the way towards certain deep and genuine problems with the preconditions of criminal law – with the kinds of social and political condition whose existence is necessary for the criminal law to have legitimacy.

The second kind of attack on the orthodox conception of the role and significance of the general part comes from those who agree that the criminal law should (and sensibly can) aspire to be 'rational' and 'principled', but differ from orthodox theorists in what they take that aspiration to involve. In particular, as Gardner's essay shows, they argue that a system of criminal law can be appropriately 'rational' and 'principled' *without* being structured by an extensive general part. For, Gardner argues, rationality need not be a matter of following highly general principles: The general part can (and should) thus be far more modest in its scope than orthodox theorists suppose, without this undermining the rationality of the special part (and see section III of Lacey's essay for a sympathetic discussion of recent moves away from the idea of a unitary general part).

My third editorial decision was to try to use this volume to bring about a more fruitful dialogue between 'critical' theorists who attack the idea that the criminal law is (in actuality, or even in genuine aspiration) rational and principled, and their opponents. As both Lacey and Norrie note early in their essays, it often seems as if 'critical' theorists and their 'liberal' opponents (although both these labels are prone to misuse, especially when being applied to theorists by those who oppose them) are talking at or past rather than to each other. Each side rejects utterly, and sometimes with contempt, what the other believes. The engagement between them is barren and destructive rather than constructive, and it generates the strong suspicion that those fervently committed to one side or the other have not done justice to those whom they criticise – that they have created easy targets for themselves by oversimplifying or distorting the others' views. A more open-minded discussion, in which opposing views are attended to more carefully than is all too often the case in these debates, might lead at least to a greater mutual understanding, and perhaps even to a realisation that there is *something* worth listening to in what the others have to say. Both Lacey and Norrie, who might be described as critically sympathetic to some of the central ideas of the radical critics, aim to assist such a dialogue, as does my essay.[6]

The contributors all provide explanatory introductions to their own essays, and I have tried to indicate how the different essays relate to the general theme of this volume. I should, however, say a little more about each of the contributions here.

Lacey's aim is to undermine the distinction, or bridge the gap, between 'critical' theorising about the criminal law and the kind of 'philosophical' theorising that 'critical' theorists attack. There is an important role for philosophical analysis of and theorising about the criminal law and its doctrines – a role that 'critical' theorists are often too quick to dismiss. Such analysis and such theorising must, however, be sensitive (more sensitive than it too often is) to the actual character of that which is to be analysed or theorised. It must attend to the historical and contingent nature of the criminal law and its doctrines, and to its character as a human practice or form of life – which is to say that it must be informed by central features of 'critical' theorists' methodology. It should also attend to the full scope of the criminal law; part of Lacey's target is the tendency amongst criminal law theorists to focus too selectively on certain limited aspects of the criminal justice system. Criminal law theorising must also be more genuinely interdisciplinary than it often tends to be: An adequate (interpretive *and* critical) theoretical approach to the criminal law must draw on the resources of a range of related disciplines. Lacey develops this general argument about the nature of criminal law theorising by discussing some developments in the history of theorising about the general part. She sketches some of the ways in which conceptions of the general part and its significance have changed over the past 200 years, and some of the current moves away from an ambitious conception of an extensive, unified general part. This discussion can be seen as exemplifying the method of theorising for which she argues: an interpretive analysis of legal doctrine (and, in this case, of legal theorising about legal doctrine) that is sensitive to its historical contingency and to its social and political context.

Husak's essay falls squarely within the tradition of theorising about the general part that 'critical' theorists aim to undermine. Indeed, one can see part of its implicit purpose as being to show how that tradition of theorising, which aims to identify the general principles by which our criminal law is and/or should be structured, is still viable. His specific target is the 'act requirement' – the (supposed) requirement, asserted by many theorists, that criminal liability must be for an act. He points up some of the difficulties in deciding what it means to say that liability is *for* an act; and he argues that we will make better sense of the law by replacing the act requirement with a 'control requirement', according to which criminal liability should be imposed only for states of affairs over which the defendant had control. This will also, he argues, further the general project of 'integrating the criminal law with moral philosophy' by making the conditions of criminal responsibility more closely akin to those of moral responsibility. His essay can be seen as a paradigm example of rational reconstruction. As he makes clear in section II of his essay, the claim that criminal liability requires control is not a purely descriptive claim about our existing legal systems, since it is not disproved by the discovery of cases in which liability is imposed for something over which the defendant had no control. Nor is it a purely evaluative claim that the law *should* be structured by such a requirement. It is, rather, the claim that the control requirement can best rationalise (in the nonpejorative sense) existing legal doctrine and practice; and such rationalisation is a process both of (descriptive) interpretation and of (evaluative) justification.

Norrie's concern is with certain fundamental 'antinomies' that, he argues, undermine 'liberal' theorising both about punishment and about the conditions of criminal liability. The central antinomy he identifies is that between the 'ideal' and the 'actual.' The key aspect of that antinomy is the profound tension that exists between the 'ideal' conception of the individual as a responsible agent (and offender) on which liberal thought depends, and the actual character of the political and social contexts within which individuals act – and by which their actions are structured and driven. Liberal theory needs the ideal individual, an autonomous agent abstracted from any concrete social context, as the agent who can justly be held liable, and be punished, for his or her wrongdoing. But at the same time it must, if even modestly honest, recognise the radical gap between the ideal responsible individual thus conceived and the actual nature of agency in a conflictual and unjust society. Norrie identifies a deep tension of this kind in classical and contemporary theorising about punishment and in contemporary discussions of intention as a central determinant of criminal liability. However, whereas other critical theorists might aim to do no more than identify the deep 'contradictions' that thus undermine a liberal ideology of law, Norrie has a more constructive purpose. He goes on to argue that we can develop a more adequate conception of the individual agent by drawing on Harré's 'social constructionist' psychology, which locates the individual firmly within, as partly constituted by, the social. Such as account would not dissolve the antinomies of liberal thought. But it would make explicit, and also intelligible, those 'ambivalences' about individual responsibility that liberal thought represses; and it might thus open the way to a more adequate (though also more untidy and far less comfortable) understanding of criminal liability.

My essay responds to some of Norrie's earlier arguments about the essentially 'contradictory' character of our criminal law. I take as my focus the orthodox doctrine that 'motive' is irrelevant to criminal liability – a doctrine that, Norrie has argued, is one site of the deep contradictions that infect liberal legal ideology. I also, however, offer a more general discussion of what should be meant by saying that some human practice (such as a legal system) is 'rational' and 'principled', or 'contradictory'; and I argue that 'critical' theorists tend to operate with an oversimple conception of rationality and are too quick to identify 'contradictions' where one should rather identify serious, but not rationality-threatening, conflicts. As far as the doctrine about the irrelevance of motive is concerned, I argue that the law is not internally contradictory in the ways that Norrie claims to identify. We can make rational and principled sense of the doctrine, as a doctrine about the proper task of adjudication, resting on an account of the proper separation of powers between the legislature and the courts. However, I also suggest that the critical theorists' charge of 'contradiction' does point us towards some deep problems with our criminal law, problems that have to do not with its *internal* coherence or consistency but with the essential *preconditions* of its legitimacy as a system that claims authority over all members of the society.

Finally, Gardner's essay mounts the second kind of attack that I noted previously on the orthodox view that an extensive general part is needed to make the criminal law 'rational' and 'principled.' He shares with orthodox theorists the ambition of making the law 'rational' and 'principled' – supported, that is, by good reasons, and structured, *when this is appropriate,* by principles that are themselves rationally justified. But he attacks the assumption, which he thinks informs much orthodox theorising about the general part, that the law is rational only insofar as it is principled – only insofar, that is, as its special part is structured by highly general principles (and definitions) that form the 'supervisory' and 'definitional' aspects of the general part. He argues that that assumption is mistaken (as is the related assumption that a Dworkinian distinction between 'principles' and 'policies' is exhaustive as well as exclusive), since it ignores the reality and significance of action-reasons (as distinct from outcome-reasons) that are *neither* instrumental reasons of policy *nor* reasons of principle. He traces the assumption that non-instrumental reasons must be reasons of principle to certain Kantian ideas, and in particular to the conception (which Kant shared with many of his opponents) of well-being as an essentially *passive* matter. He offers instead a more Aristotelian *active* conception of well-being, which will give nonprincipled action-reasons their proper place. He then applies this set of ideas to the criminal law. A recognition of the importance of action-reasons that do not depend on general principles should, he argues, lead us to rethink, and significantly reduce, the scope of the general part of the criminal law, with a corresponding increase of diversity in the special part.

I should, finally, express my thanks to those who have helped bring this project to fruition: in particular to Jules Coleman, the series editor, for his help and encouragement; but especially to the other contributors to this volume. It has been to a significant degree a cooperative enterprise. We all read, and exchanged written comments on, one another's first drafts. We met for a day in London to discuss the drafts and comments – a day that was stimulating and fruitful and as a result of which several of the papers were radically rewritten (and I think all were significantly improved). I hope that the result of all this is a collection of essays that resonate constructively with one another and that will give some idea of the character (and the liveliness) of contemporary philosophical debates about the criminal law. It should also show how much interesting and exciting work there is to be done.

Notes

1 G Williams, *Criminal Law: The General Part* (2nd ed.; London: Stevens 1961) (and see his *Textbook of Criminal Law* (2nd ed; London: Stevens 1983), Part I; J C Smith & B Hogan, *Criminal Law* (8th ed.; London: Butterworths, 1996) Part I; A J Ashworth, *Principles of Criminal Law* (2nd ed.; Oxford: Oxford University Press, 1995), chs. 4–6.

2 More precisely, the systems of law on which British and American theorists focus, i.e. English and American law, fall thus short. One general question which divides theorists is that of how far we can talk about the structure, or the basic principles, of 'criminal law' as such; or how far any analysis must be focused on particular, and historically contingent, legal systems: this is one focus of Lacey's paper, and also informs much of Norrie's work (see *Crime, Reason and History* [London: Weidenfeld & Nicolson, 1993]).

3 See D N MacCormick, 'Reconstruction after Deconstruction: A Response to CLS', (1990) 10 *Oxford Journal of Legal Studies* 539–58.

4 M Kelman, *A Guide to Critical Legal Studies* (Harvard University Press, 1987), 3.

5 See M Kelman, 'Trashing', (1984) 36 *Stanford Law Review* 293–348.

6 Both Norrie and I engage directly with some of the other's previous work. We planned at one stage to add to each of our papers a brief response to the other's criticisms of our earlier work. But, whilst we each certainly benefited from the other's comments on drafts of our papers, we decided against publishing such further responses: partly for reasons of time, but also to avoid adding further layers of argument and counter-argument to papers which were already long and complicated.

1

Contingency, Coherence, and Conceptualism

Reflections on the Encounter between 'Critique' and 'the Philosophy of the Criminal Law'

NICOLA LACEY

> Aristotle *himself has said,* speaking of the laws of his own country, that jurisprudence or the knowledge of those laws is the principal and most perfect branch of ethics.
>
> William Blackstone, *Commentaries on the Laws of England* (1765–9), Volume 1, p. 27

> Human life and philosophical explanations of it move in different planes till the explanation has become so complete as not to interfere with the thing to be explained. When they coincide, they cannot affect each other.
>
> James Fitzjames Stephen, *A History of the Criminal Law of England* (1883), Volume II, p. 84

> [T]he degree of systematization of a discipline is the prime index of the state of knowledge of its subject matter.
>
> Jerome Hall, *General Principles of Criminal Law* (1960), p. 12

Each of these contrasting reflections expresses a different view of legal theory. In this chapter, I consider the relationship between two particular approaches to criminal law theory: 'critique' and 'the philosophy of criminal law.' Whilst the title of my chapter presupposes an opposition between the two, it is in fact one of my main purposes to question that opposition. It is, of course, an opposition which bears some real relationship with the positions held by protagonists in the debate canvassed by Antony Duff in his introduction to this collection. In recent years, a number of British and American writers working within a 'critical' tradition have questioned the basis of 'philo-

I should like to express my gratitude to Lindsay Farmer, Elizabeth Frazer, Alan Norrie, and Lucia Zedner, whose close readings of earlier versions of this chapter were of enormous help in revising it; and to all my fellow contributors in this collection for their constructively critical responses to the first draft. Much remains with which each of these people will disagree, but their contributions undoubtedly improved both the quality of the argument and the clarity with which I have been able to formulate it.

sophical' theories of criminal law which emphasise and seek to elaborate upon its 'principled' nature.[1] In particular, they have questioned such theories' assumptions about the place of rationality, coherence, and systematicity as features of and ideals for both theory itself and criminal law doctrine – the intellectual framework within which the practice of criminal law is taken to be organised. Thus both the Aristotelian assimilation of jurisprudence and ethics cited approvingly by William Blackstone and Jerome Hall's equation of enlightenment with systematization have become particular targets for critical attention.[2]

At root, the critical argument is one with which, curiously, James Fitzjames Stephen might well have found himself in (at least partial) agreement:

> [I]f the philosophy of punishment is essentially contradictory in its forms, and if these forms are based upon legal ideology, then it ought to be possible to understand not only the philosophy of punishment but also the theory and practice of the criminal law as contradictory.[3]

If, as Alan Norrie suggests in this passage, the underlying state of criminal legal practices is in fact one of conflict and incoherence, a doctrinal framework or a theory which suppresses this in its movement of intellectual rationalisation cannot meet the test with which Stephen follows up the statement quoted above: 'One test of the truth of a philosophical explanation of human conduct is its complete harmony with human feeling.'[4] Yet such a test raises the further questions of the nature of the relationships between a theory and that which it purports to illuminate, and between theoretical and practical viewpoints and knowledges. As Jeanette Winterson puts it: 'The earth is round and flat at the same time. This is obvious. That it is round appears indisputable; that it is flat is our common experience, also indisputable. The globe does not supercede the map; the map does not distort the globe.'[5] The possibility has to be considered that Stephen's 'human feeling' – that feeling which structures and characterises not only the theorisation of criminal law but also the enunciation of criminal law doctrine by criminal lawyers themselves – itself suppresses or fails to acknowledge conflict and contradiction. And this possibility, too, has been the focus of critical analysis which has concerned itself with the political reasons underpinning a practical or intellectual commitment to order, consistency, and system.[6]

In this chapter, my enterprise is to use certain aspects of the debate between 'philosophers' and 'critics' as a starting point from which to draw out some general issues about the nature of 'theorising' or 'philosophising about' criminal law and criminal justice. In particular, I want to ask what we can learn about the intellectual, political, and practical significance of the notions of 'coherence' and 'systematicity' from an examination of the changing patterns of rationalising frameworks in the historical development of theories of criminal law. I shall also raise some general issues about the relationship between different intellectual disciplines contributing to the theorisation of criminal law. I do so with a view either to questioning the division between 'philosophy' and 'critique' or – which may come to the same thing – to suggesting that philosophical analysis which does not answer to some of the demands of critical method constitutes an intellectual practice which has little to do with criminal legal practices or, indeed, with any practice other than itself. Conversely, I shall argue that the view of what counts as 'rationality' or 'coherence' taken by many critics is both unduly narrow and inappropriately abstract, with the result that their own position turns out to be unsatisfactory in a curiously similar way to that of their 'philosophical' opponents.

My chapter is divided into three main parts. In the first, I shall ask the naïve question 'What are theories of criminal law?' I shall delineate a number of distinctive yet interrelated tasks, all of which have regularly announced themselves under the umbrella of 'theories of criminal law.' I shall draw on this set of distinctions in order to consider the relationship between 'philosophy' and 'critique' and the contribution of various disciplines to an adequate theoretical analysis of criminal legal practices. Second, focussing on a particular portion of the theorising enterprise which I shall denote as 'interpretive', I shall undertake a brief review of selected theorisations of criminal law from the eighteenth century to the present day. In examining these exemplary cases, I shall trace the changing patterns of theoretical and doctrinal classification, paying attention to the implicit audience for which the theorisations were developed, and the attitude to and conceptions of coherence and systematicity displayed by the various writers. My particular concern will be to map the emerging conception of a 'general part' of criminal law. This is a conception which, as Duff points out, occupies the central place in contemporary attempts to theorise criminal law; it also, significantly, raises important questions about the scope of the practices which properly form the object of criminal law theory. Its relatively recent emergence serves, however, to illuminate both the historical contingency of particular notions of what counts as a coherent or systematic approach and the difficulties inherent in some 'philosophical' theories' assumptions about their own transcendent metaphysical status. Finally, I shall consider significant moves within recent philosophical literature on criminal law theory away from the idea of a 'unitary' conception of the general part. I shall consider the origins of and motivation for this development, and I shall go on to question whether that motivation can in fact be realised within the intellectual framework of criminal law theory as it is often understood. In conclusion, I shall argue that an adequate theorisation of criminal law has to be more historically grounded, more informed by the insights of other disciplines, and more reflective about its own assumptions than is much criminal law theory in Britain and North America.[7]

I. Theories of Criminal Law

i. Different Theoretical Projects?

The briefest survey of scholarship announcing itself as 'criminal law theory' or as 'philosophy of the criminal law' suffices to reveal the broad range of work encompassed within these labels. Criminal law theory stretches from relatively technical discussion of the fundamental tenets of and issues within criminal law doctrine,[8] through more abstract attempts to conceptualise the general framework within which that doctrine operates,[9] to historical analyses of the development of criminal justice ideologies and practices[10] and normative arguments about the proper or ideal shape of that conceptual framework in a liberal, socialist, or other form of political society.[11] It includes not only work focussed on the structure of criminal law doctrine but also work addressed to the broader questions of criminalisation and penality[12]: the actual or proper subject matter of criminal law and its classification;[13] the role of the state in drawing on its power to criminalise;[14] the justification for state punishment in general or in its particular forms.[15] Many works concern themselves with some combination of these issues.[16] Criminal law theory encompasses the work of practising lawyers,[17] of legal academics in both criminal law and jurisprudence,[18] and of moral and political philosophers, linguistic philosophers, and philosophers of mind.[19] As I shall argue, the work of criminologists, historians, and sociologists also has an important bearing on criminal law theory.[20] Furthermore, criminal law theory is written for a variety of audiences: for legal practitioners;[21] for students and academics in law, sociology, criminology, and philosophy; and, though more rarely, for a wider, nonspecialist audience.[22]

One particularly vivid way of distinguishing among these different kinds of theory is that articulated by the philosopher Alan White. White delineates three projects: the scientific/empirical, the evaluative, and the analytic/conceptual. The first concerns itself, for example, with the history of the development of particular forms of liability, such as that based on intention or negligence, or strict or vicarious liability. Its disciplinary resources are primarily history and the social sciences. Second, the evaluative project concerns itself with the arguments for and against such forms of liability, asking, for example, whether liability without proof of fault is morally or politically justifiable. This, White argues, is a matter not of skill and knowledge but of judgments that can be 'argued for, supported and justified. . . . One can be brainwashed, converted, or persuaded into them. But they are not taught and learned like scientific or analytic truths.'[23]

Third, the analytic enterprise concerns itself with clarifying the logical relations internal to the concepts out of which the framework of criminal liability is constructed, tracing the contours of notions such as action, intention, and negligence and taking actual usage as a touchstone. This, White concludes, is the discrete enterprise of jurisprudence or the philosophy of law 'properly so called', as Austin might have put it. For it is the only one to which distinctively philosophical techniques of analysis are exclusively applicable. Philosophers of law, he suggests, may be compared with mapmakers: 'Philosophers are to the users of ideas, including themselves, like preachers to practitioners, critics to poets, grammarians to native speakers, map makers to explorers of the unmapped. . . .'[24]

By way of considering White's controversial conclusion, it is worth further examining the relationship between the three enterprises which he distinguishes. One way of looking at this relationship suggests a certain primacy to the 'empirical' approach. Since all three enterprises concern themselves, albeit from different perspectives, with 'criminal law', it seems obvious that each of them must start out from some general understanding of what 'criminal law' is or has been. Mapmakers, after all, have to set out with an understanding not only of what constitutes 'terrain' but also of which terrain they are to chart. Though this is least constraining in the case of evaluative theories, some such starting point must be taken if they are not to collapse into general political or moral philosophies without any specific institutional focus.[25] Thus at a minimal level all three projects presuppose an institutional conception of their subject matter.

On another view, conceptual analysis has the most salient place. Since any field of human activity such as criminal law depends on a complex set of linguistic practices, the conceptual analysis provided by White's third category may provide the basis for both the 'scientific' investigations of the first project and the evaluative assessments and prescriptions of the second.[26] Without the basic tools of construction and conceptualisation, the mapmaker's enterprise could not be imagined, let alone practised.

Or, finally, it could be argued that the evaluative perspective in fact has a covert primacy. For our (often unarticulated) moral or political presuppositions generally colour the starting points of empirical and conceptual analyses, shaping what we identify as problems or interesting issues and hence influencing the map which we ultimately produce. Mapmakers have a constructive as well as a representational role: They make choices both about which terrain to chart and what kind of chart should be produced, and these are influenced by their values and commitments as well as by their practical purposes. We could draw an analogy here not only with the existence of very different maps – for instance, those oriented to the representation of land levels, navigability of waters, or road routes – but also with those techniques of visual representation that mark out structures of power and dominion, as in the case of the (in)famous pink representing the British Empire in maps of the imperial era.

The fact that the relationship between White's three projects is more intimate than his analytic separation suggests has in part to do with a particular feature of his schema which would be controversial among – and certainly is not in practice honoured by – many philosophers. This is the idea that usage within the relevant speech community is the ultimate test of the validity of analysis of a concept. Evidently, this view presents the philosopher with acute difficulties wherever practice itself varies in an unsystematic way. In this regard it is instructive to note the contortions which White has to undertake in order to reconcile his analytic understanding of the concept of recklessness as involving 'subjective' awareness with the 'objective' conception of recklessness adopted by the House of Lords in the English case of *Caldwell.*[27] It is hard to escape the conclusion that White, here, is implicitly switching to the normative task which he formerly banished to another discipline. The example illustrates the further difficulties for White's approach to conceptual analysis which flow from a social practice such as law in which particular institutions have the power to *stipulate* meanings and (albeit imperfectly) to enforce their usage within a certain discursive arena. Even if one does not go so far as to endorse the 'critical' conclusion that illogicalities or contradictions at the heart of legal concepts are symptomatic of deeper social or political conflicts or repressions, there seems no *a priori* reason to think that judges or legislatures may not sometimes, perhaps often, stipulate or adopt both varying meanings and ones which fall short of philosophical standards of clarity. In this respect, it seems impossible for the conceptual analyst to eschew a significant, albeit limited, normative role.

The idea that conceptual analysis has to answer to the test of usage does, however, have one distinctive feature which differentiates it from the relatively ungrounded conceptual analysis which is very common in criminal law theory. This is that it requires the theorist to tell us, with some specificity, which terrain she is engaged in mapping. In other words, this kind of conceptual analyst has to tie her analysis to usage within a particular domain – typically a particular system or family of systems – and she has to have, at least in principle, an account of what it is that justifies the conceptual gathering together of that particular terrain. If she is to take the test of usage seriously, the basis of this account cannot be purely philosophical; it must be rooted in a historically and socially specific understanding of the relevant practice and its ideological and institutional framework. This is in stark contrast to theoretical analyses of the conceptual framework of criminal law which feel no need to alert the reader to the location in space and time or to the sociopolitical functions of the practice of which the analytic framework purports to be a part.[28] As White argues,[29] this can lead to an odd kind of philosophical 'legislation.'[30] The usage-based approach to conceptual analysis therefore affirms the intimacy of the relationship between social practices and philosophy and hence between the 'empirical' and the 'analytic.' In doing so, it also, crucially, opens conceptual analysis to what we might call an institution-based critique: The historian, the lawyer, the sociologist, or the anthropologist has, as it were, *locus standi* to raise questions about the theorist's understanding of the conceptual framework that he or she purports to analyse and explicate. As Norrie puts it:

> The idea of 'critique' . . . is that of starting from the forms of law in orthodox usage and showing the contradictions within that usage. From there, one moves to examine the fault lines that underlie the operative forms and to explain their existence in a particular social and historical context. In this way, one shows how the legal forms 'hang together' within criminal law discourse, and that there is an historical logic which underlies, suffuses and explains its intrinsic illogic.[31]

Thus the discrete and autonomous philosophical terrain which White maps turns out to be volcanic: The forces for its own disruption and reconstruction come from within itself.

ii. A Contextual and Interpretive Approach

Even this brief discussion suffices to show a more intimate relationship among White's three enterprises than he acknowledges, and certainly a relationship which should make us wary of according priority to any one among them. In this section, I want to go further and to suggest that the very idea that there are clear boundaries between these enterprises and indeed the disciplines which feed into them is undermined by the adoption not only of the critical method envisaged by Norrie but also, more broadly, of an understanding of social theory which is both *contextual* and *interpretive.* The idea that philosophical explanations of particular concepts should be located within the context of the social practices of which these concepts form a part is based on a particular reading of Wittgenstein's argument in the *Philosophical Investigations.* For Wittgenstein, the meaning of concepts was inextricably linked with the practices of which they are a part, and the philosophical enterprise of breaking concepts down into their component elements in order to engage in minute analysis or indeed to reconstruct them in a clearer or otherwise more satisfactory way was one which was unlikely to lead to any genuine enlightenment.[32] I shall suggest that the conception of the philosophical enterprise as properly concerned with practices and forms of life ultimately muddies the autonomy of philosophy and reconceives it as one aspect of the task of social-theoretic understanding which encompasses history and the social sciences. I shall also argue that an endorsement of this contextual method opens up a vision of an integrated approach to criminal law theory as a task of social theory of which critical method is a central part.

Moreover, I shall argue that theorists of criminal law – whether lawyers or philosophers – who seek to develop theories which answer to the contours of actual practices of criminal law are, inevitably even if implicitly, engaged in an *interpretive* enterprise. The argument for the appropriateness of an interpretive approach builds upon the argument sketched previously in relation to the institutional starting point of all projects of theorisation. In what follows, I am therefore leaving aside primarily normative or 'utopian' approaches, whose answerability to actual institutional practices is arguably exhausted at the definitional stage of the theoretical enterprise,[33] and shall concentrate exclusively on those theorisations which purport to shed light upon actual social practices of criminal law. On an interpretive understanding of these theoretical enterprises, White's distinction between the analytic/conceptual and the scientific/empirical projects begins to unravel. Since phenomena such as criminal law are human practices, consisting in the (more or less) coordinated actions of conscious agents, our access to understanding them must comprehend the understanding of those agents themselves: In an unarticulated sense, agents already have their own 'theories' of the nature and purposes of (and indeed the justifications for) the practices in which they are involved. No exclusively 'external' description of the practice, one which ignores this 'internal' point of view, can constitute an adequate theory of the practice. On this view, the 'conceptual' is, as it were, internal to the 'scientific' as well as the 'scientific' providing the location for the practice of the 'conceptual.'

But an interpretive understanding of social theory in its more thoroughgoing forms moves beyond this modest argument for a phenomenological approach. It further argues that because we have no access to the world, including the human practices within it, except through the medium of language, and because language is itself marked by the viewpoints and interpretive presuppositions of human agents, all our knowledge is relative to linguistic constructions and conceptualisations: There is no 'unmediated' access to practices such as that suggested by a pure empiricist approach.[34] On the interpretive view, then, 'theories of criminal law', whether written by or for philosophers or lawyers, are inevitably interpretations of social practices whose practitioners themselves have interpretations which are an object of the theorisation. The implication is that 'at large' philosophising which is not addressed to any particular system or practice of criminal law is, like a map of imaginary terrain, not an exercise in criminal law theory but rather an exercise in philosophising itself. It may be a stimulating intellectual or an engaging aesthetic exercise, but it is not one which particularly claims the attention of those interested in criminal law any more than the imaginary map claims the attention of an explorer with a particular journey in mind.

iii. Critique without Philosophy or Philosophy without Critique?

Having suggested a conception of criminal law theorising as an interpretive project in which 'conceptual' and 'scientific' enterprises are mutually interdependent, I now want to return to the question of the relationship between 'philosophy' and 'critique.' In the introduction to a recent collection of essays on criminal law theory, Shute, Gardner, and Horder suggest that various 'critics' have been too quick to engage in what they call 'critique without philosophy.'[35] At first sight, the opposition is puzzling. After all, the idea of 'critique' immediately associates itself with a number of theorists – Hegel, Kant, Marx, Habermas, and other members of the Frankfurt School – who either were themselves philosophers or whose ideas became the stuff of vigorous philosophical debate. In fact, the editors' argument is that the 'critics' tend to be too quick to address themselves to the 'grand' questions of injustice and oppression in criminal legal practices without engaging in the conceptual ground clearing which is a necessary preliminary to a proper understanding of those practices. Leaving aside the fact that several of the essays in the collection tend more to the normative than to the analytic enterprise which the editors, somewhat in the style of White, see as the core of criminal law theory, I want to focus on the question of whether this is indeed a proper understanding of the enterprise of critique.

Certainly, 'critical' work has more often been both motivated and informed than has analytic philosophy by the judgment that existing criminal legal practices operate in unjust or oppressive ways. It is also fair to say that this judgment is sometimes evinced rather in the rhetorical style or unarticulated assumptions of such work than in its overt argument. Nonetheless, if we look at the actual method of critical criminal law theory, it is in fact close to that of the practice-grounded, historically specific analysis of the development and implementation of conceptual schema which an interpretive approach implies.[36] For example, Kennedy's analysis of the structure of Blackstone's commentaries, Norrie's analysis of the emergence of juridical individualism, of its political and historical conditions of existence and of its impact on the conceptual framework of criminal law doctrine, and Kelman's exploration of the deep structure of apparent illogicalities in the organisation and application of criminal law's doctrinal categories are all closely engaged in conceptual analysis.[37] What distinguishes this kind of analysis from 'at large' conceptual analysis – analysis which is not grounded in any particular institutions of criminal law – is that it takes the development of conceptual frameworks themselves as social practices which form one of the objects of social-theoretic analysis.[38] In other words, one could argue that such theorists are in fact observing the Wittgensteinian precept which philosophers (including Wittgenstein himself!) often cite yet infrequently heed: the injunction to eschew the minute analysis of the 'metaphysical' structure of the component elements of a linguistic framework abstracted from its practical context in favour of an analysis which fixes rather upon the place of that conceptual framework within a complex social practice or 'form of life.'[39]

So far, I have been skating over a distinction which will be important to my argument, and whose articulation suggests that I have been being overgenerous to the 'critical' approaches which I have cited. This is the distinction between criminal legal practices and criminal law doctrine. By the latter, I mean those general rules and principles in terms of which criminal lawyers understand the organisation of their discipline and its practice. Criminal law doctrine is generally taken to comprehend the schema of classification of offences and the conceptual framework in terms of which criminal liability is constructed and justified. In much contemporary Anglo-American scholarship, criminal law doctrine is more or less assimilated with the 'general part' of criminal law. We can think of criminal law doctrine as criminal law's articulated self-conception or rationalisation: In this sense, it is already a 'theory of criminal law', albeit one which occupies a distinctive, intermediate position between criminal legal practices on the one hand and more abstract or 'external' criminal law theories on the other.

On this conception, criminal law doctrine is itself a part of criminal legal practices: To the extent that these practices are themselves informed by and structured in terms of doctrinal classifications and understandings, the latter are a part of the social practice which is being theorised.[40] Hence the construction of doctrine, like the making of maps, is a proper object of social-theoretic analysis. However, it is equally clear that doctrine is not exhaustive of the social practice of criminal law. For that practice consists also in a multiplicity of substantive and procedural rules and judgments which are not of sufficient generality to be accounted a part of doctrine. Definitions of offences in the 'special part' would be one obvious example, as would rules of evidence and practices of punishment. Moreover, it cannot be assumed *a priori* that criminal law doctrine, as expounded by commentators or indeed by practitioners, in fact systematically structures criminal legal practices in the way it professes to do. For, most obviously, it may have ideological functions which underpin a systematic 'misrepresentation' of 'practice' in 'doctrine.' This implies, of course, that doctrinal theorisation and classification is itself a social practice of central importance to a proper understanding of criminal legal practices. Indeed, this is precisely what the more sophisticated versions of 'critical legal studies' argue.

The constant danger, however, is that doctrinal self-conception and criminal legal practice may be taken to be one and the same thing. This is where both the distinction between doctrine and practice and underlying conceptions of rationality and coherence become relevant to an assessment of the contributions of critical legal theory. In focussing on legal doctrine and schemes of classification, critical legal theorists have sometimes lost sight of important questions about the broader terrain upon which doctrinal conceptions directly or indirectly impinge. Questions about the implications of legal doctrine for the pre- and post-trial criminal process – and, crucially, vice versa – are foremost among such repressed issues.[41] Equally important, critical legal theorists have sometimes failed to grasp the significance of the fact that certain areas of criminal legal practice – 'regulatory' offences of strict liability are a prime example – are unheeded by or marginalised within doctrine.[42] These are areas whose contours have escaped the systematising impulses of the doctrinal mapmakers yet which have real effects for the subjects of criminal law.[43] Furthermore, the primary focus on doctrinal 'contradictions' and on a narrow conception of rationality as formal coherence and normative consistency *within doctrine* has sometimes obscured critics' view of a deeper logic underlying the development and operation of criminal law which a broader focus on the history of criminal legal practices may reveal. In this respect, 'critical' theorists of criminal law have sometimes fallen into much the same error as 'philosophers': That is, their intellectual focus on the map and its internal structure has directed their attention away from the question of its relationship both with the terrain which it purports to characterise and with that which falls beyond its bounds.

iv. Mapping Criminal Legal Theories

Having delineated what I see as some of the features of, and difficulties confronting, theorisations of criminal law, I shall move on in the next section to trace the development of the idea of the 'general part' of criminal law in the Common Law world from the eighteenth century to the present day. Before doing so, I want to make clear a number of assumptions and concerns which will structure my discussion.

First, I shall start out from a broad conception of criminal law theory that encompasses any relatively systematic attempt to explicate the social institution of criminal law. My focus on the works of lawyers rather than those of philosophers will allow me to develop the argument sketched previously about the theoretical assumptions and views implicit in any systematic explication of criminal law doctrine. Second, in assessing some examples of such theories, I shall be particularly concerned to examine the view of, and importance attached to, systematicity and coherence in their construction. Are these theoretical precepts with some metaphysical status, or are conceptions of order and system shaped by and relative to particular historical conditions and underlying political and ethical preoccupations?[44] Third, I shall chart the slippage in theories of criminal law between the theorisation of criminal law doctrine (as if it occupied the whole of the relevant terrain) and that of criminal legal practices more broadly understood. Finally, drawing on the metaphor of mapping, I shall consider the ways in which criminal law theories of an interpretive temper have to relate to the practices which they purport to theorise.[45] Once we have abandoned a crude empiricist project in favour of an interpretive one, in what ways do practices themselves present a touchstone for the assessment of the adequacy of theory, and how is this to be judged? How can practices constitute such a touchstone if we have no 'pre-theoretical' access to them, and how are we to make sense of the deceptively simple idea that interpretive theories are theories '*of*' particular practices? Furthermore, how are the theoretical prerequisites of order and systematicity to be related to the demand that theoretical models 'correspond' or in some sense answer to the practices which are their object? Even if we grant that mapmaking, like theorising, has a constructive aspect, to the extent that maps – or theories – are not exclusively aesthetic products, the question of the relationship between map and terrain, between theory and practice, remains a pressing one.

These may seem unduly 'basic' questions, but they are ones, I believe, of which most criminal law theorists still have only a tenuous understanding.[46] Jerome Hall provides a vivid example of the problem to which I mean to direct attention. Hall opens his work on 'general principles of criminal law' with a characterisation of what constitutes 'theory':

> [A] theory signifies the knowledge of a subject, acquired without any practical objective in view; and it is especially concerned with the ultimate ideas which comprise the foundation of a science or social discipline. . . . [A] theory is a definite conceptual scheme which correlates many otherwise disconnected bits of knowledge. . . . Significance, simplicity and suggestivity in research determine preference among competing theories. . . . A theory of criminal law is constructed of a set of ideas by reference to which every penal law can be significantly 'placed', and thus explained.[47]

Later in the same chapter, Hall notes that criminal law theory is more developed in continental Europe than in the Anglo-American world, but he goes on to lament that

> . . . the orientation has been practical rather than scientific. Instead of being the subject matter of theory, the penal code has occupied the driver's seat, directing theory to make sense of every provision that has the formal markings of penal law. This has impeded scientific progress. For whilst it is true that a code to some extent reflects scientific theory, it is also true that there are inevitable gaps between them. Interests and political pressures, accidents and historical conventions have greatly influenced the codes; and inevitably these set *arbitrary* limitations on theories which took their directions from the code. (emphasis added)[48]

Note Hall's characterisation of legal theory as 'scientific' theory, and his assumption that there is a 'truth' of what counts as 'penal law' – a truth which should be in the 'driver's seat', or holding the mapmaker's pen. How, other than tautologically, is this to be squared with his earlier assertion that a theory should allow 'every penal law' to be 'placed'? And how is it to be reconciled with his criticism of the fact that the 'penal code' has been in the 'driver's seat'? What does this dissonance reveal about Hall's conception of the nature of theoretical mapping and of the construction of the objects to be mapped?

Though this is a particularly stark example of the problem with which I am concerned, we shall find it reproduced right across the terrain of criminal law theory. Historians, lawyers, and legal theorists no less than philosophers have been troubled by the difficulty attributed by Charles Gray to the late-seventeenth-century lawyer and commentarist on the Common Law, Matthew Hale:

> To an environment over-full of knowledge and half-knowledge, widened perspectives and false perspectives, theories and resistance to theory, and partisanship dressed up as thought, Hale brought a powerful impulse to digest and control. His mind sought order and system, whilst recognising at the same time the incompatibility of order and system. . . . Some concrete problems Hale solved to his satisfaction, some abstract principles he articulated. Yet the philosophic history he was reaching for eluded him, and unphilosophic history failed to hold his interest. His impulse to find a jurisprudence in legal history and to write legal history through the categories of jurisprudence was focused on *The History of the Common Law,* but that focus did not hold.[49]

II. The Development of Theories of Criminal Law

In this section, I shall undertake a brief review of four 'theories of criminal law' which more or less fit my understanding of an interpretive (though not a critical) approach. The first, that of William Blackstone, was written in England in the second half of the eighteenth century – a period in which the 'modern' English criminal law system was emerging; the second, that of James Fitzjames Stephen, was written in late-nineteenth-century England; and the third and fourth, those of Jerome Hall and Glanville Williams, represent the work, respectively, of an American and an English writer of the second half of the twentieth century. In each case, I shall trace the general shape of the conception which they developed, concentrating on their schemes of classification, their conception of 'the general part', and the nature of their implicit audience. I should emphasise that this does not pretend to be a thorough examination of the development of the general part of English and American criminal law or of Anglo-American criminal law theory. Rather, it aims to paint a series of maps with brush strokes just narrow enough to point up the general lines of movement in the social practice of criminal law theorisation, just focussed enough to illuminate the role being played by systems of classification, and just detailed enough to point up the changing representations of the criminal legal landscape and hence to sharpen our sense of the contingency and historical specificity of our contemporary understandings of criminal law doctrine.

i. Blackstone

Blackstone's *Commentaries on the Laws of England* were first published in 1765–9. Whilst Blackstone drew on the work of earlier commentators such as Coke and, in the criminal law field, Hale and Hawkins, his *Commentaries* are widely acknowledged to have been the first comprehensive and genuinely systematic account of English Common Law.[50] Blackstone was the first Vinerian Professor of Law at Oxford University, and the *Commentaries* were originally written as lectures – indeed, they open with an impassioned plea for the teaching of the Common Law in English universities, and for the place of legal studies within the conception of a liberal education. However, Blackstone's intended audience certainly went well beyond students of law in a narrow sense: He saw a knowledge of law as the civic duty of all those in positions of status, power, and responsibility, and the aim of his *Commentaries* was to provide a statement of the Common Law sufficiently accessible and systematic to reach this wider audience. Drawing on what must have been a chaotic array of written resources, Blackstone sought to articulate what he saw as the underlying wisdom and coherence of the Common Law, and hence to defend it in the social context of encroachment both by the legislative forays of an increasingly active Parliament and by the principles of equity. He sought to enunciate the Common Law in a way that would illuminate 'the general spirit of laws and the principles of universal jurisprudence, combined with an accurate knowledge of our own municipal constitutions, their original, reason and history.'[51] He saw his course as providing 'a general map of the law, marking out the shape of the country, it's [*sic*] connexions and boundaries, it's [*sic*] greater divisions and principal cities: it is not [its] business to describe minutely the subordinate limits, or to fix the longitude and latitude of every inconsiderable hamlet.'[52]

In these passages we see Blackstone's commitment to the mapping enterprise: one which answers to its terrain, yet one which both constitutes a particular interpretation of that terrain and responds to the intellectual demands of coherence and simplicity in a way reminiscent of the passage from Jerome Hall quoted at the opening of this chapter. Blackstone has, of course, been seen as the supreme apologist for the Common Law[53] – its rationaliser on the cusp of the turn towards legislative primacy which would come with the further development of parliamentary democracy; its reconciler as between the feudal world left behind and competing, Hobbesian/positivist and Lockean/naturalist, versions of the liberal vision which was beginning to be realised. Whilst he himself was neither a liberal nor a philosopher, Blackstone's genius arguably lay in his success in giving legal form and expression to the modern criminal law system, and in drawing out of the Common Law certain principles which might inform, and improve the quality of, the growing field of criminal legislation.[54] Blackstone was engaged in a process not dissimilar to that of many criminal law theorists today: Each is concerned with the presentation of his or her subject in the best possible light, and the difference between Blackstone and later writers in terms of how far they acknowledge difficulties in the application of their theoretical schemata is arguably a matter of degree rather than a qualitative one. Blackstone's eulogistic treatment of the Common Law and his vision of its evolutionary progress towards ever greater degrees of humanity and coherence are extreme. But the basic problem which he confronted – that of reconciling his intellectual (and indeed political) ambition to produce a systematic account with the diverse and chaotic nature of his data – is very familiar.

Blackstone's treatment of criminal law, conceptualised as dealing with 'public wrongs', occupies the fourth volume of the *Commentaries*. Only the first three chapters, which constitute about 10 percent of the total, are concerned with what approximates to what is now understood as 'the general part.' The first chapter is essentially introductory and deals with the nature of crimes and their punishment; the second deals with persons capable of committing crimes; and the third with principals and accessories. Blackstone conceptualised crime as a voluntary act consisting in a vicious will and an unlawful act consequent upon that will. All pleas and excuses are seen as flowing from the want of a sufficient will. These excuses arise in three kinds of case: those such as infancy or lunacy in which there is a defect of understanding; those such as mistake or ignorance in which the understanding and will of the subject are not engaged; and those such as compulsion or necessity, in which the will is constrained by some outward force or violence.[55] Blackstone's general conception therefore focuses rather upon what would now be conceptualised as '*actus reus*' and 'defence' than upon '*mens rea*': His conception of the 'vicious will' and of reasons for its absence relates to the wickedness or lack of wickedness of *acts*. Beyond his superficially familiar picture of the act component of criminal liability, his further discussion of excuses and of what would today be thought of as 'mental states' is woven in a relatively uneven way into the tapestry of his accounts of substantive offences, often in the context of a discussion about the distinction between felonies and misdemeanours.[56]

The first three chapters of Volume IV are succeeded by a detailed treatment of substantive offences which occupies about half of the text. The offences are organised in terms of the interests which they affect, beginning with offences against God and religion, moving through injuries against king and government, those against public justice and public order, and finally reaching those against the person, habitations, and property. In each case, the main focus of the discussion is on the nature of the conduct and what makes it wrongful. There is no systematic analysis in terms of anything resembling the analytic framework of *actus reus/mens rea*/defence which dominates criminal law theory today.[57] Blackstone's analysis of substantive offences is integrated with his discussion of procedural matters such as form of trial and penalties. The remaining very substantial portion of the volume is a treatment of procedural matters such as jurisdiction, courts, and other issues pertaining to the pre-trial, trial, and post-trial stages of the administration of criminal justice. Blackstone therefore focuses on criminal procedure to a very substantial degree, and his integration of procedural issues with the treatment of substantive offences marks a view of the terrain of criminal law significantly different from that dominant in the Anglo-American world today.

What notions of systematicity and coherence are exemplified by Blackstone's theorisation of criminal law? To modern eyes, Volume IV might look more like a textbook on criminal law and procedure than a theorisation of its subject matter. The emphasis on the detailed treatment of substantive offences and the embryonic nature of the discussion of 'principles of liability' make the work look more like a description of criminal laws than a systematic theory.[58] This, however, would be a serious misunderstanding of the nature of Blackstone's work. First, his arguments clearly disclose a conception of criminal law which goes beyond the mere description of its elements and which, on occasion, he uses to engage in criticism of criminal legal practices or to develop arguments for reform. Take, for example, the following statement:

> In proportion to the importance of the criminal law, ought also to be the care and attention of the legislature on properly forming and enforcing it. It should be founded upon principles that are permanent, uniform and universal; and always conformable to the dictates of truth and justice, the feelings of humanity, and the indelible rights of mankind; though it sometimes (provided there be no transgression of these eternal boundaries) may be modified, narrowed or enlarged, according to the local or occasional necessities of the state which it is meant to govern.[59]

Blackstone goes on to argue that the vagaries of politics and the temptations of a resort to unprincipled criminalisation have meant that criminal law systems tend to be 'in every country of Europe more rude and imperfect than the civil.' Certainly, he engaged in that familiar criminal law theorist's practice of shaping the presentation of his data so as to meet his conception (examples include his treatment of the administration of pardons and steps for mitigating the severity of punishment[60]). Yet he also articulated arguments for legal reform and criticised aspects of contemporary criminal law, sometimes in trenchant terms (for example in his condemnation of the 'outrageous [capital] penalties' pertaining to the offence of breaking down the mound of a fishpond and allowing fish to escape[61]). It is also worth noting that, notwithstanding both their relative novelty and their great increase during the two centuries before he was writing, Blackstone fully incorporated misdemeanours into his analysis (though he did question the consistency of the summary courts with the 'genius of the common law'!).[62] In this respect he confronts the challenge of answerability to practices more squarely than do many contemporary criminal law theorists, whose tendency is to marginalise or even to ignore the less serious offences.

Second, to see a lack of systematic theorisation in Blackstone is to miss the specific shape and motivation of his scheme by judging it in terms of the elements thought to be central to criminal law in the late twentieth century. In contemporary debate, as we shall see, criminal law theory is more or less assimilated to the explication of the 'general part' of criminal law. With the exception of normative philosophical treatises concerning the limits of criminal law,[63] the systematic theorisation of substantive offences, let alone of the law of criminal procedure and punishment, is seen as the business of expository legal scholarship rather than as a feature of criminal law theory.[64] This, doubtless, is due to the specific imperatives of justification and rationalisation of criminal law power in the modern world – imperatives which I shall consider later. For Blackstone, these imperatives were different. The challenge which he confronted was that of moving beyond the earlier classification of the Common Law in terms of forms of action or writs, and of articulating a system of criminal legal classification based on the general notion of a public wrong – a wrong of concern to the whole community – elaborated in terms of the interests threatened and protected by criminal law. This system would provide a mapping of the relations between individual and polity in a way which gave an adequate place both to concerns with public order and to emergent conceptions of individual right, whilst maintaining a central focus on the framework of criminal procedure. What needed rationalising and justifying was not so much the state's imposition of criminalising power on the free individual – the major problematic of modern liberal conceptions of the general part – but rather a conception of criminalisation which focused on substantive interests rather than exclusively on procedural forms, and which illustrated the Common Law's general ability to evolve and progress in the context of changing political and historical conditions and, in particular, to adapt to the changing needs of government. Blackstone's *Commentaries* are as much theorised as the later conceptions which we shall examine. But what needed to be rendered and represented as coherent and rational was, given historical differences, itself different.

ii. Stephen

The second theorisation of criminal law I shall consider is that of James Fitzjames Stephen's monumental *History of the Criminal Law of England,* published in three volumes in 1883. Stephen was a High Court judge, as well as a prolific writer on both criminal law and public policy issues surrounding criminalisation. He was a strong advocate of codification of the criminal law and undertook the writing of a draft code which was published as his *Digest of Criminal Law.* His legal works are clearly addressed to a specialist audience, but he also directed his trenchant writings on the nature of crime and the denunciatory role of punishment to a broader, educated audience.[65]

The first volume of Stephen's *History* maps the early history of criminal law, with particular reference to the development of the criminal jurisdiction and the nature of criminal procedure, trial, and punishment in England: It concludes with a comparison of English and French criminal procedure. Volume II traces the limits of criminal jurisdiction in terms of persons, time, and place: It then considers 'crime and punishment in general', responsibility and insanity, the sources of criminal law, 'leading points in the history of the substantive criminal law', and the liability of secondary parties and the inchoate offences; finally it moves to an analysis of crimes against the state, of sedition, and of crimes against religion. Volume III is concerned primarily with substantive offences, organised in terms of the interests they affect – homicide and offences against the person, crimes against property, offences relating to 'trade and labour', miscellaneous offences, and police offences triable summarily. There is then a discussion of Indian criminal law, and a chapter considering the case for codification of the criminal law. The volume closes with a discussion of some exemplary cases.

In a work amounting in total to well over 1,300 pages, consideration of what is now understood as 'the general part' takes up a mere 170 pages,[66] with the rest being relatively evenly divided between the treatment of substantive offences and that of criminal procedure, broadly understood. Notwithstanding their rather different audiences and orientation, the proportionate presentation of material is very similar in both the *Commentaries* (of which Volume IV is concerned with criminal law) and the *Digest.* In the former, about half the relevant volume is concerned with substantive offences (this time including inchoate offences); about one-third is a treatment of evidence and procedure; and the remaining sixth deals with the 'general nature of criminal liability.' The *Digest* is divided into six parts of approximately equal length, of which all but the first are concerned with offences, classified in accordance with the interests which they threaten. The first part, entitled 'Preliminary', deals with 'general exceptions' such as those based on incapacity, ignorance, or compulsion; parties to crime; inchoate offences; and punishments (this last occupying well over half of the part).

Having noted the general distribution of Stephen's attention as between general part, special part, and criminal process, I shall now concentrate on the nature of his treatment of the general part in the *History.* Chapter XVII opens with a discussion of the nature of crime, in which he defends a trenchantly positivistic view of crime as 'an act or omission punished by law,'[67] whilst acknowledging the role of conventional morality in the understanding of criminal law:

> . . . there is a moral as well as a legal classification of crimes, and the merits and defects of legal definitions cannot be understood unless the moral view of the subject is understood. Law and morals are not and cannot be made co-extensive, or even completely harmonious. Law may be intended to supplement or to correct morality. There may in some cases be an inevitable conflict between them, but . . . it is essential to a just criticism of the law to understand what may be called the natural distribution of the class of actions to which it applies.[68]

He identifies the core of criminal law as its concern with conduct dangerous to the community, involving some 'definite, gross, undeniable injury to someone.'[69] Beyond this, his aim is to trace the principles of criminal legislation appropriate in a democratic society, to consider the relationship between law and morality, and to note the need for and appropriateness of judicial discretion in punishment. We come to what would now be regarded as the 'general part' in Chapter XVIII, entitled 'Criminal Responsibility.' Stephen here announces (in a formulation remarkably close to that of Hawkins's seventeenth-century *Pleas of the Crown*) the general presumption that 'people are responsible for their actions' but notes that there are certain exceptions to this. He continues,

> In considering this matter it will be necessary to depart from the method which I have hitherto followed of tracing out historically the growth of institutions and practices, and so explaining both their origin and their present form. The result in this case is more interesting and important than the process by which it was arrived at, and the result can be both described and criticised with less reference to the process than is possible in regard to other parts of the law.[70]

After this evasion of the history of the general part, he goes on to criticise as misleading the idea that '*actus non facit reum nisi mens sit rea*' – something which he famously saw as not so much a 'maxim' as a 'minim.'[71] He does, however, consider a number of philosophical arguments relevant to the construction of criminal responsibility. Whilst it is possible to make some generalisations about the mental conditions of responsibility,

> [i]t is common to discuss this subject as if the law itself depended upon the result of discussion as to the freedom of the will, the origin of moral distinctions and the nature of conscience. Such discussions cannot be altogether avoided, but in legal inquiries they ought to be noticed principally in order to show that the law does not really depend upon them.[72]

Responsibility must thus be understood in terms of 'actual liability to legal punishment' and be traced by means of a positive analysis of English law rather than of 'some abstract or imaginary system':

> General theories as to what ought to be the conditions of criminal responsibility may not be useless, but they must depend on the tastes of those who form them, and they cannot, so far as I can see, be said in any distinct sense to be either true or false. If the question be asked with reference to any definite body of law, it can, of course, be answered with a greater or less degree of confidence and accuracy, though even in this case there must be some degree of vagueness. . . .[73]

In the context of his scepticism about 'general theories', it is perhaps hardly surprising that Stephen's basic statement of the general principles of criminal liability occupies approximately half a page, with the rest of the chapter consisting in a discussion of the nature of involuntary actions – a discussion which owes a clear intellectual debt to the simple schema developed by Blackstone. Many doctrinal issues arising out of this general discussion are said to be deferred until the analysis of specific offences, in the context of which Stephen argues that they may be better understood.

The foregoing discussion might be taken to suggest that Stephen's *History* is an entirely descriptive work, disclosing no 'theory of criminal law' whatsoever. This, however, would be a mistaken interpretation. Stephen, no less than Blackstone, has an elaborate theory of criminal law, and one which entails its own concern with order, system, and coherence. The focus of these theoretical requirements is not directed to the 'general part', because the ethical and political questions to which an elaboration of the general part are addressed are not those which are central to Stephen's concerns. The historical development traced in the chapter following those on insanity and sources notes (perhaps somewhat surprisingly in the light of the foregoing) that the 'main doctrinal principles' were in place by the mid–eighteenth century[74] and is concerned to emphasise the unsatisfactory nature of the incremental and *ad hoc* development of a statutory code of criminal law in response to shortcomings of the Common Law and particular emerging social problems. Conservative and authoritarian as he was, and writing in an era deeply touched by utilitarian philosophy, Stephen's implicit problematic was not the propriety of imposing criminalising power on the free individual. Rather, he is concerned to trace the broad patterns of criminalisation from the thirteenth to the nineteenth centuries, mapping the route from a focus on procedural forms to that upon substantive offences, the voyage from fixity and great severity in punishment towards greater leniency tempered by the exercise of judicial discretion. His positivistic approach suits his authoritarian politics: Criminal law is seen as a tool in the hands of the legislator, and a tool of particular utility in the promotion of social order. Whilst Stephen's conception of the subject of criminal law is undoubtedly individualistic, it remains rooted in the old view that an act presumptively discloses the subject's will and hence that the basis for judgments of criminal culpability lies primarily in the quality of *conduct.* Thus, notwithstanding case law developments in the nineteenth century moving, particularly in the law of homicide, towards a distinction between acts and mental states, Stephen recognises this framework only to a partial degree. His analysis therefore rests somewhere between the models later identified by Fletcher as those of 'manifest' and of 'subjective' criminality.[75]

Notwithstanding his anti-theoretical pretensions, then, Stephen discloses his own concern with order, coherence, and system. These are the concerns of a practising lawyer, interested in the certainty and consistency of criminal law; of a judge, concerned to delineate a clear and powerful role for the judiciary notwithstanding the propriety of legislative supremacy in law making (hence the focus on judicial discretion in sentencing); of a Victorian conservative, concerned to affirm the centrality of criminalisation to the maintenance of social order. They are also, perhaps even more important, the concerns of the advocate of codification, who saw no difficulty in reconciling parliamentary supremacy with the will of the people, because

> In these islands, where the legislature tends to represent directly the will of a large proportion of the community, it is unnecessary to distinguish between the morality of the legislature and that of the persons legislated for, for the two may be considered as practically identical.[76]

Stephen's implicit theoretical concern is that of Austin: the systematisation of the law through the reduction and rationalisation of its bulk by means of the production of an accessible and intelligible Code, with the aim of integration of substance and procedure (hence the large space devoted to the latter).[77] It is worth noting that even Stephen's relatively weak impulse to systematise at the level of 'general principles of liability' was sufficient to engender a certain selectivity of subject matter. His *Digest* was concerned only with indictable offences, and little of the regulatory legislation which had grown apace in the nineteenth century finds a place in his lengthy discussions in either the *History* or the *Commentaries.*[78] Even though his own Code, unlike that of Austin, eschewed mention of a distinction between special and general parts, he may, in fact, have been closer to proceeding from, even if not expounding, assumptions about the importance of 'general principles' than he liked to admit.

iii. Hall and Williams

We now move to the latter half of the twentieth century, and thus to the period in which the idea of a 'general part' as the core organising framework for theories of criminal law reaches its summit in the Anglo-American world. I have chosen to focus on two theorisations, both written in the 1950s, but on different sides of the Atlantic Ocean. Whilst Hall's *General Principles of Criminal Law* and Williams's *Criminal Law: The General Part* are strikingly similar in their assumptions about the centrality of the general part for a proper understanding of criminal law, their rather different approaches to it are instructive in the variety even among organising frameworks which form themselves around this particular model.

The first edition of Williams's book, published in 1953, ran to more than 700 pages; the second edition, published in 1961, was 200 hundred pages longer. A leading academic lawyer with some interest in legal theory, Williams defined the 'general part' – a notion whose invention he attributed to continental legal discourse – as general rules applying to more than one crime. He expressed the aim of his work as that of bringing together all authorities on the general part so as to throw them into relief and direct practitioners' attention to them. The bulk of the discussion is both legalistic and positivistic: Williams's analysis is grounded in cases or in assertions which are commonsensical rather than philosophical in tone, and when in search of critical resources, he casts his net into the pool of comparative law rather than into that of legal theory.[79] *Mens rea,* for example, though delineated as intent or recklessness, is further described merely as 'the mental element necessary for a particular crime.' Williams's views on the accuracy and utility of the Latin maxim *actus non facit reum nisi mens sit rea,* we can conclude, would have been hardly more complimentary than those of Stephen.[80]

Eschewing even a brief preliminary discussion of 'the nature of criminal law',[81] Williams deals with *actus reus, mens rea,* defences, capacity, strict and vicarious liability, the liability of corporations, the principle of legality, preventive justice and the rule of law (binding over), and the burden of proof. Apart from that which is necessary to the analysis of the last few topics, there is no discussion of criminal procedure or the rules of evidence. The general method is to illustrate the 'general principles' by reference to their application in particular cases – negligence in the context of manslaughter, intent in relation to larceny, and so on. Williams is relatively uninterested in detailed historical excursions; he remarks that the idea of *mens rea* goes back at least to the time of Coke, which is 'as far back as any modern lawyer needs to go.'[82] And he is positively dismissive of the need for detailed philosophical let alone psychological or other social-scientific inquiries; his discussion of intention proceeds from a stipulated definition of intent as knowledge of circumstances and desire for consequences, and he remarks that '[t]he definition of intention is not a matter of investigating psychological facts: it is (as definition always is) a question of verbal usage and convenience.'[83] Nor is there very much discussion of the broad liberal rationale which underpins his normative focus on the general part, and of which in much of his other work Williams is a staunch defender. Indeed, in his later work, this normative commitment quite distorted his positivistic vision in relation to matters such as the dilution of subjective principles of liability by the widening terrain of negligence and objective recklessness.[84] In *Criminal Law: The General Part,* however, Williams resisted any impulse to systematise at the level of a substantive conception of the nature and purposes of criminal law. He (implicitly) defends his focus on the issue of 'responsibility' by a process of oblique reasoning: He notes the partial validity of a number of competing theories – those based on the need to prevent, deter, incapacitate, or reform offenders, and those based on the idea of retributive justice – and simply notes the importance of responsibility to each of these theories (with the possible exception of a thoroughgoing reformism). Many of Williams's critical arguments are couched in terms of an appeal to 'principle' or 'a better view' the basis of which it is not thought necessary to spell out.[85]

The legalistic tone of Williams's account, his overt address to a practitioner audience,[86] and the level of detail and specificity with which he examines the general part might be taken to connote an approach which is expository rather than theoretical. As in the cases of Blackstone and Stephen, however, such a reading would miss an important aspect of what gave Williams's map its meaning and importance at the time of its writing. For whilst Williams's treatment is indeed extraordinarily comprehensive[87] and hence encounters the problem of answerability to practices in a less vivid way than, for example, his later *Textbook of Criminal Law* (1983), the theoretical assumptions on which his work is based may relatively easily be unearthed. First of all, like Stephen, Williams is a keen advocate of codification. But Williams's view of the advantages of codification is subtly different from that of his positivist ancestor. For Williams, the general part would be the cornerstone of the project of rationalisation through codification and would provide a basis for immanent critique of existing criminal law. For example, in his treatment of strict and vicarious liability, Williams describes them as instances of the disadvantages of living without a Code enshrining 'general principles and policies': He cites the system of Queensland as one in which principled codification has been used as a means to check the development of 'these over-severe doctrines.'[88] In his discussion of the principle of legality, Williams deplores the fact that, 'like everything else in criminal law', there is no agreement on general principles, so that problems caused by uncertain drafting or retrospectivity, and the dubious propriety of institutions of preventive justice such as binding over, cannot properly be addressed within the current system.[89] Interestingly, Williams sees as a limitation of nineteenth-century draft Codes such as that of Stephen the fact that they focussed only on indictable offences, and he cites the growth of summary jurisdiction as one of the main arguments in favour of the need for an accessible and systematic Code.[90] Notwithstanding Williams's professedly pluralistic approach to the rationale for criminalisation, therefore, the implicit role of the general part in his vision of codification is a normative one. For codification within the framework of the general part speaks both to the individualistic and egalitarian liberal concerns which have posed an ethical challenge to criminalising power in the latter part of the twentieth century and to the practical difficulties of accessibility and clarity posed by an ever-expanding terrain of criminalisation.

Second, and more important, however, we should note an extraordinary shift in the balance of concern among issues already seen as putatively within the general part by the late nineteenth century. Williams moves from the focus on action and conduct, voluntariness and exceptions to it, which characterised the approach of both Blackstone and Stephen, to a focus on *the mental conditions of individual responsibility.* The signs of this shift are evident in Williams's opening words: 'The chief problems in the general part of criminal law pertain to the requirement of a criminal state of mind.'[91] This conviction is further reflected in the fact that after a 'preliminary exploration' of *actus reus* (consisting in 29 pages), Williams moves on to devote the next 200 pages to matters exclusively concerned with *mens rea*. Furthermore, his discussion both of strict and vicarious responsibility, and of defences such as drunkenness and mental disorder, are oriented to a significant degree around the questions raised by such defences about the defendant's mental state rather than about the wickedness of his or her act. The simple schema of defences explained in terms of exceptions to the presumption of voluntariness is thus displaced in favour of a more complex view, in which questions about mental responsibility as well as about voluntariness of action are relevant to the construction of defences – a distinction which opens the way for Williams's crisp differentiation of notions of justification and excuse.[92]

A complete explanation of this remarkable shift in focus from action or conduct to mental responsibility is well beyond the scope of this chapter.[93] But it is worth speculating on its relationship both to social, political, and economic changes and to the development of other intellectual and practical disciplines during the course of the twentieth century. Three interrelated factors are particularly worthy of consideration.

First, the growth of the discipline of psychology can hardly be doubted to have had an impact on legal understandings of responsibility and of the 'fair terms' under which criminal liability can be imposed.

Second, a strong conception of individual (mental) responsibility had the capacity to rationalise both the autonomy of criminal law and the distinctive role of the legal profession. As far as the former is concerned, a discrete notion of individual criminal responsibility served to keep at bay the determinist, reformist discourses whose emergence at the beginning of the twentieth century David Garland has charted.[94] The doctrine of *mens rea* protected criminal law's autonomy in the face of the multiplication of rehabilitative and other welfare-oriented discourses which impinged on the same terrain and which legitimised regulatory responses to human behaviour irrespective of individual responsibility or desert. Moreover, the *mens rea* doctrine helped to rationalise the autonomy of the legal profession in the face of diversifying modes of enforcement and regulation prompted by the continued growth of the summary jurisdiction and the development of administrative regulatory frameworks parallel (and sometimes internal) to the criminal process. In a (broadly speaking) liberal culture, the idea that criminality proceeds from individual characteristics or social conditions for which the individual agent is not in any strong sense responsible poses a challenge to the specificity of criminal law. For it points in the direction of the assimilation of criminal law with broader strategies of social welfare and social control. This potential assimilation has been facilitated by the rapid increase in the scope of criminal legislation during the twentieth century, and in particular by the growth of 'regulatory' offences. We may speculate, then, that the development of a sophisticated *mens rea* doctrine contributed to the maintenance of a discrete area of specialist social knowledge and practice, answering both the demands of legal professional interests and those of a political establishment whose legitimising ideology was predominantly individualist.

Finally, the rapid social change and increase in social mobility promoted by industrial and economic development and accelerated by two world wars, along with the increasing currency of egalitarian political ideologies and of value pluralism within democratic politics, had given a new spin to the ethical demands of the individualism already expressed in nineteenth century *laissez faire* liberalism. In particular, these social and political changes favoured the construction of the unequal impact of criminalisation as an ethical challenge to criminal law's legitimacy. This was a challenge which could be overcome only by the development of a firmer conception of the basis on which criminal responsibility could be attributed to individuals. In order to meet the demands of pluralism and to accommodate the expanding terrain of criminal regulation, this conception had to be one which was independent of the substance of criminal law's prohibitions.

In short, the demands that the state's power to criminalise be fairly imposed on individual members of society, that the legal requirements geared to meeting this demand answer adequately to the growth in social-scientific knowledge, and that criminal law be distinguished from a general technique of managing the population and responding to social problems fed the development of the *mens rea* doctrine. The self-conception expressed in doctrine thus acted (and still acts) as an ideological counterbalance to the increasingly managerialist reality of criminal legal practices in a world in which resources are strictly limited and hence, for example, plea bargaining and modes of diversion from the formal criminal process are endemic, and trial by jury is relatively rare. The development towards general principles of responsibility, of course, could not entirely suppress underlying tensions between individual and social, agency-based and deterministic models of criminal justice, and may be interpreted as part of a balancing strategy which is ultimately doomed to failure.[95] But the fragility of the equilibrium was not yet apparent in the 1950s, and this helps to explain the confidence and seriousness with which Williams was able to assert the primacy of a unitary general part as the keystone of criminal law's (actual and potential) coherence and legitimacy.

Jerome Hall, like Williams, was an academic lawyer, albeit one of a more theoretical turn of mind. His *General Principles of Criminal Law* was written with an academic rather than a practitioner audience in view, and it engages explicitly with the methodological problems of theorisation which escape

Williams's notice. Hall develops a conception of penal law as proscribing and punishing harms which may be imputed to a normal adult who has voluntarily committed them with criminal intent. According to Hall, penal law consists in three different levels: rules (which define specific offences), doctrines (which articulate defences and the principles of inchoate and participatory liability), and principles (which conceptualise the notions of act, *mens rea,* the requirement of concurrence between the act, *mens rea,* harm, and causation). Doctrines and principles constitute the 'general part.' These general norms are the cornerstone of a science of criminal law because they enable us to give a complete and systematic description. In this sense, they 'stand outside' the actual norms of penal law, yet they are related to the special part in that they are inferred from it.[96]

Whilst features such as the centrality of the general part to Hall's notion of how to theorise criminal law, the primacy accorded to questions of *mens rea,* and the downgrading of procedural issues as compared with earlier treatments[97] are strikingly similar to Williams's work, some significant differences can also be noted. As I have already mentioned, unlike Williams, Stephen, or Blackstone, Hall is self-consciously engaged in a theoretical enterprise, and in particular in that of constructing a descriptive or 'scientific' model which bridges the valley between practices of criminal law and the systematising precepts of theory. He therefore explicitly confronts the difficulties for such a theoretical enterprise. These, he suggests, are of two main kinds. First, the descriptive theorist is inevitably influenced in her selection of materials by her own preferences. The only solution here is to articulate these preferences, and Hall accordingly announces from the start his focus on a conception of *mens rea* which proceeds from a commitment to the principle of legality. This Hall takes to entail a conception encompassing only aware mental states such as intent and recklessness and hence excluding negligence. Second, the variety of actual offences comprehended in the criminal Code may be such as not to admit of 'scientific' rationalisation: In other words, the theoretical requirement of coherence may be impossible to square with the disorder of the world. To this problem, the solution is selectivity of the portions of criminal law to be theorised. Hall never confronts the tension between this admission and his opening remarks about the purpose of descriptive theory being to allow each penal law to be 'placed': Indeed, the only possible solution seems to be that of definitional fiat, with the consequent marginalisation of whole tracts of social practice actually conceptualised by its practitioners and subjects as 'penal law.'[98]

Another difference between Hall and Williams is that Hall's account is prefaced by a historical analysis of criminal law doctrine which bears on its face a strong evolutionary vision – a vision which plays an important role in the construction of Hall's contemporary theorisation. From Bracton through Hale and Hawkins, via Blackstone to Bentham, Austin, and Stephen, Hall traces a journey of inexorable progress and improvement. At root, this progress consists in the gradual refinement of schemes of classification and culminates in the full realisation of the principle of legality through the articulation of general principles of criminal responsibility. Whilst Hall notes imperfections and gaps – the relatively small amount of space devoted to the conceptualisation of harms and injuries, or to the problem of causation, particularly in nineteenth-century scholarship – the general trajectory is one of a gradual advance towards a fully systematised conception. This is a conception which admits of (or perhaps constitutes) a 'scientific theorisation':

> Progress toward systematization resulted from discovering that crimes can be decomposed, i.e. analyzed into several elementary 'material' (essential) ideas; then, that certain ideas are common to two or more offenses. . . . It was next perceived that certain generalizations applied to all the specific prescriptions. These became the 'general part' of the criminal law, and the rules were placed in the 'special part' of penal codes. There was also considerable elucidation of the fundamental principles upon which the entire structure of the criminal law rests. Beyond all that, however, there remains the present paramount challenge of inclusive systematization, disclosing the interrelations of the various parts of penal law – in short, the construction of a coherent theory of that law.[99]

What impedes this ideal theoretic construction is a collection of inconvenient facts: that codes are multifarious, that they are addressed to lawyers and practitioners with practical ends in view, and that they are often driven by procedural concerns. The 'unfortunate' result is that

> orientation towards practice and procedure has induced scientifically untenable bifurcations, e.g. the separation of excuse and justification from a supposed complete definition of the specific crimes. It has produced other unresolved antinomies in extant criminal theory, such as . . . zealous efforts to combine negligence and conscious harm-doing within a single conception of 'fault.'[100]

When Hall moves on to consider the principle of selection which would allow these problems to be transcended,[101] it turns out that it consists not in a genuinely mediating principle between practice and theorisation but in the requisites and axioms of theory itself:

> *Since this theory is both descriptive and systematic, it requires a unified substantive subject matter, and that need functions as a definite principle of selection among verbally or practically designated 'penal' laws.* Such a theory is therefore not directed by the 'penal code'; it is directed towards that code. Since the theory is descriptive, normative and scientifically oriented, it selects 'penal laws' which exhibit common characteristics by virtue of their reference to certain classes of conduct and harm. By adhering to common empirical-normative references, the theorist gathers together penal laws which are often widely separated or indiscriminately lumped together; and . . . he also excludes many so-called 'penal laws' from the field of penal law. Transcending the practical logic and criteria of codes and procedure, descriptive theory seeks to provide an organised body of knowledge that is no less helpful to the practitioner than it is valid for the scholar.[102] (emphasis added)

In a final *reductio ad absurdum* of this theoretical stance, Hall asserts that criminal laws are either 'merely formal or they are also true or "real" penal laws: i.e. they conform to the principles of penal law.'[103] In Hall, the general part has reached its apogee as theoretical cornerstone, encompassing a theory of criminalisation as well as a theory of responsibility. Yet this very primacy means that its limitations as an organising framework for 'theory' are far more apparent than they are in Williams.

Finally, however, we can also perceive in another difference between Hall and Williams the seeds for one of the next developments in criminal law theory. Hall has an extraordinarily inclusive conception of the disciplinary resources of criminal law theory. Whilst Williams's resources are those of analytical jurisprudence and positivist legal scholarship, Hall's conception bears the marks of the social sciences' influence in twentieth-century American legal scholarship. Thus he sees advances in the philosophy of science, psychiatry, and the social sciences as key insights to be incorporated into the theorisation of criminal law. Consequently, Hall includes a chapter on criminology and penal theory – enterprises that he describes as 'interdependent phases of a single body of [criminal legal] knowledge.'[104] Since penal law defines the subject matter of criminology, and as criminological explanations of the conduct in question form the basis for application of penal law, Hall envisages a synthesis of the normative/ethical orientation of classical criminology, the analytical/conceptual framework of imperative theories of law, and the empirical orientation of the sociological school, organised around a common subject matter.[105] There is therefore an enormous gulf between Williams and Hall in terms of their theoretical ambitions and pretensions. In Williams, these are modest. In Hall, they are extravagant: 'penal theory systematizes and elucidates the structure, factual meaning and ethical rationale of penal law.'[106] Hall envisages an 'inclusive socio-legal discipline'[107] which would acknowledge that the various parts of the legal structure are assembled from a nonlegal realm of fact, value, and meaning. In this, he foreshadows the shape of criminal-theoretic maps to come. Yet, ironically, this vision has little to do with the analytically driven 'science' which he himself struggles to develop.

iv. A Pause in the Journey

Before moving on to consider the contemporary state of criminal law theory, I want to return to the metaphor of mapping in order to draw out some general points from the foregoing discussion of the history of doctrinal theories and classification systems in criminal law scholarship. First, our consideration of the work of Blackstone, Stephen, and Williams has shown that even the most detailed of expository legal scholarship implicitly contains theorisations of criminal law. As such, even the most detailed and system-grounded theorisations meet the methodological problem of answerability to practices outlined at the end of the previous section. In this respect, the analogy between maps and theories is instructive. A theory, after all, is not the same as the practice which it explicates, any more than a map is the same as a terrain: 'All lines on a map, we must acknowledge, are imaginary; they are ideas of order imposed on the sloshing flood of time and space. Lines on a map are talismanic and represent the magical thinking of quantitative and rational people.'[108]

By focussing on criminal law doctrine – itself a theorised notion – lawyers' systematisations of criminal law seek to mediate the theory/practice dichotomy. But such a mediation buys its success at the cost of rationalising only a part of its potential terrain. Moreover, it is interesting to note that the increasing emphasis upon systematisation structured around the 'general part', and around the '*mens rea* principle' in particular, has developed during a period in which the criminal law terrain which lies outside this doctrinal paradigm has massively increased in scope and in practical importance. This fact lends some support to the critical hypothesis set out in the early part of this chapter: that doctrinal rationalisations serve to repress aspects of practices which raise intractable problems of legitimation. The map is most necessary to the bewildered traveller, and its magic lies precisely in its power to mitigate the bewilderment by reshaping the world in terms which are intellectually and psychically palatable and which conduce to practical orientation, even if they are extraordinarily partial.

Second, our historical excursus has revealed that the shape of theoretical precepts of coherence, rationalisation, and systematicity are themselves relative to the practical, political, and ethical motivations and underpinnings of particular theories. There are no absolute criteria of coherence or systematicity: What appears coherent or systematic depends upon a particular understanding of the practice being theorised. Different magics realise themselves in different logics: A map oriented to the navigation of waterways is of little use to a person driving a car, just as a map which expresses different geological and geographical formations looks very different from one which traces the boundaries of nation-states.

Hence, third, our selective survey has shown that the conceptualisation of criminal law as based primarily on a 'general part' of broad and coherent principles applicable across the terrain of criminal law is merely one, historically contingent, theorisation. It is one whose power to orient us and to illuminate our journeys across criminal law doctrine and practice is not a product of timeless laws of logic or metaphysical truths. Its power is rather relative to the existing state of criminal law doctrine, to contemporary developments in intellectual disciplines, and to the social, political, and economic conditions underpinning criminal law as a social practice in certain societies of the late twentieth century. Certainly, it is possible to represent, as Hall does, the gradual development of criminal law doctrine as one of progress towards a more significant general part, and hence to characterise early classification systems as 'primitive' or 'undeveloped.' But this reverse historical mapping is what we might call 'chronologically ethnocentric': It proceeds from the ideological premises of contemporary legal culture. Furthermore, it has the effect of obscuring other motivating features of criminal legal theorisation – features such as the importance at certain moments of arguments about procedure, for codification, for the inclusion of certain forms of conduct within criminal law, for certain practices of punishment. It also fails to attend to aspects of criminal law theory – notably the analysis and rationalisation of the conduct encompassed by criminal law and the analysis of the logic and power of procedural forms – which have gradually been attenuated or lost. With a firm grasp of the historical contingency of our contemporary conception of and commitment to 'the general part', we are better equipped to return to the present day and to consider the shape of maps in recent criminal law theory.

III. Contemporary Criminal Law Theory: Postmodernism, Value Pluralism, and the General Part

The foregoing discussion has revealed a number of broad trajectories in the development of criminal law theory: a move from a focus on procedure to an approach based on substantive offences and then on formal principles of liability; a growing concentration on the 'general part' and on the *mens rea* as opposed to the *actus reus* elements within that part; and, over the last century, a diminishing concern with the mapping of the special part and with the scrutiny and classification of the harms, interests, and injuries comprehended within the definitions of substantive offences. This increasingly focussed mapping has, in effect, carved out a specialist terrain of highly technical doctrinal argument, in which legal and philosophical modes of analysis are often hard to distinguish from each other. It has also contributed to a situation in which a concentration on the proper *conditions* of responsibility has shifted attention away from *patterns and practices of the attribution of criminal responsibility:* Indeed, conditions of responsibility are sometimes treated as if they *constituted* the practice of attribution. In stark contrast to the focus of Blackstone or even Stephen, insofar as changing patterns in substantive criminalisation have formed the object of contemporary scholarship, it has been among criminologists and sociologists rather than criminal law theorists. This has facilitated the theoretical and doctrinal construction of criminal law as an autonomous, coherent, and principled practice and, notwithstanding the fragmentation of both criminal law and the social world of which it forms a part, has perpetuated the image of a strong link between criminal law and widely shared 'community values.' This vision of autonomy and coherence is, however, far more central to both philosophical and doctrinal analyses than to socio-legal analyses which map a broader terrain.[109]

However, as we saw in the early parts of this chapter, the practice of presenting criminal law as coherent, rational, and systematic has recently come under attack from exponents of critical legal theory. By subjecting criminal law doctrine to both philosophical deconstruction and historically grounded analysis, 'critical' scholars have attempted to reveal its underlying tensions, compromises, and contradictions, its instabilities and its indeterminacies, its hidden contingencies discursively reconstructed as transcendent rather than practical truths. In this section, I want to consider certain developments in criminal law theory which do not see themselves as within the 'critical' tradition yet which bear some apparent relationship to the critics' diagnosis of multiplicity and lack of systematicity in criminal law. I then want to consider the relationship between these developments and critical legal theory and, in turn, to raise some questions about the social, political, and historical conditions under which the impulse to highly systematic classification in theorisations of criminal law is transformed or weakened.[110] In conclusion, I shall develop some arguments about the disciplinary resources and the substantive scope of an analysis which may hope to illuminate criminal legal practices and their relationship both to predominant doctrinal and other theoretical rationalisations and to broader practices of criminalisation.

In considering some recent contributions to criminal law theory, I want to concentrate on two distinct but interrelated themes. First, I shall examine the move away from the idea that the 'general part' has to be systematic in the sense of being *unitary.* Second, I shall examine the move towards a greater focus on the 'special part' as an object of criminal law theory. I shall suggest that each of these developments speaks to some of the same concerns as critical legal theory, and that each may be located within a general trend in intellectual culture away from the pretensions of 'grand theory.' I shall argue that these intellectual trends in turn relate to material social developments – both towards a more extensive and hence fragmented criminal law, which poses increasingly severe problems for theoretical rationalisation, and towards forms of social organisation in which certain kinds of order and predictability are increasingly scarce commodities. Finally, I shall suggest that these intellectual trends lay the ground for an approach to criminal law theory which, if less rigid in its demands for coherence and unity, is nonetheless systematic in its demand that a concern with the conditions for the attribution of responsibility be integrated with a concern to trace the substantive patterns of criminalisation and practices of punishment. What I shall diagnose, then, is a changing conception of what counts as, or should be included in, a 'systematic' account – one which takes the form of an (inchoate) movement towards a theory of criminal law*s* and of criminal legal practice*s*. I shall argue for a conception of such a theory in which the analysis of historical, political, and social conditions and forces is as much a part of the theoretical mapmaker's toolbox as are philosophy and legal doctrinal analysis.

i. The Loosening Grip of the General Part?

Whether illustrative of continuity or of discontinuity, the selection of examples in the mapping of a history is bound to be shaped by the concerns of the mapmaker. This is doubtless true in my own case. However, I think that it is conducive to the drawing of a thought-provoking map to see something of a turning point in 1978, with the publication of George Fletcher's *Rethinking Criminal Law.* Whilst most certainly concerned both with 'grand theories' of criminal responsibility and with an assessment of the relative merits of competing such theories, the organisation and approach of Fletcher's 900-page volume was a striking departure from that of earlier criminal law texts.[111] In the first place, his starting point was not a consideration of 'the nature of criminal law' or even of 'the principles of criminal responsibility.' Rather, he set out from a detailed case study of the law of theft, tracing its historical development from the early Common Law onwards and identifying certain pervasive problems of interpretation as they arose at different moments of that history. Out of this specific case study, Fletcher distilled two 'patterns of criminality' which, with the addition of a third distilled from the law of homicide, he used to map, analyse, and assess different approaches to the construction of criminal liability in American and in German law. Moving through this detailed consideration of theft and homicide, Fletcher did not arrive at the 'general part' until almost 400 pages into his book. And whilst the analysis of the general part occupied the rest of the volume, it was not organised along the familiar lines of *actus reus, mens rea,* and defence but rather in terms of a conceptual framework based on the notions of wrongdoing and its attribution to agents. This framework entailed that questions about the nature and meaning of punishment lay at the heart of Fletcher's conception of the general part.

Fletcher's pathbreaking study did not, it must be noted, change the pattern of organisation of other widely used English and American criminal law texts, the majority of which continue to employ a system of classification which owes a deep intellectual debt to Williams's *The General Part.*[112] Nonetheless, a recognition of different principles of attribution or responsibility as *co-existing within* rather than as *competing explanations of* the general part has arguably gained increasing currency in theoretical work on criminal law over the past fifteen years. I shall take as my touchstone here a recent book which includes articles by some of the most influential criminal law theorists in Britain and America – *Action and Value in Criminal Law.*[113] This collection reflects both the density of the contemporary theoretical focus on the general part and the methodological problems about general theorisation which I have already considered. However, several of the articles also concern themselves with the tendency to inappropriate or exaggerated systematisation in criminal law theory and propose various responses which would render such theory more pluralistic and (hence) more answerable to the demands of multifarious criminal legal practices. In what follows, I shall briefly review these features of the collection before moving to a more detailed consideration of its status as a symptom of the incipient development towards more pluralistic theorisations.

With one exception,[114] all the contributions to *Action and Value in Criminal Law* concern themselves with theoretical questions pertaining to the component elements of the contemporary conception of the general part: *actus reus, mens rea,* and defence. The collection is therefore a paradigm of the typical focus of contemporary criminal law theory. Insofar as the object of the articles' theorisation moves beyond that of criminal law doctrine, the main question canvassed is that of punishment. This reflects the way in which the arguments which underpin 'the principle of responsibility' have direct connections with and implications for the practice of punishment – a connection which is perhaps most clearly expressed in the work of writers such as von Hirsch and Ashworth who have defended desert-based penal theories.[115] Questions of evidence and procedure, like those about the conduct which forms the substantive object of criminal law, are strikingly absent from the collection.

Similarly, many of the articles in the collection exemplify the methodological difficulties in mediating the relationship between theory and practice we have already identified. In this respect, Brudner's essay is an instructive example not only of the move towards pluralism to be discussed below but also of the difficulties of philosophical analysis which feels no apparent need to ground itself in either a particular system or a particular type of system identified in terms of a moment of history or a certain political ideology. Whilst Brudner is clearly concerned, roughly speaking, with liberal systems,[116] his selection of examples is not grounded in a particular system and is quite often inaccurate, at least in relation to the English system.[117]

An interesting though rather different example of the puzzle about the relationship between philosophical theory and legal practice is provided by Moore's essay on foreseeability.[118] Moore provides a philosophical analysis which purports to show the complete indeterminacy of the concept of foreseeability because of the malleability of the action descriptions onto which judgments of foreseeability are mapped. Without some typology of those action descriptions, he argues, foreseeability tests are meaningless and should be abandoned. As the editors note, his argument here has something in common with the diagnoses of 'incoherence' which characterise the work of the sceptical critics whom Moore stigmatises as the 'stray dogs' of the intellectual world.[119] More important, however, one wonders just what Moore thinks is going in the many cases in which courts and juries rely, apparently without appalling difficulty, on the tests whose incoherence he claims to demonstrate. *Some* form of meaningful social practice is going on here, and one would think that the attempt at its interpretive reconstruction is one role of criminal law theory. In this respect, conceptually minded philosophers all too often fall into the error of which they accuse their critical legal counterparts: that of 'deconstruction' without 'reconstruction.'[120]

Let us turn, then, to the move towards a more modest or pluralistic approach to the general part – a theme which characterises several of the contributions to *Action and Value in Criminal Law* and one that is echoed in both the editors' introduction and the recent work of one of the editors, John Gardner. It is, for example, taken up by Gardner in his contribution to the present collection, and by Gardner and Jung in an article reviewing Duff's *Intention, Agency and Criminal Liability* – a review which takes issue, among other things, with Duff's assumption of the need for a unitary conception of *mens rea.*[121] The nature of contemporary doubt about the notion of a unitary 'general part', and about the pretensions of a theory of the general part to constitute a theory of criminal law, is particularly clearly expressed by Gardner and Jung. They question Duff's attempt to produce a unitary theory of criminal responsibility based on the paradigm of intended actions, arguing instead for a more modest conception of the general part. This conception focuses only on the threshold conditions for liability and in particular on the issues of voluntariness, capacity, infancy, and sanity. In this respect Gardner and Jung's argument resembles a call for a return to the Blackstonian conception of the general part.[122]

Gardner and Jung also tackle some central issues concerning methodology in criminal law theory. They question the 'philosophical' status of Duff's analysis by highlighting the tension between his engagement with the empirical, analytic, and evaluative projects distinguished by White: his appeal to and exposition and clarification of existing criminal law doctrine, his attempt to construct a systematic conceptual/philosophical account, and his attempt to render that account consistent with the precepts of an adequate moral theory. Gardner and Jung suggest that the combination of the ambition of Duff's conception of the general part with his insistence on the answerability of theory to practice – an insistence which leads him to ground much of his argument in an analysis of actual cases – means that his theory falls between two stools. Although they sometimes write as if philosophers of action should be concerned only with logic within conceptual frameworks and not with answerability to practices, Gardner and Jung's point here seems to be that in the movement between conceptualisations and values enshrined in existing practices and the intellectual demands of a theoretical system, Duff's balance is too strongly geared to the former. In the final analysis, his project fails because he misreads existing practices as themselves based on a principled conception of a unitary general part. As Laing has suggested, however,[123] there is a similar tension in Gardner and Jung's own account. Their argument that voluntariness as a threshold condition poses a more promising basis for the construction of criminal law theory than does a broad notion of responsibility appears to be premised on an appeal to practices not dissimilar to that made by Duff. If, as Laing suggests, voluntariness, no less than responsibility, turns out, as realised in criminal legal practices, to be a multifaceted notion, it will present the theorist with much the same difficulties. Hence, Laing argues, Gardner and Jung's analysis leads them along a path to a scepticism about systematising theory which they do not in fact want to follow.

Similar doubts about the prospects for a unitary theory of criminal culpability are expressed by Gardner and his co-authors, Shute and Horder, in their introduction to *Action and Value in Criminal Law.* Take, for example, their comment on Robinson's essay.[124] This essay is itself an attempt to develop a more differentiated account of the component elements of the general part. Robinson questions the simple conceptualisation of the general part in terms of a distinction between *actus reus* and *mens rea* – a distinction which, he suggests, has neither a functional nor a conceptual unity. He then proposes a more complex conceptualisation which breaks down both *actus reus* and *mens rea* into four separate analytic concerns: *Actus reus* encompasses the act requirement, rules about omissions liability, the voluntariness requirement, and objective elements of defences; *mens rea* comprises present-conduct intention, present-circumstance culpability, future-result culpability, and future-conduct intention. Robinson suggests that this more complex classification maps functionally onto the appropriate framework for analysing crimes. This he takes to be a framework distinguishing conduct, circumstance, and result and one which acknowledges three distinct functions of criminal law doctrine: the articulation of rules, the setting of conditions for liability, and the setting of a general system of grading offences.

Shute, Gardner, and Horder question not only whether the adoption of such a classification would clarify criminal legal practice but also whether one can say *anything* about the 'logical structure of crimes in general.'[125] This perhaps sits unhappily with their introductory commitment to the value of the project of tracing the 'internal logic' of social practices such as criminal law.[126] And because they are clearly anything but sceptical about criminal law theory, it follows that they think that its focus should be elsewhere than on the general part.[127] A glimpse of their commitment to a more pluralistic approach is given in their comment on Brudner's contribution to the collection.[128] Brudner suggests that theories of criminal law have gone awry in their attempt to rest the entire weight of their rationalisation on criminal law's concern with *either* autonomy *or* welfare. This has led in turn to one of two problems. Sometimes it has engendered a distortion of the actualities of criminal legal practices through the marginalisation or exclusion of portions of those practices which do not fit with the favoured model: The (non)treatment of strict liability in autonomy-focussed theories is a clear example. On other occasions it has led to a false diagnosis of lack of principle and contradiction. The diagnosis is false,

Brudner suggests, because the autonomy- and welfare-protecting concerns of criminal law are in fact not only complementary but also mutually dependent. A better approach – one which he labels 'dialogic community' – recognises this by espousing a pluralistic conception of criminal law. The editors' response to this suggestion is that it does not go far enough: that welfare and autonomy are not exhaustive of the values which criminal law seeks to respect and promote.[129] They therefore evince a commitment to a yet more pluralistic theory of criminal law, and to one which, by implication, is as much concerned with the shape of the special as of the general part.[130]

ii. From the Formal Structure of Liability to Substantive Patterns of Criminalisation?

Thus whilst many of the contributions to *Action and Value in Criminal Law* reflect the dominant concern with responsibility which characterises Williams's focus on the general part, an incipient turn to a more modest conception of the general part in terms of threshold conditions of liability and/or to a more pluralistic conception is presaged in both the introduction and several of the essays. This in turn foreshadows, I suggest, a shift in criminal law theory towards a greater focus on conduct and thus on the special part of criminal law. This inevitably entails a certain kind of shift from form to substance. If, as the editors suggest, little that is general and systematic can be said of the *structure* of criminal liability, the theorisation of criminal law will have to concern itself also with the *actual forms* which criminal liability takes. Furthermore, it will have to concern itself with the *connections* between the formal aspects of criminal liability and the substantive patterns of criminalisation – a connection which is generally ignored in both 'critical' and 'philosophical' criminal law theory.[131] It is worth noting, however, that insofar as a shift towards this kind of focus can already be detected, it is one which continues to marginalise the dominant concerns of criminal law practitioners: criminal procedure, the rules of evidence, and sentencing practice.

The idea that forms of liability and their substantive objects are entirely separate is, it seems to me, an odd one which is contradicted not only by the history of criminal legal practices but also by the tenets of critical method. To take just one example: The attempt to render corporations criminally responsible is one which has certainly encountered difficulties in terms of the formal structure of criminal liability; yet the political and ethical motivation for such criminalisation has itself gradually driven changes in the legal interpretation of those formal requirements.[132] In other words, the political arguments for criminalising corporations have influenced the development of doctrine, just as the earlier form of that doctrine reflected a substantive judgment about the proper objects of criminalising power – that is, individuals. More generally, can it really be doubted that views about who should be criminalised for what, and about what the practical (penal) implication of that liability should be,[133] are on the implicit agenda in all criminal law cases, playing an interpretive role which is certainly structured but equally certainly not determined by doctrinal categories? The unearthing of this suppressed role is, of course, one of the main concerns of 'critical' approaches; but it is one which cannot be attempted within the constraints of an exclusive focus upon the formal structure of criminal law doctrine.[134] In short, a rigid separation of doctrinal and criminalisation theory obscures the existence of connections which are central to an adequately historicised understanding of criminal law.

What I am both advocating, and arguing to be implicit in the incipient developments analysed previously, is therefore criminal law theory which is interpretive in the sense outlined in the earlier part of this chapter: criminal law theory which constitutes an attempt to map existing institutional practices. As well as taking a broad view of the terrain to be charted, such an approach would have an enriched conception of the disciplinary resources relevant to criminal law theory. Hence analysis of the political, social, and economic forces underlying patterns of criminalisation and prevailing understandings of the role and functions of criminal law, and with them much of the terrain of criminology, criminal justice studies, and penology, will, I predict, force themselves on the attention of criminal law theorists who follow through their own arguments about the shortcomings of unitary theories of the general part. Whilst it is too soon to attempt a general review of any such development, it is perhaps worth citing some examples which may count as evidence of the move to such a pluralistic disciplinary approach. One is Schonsheck's recent work in normative criminal law theory, which mounts a powerful argument for the integration of questions about the proper scope of criminal law and sociological understandings of its actual and likely impact *as enforced.*[135] Another is the appearance of a number of collections of essays which blend the concerns traditionally associated with criminal law theory, criminology, and penology and which focus upon particular hills, plains, and islands within the criminal legal terrain, rather than on that terrain as a whole.[136] Once again, it is important to emphasise that the move towards a criminal law theory which is both less unitary and more inclusive in its conception of its subject matter does not represent an abandonment of the commitment to coherence or system: It simply evinces a different conception of those intellectual and practical demands.

iii. Politics, Pluralism, and the 'Postmodern' Moment

I now turn, finally, to the question of the origins of the incipient move in criminal law theory towards a broader and less rigidly systematised approach. Whilst this is a move within the conceptualisation of doctrinal categories, there are strong reasons for thinking that it is related – albeit obliquely – to the development of substantive offences and the administration of criminal justice. Inevitably, I am painting here with broad brush strokes. The following remarks, however, provide a tentative sketch of the issues which would need to be addressed in any full interpretation of the development of systems of classification as the products of underlying sociopolitical forces which shape the motivations and concerns not only of philosophers and legal theorists but also of legislators and lawyers.

Whatever the intellectual merits of movements such as 'pragmatism', 'deconstruction', 'poststructuralism', and 'postmodernism', it can hardly be denied that the contemporary practice of social theory is significantly marked by them.[137] Whilst the relationship between these approaches is contested, a common theme amongst them is a scepticism about the pretensions of so-called 'meta-narratives' or 'grand theories' either to illuminate the nature of social practices or to ground the claims to 'truth' and 'knowledge' which they generate. Many of these theories, of course, move well beyond the interpretivism which I have defended. Furthermore, it is debatable how far these approaches themselves dispense with generalisations and assumptions such as those of the 'meta-narratives' which they criticise. Nonetheless, their emergence and currency in the academy is itself a symptom which calls for interpretation. The link between these sceptical, localised, deconstructive social theories and the approach of critical legal theory and the further resonance between the disintegrating approach of critical legal theory and the move to a less unitary conceptualisation of the general part of criminal law are quite striking. As Gardner argues in the present volume, this is not to imply that no criteria of rationality or coherence can be applied to criminal law theories. It is, however, to suggest that what motivates a rekindled emphasis on the special part in the reconstruction of such theories is not unrelated to the impulse which feeds the scepticism of postmodernism and the pragmatic resistance to the metaphysical pretensions of philosophy in contemporary social theory. It also suggests a link between the development of postmodernism in social theory and the increased emphasis on value pluralism and multiculturalism in liberal political theory.[138]

This raises the further question of the social and political conditions under which such intellectual discourses arise and find an audience – in which the postmodern map is thought to chart a meaningful and navigable terrain.[139] In other words, it raises the question of the relationship between postmodernism, understood as a collection of intellectual discourses, and postmodernity, understood as a moment in the development of 'advanced', post-industrial countries. The most frequently canvassed possibility focuses on the physical, informational, and even emotional mobility fostered by modern transport and electronic technology, the disintegration of traditional forms of life and fixed identities, and the sense of insecurity which this, along with mass unemployment and unpredictable shifts in the globalised economy, engenders.[140] These features of the (post)modern world, it may be argued, have an impact on the style of theorisation which is palatable to the intellectual community. In a world in which certainty and predictability are scarce commodities, the development of theory which either celebrates uncertainty, incoherence, and diversity or which at least attenuates the demand for order and coherence in intellectual systems may not only reflect interpretive judgments but also constitute an adaptive mechanism. The fact that such theorising itself calls forth vigorous (and sometimes intemperate) resistance on the part of those still committed to the older notions of system and rationalisation, stability, and (T)ruth is certainly not a sufficient counter to this hypothesis; resistance and repression are, after all, mechanisms which fulfill similar psychic functions to that of adaptation. In the criminal law sphere, this would lead us to expect precisely what we see: a theoretical practice polarised in terms of approaches which explore multiplicity, incoherence, and indeterminacy,[141] and those which lay an ever greater stress on order, rationality, and system. These comments can be no more than speculative. They are, however, premised on the view that the challenge to think through the genesis of current developments in criminal law theory is no less important than is that of engaging in a politically and historically informed interpretation of the systematising efforts of past criminal law theorists such as Blackstone and Stephen.

The further project of mapping the relationship between doctrinal rationalisations and distinctive developments in contemporary patterns of criminalisation now seems to me the most pressing challenge for the theorisation of contemporary criminal law and criminal justice. Such a project would concern itself with substantive practices of criminalisation at not only legislative and judicial but also executive and penal levels. It would also address the patterns of that social interpretation which is an inextricable part of the formal exercise of criminalising power.[142] It would, therefore, locate the genesis of theorisations of criminal law within specific socioeconomic and political developments; and it would be both critical and sociolegal.[143] It is a mapmaking task which is, however, in its early stages, and one which has hardly impinged on the consciousness of philosophically inclined theorists of criminal law.

Conclusion

The most systematic and accessible of articles ideally concludes with a crisp reiteration of its principal themes and the main arguments which it has advanced, just as the most systematic map books include a small-scale overview of the territory charted. Since this chapter has surveyed several different terrains, the best that can be done by way of conclusion is to identify each of them, marking out, in the style of Blackstone, their principal geographic features and the paths which I have suggested should be followed in traversing them.

First, I have considered the nature of the enterprise(s) of criminal law theory, in terms both of an analysis of their various components and their relationship with one another, and of a historical overview of actual approaches to criminal law theorisation of a particular kind. My argument has focussed on approaches which seek to interpret actual criminal legal practices – a method which I defended as both the most illuminating and, in some sense, the inevitable form of criminal law theory which deserves the name. With this focus in mind, I argued that criminal law theory is produced equally by philosophers and by doctrinal scholars, and, moreover, that both detailed and relatively abstract approaches confront similar methodological difficulties in terms of their answerability to practices and their balancing of this (vaguely understood) requirement with the theoretical precepts of systematicity, consistency, and coherence. My historical analysis served as a basis for considering the problems posed by this question about the mediation of the terrain of practices by the map of theory. And, by tracing significant changes in the patterns of systems of classification informing criminal law doctrine and its further theorisations, the historical voyage served to sharpen our awareness of the contingency and specificity of contemporary approaches to classification. In particular, it helped to illuminate the contemporary predominance of a certain conception of 'the general part', the normative assumptions implicit in the reading of the history of criminal law doctrine as one of inexorable progress towards the coherent rationalisation of the general part (i.e., in an implicit reading of earlier systems of classification as deficient or theoretically unsophisticated), and the relativity of notions of order and system to particular political concerns and historical conditions underpinning the development and defense of different systems of classification.

Second, I have drawn on a methodology similar to that used in the historical analysis, though inevitably more tentatively applied, to interpret contemporary developments in criminal law theory. These were developments towards both a partial rejection of systematisation and rationalisation as a basis for theory (one way of reading critical legal studies) and (among a different group of theorists) an attenuation of the demands of unitariness in the general part and a shift towards a more modest conception of that part, along with a focus on the special part, as the basis for criminal law theory. Whilst I made some speculative suggestions about the origins of these intellectual developments and their relationship to one another, the main burden of my argument was rather that the movement away from a monolithic 'grand theory' of the general part will produce the theoretical advantages it promises only if it is pursued in terms of an interpretive methodology which has learnt some crucial lessons from the critical tradition in criminal law (and other social) theorising. Such a methodology would be characterised by three main features. First, it would maintain a rigorous self-reflexivity at the level of method, particularly in relation to the question of the mediation between practices, doctrine, and theory. Second, it would have an inclusive conception of its subject matter as one which ranged across all social practices relevant to criminalisation – law making, legal interpretation, legal doctrine, law enforcement, trial processes, sentencing, and punishment. In this context, I argued that the interpretation of criminal procedure has come to be the repressed aspect of contemporary criminal law theory, and my analysis implied the desirability of a renewed focus on criminal procedure as a central aspect of criminal law theory. Third, it would take a broad view of its own disciplinary resources – one in which history and the social sciences are as central as is philosophy, and indeed in which the boundaries between philosophical and social-scientific or historical terrains are either more or less invisible or, at least, do not require the passport of a professional qualification to be crossed.

With such a methodology, contributions to criminal law theory would doubtless look less satisfyingly coherent and systematic than those of, say, philosophers of the conceptual/analytic school. The political and ethical conclusions which we would be able to draw from such theory would, likewise, doubtless be more complicated and indeed uncertain than seem the prescriptions generated by normative philosophical theories which do not concern themselves closely with the actuality of criminal legal practices. Purely from the point of view of theory, or perhaps of theor*ists,* there would therefore certainly be costs. But to count these as a decisive reason against such a development would be to interpret theory as addressed exclusively to theorists. Such an interpretation may well be sociologically valid, but it is no more attractive from a practical or ethical point of view than the idea that maps are made exclusively for mapmakers. If we think, on the other hand, that theories, like maps, are for citizens as well as for scholars, we should not rely on essentially formal theoretical criteria to shape our theoretical practices. The outcome may be a less aesthetically pleasing map, but it will be one which relates more closely to a greater part of the terrain occupied by real subjects of criminal legal practices than do the beautiful local and imaginary maps produced by contemporary theorists of criminal law.

Notes

1 See, for example, Kelman (1981); Lacey, Wells, and Meure (1990): Chapter 1; Nelken (1987); Norrie (1993).

2 Note also Hall's comment that 'One test of the validity of a theory is that of its coherence' (Hall 1960: 21).

3 Norrie (1993): xiii.

4 James Fitzjames Stephen (1883): Volume II, 84.
5 Jeanette Winterson (1989): 87.
6 See Kennedy (1979): 211–16; in relation to criminal law, see references at note 1, and Lacey (1993).
7 Many of the arguments I shall develop bear on my own contribution to such theory: Lacey (1988).
8 Williams (1961), Kelman (1981), Norrie (1993).
9 Duff (1990), Hart (1968).
10 Norrie (1991).
11 Sistare (1989).
12 Box (1983, 1987), Cohen (1985), Foucault (1979), Garland (1985, 1990), Loveland (1995), McVeigh et al. (forthcoming).
13 Hart (1963), Devlin (1965).
14 Feinberg (1984–8), Schonsheck 1994.
15 Duff (1986), Lacey (1988), von Hirsch (1993).
16 Cf. the variety of enterprises comprehended within Shute, Gardner, and Horder (1993a), notwithstanding the editors' introductory focus on conceptual analysis as the basis for philosophy of criminal law (Shute et al. 1993: 1–2).
17 Devlin (1965), Stephen (1883).
18 Fletcher (1978), Hall (1960).
19 Feinberg (1984–8), White (1985), Duff (1986).
20 Cohen (1985), Foucault (1979), Garland (1990).
21 See, for example, the preface to Williams (1961).
22 Cf. Devlin (1965), Hart (1963).
23 White (1985): 5–6.
24 White (1985): 13.
25 See Lacey (1988): Chapter 1.
26 This seems to be roughly the view articulated by Shute et al. (1993). My reference to the importance of the linguistic basis of criminal legal practices should not be taken to imply that such practices constitute an exclusively linguistic realm.
27 [1981] 1 *ALL ER* 961; see White (1985): 106–7.
28 For a good example of the 'pure' philosophical approach, see Hornsby (1993). Unlike some of the other philosophers discussed in this chapter, however, Hornsby is clear-sighted about the distinction between the conceptual and normative philosophical projects. She also recognises the discrete ambit of her philosophical analysis: In a more recent paper she argues, for example, that '(a)n account of action suited to answering questions about the criminal law must be one which combines suitably with an account of all the moral psychological notions and (I should say) with an understanding of the social world' (Hornsby 1995). A good example of an approach which blurs the distinction between conceptual-analytic and normative projects, and yet which fails to identify with any precision the terrain which it attempts to map, is Moore (1993a). The book opens by identifying its analytic object in the following general terms: 'In today's highly regulated, industrialized society, a criminal code typically prohibits approximately 7,000 types of actions' (p. 1).
29 White (1985): 21

30 A good example here would be the approach taken in Moore (1993a). For a critical analysis of Moore's approach, see Hornsby (1994).

31 Norrie (1993): xiv.

32 Wittgenstein (1963) – see in particular paragraphs 23, 199.

33 For further discussion, see Lacey (1988): Chapter 1.

34 For a helpful discussion of interpretive approaches, see Frazer (1997).

35 Shute et al. (1993): 1–2.

36 Cf. Nelken (1987).

37 Kennedy (1979), Norrie (1991, 1993), Kelman (1981).

38 This is not to imply that all conceptual analysis has to engage with historical or contextual questions; it is rather to assume that such philosophical analysis is of oblique and limited relevance to criminal law theory. See note 28.

39 Cf. Duff (1993): 84.

40 Cf. the focus in much of Michel Foucault's work on the historical significance of systems of classification and the organisation of knowledge: Foucault (1972, 1973).

41 For further argument on this point, see Lacey (1993).

42 See Lacey, Wells, and Meure (1990): Chapter 1; Lacey (1995).

43 For a development of this point in relation to Norrie (1993), see Lacey (1994).

44 Cf. Foucault (1972, 1973, 1979).

45 Jeanette Winterson touches on a part of the problem I have in mind: 'Maps are constantly being re-made as knowledge appears to increase. But is knowledge increasing or is detail accumulating?' (Winterson 1989: 88). The idea that legal theory can be likened to mapmaking has a long history; see, for example, the quotations from White at note 24 and from Blackstone at note 52. For a sophisticated discussion of both laws and legal theories as maps, see Santos (1995): Part Three; and for a thoughtful application of the metaphor to the history of criminal law, see Farmer (1996b). The metaphor of mapping captures the sense in which theories of criminal law are inevitably interpretive as opposed to purely representational or descriptive, whilst being simultaneously held to both certain 'scientific' benchmarks and distinctive practical demands in terms of answerability to the phenomena which they seek to explicate. Interestingly, however, the 'scientific' apparatus of criminal law theory knows no equivalent to the mathematical processes of measurement, scaling, and so on which are central to mapmaking, and both the methodology of criminal law theory and the interpretation of the requirement of answerability to practices – the distinction between Winterson's 'knowledge' and 'detail' – are consequently more opaque and more contested than are their analogues in mapmaking.

46 They are not, of course, problems unique to criminal law theory. In the field of civil law, see for example Coleman (1992), reviewed by Cane (1993) and Fletcher (1993).

47 Hall (1960): 1.

48 Ibid.: 13.

49 Hale (1713): xvii–xviii.

50 Indeed, their recognition and reception as such raises as many interesting questions as their content. These issues are, however, beyond the scope of my chapter.

51 Blackstone (1765–9): Vol. I, ii.

52 Ibid.: Volume I, 35.

53 Kennedy (1979).

54 In the view of Duncan Kennedy (1979), Blackstone already gave expression to the idea of the liberal individual as the subject of criminal law; cf. Norrie's argument that the basic ontological component of liberalism is an essentially juridical conception of the individual subject (Norrie 1990). Kennedy's reading of Blackstone is, however, questioned by some legal historians; see, for example, Cairns's (1988) account of the eighteenth-century scholar John Millar's treatment of criminal law as one which expresses the centrality of individual rights more clearly than does Blackstone's. And Lindsay Farmer (1996b: Chapter 5) provides persuasive arguments against the view that Blackstone conceived of the subject of criminal law as an autonomous, will-driven individual.

55 Blackstone (1765–9): Volume IV, 21.

56 See, for example, ibid., 183 (excusable homicide *per infortunium*); 207–8 (malice prepense as a precondition for mayhem); 220 (the meaning of 'malicious' and 'unlawful' in the context of arson); 226–7 (felonious intent in burglary); 243 ('spirit of wanton cruelty or black and diabolical revenge' in criminal damage); 232 (*lucri causa* in theft).

57 Blackstone's treatment of the law of murder (ibid., 194–200), which looks superficially very much like a modern *actus reus-mens rea* analysis, in fact constitutes a useful illustration of the difference between Blackstone's and the modern conception. As in the discussion at note 54, the key issue here has to do with Blackstone's conception of the vicious will, which, as Farmer (1996b: Chapter 5) argues, relates rather to the wicked quality of the act than to the responsibility of the actor understood in terms of a mental state.

58 This is not to imply the fallacious empiricist view that there can ever be purely representational, unmediated description; rather, I assume that interpretivism entails a spectrum of approaches paying greater and lesser attention to detail as opposed to selective rationalisation. Even at the most detailed end of this spectrum, the process of interpretation – and hence of theorisation – is in play.

59 Blackstone (1765–9): Volume IV, 2–3.

60 See the discussion by Green, introducing Volume IV of the *Commentaries* (Blackstone 1765–9). It should, however, be noted that some justification for Blackstone's favourable presentation of the practice of pardoning is provided by the importance of the prerogative of mercy in the administration of criminal justice in the eighteenth century; see Hay (1975).

61 Blackstone (1765–9): Volume IV, 4.

62 Ibid., 284. This is not to say that Blackstone excluded the possibility that a (reformed) summary jurisdiction might be consistent with that genius.

63 For example, Feinberg (1984–8); Schonsheck (1994).

64 On the relationship between form and substance, see Norrie (1993): xiv and text following note 131. A significant and valuable exception to the modern trend is Jeremy Horder's historical analysis of the development of the doctrine of provocation (Horder 1992).

65 The reason for focussing on Stephen's *History* rather than on his other works such as the *Digest* (Stephen 1950b) or *Commentaries* (Stephen 1950a) is that the *History* both gives a flavour of Stephen's general theory of criminal law and shows us his views of

the trajectory of criminal law towards its form in the late nineteenth century. I shall, however, draw analogies and comparisons between Stephen's approach in the *History* and in his other work where this seems useful or necessary.

66 In this computation, as with that of Blackstone, I have included Stephen's discussion of the general nature of criminal law, much of which is not doctrinally oriented and which is therefore not squarely within the conception of 'the general part' adopted, for instance, by Glanville Williams.

67 Stephen (1883): Vol. II, 76.

68 Ibid., 75.

69 Ibid., 78.

70 Ibid., 94.

71 See ibid., 94, discussed in Farmer (1996b): 166 n.103. Stephen's evasion of the history of the principle of responsibility seems odd when compared with the importance he attaches to the history of other aspects of criminal law – particularly so given that he offers no reasons for his assertion that 'the result . . . is more interesting and important than the process by which it was arrived at.'

72 Stephen (1883): Vol. II, 196.

73 Ibid., 96.

74 Ibid., 214.

75 Fletcher (1978). For further discussion of the development of the law of homicide in the nineteenth century, see Farmer (1996b): Chapter 5.

76 Stephen (1883): Vol. II, 77.

77 See Austin (1885), 1048. On Victorian attitudes towards crime and projects of codification, see Wiener (1990).

78 This is not to imply that Stephen ignored regulatory legislation throughout his work; see Stephen (1877).

79 Williams's work includes many references to the Criminal Codes of Commonwealth countries; it also includes several discussions of U.S. doctrine.

80 See Williams (1961): 31.

81 This is a discussion I included within my assessment of both Blackstone's and Stephen's treatment of 'the general part.'

82 Williams (1961): 30.

83 Ibid., 34. Cf. Hart's (contemporary) discussion of definition in jurisprudence (Hart 1957). For further discussion of the (recurring) issue of definition in criminal law, see Farmer (1996a).

84 See Williams (1983); for an analysis of the distorting effects of Williams's implicit commitment to a particular 'theory of criminal law', see Lacey (1985).

85 For good examples of this pervasive rhetorical technique, see Williams (1961): 245–6, 900–1.

86 Ibid, v.

87 Indeed it might be thought an instance of Winterson's accumulation of 'detail' rather than increase of 'knowledge'; see note 45.

88 Williams (1961): 286.

89 Ibid., 575ff, 716–21.

90 Stephen (1950b).

91 Ibid., 1.

92 Ibid., 760.
93 For evidence of the influence of this shift, see Ashworth (1995), Clarkson and Keating (1994), Smith and Hogan (1992).
94 Garland (1985).
95 See Norrie (1993).
96 Hall (1960): 23.
97 See ibid., 20, for a dismissal of procedure as merely 'practical.'
98 See the passages cited at notes 47 and 48.
99 Ibid., 12–13; for further instances of the evolutionary view, see 103, 609.
100 Ibid., 14.
101 Cf. Hall's discussion of *mens rea:* ibid., 72–3.
102 Ibid., 15–16.
103 Ibid., 615.
104 Ibid., 601.
105 Ibid., 607.
106 Ibid., 26.
107 Ibid., 615.
108 Janette Turner Hospital (1992): 1.
109 For example, criminological and penological research charts the impact and enforcement of criminal law.
110 On the historical conditions of existence of deconstruction, see Teubner (forthcoming).
111 It is worth noting, however, that Fletcher owes an intellectual debt to Hall, whose *Theft, Law and Society* (1952) constitutes the starting point for Fletcher's analysis.
112 See Ashworth (1995), Williams (1983), Smith and Hogan (1992); see in particular Clarkson and Keating (1994), one of the most interdisciplinary criminal law texts in England and Wales, yet one in which substantive offences occupy only 250 out of a total of 800 pages, whilst 'general principles', defences, parties, inchoate offences, and causation occupy well over 400. Although in Lacey, Wells, and Meure (1990) the balance of treatment is far more heavily weighted towards the consideration of substantive areas and patterns of criminalisation, the text is nonetheless introduced by a chapter setting out (and criticising) the 'general principles.' For 'critics' as much as for 'mainstream' scholars, the 'general principles' have defined the starting point of enquiry.
113 Shute, Gardner, and Horder (1993a).
114 The exception is the article by Brudner.
115 See von Hirsch (1993), Ashworth (1994).
116 Indeed, one can question how far Brudner's account really moves away from the ethical fulcrum of individual autonomy. For example, his basic argument about what is valuable about welfare is one that proceeds directly from the notion of an individual agent. See Brudner (1993): 48–9.
117 See, for example, Brudner's discussions of consent to grave harm (p. 23) and of drunkenness (p. 35). Whilst doctrinal accuracy is not a test for philosophical adequacy, if philosophers purport to produce interpretive theories, or choose to use actual examples to illustrate, explicate, or confirm their analyses, they had better be accurate than not. If accuracy does not matter, why choose legal examples at all? And if the examples do not need to be legal, what makes these contributions philosophies *of criminal law*?

118 Moore (1993b).

119 Moore is well known for his acerbic characterisations of positions which he sees as falling below appropriate standards of philosophical rigour (see, for example, the terms in which he introduces his discussion of interpretivism in social theory: Moore 1989). It is amusing to speculate whether, on this occasion, Moore's failure explicitly to include within his contemptuous aside stray dogs of the female persuasion flows from chivalry, a pervasive resistance to anything which risks being seen as 'politically correct', fastidiousness about the use of certain words, or analogical adoption of Anglo-American canons of statutory interpretation.

120 For an attempt to reconstruct another case of apparent doctrinal incoherence in terms of broader notions of logic and rationality, see Lacey (1993).

121 Gardner and Jung (1991), reviewing Duff (1990).

122 The same might be said for Horder's historical work (1992) on provocation.

123 Laing (1994).

124 Robinson (1993).

125 Shute et al. (1993): 14.

126 Shute et al. (1993): 2.

127 Unfortunately, their introduction gives little indication of where that focus should lie other than in the notion of voluntariness.

128 Brudner (1993).

129 For example, the editors question whether they could encompass environmental concerns: Shute et al. (1993): 5.

130 The move towards more pluralistic approaches to criminal law theory therefore finds significant expression in *Action and Value in Criminal Law.* However, arguments such as Brudner's also serve to illustrate some of the dilemmas of pluralist theory. For if the pluralism in fact divides up along lines already closely associated with marginalisation of certain criminal legal practices as, as Hall might have put it, 'not real', is there not much the same risk of banishing them to another discipline as exists in purportedly unitary theories? The editors are right to point out that Brudner's analysis incorporates the regulatory and strict liability offences within its philosophical schema (see Shute et al. 1993: 4). But in the absence of any socially and historically grounded attempt to map (legislative and interpretive) patterns of criminalisation, the net result of such a re-theorisation may not be so different from that of Hall; some 'penal laws' just aren't penal laws in the paradigm sense. This is a difficulty which perhaps feeds both the editors' preference for a less ambitious conception of the general part, and the 'definitional minimalism' favoured by Tur (1993), in another essay which exemplifies the sort of development I am attempting to map. Tur argues against a conception of *mens rea* which prioritises either a subjective or an objective approach, arguing that the two can and do co-exist very happily in English criminal law. Whilst his talk of 'synthesis' certainly expresses an impulse for system and unity, this is a far less constraining systematisation and (as Tur shows) one which distorts criminal legal practices considerably less than its 'objectivist' or 'subjectivist' counterparts.

131 Cf. Alan Norrie's comment in the preface to his *Crime, Reason and History* (1993) that his focus on the form of criminal law is complementary to the substantive focus of Lacey, Wells, and Meure (1990). This idea of complementarity is premissed on the sep-

arability of the two kinds of issues. It is precisely this premise which I want to question. This is not, however, to deny what might be called the 'functionalism' of the formalism of modern criminal law doctrine; see text preceding note 95.

132 See Wells (1993).

133 Criminal 'liability' is, after all, liability to punishment.

134 See Lacey (1994).

135 Schonsheck (1994).

136 See, for example, McVeigh, Rush, and Young (forthcoming), Loveland 1995. See also Ashworth's recent study of the criminal process, which attempts to structure an understanding of diverse criminal justice practices in terms of an emerging culture of human rights located within the doctrine of the European Court of Human Rights (Ashworth 1994).

137 See, for example, Rorty (1979, 1989, 1991), Lyotard (1984), Derrida (1976, 1978), Featherstone (1988), Harvey (1989).

138 See, for example, Raz (1986, 1995).

139 Cf. Alan Norrie's powerful argument for reading the history of philosophy as itself a part of the data for critical social theory: Norrie (1990).

140 See, for example, Giddens (1990), Wagner (1993), Lash and Urry (1993).

141 I do not mean, by grouping these three ideas together, to imply their equivalence. Whilst they certainly emphasise contingency, indeterminacy, and multiplicity, both postmodern and deconstructive theories operate with their own conceptions of coherence and map a distinctive logic in their diagnosis of what might be called the unreason of modern rationalism.

142 Cf. Sumner's call for a move to a 'sociology of censures': Sumner (1994).

143 For a further development of this argument, see Lacey (1995); see also Loveland 1995, Christie (1993), and Cohen (1985) for examples of what I take to be this kind of socially informed theoretical research.

References

Ashworth, Andrew (1994). *The Criminal Process: An Evaluative Study* (Oxford University Press).

(1995). *Principles of Criminal Law* (Second Edition, Oxford University Press).

Austin, John (1885). *Lectures on Jurisprudence,* Volume II (John Murray, London).

Blackstone, William (1765–9). *Commentaries on the Laws of England* Volumes I & IV (University of Chicago Press 1979).

Box, Steven (1983). *Power, Crime and Mystification* (Tavistock, London).

(1987). *Recession, Crime and Punishment* (Macmillan, London).

Brudner, Alan (1993). 'Agency and Welfare in the Penal Law', in Shute et al. (eds.), 21–53.

Cairns, John W. (1988). 'John Millar's Lectures on Scots Criminal Law', 8 *Oxford Journal of Legal Studies* 364.

Cane, Peter (1993). 'Markets and Morals in Contract and Tort', 13 *Legal Studies* 396.

Christie, Nils (1993). *Crime Control as Industry* (Routledge, London).

Cohen, Stanley (1985). *Visions of Social Control* (Polity Press, Oxford).

Coleman, Jules (1992). *Risks and Wrongs* (Cambridge University Press).

Clarkson, C.M.V., and H. M. Keating (1994). *Criminal Law: Text and Materials* (Third Edition, Sweet & Maxwell, London).
Derrida, Jacques (1976), *Of Grammatology* (Johns Hopkins University Press).
(1978). *Writing and Difference* (University of Chicago Press).
Devlin, Patrick (1965). *The Enforcement of Morals* (Oxford University Press).
Duff, R. A. (1986). *Trials and Punishments* (Cambridge University Press).
(1990). *Intention, Agency and Criminal Liability* (Blackwell, Oxford).
(1993). 'Acting, Trying and Criminal Liability', in Shute et al. (eds.), 75–106.
Farmer, Lindsay (1996a). 'The Obsession with Definition: The Nature of Crime and Critical Legal Theory' *5 Social and Legal Studies* 57–73.
(1996b). *Criminal Law, Tradition and Legal Order: Crime and the Genius of Scots Law* (Cambridge University Press).
Featherstone, Mike (1988). 'In Pursuit of the Postmodern' 5 *Theory, Culture and Society.*
Feinberg, Joel (1984–8). *The Moral Limits of the Criminal Law,* Volumes I–IV (Oxford University Press, New York).
Fletcher, George P. (1978). *Rethinking Criminal Law* (Little, Brown, Boston & Toronto).
(1993). Review of Coleman (1992), 106 *Harvard Law Review* 1658.
Foucault, Michel (1972). *The Archaeology of Knowledge* (transl. A. Sheridan) (Tavistock, London).
(1973). *The Order of Things* (Vintage Books, New York).
(1979). *Discipline and Punish* (transl. A. Sheridan) (Penguin, Harmondsworth).
Frazer, Elizabeth (1997). 'Method Matters: Feminism, Interpretation and Politics', in A. Vincent (ed.), *Political Theory: Tradition, Diversity, Ideology* (Cambridge University Press).
Gardner, John, and Heike Jung (1991). 'Making Sense of *Mens Rea:* Antony Duff's Account' 11 *Oxford Journal of Legal Studies* 559.
Garland, David (1985). *Punishment and Welfare* (Gower, Aldershot).
(1990). *Punishment and Modern Society* (Oxford University Press).
Giddens, Antony (1990). *Consequences of Modernity* (Cambridge University Press).
Hale, Matthew (1713). *The History of the Common Law of England,* with an Introduction by Charles M. Gray (University of Chicago Press 1971).
Hall, Jerome (1952). *Theft, Law and Society* (Bobbs-Merrill, New York).
(1960). *General Principles of Criminal Law* (Second Edition, Bobbs-Merrill, Indianapolis and New York).
Hart, H.L.A. (1953). 'Definition and Theory in Jurisprudence', in his *Essays in Jurisprudence and Philosophy* (Oxford, Clarendon Press, 1983), 21–48.
(1963). *Law, Liberty and Morality* (Oxford University Press).
(1968). *Punishment and Responsibility* (Oxford University Press).
Harvey, David (1989). *The Condition of Postmodernity* (Basil Blackwell, Oxford).
Hay, Douglas (1975). 'Property, Authority and the Criminal Law', in Hay, P. Linebaugh, and E. P. Thompson (eds.), *Albion's Fatal Tree* (Harmondsworth, Penguin), 17–63.
Horder, Jeremy (1992). *Provocation and Responsibility* (Clarendon Press, Oxford).
Hornsby, Jennifer (1993). 'On What's Intentionally Done', in Shute et al. (eds.), p. 55.
(1994). 'Action and Aberration', 142 *University of Pennsylvania Law Review* 1719.
(1995). 'The Poverty of Action Theory', Inaugural Lecture, Birkbeck College, University of London.

Kelman, Mark (1981). 'Interpretive Construction in the Substantive Criminal Law' 33 *Stanford Law Review* 591.

Kennedy, Duncan (1979). 'The Structure of Blackstone's Commentaries' 28 *Buffalo Law Review* 205.

Lacey, Nicola (1985). 'The Territory of the Criminal Law' 5 *Oxford Journal of Legal Studies* 453.

(1988). *State Punishment* (Routledge, London).

(1993). 'A Clear Concept of Intention: Elusive or Illusory?' 56 *Modern Law Review* 621.

(1994). 'Abstraction in Context' 14 *Oxford Journal of Legal Studies*, 255–67.

(1995) 'Contingency and Criminalisation', in Loveland (ed.), 1–27.

Lacey, Nicola, Celia Wells, and Dirk Meure (1990). *Reconstructing Criminal Law* (Weidenfeld & Nicolson, London).

Laing, J. A. (1994). 'The Prospects of a Theory of Criminal Culpability' 14 *Oxford Journal of Legal Studies* 57.

Lash, John, and Scott Urry (1993). *Economies of Signs and Space* (Open University Press, Milton Keynes).

Loveland, Ian (ed.) (1995). *Frontiers of Criminality* (Sweet & Maxwell, London).

Lyotard, Jean-François (1984). *The Postmodern Condition: A Report on Knowledge* (University of Minnesota Press).

McVeigh, Shaun, Peter Rush, and Alison Young (eds.) (forthcoming). *Criminal Legal Doctrines.*

Moore, Michael S. (1989). 'The Interpretive Turn in Modern Theory: A Turn for the Worse?' 41 *Stanford Law Review* 871.

(1993a). *Act and Crime: The Philosophy of Action and Its Implications for Criminal Law* (Clarendon Press, Oxford).

(1993b). 'Foreseeing Harm Opaquely', in Shute et al. (eds.), 125–55.

Nelken, David (1987). 'Critical Criminal Law' 14 *Journal of Law and Society* 105.

Norrie, Alan (1991). *Law, Ideology and Punishment* (Kluwer, Dordrecht).

(1993). *Crime Reason and History* (Weidenfeld & Nicolson, London).

Raz, Joseph (1986). *The Morality of Freedom* (Oxford, Clarendon Press).

(1995). *Ethics in the Public Domain* (Oxford, Clarendon Press).

Robinson, Paul H. (1993). 'Should the Criminal Law Abandon the Actus Reus–Mens Rea Distinction?', in Shute et al. (eds.), 187–211.

Rorty, Richard (1979). *Philosophy and the Mirror of Nature* (Princeton University Press).

(1989). *Contingency, Irony and Solidarity* (Cambridge University Press).

(1991). *Objectivity, Relativism and Truth* (Cambridge University Press).

Santos, Boaventura de Sousa (1995). *Toward a New Common Sense* (Routledge, London and New York).

Schonsheck, Jonathan (1994). *On Criminalization* (Kluwer, Dordrecht).

Shute, Stephen, John Gardner, and Jeremy Horder (eds.) (1993a). *Action and Value in Criminal Law* (Clarendon Press, Oxford).

(1993). 'Introduction: The Logic of Criminal Law', in Shute et al. (eds.), 1–20.

Sistare, C. T. (1989). *Responsibility and Criminal Liability* (Kluwer, Dordrecht).

Smith, J. C., and Brian Hogan (1992). *Criminal Law* (Seventh Edition, Butterworths, London).

Stephen, James Fitzjames (1883). *A History of the Criminal Law of England,* Volume II (Macmillan, London).

(1950a). *Commentaries on the Laws of England,* Volume IV, ed. L. Crispin Warmington (Butterworths, London).

(1950b). *A Digest of the Criminal Law (Indictable Offences)* 9th edition, ed. Lewis Frederick Sturge (Sweet and Maxwell, London).

(1877). 'Suggestions as to the Reform of the Criminal Law' *Nineteenth Century* (2) pp. 735–59.

Sumner, Colin (1994). *The Sociology of Deviance: An Obituary* (Open University Press, Buckingham).

Teubner, Gunther (forthcoming). 'The King's Many Bodies: The Self-Deconstruction of Law's Hierarchy', *Law and Society Review.*

Tur, Richard H.S. (1993). 'Subjectivisim and Objectivism: Towards Synthesis', in Shute et al. (eds.), 213–37.

Turner Hospital, Janette (1992). *Isobars* (Virago Press, London).

von Hirsch, Andrew (1993). *Censure and Sanctions* (Clarendon Press, Oxford).

Wagner, Peter (1993). *A Sociology of Modernity: Liberty and Discipline* (Routledge, London).

Wells, Celia (1993). *Corporations and Criminal Responsibility* (Clarendon Press, Oxford).

White, Alan R. (1985). *Grounds of Liability* (Clarendon Press, Oxford).

Wiener, Martin J. (1990). *Reconstructing the Criminal: Culture Law and Policy in England, 1830–1914* (Cambridge University Press).

Williams, Glanville (1961). *Criminal Law: The General Part* (Second Edition, Stevens, London).

(1983). *A Textbook of Criminal Law* (Second Edition, London, Sweet & Maxwell).

Winterson, Jeanette (1989). *Sexing the Cherry* (Bloomsbury, London).

Wittgenstein, Ludwig (1963). *Philosophical Investigations* (transl. G. E. Anscombe) (Basil Blackwell, Oxford).

2

Does Criminal Liability Require an Act?

DOUGLAS HUSAK

Does criminal liability require an act? Most legal philosophers apparently believe so. I am unpersuaded. My defense of a negative answer will begin with a clarification of the question itself. If my efforts to interpret this question are successful, I hope it will become relatively clear that criminal liability does not require an act. My conclusion, however, is not designed to support those critical theorists who maintain that the criminal law is unprincipled.[1] I will argue that the considerations frequently advanced on behalf of the act requirement actually establish a somewhat different principle – which I will call the *control requirement.*

I am hopeful that the control requirement proves superior to the act requirement in helping to organize and understand the substantive criminal law. Critical theorists are likely to disagree; they question the rationality and coherence of such principles as I defend. Whether the control requirement should be accepted as rational and coherent depends on two factors. First, the implications of the control requirement must be tested against the general rules and doctrines of the criminal law. I begin this assessment here, although a great deal of work remains to be done. Second, critical theorists must be pressed to explain what they mean by coherence and rationality – the features that the criminal law is alleged to lack. I do not explore these latter issues.[2]

In section I of this chapter, I will describe some of the difficulties that arise in assessing the thesis that criminal liability requires an act and discuss the role that this thesis has played in attempts to distinguish the conditions of moral and criminal responsibility.[3] In section II, I will clarify the thesis that criminal liability requires an act. In section III, I will examine the reasons for believing that criminal liability *ought* to require an act and will contend that these arguments actually support a somewhat different conclusion: that criminal liability ought to require control. I will provide a partial explication of the control requirement

Special thanks to each of the contributors of this volume for their extremely helpful criticisms and suggestions.

in section IV. In section V, I will contrast the implications of the act requirement with those of the control requirement for the justifiability of *status* criminality: offenses that proscribe what a person *is* rather than what he or she *does*. In section VI, I will contrast the implications of the act requirement with those of the control requirement for the justifiability of thought crimes: offenses that proscribe what a person intends. In these two contexts, at least, the control requirement appears to be preferable to the act requirement. In the course of defending my views, I will frequently refer to the contributions of Michael Moore, whose recent defense of the act requirement is the most thoughtful and sophisticated to date.[4]

I. The Act Requirement and the Alleged Distinction between Moral and Criminal Responsibility

Modern criminal codes are seemingly unambiguous in requiring an act for criminal liability.[5] Thus it may be surprising that some criminal theorists disagree about this matter. How might this continued disagreement be explained? Any number of possible explanations might be given; I will discuss only two.[6] The contrast between these two explanations is best understood by the different emphases they place on the original question. The first explanation focuses on the difficulties in deciding whether criminal liability requires an *act;* the second explanation stresses the problems in deciding whether criminal liability *requires* an act. Throughout most of this chapter, I will concentrate on the (relatively unexplored) uncertainties that stem from the latter of these two explanations. The thesis that criminal liability *requires* an act is surprisingly hard to interpret and apply. First, however, it may be helpful to comment briefly on the former explanation and on the role it has played in the larger project of contrasting the conditions of moral and criminal responsibility.

The first general explanation of why commentators are uncertain about whether criminal liability requires an act locates the controversy in disagreement about the nature of action. What are acts?[7] Philosophers have defended many different conceptions,[8] and their lack of consensus might contribute to uncertainty about whether criminal liability requires an act. Criminal liability may require an act according to one conception of action but not according to a competing conception. Thus it seems unlikely that the debate will be resolved without agreement on a particular conception of action. If so, there is little reason for optimism that the matter will be settled in the foreseeable future.

Unfortunately, the prospects for resolving the debate about whether criminal liability requires an act are even more bleak than these remarks suggest. Commentators disagree not only about the nature of action but also about the criteria by which one conception of action should be preferred to another. Their disagreement about these criteria is part of a larger, more fundamental schism in legal philosophy, a schism about the relevance of analytic philosophy to law in general and to the criminal law in particular. This schism, as I propose to understand it, is about the strengths and weaknesses of what I will call the project of *integrating* the criminal law with moral philosophy.

Theorists who endeavor to integrate the criminal law with moral philosophy seek to identify the conditions of criminal responsibility by applying the most philosophically defensible analyses of various concepts. Moral philosophy and criminal law share a common vocabulary. A partial list of the concepts in criminal law that have received extensive attention from moral philosophers includes act, intention, cause, voluntariness, excuse, justification, blame, and desert. Legal theorists might borrow philosophical analyses of these several concepts to identify the conditions of criminal responsibility. In particular, accounts of action by moral philosophers might be invoked in order to understand the law's act requirement.[9] *Perhaps* the criminal law uses a special conception of action, different from that explicated by philosophers. But what could it mean to say that the sense of "action" required for criminal responsibility is different from that developed by moral philosophers, other than to admit that the criminal law does not *really* require action after all? More generally, what could it mean to say that the sense of "responsibility" required for criminal responsibility is different from that developed by moral philosophers, other than to admit that the criminal law does not really require responsibility after all?

Despite its plausibility and appeal, many commentators resist the project of integrating the criminal law with moral philosophy. They have sought to differentiate the conditions of moral and criminal responsibility by denying that philosophical analyses are especially relevant to our understanding of legal concepts. Opposition to this project has come both from philosophers and from legal theorists.[10] Why is there reluctance to use philosophical analyses to help understand legal terminology? Although many possible answers might be given,[11] it is noteworthy that the act requirement has played a central role in attempts to undermine the project of integrating the criminal law with moral philosophy. More specifically, the act requirement is frequently invoked in attempts to differentiate the conditions of moral and criminal responsibility. The latter, it is often claimed, requires an act, whereas the former does not. Rollin Perkins expresses this view as follows: "In the field of ethics, as in the teachings of the Church, guilt depends upon the state of mind alone. . . . But there is no criminal guilt without some socially-harmful result of the guilty mind."[12] In a similar vein, W. Hitchler writes: "In requiring a physical act as a condition of liability[,] the criminal law differs from . . . principles of ethics or moral philosophy, by which the mental element is sufficient to constitute guilt. The moral law has to be expressed in the form 'Be this,' and not in the form 'Do this.'"[13] This claim, if correct, would appear to undermine the project of integrating the criminal law with moral philosophy.

But *is* this claim correct? In fact, this claim contains two distinct contentions – the first about criminal responsibility, which is said to require an act, and the second about moral responsibility, which is said not to require an act. Suppose for the sake of argument that the first contention is correct and that criminal responsibility indeed requires an act. Is the second contention correct as well? Does moral responsibility *not* require an act? If moral responsibility requires an act, these theorists are mistaken in supposing that they have identified a difference between the conditions of criminal and moral responsibility.

The claim that moral responsibility does not require an act is often trumpeted as an important insight, as revealing something deep and significant about the different structures of moral and criminal theory. On closer scrutiny, however, I believe that this claim turns out to be relatively uninteresting and does not really undermine the larger project of integrating the criminal law with moral philosophy. No one should doubt that moral theory purports to evaluate a more diverse range of objects than those evaluated by the criminal law. To cite just a few examples, moral philosophers might endeavor to evaluate actions, intentions, motivations, tryings, emotions, persons, characters, dispositions, thoughts, and even possible worlds.[14] Clearly, neither the law in general nor the criminal law in particular endeavors to evaluate each of these diverse objects. Moral philosophy, in other words, is significantly broader in scope than the criminal law. Why the scope of moral philosophy and that of criminal law are so different presents something of a puzzle and requires an explanation from theorists who sympathize with the project of integrating the criminal law with moral philosophy. If a person can be *morally* responsible for his or her character, for example, why is *criminal* liability for character almost universally rejected as unjustifiable? Still, the proposition that moral philosophy has a wider scope can scarcely be doubted. Perhaps the contention that the act requirement differentiates moral philosophy from the criminal law is designed to serve as a reminder of this fact.

In any event, acts are *one* of the objects of moral evaluation – even if many kinds of non-acts are objects of moral evaluation as well. That part of moral philosophy which evaluates acts might be called *act-morality.*[15] The relationship between act-morality and those parts of moral philosophy that evaluate other objects is controversial. In particular, one object of moral evaluation might be primary and basic, or it might be reducible to another, or it might stand in various complex relations to other objects of evaluation.[16] But these important speculations do not challenge the central point that one part of moral philosophy evaluates acts. Hitchler is surely mistaken to hold that "the moral law" *must* be expressed in the form "Be this" and not in the form "Do this." Can he seriously believe that a rule of the form "One ought not to do this" *cannot* qualify as a *moral* rule? Hitchler's view has the radical and unacceptable consequence that judgments made in the criminal law are immune from moral evaluation, given that the subject matters of morality and law are mutually exclusive.

The statement that an act is required in act-morality is a tautology; without an act, there is nothing to evaluate. By definition, moral evaluation that takes place despite the absence of an act must involve a different part of moral philosophy from act-morality. Thus the claim that criminal liability requires an act can hardly suffice to differentiate the criminal law from at least one *part* of moral philosophy. This claim might suffice to differentiate the criminal law from those parts of moral philosophy that do not evaluate acts, but it is no great insight to notice that those parts of moral philosophy that do not evaluate acts need not require an act. Even if the criminal law *did* require an act, this fact would not differentiate the conditions of criminal responsibility from those of act-morality.

Despite my sympathy with the general project of integrating the criminal law with moral philosophy, in what follows I will not employ a metaphysical conception of action to help answer my question of whether criminal liability requires an act. My reason is simple. Any answer that depends on a particular conception of action would be bound to attract controversy[17] and to deflect attention from those substantive issues to which this account is to be applied.[18] I hope that the best philosophical account of action will prove useful and illuminating for purposes of legal analysis. Fortunately, however, no such account is needed in order to make ample progress in answering the question at hand. I believe that surprisingly little of the disagreement about whether criminal liability requires an act arises from the lack of consensus about the nature of action. There are remarkably few instances in which a clear instance of criminal liability requires an act according to one philosophically respectable conception but does not require an act according to another philosophically respectable conception, so that the question of whether criminal liability requires an act forces the theorist to choose between these conceptions of action. I do not deny that *some* such cases may exist. But I think that insight can be gained by examining cases in which *no* reasonable person would contest that an act has or has not been performed. Reasons can be given in favor of the truth or falsity of the thesis that criminal liability requires an act on *any* conception that satisfies the minimal constraints to which a philosophically acceptable account of action must conform.

I contend that metaphysical confusion about the nature of action provides only a partial explanation of continued disagreement about the act requirement. In this chapter I will be especially concerned with the relatively unexplored source of disagreement that arises from uncertainty about what is meant by the thesis that criminal liability *requires* an act. I will proceed by supposing that theorists have a pretty good understanding of what acts are – but still may be uncertain about whether an act is required for criminal liability.

II. The Act Requirement

Much of criminal theorists' disagreement about whether criminal liability requires an act arises from their lack of clarity about what it means to say that criminal liability *requires* an act. In this section, I hope to gain a better understanding of how this thesis should be interpreted.[19]

Two sources of confusion surround the thesis that criminal liability requires an act. I will describe the first source of confusion as uncertainty about the *status* of the act requirement. I will describe the second source of confusion as uncertainty about the *nature* of the act that satisfies the act requirement. I will comment on each source of confusion in turn. Many of my remarks will address Michael Moore's impressive defense of the act requirement.[20] Few contemporary theorists have gone to greater lengths to integrate the criminal law with moral philosophy.[21]

The Status of the Act Requirement

By inquiring about the *status* of the thesis that criminal liability requires an act, I mean to ask whether this thesis should be construed descriptively, conceptually, evaluatively, or as some combination of these alternatives. Perhaps the most straightforward interpretation of this thesis is that it is solely a descriptive generalization; it is designed to describe the existing state of Anglo-American criminal law. This interpretation suggests that theorists have noticed a striking feature of each case in which criminal liability has in fact been imposed: In every instance, the defendant has performed an act. The thesis that criminal liability requires an act is simply an inductive generalization from this extensive survey. Whether there are good reasons for believing that criminal liability *ought* to require an act is quite another matter. This latter, evaluative question is to be decided independently of whether criminal liability *in fact* requires an act.

For at least three reasons, however, this thesis should not be construed solely as a descriptive generalization. First, no theorist has actually invested the immense time and effort needed to perform the requisite survey – especially because many cases are unreported. As so construed, the act requirement may be highly corroborated, but – because many cases remain to be examined – no one should profess tremendous confidence in its truth. In addition, the thesis itself is misleadingly expressed if it is interpreted simply as an inductive generalization from existing cases. A survey of cases in which criminal liability has in fact been imposed might support the claim that criminal liability always *includes* an act, but it can hardly establish the thesis that criminal liability *requires* an act. Requirements suggest necessity, and it is hard to see how the alleged necessity of an act to criminal liability could be detected by empirical, inductive means. Finally, the thesis as so construed is almost certainly false. In a few notorious instances, persons have been held criminally liable despite the apparent absence of an act. Perhaps the most well-known such case is *Larsonneur.*[22] In this case, a defendant was held liable for "being found in the United Kingdom" without permission, contrary to the Aliens Order. The defendant left England and moved to Ireland, whence she was deported and returned to England, where she was arrested and taken in custody by the English police. A defendant who was taken to a cell by the police and arrested for having been "found" there has almost certainly not performed an act.[23]

For these three reasons, the thesis that criminal liability requires an act should not be construed solely as a descriptive generalization inductively derived from a survey of cases in which criminal liability has actually been imposed. What are the alternatives to this deficient interpretation? Perhaps the thesis that criminal liability requires an act is better construed as a conceptual truth. According to this interpretation, an adequate analysis of the concept of criminal liability entails that such liability requires an act. Although this interpretation overcomes some of the difficulties with construing the thesis as a descriptive generalization, it is clearly deficient as well.[24] Presumably, it is possible to *imagine* a case of criminal liability in which the defendant had not acted; the thought-experiment that criminal liability might be imposed despite the absence of an act does not appear to yield a contradiction.[25]

Perhaps, then, this thesis is best construed as purely evaluative. According to this third interpretation, each imposition of criminal liability *ought* to require an act. This interpretation overcomes each of the three difficulties cited previously. Because the thesis is not an inductive generalization from existing law, the theorist might subscribe to it without having read a single case. In addition, it explains why the thesis is expressed in terms of a *requirement;* an ought-statement is frequently said to give rise to a kind of necessity. Finally, counterexamples from existing law do not count against an evaluative claim; what the law *is* does not entail what the law *ought to be.* Despite these advantages, this interpretation must be rejected as well. Although those commentators who endorse the act requirement construe it as *partly* evaluative, they do not construe it as *purely* evaluative. In asking whether criminal liability requires an act, theorists should be understood to raise a question not about an ideal system of criminal justice but rather about *our* (Anglo-American) systems of criminal law. Anglo-American cases cited in support of this thesis would be irrelevant if the act requirement functioned solely as a constraint on an ideal system of criminal justice. Thus this thesis should not be construed as totally lacking in descriptive content.

What remaining alternatives are available, if this thesis should be interpreted neither as a descriptive generalization, nor as an analytical truth, nor as a pure evaluation? No answer is beyond controversy. I propose that this thesis should be construed as a hybrid of description and evaluation. This thesis is meant to describe the vast majority of cases in Anglo-American law – not merely an ideal system, but *our* systems of criminal law. But the thesis should be understood to include some evaluative content as well. Although the thesis is compatible with the existence of a few examples of criminal liability that do not include an act, such cases must be regarded as mistakes and aberrations.[26] This interpretation of the status of the act requirement captures the overwhelming response of commentators to *Larsonneur*.[27] There would be no basis for using the act requirement to identify real or hypothetical instances of criminal liability that have been decided incorrectly unless the act requirement itself included some evaluative content.

I believe that this interpretation of the status of the act requirement is compatible with the understanding of thoughtful commentators. Michael Moore provides a useful illustration. Moore contends that "there can be no criminal offence without the doing of a voluntary act."[28] This supposed requirement is not a logical necessity; he regards the "can be" in this thesis as a "contingent fact about Anglo-American criminal law."[29] Why, then, is the "can be" not better construed as an "is"? The answer is that this "is" is also an "ought to be." Even before the subsequent chapter that provides a "normative defence of the act requirement,"[30] Moore apparently supposes this requirement to have some evaluative content. After admitting that criminal liability has sometimes been imposed on persons who have *not* acted, Moore writes: "This raises the possibility that perhaps Anglo-American criminal law is mistaken in those rare instances. . . . Perhaps there ought not to be such crimes."[31] Of course, there would be no basis to suspect that exceptions to the act requirement constitute mistakes unless that requirement were partly evaluative. If this requirement had no evaluative component, exceptions would not be mistakes, but just – exceptions.

The Nature of the Act That Satisfies the Act Requirement

I have proposed that the act requirement has the status of a hybrid of description and evaluation. But this conclusion addresses only one confusion about how to interpret the act requirement. A different set of problems emerges in providing an account of the nature of the act that satisfies the act requirement. *Some* such account is needed. Surely criminal liability has not been imposed on someone who has never performed a single act in the course of his or her entire lifetime – a newborn infant, for example. Clearly the act requirement should not be construed to express the obvious (but contingent) truth that anyone ever found criminally liable has in fact acted at some time or another. What, then, does the act requirement express?

An example may help to illustrate this uncertainty. Suppose that legislators in a given jurisdiction become convinced that existing statutes were ineffective in punishing persons who had been disloyal to the monarch and propose a new statute that defined treason as "compassing the death of the king." One legislator, especially adept at criminal theory, objects to this new statute on the ground that it violates the act requirement. In order to mollify his concerns, the legislators agree to amend the statute to include an additional clause that allows liability to be imposed only on persons who had performed the act of eating at some time prior to the moment at which they compassed the death of the king. Surely this additional clause would fail to satisfy any of the concerns that have led theorists to endorse the act requirement in the first place. This device to achieve conformity with the act requirement is clearly a ruse. But why is it so easy to identify this device as a ruse? Whether this device qualifies as a ruse can be decided only by providing an account of the nature of the act that satisfies the act requirement. Such an account will further clarify the act requirement itself.

The act requirement must be interpreted to state that criminal liability requires not only that some act be performed but also that this act must bear some specific relation to criminal liability. The nature of this "specific relation" is not patently obvious. I propose that this connection is best expressed by the "for" relation. In other words, the act requirement is not satisfied unless criminal liability is imposed *for* an act. I am unsure how to defend my proposal to understand the act requirement.[32] But an act would seem unnecessary, superfluous, or extraneous to liability unless punishment were imposed *for* it. Although an act might be included in the offense, I do not see how it could be said to be *required.* This interpretation helps to expose the ruse in the foregoing device to reconcile the treason statute with the act requirement. Unless liability under the statute were *for* the act of eating by a person who compassed the death of the king, the act requirement would not be satisfied – even though the statute had been amended to include an act.

Whether or not a given case of criminal liability satisfies this condition may be hard to determine. Few ruses are as easy to expose as my contrived example; tremendous confusion can arise in identifying what punishment is *for.*[33] Moreover, in holding that the act requirement is unsatisfied unless liability is imposed *for* an act, I hope not to be misunderstood to insist that liability must be imposed for an act *alone.* An act may be necessary but not sufficient for criminal liability. Of course, criminal liability is typically imposed for an act accompanied by a culpable state. When a culpable state is required – as in all crimes in which liability is not strict – liability is just as much *for* the culpable state as *for* the act. I see no basis for privileging either the act or the culpable state, or for claiming that one plays a primary and the other a subordinate role.[34] Nor do I see any basis for apportioning liability between the act and the culpable state. Liability is best conceptualized as *for* the union of an act with a culpable state.

An ambiguity arises in asking what liability is for.[35] One might be inquiring (1) for the sake of what purpose or objective is liability imposed? This question invites the theorist to provide a forward-looking rationale or justification for imposing liability. Different areas of the law may have distinct goals or objectives. In tort law, for example, theorists in the "law and economics" school argue that the rationale for imposing liability is to promote efficient behavior. This is not, however, the sense in which I propose that the act requirement is unsatisfied unless liability is imposed for an act. In asking what liability is for, one might be inquiring (2) in virtue of what is liability imposed? This question invites the theorist to provide a backward-looking rationale or justification for imposing liability. It asks, I think, for a desert basis for liability: In virtue of what is liability deserved?[36] In tort law, again, I think it is reasonably clear that liability is for the injury suffered by the plaintiff. In this context, the preposition "for" requires not a goal but an untoward state of affairs.

Moore appears to disagree with my proposal about the relation between the act and criminal liability that is needed to satisfy the act requirement. In other words, Moore seems to believe that the act requirement can be satisfied even though liability is not imposed *for* an act. Clues that he disagrees with my proposal to interpret the act requirement in terms of the "for" relation can be gleaned from his section titled "Supposed Counter-examples to There Being Any Act Requirement."[37] Here Moore responds to those theorists who have proposed that the act requirement admits of exceptions.[38] Among these "supposed counterexamples" to the act requirement are "crimes of possession, of omission, of status, and of mental action."[39]

Moore begins by discussing the allegation that criminal attempts are "Crimes of Mental State" that suffice as counterexamples to the act requirement.[40] He writes:

> It might be objected that we in effect do punish people for thoughts alone when we define crimes in a way not requiring the doing of any wrongful act. In attempts, for example, the acts that amount to an attempt may well be innocent on their face – such as walking towards a building with matches in one's pocket and the day's newspaper under one arm. Yet such acts become criminal – say, attempted arson – if done with a culpable intention, such as the intent to burn the building with the paper and matches. The objection is that in such instances we are in reality punishing for the intention alone.[41]

Clearly, Moore is unpersuaded that attempts provide counterexamples to the act requirement. What is less clear is *why* he is unpersuaded. Two incompatible answers might be given. First, he might believe that liability for attempts satisfies the act requirement even though it is not imposed *for* an act. Second, he might believe that liability for attempts satisfies the act requirement because it *is* imposed for an act. With the difference between these answers in mind, consider Moore's subsequent remarks:

> Such an objection misses the formal, doctrinal nature of the question here examined. . . . The question is only whether our criminal law requires that some action be done before liability to punishment attaches. Even for crimes like the Federal Interstate

Travel Act – where the act prohibited (travelling interstate) is wholly innocent but is made criminal by an intention to bribe officials or do other corrupt acts – the answer to the doctrinal question is that some act must be done before criminal liability attaches.[42]

From these remarks, Moore appears to believe that the action that "must be done before criminal liability attaches" need bear *no* specific relation to liability in order to satisfy the act requirement.

Much the same impression emerges in the context of Moore's response to the allegation that possessory crimes constitute a counterexample to the act requirement. Possession, after all, does not *seem* to be an act. According to Moore, however:

Possession crimes are generally defined so that either an act (of acquiring possession) or an omission (to rid oneself of possession) are prerequisites to liability. Thus it is not the *state* of possession that is being punished, but either the act of taking possession, or (in the cases where the defendant comes into possession without doing anything) the omission to rid oneself of possession. Possession crimes, so construed, present no counter-examples to the act requirement, or at least none greater than that presented by omissions generally.[43]

Moore is aware that not all critics of the act requirement are likely to be convinced by this treatment of possessory crimes:

The objection often voiced to this traditional accommodation of possession crimes to the act requirement is that we aren't really punishing acts of acquisition of, or omissions to dispose of, things like burglary tools, stolen goods, etc. Really, we are punishing the possession itself, however the crimes are formally construed.[44]

When the theorist to whom Moore responds objects that, "really, we are punishing the possession itself," I interpret him to speak elliptically. Literally, possession cannot be punished; only persons can be punished. Persons are always punished *for* something. Thus I interpret the unpersuaded theorist to object that "really, we are punishing the person *for* the possession itself." The omitted preposition is implicit.

As with the comparable objection based on liability for attempts, Moore regards this criticism of his treatment of possessory crimes as "confused."[45] He responds by questioning the need to determine "what is "really" being punished in possession crimes."[46] He seems to believe that all allegations about what is "really" being punished are beside the point. In other words, he seems to believe that all allegations about what punishment is *for* are beside the point. He continues: "The compatibility of possession crimes with [the act requirement] is a formal matter, and, formally, possession is defined so as to include an act or an omission."[47]

Moore responds that both these alleged counterexamples fail because they do not construe the act requirement as a "formal, doctrinal matter."[48] What does this mean? Because Moore himself does not elaborate, any answer must be tentative. For present purposes, one matter is especially significant. Does Moore's proposal to understand the act requirement as a "formal doctrinal matter" represent an *alternative* to my proposal that the act must relate to liability by what I have called the "for" relation?

A commentator who proposes that criminal attempts and possessory crimes provide counterexamples to the act requirement is well aware that these offenses are generally construed to include acts. But a theorist can believe that these offenses provide counterexamples to the act requirement nonetheless, because the acts that are involved are not what is "really" being punished. That is, criminal liability is not imposed *for* the acts that have been committed but rather *for* the culpable state of mind, in the case of attempts, or *for* the state of possession, in the case of possessory crimes. In other words, the theorist who scratches beneath the surface and is not persuaded by superficial appearances can appreciate that liability in these cases is *really* imposed *for* something other than an act. Moore, in contrast, interprets the act requirement as "formal and doctrinal." I construe this remark to mean that he is content to trust appearances and is skeptical of the theorist who regards them as misleading or deceptive. As long as the crimes of attempt and possession are in fact defined by positive law to include an act, the act requirement is satisfied, whatever speculation one may entertain about what liability is "really" imposed *for.*

Positive law, however, does not always confirm Moore's thesis. Moore is correct about how "possession crimes are *generally* defined."[49] But what about those possessory crimes that are *not* defined in accordance with this generalization? Consider *State v. Cleppe,*[50] in which neither intent nor knowledge was held to be an element of the crime of possession of a controlled substance. Or *Chajutin v. Whitehead,*[51] in which a defendant was summarily convicted for possession of an altered passport he did not know to have been altered. Are we to believe that the act requirement is preserved here because the defendants performed the omissions of failure to divest themselves of something they did not know they had? Why accept this strained account? Such cases are more plausibly treated as counterexamples to the act requirement, when construed as a descriptive generalization. Of course, Moore might be correct to regard the judgments in these cases as mistaken. But counterexamples cannot be dismissed so easily if a claim is construed as "formal and doctrinal." If positive law serves as the test of the act requirement, the better conclusion is that some possessory offenses are exceptions to it.

In any event, the foregoing interpretation cannot capture what Moore means by describing the act requirement as "formal and doctrinal." In an instructive footnote, Moore admits that "in one respect the answer [to the question of whether our criminal law requires that some action be done before liability to punishment attaches] is not as formal as might be thought."[52] A given offense should "not treat the act that must be done to trigger liability as a mere formality."[53] As an example, Moore writes that "[the Federal Interstate Travel Act does] not say, for example, that it is a crime to intend to bribe an official while at the same time whistling Dixie, combing one's hair, or washing one's cat. *That* would be to treat the act requirement as an empty formality."[54]

This footnote raises more questions than it answers. Moore's comment that "in one respect the answer [to the question of whether our criminal law requires that some action be done before liability to punishment attaches] is not as formal as might be thought" is puzzling. Whether a claim is "formal," as I understand it, is not a matter that admits of degrees. Either the act requirement is formal or it is not; one cannot have it both ways and treat the requirement as *more or less* formal.

Moreover, the theorist should demand an account of the precise circumstances under which a given offense does *not* treat the included act as a "mere formality." Moore's example of the Federal Interstate Travel Act is helpful but only hints at an answer. According to Moore, the act that is required for liability is not a mere formality if it "executes, however slightly, the culpable intention."[55] In other words, as long as the included act "executes" a "culpable intention," the act requirement is satisfied as something other than an "empty formality."

Can this be correct? I think not. One difficulty is that the act which satisfies the requirement cannot always "execute a culpable intention" for the simple reason that there may be no "culpable intention" to "execute." Crimes of strict liability lack culpable intentions. Of course, Moore may join those many commentators who regard strict liability crimes as morally objectionable. But moral objections seem beside the point in construing the act requirement in terms of positive law. A crime of strict liability, however objectionable from a moral point of view, lacks a culpable intention to execute.

In addition, one must ask why the presence of an act that executes a culpable intention makes the act more than a "mere formality." The answer, I think, is that it is plausible to construe liability as *for* an act that executes a culpable intention. The reason that the foregoing examples of "whistling Dixie" or "eating food" are ruses that do not satisfy the act requirement is that liability cannot plausibly be thought to be imposed *for* these acts. Because these acts do not "execute a culpable intention," liability is not imposed for them. On this interpretation, of course, Moore's proposal is not a genuine *alternative* to mine; it construes the act requirement as satisfied only when the act executes a culpable intention – which occurs when liability is imposed *for* the included act.

Quite apart from whether or not I have understood Moore correctly, I reach two conclusions about how the act requirement should be interpreted. First, the requirement has the status of a hybrid of description and evaluation. That is to say, the thesis accurately describes the vast majority of cases actually decided in Anglo-American law. But a few counterexamples do not falsify this thesis, because it is not *purely* descriptive. Because this thesis is partly evaluative, the handful of exceptions to the act requirement in Anglo-American law can be dismissed as aberrations and mistakes. Second, I have provided an account of the nature of the act that is needed to satisfy the requirement. The act requirement is unsatisfied unless liability is imposed *for* an act.

III. The Evaluative Component of the Act Requirement

I have argued that the thesis that criminal liability requires an act must be understood as partly evaluative. I now address the important normative issues that are involved in assessing this component of the thesis. Is it true that criminal liability *ought* to require an act? This question should be understood in light of my attempts to clarify the meaning of the act requirement. That is, the act requirement is not satisfied unless criminal liability is imposed only *for* acts, and not for any non-acts. The corresponding evaluative thesis is that criminal liability *ought* to be imposed only *for* acts and ought not to be imposed for any non-acts. I hope to make progress in assessing this evaluative thesis without taking a stand on the more difficult metaphysical issues that have divided philosophers about the nature of action.

Attempts to show that criminal liability ought to require an act must identify a feature peculiar to acts in virtue of which they are the unique objects of criminal liability and the sole bases of deserved punishment. A simple argument supports this conclusion. By definition, violations of the criminal law are subject to punishment. The infliction of punishment requires a moral justification. I assume that such a justification must be based on the desert of the offender.[56] Thus a defense of the thesis that criminal liability ought to require an act must establish that persons deserve to be punished only for their actions. What reasons can be given in favor of this evaluative thesis?

In this section, I will claim that no such feature of action can be identified – there is no good reason to believe that actions should be the sole basis of criminal liability and deserved punishment. A definitive argument in favor of my claim would provide a philosophically rigorous account of the nature of action and show that there is no feature of action in virtue of which it can qualify as the unique object of criminal liability. But the strategy I will pursue is less ambitious. I will argue that the feature that theorists have identified as essential to criminal liability and deserved punishment does not support the act requirement. This feature is not unique to acts; that is, some non-acts share it. Moreover, not all acts appear to share this feature; that is, some acts seem to lack it. If I am correct, the arguments that theorists have provided in favor of the act requirement fail to show that criminal liability should be imposed only for acts. No principled reason has been given not to punish persons for some of their non-acts.

My claim is easily misunderstood. I fully acknowledge the enormous *practical* difficulties in punishing persons for given kinds of non-acts. Most of these practical difficulties involve law enforcement. Many theorists have noted that punishment for many kinds of non-acts would be likely to involve invasions of privacy that are intolerable in a free society. I concede this point without modifying my basic claim. The fact that a given offense is likely to be enforced by objectionable means does not entail that the offense is illegitimate in principle. It is one thing to say that a person is punished for something for which he lacks responsibility and quite another to say that his privacy has been violated by the means by which his responsibility has been established.

Once again, Moore has gone to greater lengths than any other theorist to provide a detailed answer to the question "why those, and only those, who act are deserving of punishment."[57] His reply begins by contrasting two "views of morality." He describes the first as the "classical view" or the "virtue-based conception."[58] According to this view, "morality is primarily concerned with the virtue of individual persons."[59] Actions are important on this conception, but "only as subsidiary means of promoting persons' virtue."[60] Moore describes the second view of morality as the "non-classical" view.[61] According to this view – which appears to coincide with what I have called act-morality – "morality is fundamentally a matter of norms. Such norms do not have as their subjects virtuous character."[62] Instead, these norms prohibit or permit actions. In contrast to the classical conception, "the sufficiency of action for responsibility falls out easily from this non-classical view of morality."[63]

Moore invokes this distinction between these two "views of morality" to conclude that "desert must be such that we deserve punishment for violations of morality's norms of obligation, but we do not deserve punishment for violation of morality's ideals of virtuous character."[64] His argument, as I understand it, has two parts – one negative, the other positive. The negative part of his argument attempts to show that persons do *not* deserve punishment under the classical view. Moore contends that although we "rightly judge people morally by their characters in non-legal contexts,"[65] the *law* should not punish persons pursuant to such judgments. He maintains that

> no one deserves to be punished for lacking grace – or for lacking any other virtue. Those who lack virtue, but do not exhibit it through bad actions, have done no wrong. They have wronged themselves, by being less worthy persons than they should be; but they have not wronged anyone else. . . . Without wrongdoing, what is there to exact retribution for?[66]

Thus Moore concludes that a person should *not* be punished *for* his lack of virtue or bad *character*. But why *should* a person be punished *for* his bad *acts*? Moore's positive argument is that actions alone exhibit the feature in virtue of which persons deserve to be punished. That feature is *choice*. According to

Moore, "it is the choice to do evil on a particular occasion that makes a person morally responsible for any wrong that flows from such choice, irrespective of whether such choice expresses bad character or not."[67]

Surely, however, this dichotomy is incomplete. The claim that punishment is justifiable for acts is not made more plausible by discrediting the claim that punishment is justifiable for the lack of virtue. These are not the only two alternatives; bad acts and the lack of virtue do not exhaust the many possible objects of moral evaluation. As indicated previously, moral philosophers have sought to evaluate a wide range of diverse objects and states of affairs. Perhaps persons deserve punishment for a number of such objects of evaluation, even if they do not merit liability for the lack of virtue.

Moreover, Moore's negative argument for concluding that punishment cannot be deserved for non-acts (in particular, the lack of virtue) appears circular. Moore believes that those who lack virtue but do not exhibit it through bad actions do not deserve punishment because "they have done no wrong."[68] Of course, persons who have not performed a bad action have *done* no wrong. Because they have not acted, they cannot have engaged in wrong*doing*. But why should criminal liability require a wrong*doing*? Perhaps Moore's reply is that only a *doing* can *be* wrong. Or perhaps his answer is that only a *doing* can *wrong* anyone. On Moore's own account, however, these replies cannot be correct. Recall that Moore allows that one can wrong *oneself* without acting,[69] even though he believes that one cannot wrong anyone *else* without acting. Apparently, then, nondoings *can* be wrong, and one *can* wrong someone without acting. Moore contends only that one cannot wrong *others* without acting. Why this should be so is mysterious. I see no reason to believe that the conditions for wronging others are unlike the conditions for wronging oneself. Thus I find no noncircular reason to conclude that criminal liability requires a wrong*doing*. If other states of a person can be wrongful, why should criminal liability be withheld because these other states do not consist in a *doing*?

Most important, I believe that Moore's positive argument derives the wrong conclusion from a premiss that is nearly correct. Moore is on the right track to identify *choice* as the crucial feature that separates appropriate from inappropriate objects of deserved punishment and liability. Why does he believe that choice is so fundamental, and that blame and retribution are unjustifiable for states of affairs that are *not* objects of choice? The answer, I think, is that persons typically have *control* over their choices, and persons are responsible and deserve punishment only for those states of affairs over which they exercise control.[70] I submit that the absence of control, and not the absence of action, establishes the outer boundary of deserved punishment and responsibility. I claim, in other words, that what I will call the *control requirement* should be substituted for the act requirement as a necessary condition of criminal liability and deserved punishment.

Moore is not the only theorist to defend the act requirement by premisses that in fact support the requirement of control. According to David Richards, "the subject of criminal liability is to be limited to conduct over which an agent has planful control. Accordingly, penal liability should be limited to such acts or omissions to act."[71] Richards is correct until the final "accordingly." The limitation of liability to those states of affairs "over which an agent has planful control" does not restrict liability to acts – or even to acts and omissions. Instead, this limitation confines liability to *any* state of affairs over which an agent has control.

I have suggested that Moore's positive argument actually provides more support for the control requirement than for the act requirement. But his claim that persons are responsible only for their choices is not equivalent to my claim that persons are responsible only for those states of affairs over which they have control. A person may have control over a state of affairs and thus be eligible for responsibility for it, even without having made a choice. Criminal negligence provides an example. Suppose that Smith kills Jones by starting a fire after falling asleep with a lit cigarette. Surely Smith has not made what Moore describes as "a *choice* to do evil."[72] But Smith is (and ought to be) criminally liable for his negligence nonetheless, because he presumably had a sufficient degree of control over whether he would create an unreasonable risk of harm resulting in Jones's death.[73]

Moreover, Moore himself acknowledges, in a subsequent article in which he argues that persons are more responsible for having caused an untoward result in the world than for having tried but failed to cause that untoward result,[74] that the concept of control serves to identify the boundaries of liability and deserved punishment. Many theorists believe that persons who act with the same degree of culpability are no more responsible for having killed than for having attempted to kill. Their arguments are familiar to criminal theorists and to moral philosophers alike. Whether an attempted killer succeeds in actually killing his intended victim is frequently said to be a matter of luck, and luck should play no role in impositions of criminal liability and deserved punishment.[75] Moore devises a plausible reply to this seductive train of thought. He responds that, in the relevant sense, intentional killers actually *have* control over the deaths they cause. Moore thinks that "when we proximately cause just the harm we intended to cause by our action, we have not lacked *control* as we use that phrase in ordinary moral assessments."[76] Those theorists who claim that intentional killers *lack* control over the deaths they cause employ an unexplicated and overly stringent standard of control.

My point here is not to take sides on whether Moore is right or wrong in suggesting that persons typically have control over the consequences of their actions. Rather, my point is that Moore's premiss that intentional killers have control over the deaths they cause provides a reason to believe that they are blameworthy and deserving of punishment for these deaths only if persons can be responsible and deserving of punishment for those states of affairs over which they have control. An argument that persons have control over a state of affairs (for example, the consequences of their actions) establishes that persons may be responsible for that state of affairs. I conclude that the normative argument which theorists such as Moore invoke in favor of the act requirement actually supports a somewhat different thesis – that criminal liability requires control.

IV. The Control Requirement

In this section, I will elaborate on the requirement I propose to substitute for the act requirement – the requirement of control. I am painfully aware that my explication of control is incomplete and leaves many fundamental questions unanswered.[77] A comprehensive analysis of the concept of control would necessitate a treatise comparable in length and complexity to Moore's 413-page *Act and Crime.* Nonetheless, a few observations are in order.

The control requirement, as I construe it here, has the same status that I have assigned to the act requirement, its rival and counterpart. The thesis that criminal liability requires control is a necessary but not a sufficient condition for deserved punishment.[78] This requirement should be understood as a hybrid of description and evaluation. It should be rejected unless it accurately describes the great bulk of Anglo-American law. As a matter of fact, control is present whenever criminal liability is imposed. But this thesis also includes an evaluative component. A handful of counter-examples to this descriptive generalization do not suffice to refute it, as long as there is good reason to believe that these cases qualify as mistakes. Any such cases should be regarded as mistakes because criminal liability ought to require control.

Substitution of the control requirement for the act requirement promotes the project of integrating the criminal law with moral philosophy. Theorists who sympathize with this project and yet defend the act requirement must struggle to explain why the criminal law should impose liability only for acts – because persons may be morally responsible for a great many states of affairs other than their acts. Control, however, is more plausibly regarded as a condition of both moral and criminal responsibility.

What does it mean to lack *control* over a state of affairs, and why should control be required for moral or criminal responsibility? Philosophers have long appreciated that "'ought' implies 'can.'" "Can" is implied by either a moral or a criminal "ought." The core idea behind the control requirement is that a person lacks responsibility for those states of affairs he or she is unable to prevent from taking place or obtaining. If the state of affairs for which he is responsible is an action, he must have been able not to perform that action. If the state of affairs is a status, he must have been able not to have that status; if the state of affairs is a thought, he must have been able not to have that thought,[79] and so on for any state of affairs for which a person is responsible. But what sense of "can" is implied by "ought"? In what follows, I will try to avoid the extraordinarily difficult metaphysical questions that arise in attempts to reconcile freedom and determinism. I have nothing especially new or insightful to contribute to these debates. In any event, I am not wholly persuaded that control in the relevant sense requires that agents "could have done otherwise."[80] Instead, I propose to explicate control in terms of what it is reasonable to expect of persons. A person lacks control over a state of affairs and neither is nor ought to be criminally liable for it if it is unreasonable to expect him or her to have prevented that state of affairs from obtaining.

Two related features of this explication of control are noteworthy. First, the determination of whether an agent has control over a state of affairs is rarely a matter of empirical fact. On a few occasions, the absence of control can be established by the laws of physics; for example, a person lacks control over whether he or she may be in two places at the same time. But most of the hard questions about control depend on normative assessments of what it is reasonable to expect from persons. Commentators can and do differ about how these questions should be answered. Their answers have changed over time and will continue to evolve.[81] Second, the issue of whether an agent has control over a state of affairs admits of degrees. A person may have more control over some kinds of states of affairs than over other kinds of states of affairs, and one person may have more control over the same kind of state of affairs than another person. Because the determination of whether a person has control over a state of affairs is a normative inquiry that admits of degrees, theorists must decide how *much* control over a state of affairs a person must possess before he or she can become responsible for it.

These two features of control stand in stark contrast to what many (but not all) commentators have said about the concept of action. Many theorists regard the issue of whether an agent has performed an act to be solely a matter of fact.[82] Determining whether an agent has acted is just as much an empirical inquiry as measuring his or her shoe size. Moreover, the issue of whether an agent has performed an act is seldom thought to admit of degrees. Philosophers of action acknowledge the existence of stubborn, borderline cases. Even here, however, theorists presuppose that either an agent has acted or has not; little or no sense can be made of the claim that one agent has performed *more* or *less* of an action than another agent. Because I have sought to minimize my metaphysical commitments about the nature of action, I do not insist that action *must* differ from control in these two respects. Whether a person has control over a state of affairs, however, is unlike what is typically said about action; it is a normative inquiry that admits of degrees.[83]

I do not attempt to identify in abstract terms how much control a person must have over a state of affairs before he or she can become responsible for it. No *general* answer can be given to the problem of "where to draw the line." All

I can hope to accomplish is to point out some of the many factors that affect this complex determination. In particular, less control is needed before responsibility is imposed for an especially bad state of affairs than for a not-so-bad state of affairs. If so, the determination of how much control over a state of affairs is needed before responsibility may be imposed cannot be answered without a judgment about the importance of preventing that state of affairs from obtaining. Small wonder that a comprehensive account of the control requirement is so difficult to defend. Without a theory of the interests protected by various laws, and the relative importance of respecting them, no account of control is complete.

How, then, should an explication of control proceed? Perhaps the best strategy is to examine briefly the role played by control in several diverse contexts in which judgments of criminal responsibility have long been recognized as controversial. I will be especially concerned to contrast the role of control with that played by action in order to support my thesis that the control requirement is preferable to the act requirement. In the remainder of this section, I will discuss several situations in which action is seemingly present, but control is absent. Liability is unjustifiable here, despite action on the part of the defendant. In the final two sections, I will examine situations in which control is present, but action is almost certainly absent. If a defendant possesses a sufficient degree of control, liability may be justifiable despite the absence of action. I do not pretend that the application of the control requirement to these diverse contexts will produce simple solutions. The crucial test of my thesis is not whether it makes hard cases easy but whether it raises questions that are relevant to the problem at hand. According to my approach, the right question is not whether the defendant failed to act but whether he or she lacked sufficient control over a state of affairs to be responsible for it.

Consider the role played by the act and control requirements in the typical situation in which criminal liability is imposed for an act. As I have indicated, criminal liability for an act (as for any state of affairs) is incompatible with the control requirement unless it is reasonable to expect the person not to have performed that act. The implications of the two requirements largely coincide, because persons control virtually all of their acts. If persons do not control *all* of their acts, however, the implications of the two requirements will diverge. Arguably, persons lack control over some of their acts – those that are nonvoluntary. There is some dispute among philosophers about whether nonvoluntary acts actually exist.[84] According to some accounts, so-called nonvoluntary acts are not really acts. Several commentators contend that when conduct is involuntary, "we are tempted . . . to say that no true human action has been performed at all."[85] But most criminal codes, such as the Model Penal Code, allow that action can be nonvoluntary.[86] No criminal theorist openly tolerates liability for any nonvoluntary acts that indeed exist.[87]

When is an act voluntary or nonvoluntary?[88] Most criminal theorists regard an act as voluntary when it is produced by volition or the will.[89] Why should the will loom so large in determinations of voluntariness? The answer must be that persons have control over their wills; if a person lacked control over his or her will, there would be no inclination to identify it as the source of voluntary action. Anglo-American law tends to require the complete non-involvement of the will and a total loss of control before an act can be countenanced as non-voluntary. Under these extreme circumstances, an act clearly ceases to be a state of affairs for which punishment can be deserved. Thus criminal liability ought not to be imposed in those cases, real or imaginary, in which action is present, but control is not. These considerations suggest that the absence of control, rather than the absence of action, is the central feature that renders criminal liability unjustifiable. In other words, the control requirement provides a better explanation than the act requirement of why punishment for non-voluntary acts is unjustified.

It is noteworthy that the accounts of voluntariness provided by criminal theorists differ substantially from those proposed by most philosophers, threatening to undermine the project of integrating the criminal law with moral philosophy. Joel Feinberg, for example, analyzes voluntariness as "a variable concept, determined by higher and lower cut-off points depending on the nature of the circumstances, the interests at stake, and the moral or legal purposes to be served."[90] According to this analysis, an act can be nonvoluntary even though it is produced by the will. Such accounts of voluntariness, which Alan Norrie has called moral conceptions,[91] resemble my control requirement; they transform determinations of voluntariness into normative inquiries that admit of degrees. If adopted and applied throughout the criminal law, the moral conception of voluntariness would do much of the work I have assigned to the concept of control.[92] The determination of whether an act is voluntary would no longer depend solely on whether it is caused by the will but on whether a person could reasonably be expected not to perform it.

On several occasions, however, criminal liability is precluded even though a person exercises enough control over his or her acts to make them voluntary. In some of these situations, liability is unjustifiable not because a defendant lacks all control but because it is unreasonable to expect him to exercise the control he or she has. I will briefly comment on three such situations.[93] The first is duress. Theorists no longer engage in the fiction that the will of the defendant who acts under duress must be overborne. Instead, modern statutes grant the defense when a defendant is coerced by a threat "which a person of reasonable firmness would have been unable to resist."[94] In other words, the defense is unavailable when it is reasonable to expect the defendant not to have committed the crime. Rather than attempt to specify as a matter of law the myriad circumstances under which threats should be resisted, the current trend is to leave these complex matters to the trier of fact. Judgments about when a person lacks sufficient control over a state of affairs to be responsible for it are too difficult to capture in a simple statutory rule.

Next, consider the vexing topic of vicarious liability. Commentators have disagreed about whether criminal liability is justifiable in a range of cases in which corporate officers were convicted of so-called regulatory offenses, such as prohibitions of the sale of adulterated food.[95] I do not believe that the justifiability of punishment in these cases should depend on whether the defendants performed an act; I see no reason to embrace the fiction that an officer acts whenever his or her corporation is guilty of a regulatory offense.[96] Instead, the justifiability of punishment should depend on whether the defendants had a sufficient degree of control over the sale to be responsible for it.[97] Vicarious criminal liability would be manifestly unjust if imposed on a defendant who was "powerless" to have prevented the violation.[98]

Third, consider the plethora of issues involving drug and alcohol addiction. Commentators have disagreed about whether criminal liability is justifiable in a host of cases in which persons have violated a number of laws as a result of their addiction to various substances – including statutes proscribing drug possession itself.[99] I do not believe that the justifiability of punishment in these cases should depend on whether drug possession by addicts can be said to qualify as voluntary action. Instead, the justifiability of liability should turn on whether addicted defendants exercise a sufficient degree of control over their use of drugs to be responsible for it. Surely withdrawal symptoms *might* be so unpleasant that an addict could not reasonably be expected to control his or her use of an illicit substance. Whether the withdrawal symptoms caused by the repeated use of various addictive substances are sufficiently severe to undermine control is partly an empirical question.[100] Addiction per se does not preclude control; everyone agrees that persons addicted to caffeine retain control. Whether the degree of control needed for responsibility is undermined by addiction to opiates or tobacco is far less clear.

Even a moment's reflection about the foregoing three issues should be sufficient to appreciate that the implications of the control requirement for the substantive criminal law are likely to differ from those of the act requirement. For the most part, however, the implications of these two principles coincide. As a very crude generalization, persons possess control over most of their actions and lack control over most of what remains. For this reason, acts might be called the paradigm objects of responsibility; it is no surprise that criminal liability is typically imposed *for* an act. Nonetheless, the implications of the control requirement differ from those of the act requirement in a number of additional respects that are worthy of note. When measured against the control requirement, the act requirement, I have argued, is too broad. In the remaining sections of this chapter, I will argue that the act requirement is too narrow. I will defend the claim that criminal liability might be imposed for two kinds of states of affairs over which persons sometimes exercise sufficient control, despite the absence of an act.

My thesis that liability may be appropriate for a non-act over which a defendant has control is not really so novel. Omissions provide the clearest example of a state of affairs other than action over which persons can exercise a sufficient degree of control to be responsible. This claim can be supported without the need to examine those controversial cases in which homicide statutes are construed to impose liability on bad samaritans, or on persons who violate legal duties of care owed to victims to whom they have special relationships.[101] The more obvious cases are those in which an omission is explicitly punished by law, as when a statute proscribes the failure to pay a tax. Because persons have sufficient control over whether or not they will pay their taxes, no one disputes the justifiability of liability here, despite the absence of an act.

Defenders of the act requirement must strain to explain liability for omissions.[102] *Some* explanation is required, if the act requirement is to be preserved. A few theorists, however, simply include omissions as exceptions to that requirement, without acknowledging the need for further explanation. Moore, for example, admits that it is simply "not plausible" to deny that we "have some positive duties"[103] and thus allows that the act requirement is appropriately subject "to an exception in the case of certain omissions."[104] But if Anglo-American law should allow liability for any omissions – as Moore and virtually all commentators concede – the normative basis for this exception to the act requirement must be identified. I believe that this normative basis is easily described. Criminal liability should sometimes be imposed for omissions because persons are able to exercise control over a state of affairs by not acting, and persons may be subject to moral and criminal condemnation for some of those untoward states of affairs over which they exercise sufficient control.[105] This basis can be extended far beyond the category of omissions, thus opening the door to further kinds of exceptions to the act requirement. In what follows, I will extend this basis to two kinds of states of affairs other than omissions. That is, acts and omissions do not exhaust the states of affairs over which persons exercise a sufficient degree of control to become eligible for deserved punishment.

V. Criminal Liability for Status

I have suggested that the arguments offered in support of the act requirement actually support a somewhat different requirement – the requirement of control. I propose that criminal liability should be imposed only *for* those states of affairs over which persons have the requisite degree of control. The control requirement cannot be used to show that persons should be punished only for their acts, because persons may sometimes exercise control over a state of affairs without acting. No reason to oppose criminal liability for such states of affairs can be derived from the arguments that theorists have advanced in favor of the act requirement.

In this section, I will examine one of several kinds of states of affairs other than action over which persons sometimes exercise a sufficient degree of control: their *status.*[106] By a *status,* I mean a property that describes what a person *is,* rather than what he or she *does.*[107] A given person *is* any number of things; that is, he *has* any number of statuses. He *is* a given age, or is a resident of a particular place, or is a member of a particular political party. By a *status crime,* I mean a crime that punishes a person *for* his status, that is, *for* what that person *is.* Whether a given crime, real or hypothetical, qualifies as a status crime can be decided by a linguistic test. Does the offense impose liability for a state that is defined by some form of the verb "to be"? If so, the offense is an instance of status criminality.

For present purposes, two distinctions between kinds of statuses are of crucial significance. First, those kinds of statuses over which persons *lack* control must be distinguished from those kinds of statuses over which persons *have* control. There are obvious examples of each kind of status, although there are many borderline cases as well. For example, people lack control over their age. I will refer to an instance of such a status as an *uncontrolled status.* Not all statuses are uncontrolled.[108] For example, a male typically has control over whether or not he has a beard. I will refer to an instance of such a status as a *controlled status.*

The distinction between an uncontrolled status and a controlled status is best construed as a distinction between status-tokens, not status-types. Few status-types can be categorized as one or the other. Consider, for example, the status of having four toes. Smith might acquire this status as a result of a birth defect, whereas Jones might acquire this status by deliberately shooting himself in the foot. Smith's status-token would be uncontrolled whereas Jones's status-token would be controlled. Moreover, whether a given status-type is controlled or uncontrolled can change over time, usually as the result of technological innovation. Sex-change operations allow some degree of choice over a status that once was thought to be utterly beyond personal control.

The second crucial distinction is between those statuses that *are* reducible to one or more act(s) of the agent and those statuses that are *not* reducible to one or more act(s) of the agent. Again, there are obvious examples of both kinds of status, although there are many borderline cases as well. Consider, for example, the status of *being* one of the persons who have climbed Mt. Everest. Persons attain this status simply by virtue of having performed the relevant act – namely, the act of having climbed Mt. Everest. There is nothing more to the acquisition of this status than having performed the act(s) to which the status is reducible. I will describe an instance of such a status as a *reducible status.* Not all statuses are reducible. Consider, for example, the status of being tall. Typically, at least, one does not gain this status simply by virtue of having performed any act(s). I will describe an instance of such a status as an *irreducible status.*

Many statuses typically require acts but are not reducible to them. In fact, fewer statuses are wholly reducible than might be supposed. Consider, for example, the status of *being* a convicted felon. Persons do not attain this status simply by virtue of having performed a felonious act. A person does not acquire this status unless he or she has been convicted, and being convicted is not an act that the individual performs. Conviction is something that happens *to* someone; it is not something that someone *does.* In fact, a person may actually acquire this status even though he or she has not performed the act of committing a felony – given that some persons are mistakenly convicted and gain felonious status through a miscarriage of justice. So this status cannot be reduced to the performance of one or more acts.

The distinction between reducible and irreducible statuses is needed to salvage my thesis from the charge of triviality. Any attempt to show that persons are responsible for some of their statuses would be uninteresting if a person were responsible only for those statuses that are reducible. Because such statuses can be reduced to the performance of one or more acts, there would be little difference between holding a person responsible for his status and holding him responsible for the act(s) to which his status could be reduced.[109] There is little more than a verbal difference between holding someone responsible for the act of having assassinated a president and for the status of being a person who has assassinated a president.[110]

These two distinctions between kinds of status cut across each other. Hence there exist four possible kinds of status: irreducible controlled, reducible controlled, irreducible uncontrolled, and reducible uncontrolled statuses. Because I have proposed that the lack of control should preclude criminal liability, I hope it is clear that punishment should not be imposed for any status that is uncontrolled. Punishment for an uncontrolled status is just as objectionable as punishment for a nonvoluntary act.

As a descriptive generalization, the claim that no one has ever been punished for an uncontrolled status is false. *Larsonneur* provides a probable counterexample.[111] Larsonneur was held criminally responsible for the status of *being* found in the United Kingdom after having been brought there against her will. Of course, this judgment was mistaken; liability was imposed unjustly. But much of the criticism of *Larsonneur* has missed the point. The injustice in *Larsonneur* does not derive from the fact that the defendant was punished without having acted, or even from the fact that she was punished for a status. Instead, the injustice derives from the fact that the defendant was punished for a status over which she lacked control – that is, for an uncontrolled status. Had she voluntarily come to England, the imposition of liability for *being* found there would not have raised an eyebrow. The lack of control, rather than the absence of an act or the presence of a status, is the real basis of the injustice in *Larsonneur.*

Punishment for a controlled status, however, is quite another matter. Punishment for a controlled status is just as legitimate as punishment for a voluntary act. As indicated previously, however, instances of the class of reducible status crimes are uninteresting. My nontrivial (and I hope interesting) proposal is that there is no principled reason why criminal liability should not be imposed *for* an irreducible controlled status.[112]

Many irreducible controlled status crimes exist.[113] As defined in some jurisdictions, prostitution is an example of an irreducible controlled status crime. The New Jersey Criminal Code provides that "a person is guilty of prostitution . . . if he or she . . . is an inmate of a house of prostitution."[114] This statute creates a status crime. Liability is imposed not *for* an act of prostitution but *for* what a person *is:* an inmate in a house of prostitution. In case the grammatical form of this statute is not decisive on this matter, the commentaries to the Code are explicit. These commentaries provide that "the point of making it an offense to be an inmate is to dispense with proof of a particular sexual episode or solicitation, when the woman is associated with the house in a way that amounts to a general holding out of her availability for sexual purposes."[115] Thus this status is irreducible; *being* an inmate in a house of prostitution is not reducible to the performance of one or more acts. Moreover, this status is controlled; whether a person is or is not an inmate in a house of prostitution is a matter over which she has control.[116] Thus this statute creates an example of what I have called an irreducible controlled status crime. I see no reason to deem this statute an unjustifiable exercise of state authority.[117]

Of course, the justifiability of this irreducible controlled status crime is precluded by the act requirement, construed as an evaluation. One might expect theorists who have defended the act requirement to have produced powerful arguments against the justifiability of such offenses. Unfortunately, no such arguments can be found. Consider the burden that any such argument must bear. Commentators should agree that persons might be *morally* responsible for what they are. Recall that Hitchler went so far as to claim that persons can be morally responsible *only* for what they are.[118] Thus, an argument against the justifiability of controlled status criminality must show why a person should not be criminally responsible for something for which he or she is morally responsible. Any such argument threatens to undermine the project of integrating the criminal law with moral philosophy.

Once again, Moore's comments on status criminality are instructive, as they indicate the deficiencies in his defense of the act requirement. Moore grudgingly countenances the existence of status crimes, such as "being a vagrant" or "being a drunkard."[119] But he seems content to note that these crimes are "rarely enacted" and "were once more prevalent than they are today."[120] He quotes with approval Herbert Packer's observation that "laws of this sort are in fact very much on the way out."[121] But rare though they may be, Moore recognizes that such crimes *do* exist. Thus they constitute an additional exception to the act requirement, construed as a descriptive generalization. For some reason, however, Moore does not acknowledge this additional exception when he summarizes his views about the existing state of the law. He concludes: "The most one can say of the Anglo-American criminal law's act requirement is that either an act or an omission is required for liability."[122]

Why does Moore not include status crimes alongside omissions as genuine exceptions to the act requirement, when the latter is construed as a descriptive generalization? Perhaps Moore believes that crimes of status need not be mentioned because such offenses would, if challenged, be found unconstitutional. He writes: "Not only are such laws rarely enacted today, but in America a number of constitutional infirmities are regularly found to afflict such laws so that even where they do remain on the books they are not valid."[123]

Perhaps Moore would be correct to regard crimes of status as unimportant exceptions to the act requirement if he were right that all such crimes are unconstitutional. However, no such sweeping condemnation of status criminality can be supported.[124] English law continues to include many such offenses.[125] Even American jurisdictions occasionally enact and enforce status crimes. According to one commentator, "[Status crimes], though occasionally held invalid . . . have often been upheld notwithstanding their definition of crime in terms of 'being' rather than 'acting.'"[126]

My position is easily misunderstood. To claim that controlled status criminality can be a justifiable exercise of state authority is not to endorse any such crime wholeheartedly. The control requirement, like the act requirement, is put forward as a *necessary,* but not a *sufficient,* condition for the justified exercise of state authority. No one who defends the act requirement believes that it must be legitimate to impose liability for *any* act, such as scratching one's head. The same is true of status criminality. To punish someone for the controlled status of being a member of the Republican Party would be no less outrageous than to punish someone for the act of voting in favor of a Republican candidate. On some occasions, however, I see no principled reason to deny that persons may be criminally liable for their status.

VI. Criminal Liability for Thoughts

I will conclude by commenting briefly on a final category of criminality that is clearly precluded by the act requirement but that might be compatible with the control requirement – punishment for thoughts. Unlike status crimes, which have received a lukewarm reception, scarcely a kind word in favor of thought crimes has ever been voiced by Anglo-American commentators.[127] As a descriptive generalization, the claim that Anglo-American law does not explicitly impose liability for thoughts may be unassailable. There may never have been a time in the history of the common law when liability for thoughts was openly condoned.[128] Theorists are likely to recoil in horror at the prospect of punishing a person for a mere thought. The very suggestion that criminal liability for thoughts might ever be justifiable is bound to strike many commentators as a *reductio* of the control requirement.

Thus I enter into the following discussion with trepidation. "Thought crimes" have been denounced so universally that it is hard to believe that every criminal theorist could have been mistaken about them. On the other hand, the rejection of thought crimes has been taken for granted for so long that commentators have not been challenged to defend their consensus.[129] If punishment for thoughts is really so outrageous, the normative basis for this conclusion should be easy to demonstrate.

By this point, I hope it is clear that one defense of this conclusion – by far the most popular – is unsound. No one should argue that punishment for thoughts is unjust simply because thoughts are not acts, and only acts are the proper objects of criminal liability. I have argued that the major premiss of this syllogism – the act requirement, construed evaluatively – should be rejected. Some basis other than the act requirement for the alleged unjustifiability of thought crimes must be found.

What might this basis be? The more cautious strategy would be to attempt to interpret the control requirement so that it became incompatible with punishment for thoughts. Indeed, the best reason to resist criminal liability for the vast majority of thoughts is that persons lack the requisite degree of control over most of their mental processes to be responsible for them. Consider beliefs. A person cannot control whether or not he or she believes the Earth to be round, for example.[130] A person simply evaluates the evidence and forms a judgment about the shape of the Earth, without exercising much if any control over the outcome. For this reason, liability for beliefs would be unjustifiable. The control requirement would bar punishment for the lack of a belief in God, for example – quite apart from the fact that such an offense would violate the act requirement as well.

But this more cautious strategy would be disingenuous, because no sweeping condemnation of punishment for thoughts can be derived from the control requirement. I will call those thoughts that are sufficiently under the control of persons "mental acts." Clearly, some mental acts exist. For example, whether a person decides to rob a bank, deliberates over time, anticipates every contingency, and carefully plans an escape seems no less under individual control than whether he or she commits any number of acts that unquestionably are the proper objects of criminal liability.

Moreover, many philosophers have agreed that persons can be *morally* responsible for their mental acts.[131] The prospective bank robber just described seems appropriately subject to blame for his deliberations – or so I shall suppose. If so, the question arises whether such a person might be *criminally* responsible for his mental acts as well. The defense of a negative answer to this question must bear a burden similar to that discussed in the context of status criminality. Because mental acts are appropriate objects of moral responsibility, an argument against the justifiability of criminal liability for mental acts must show why a person should not be criminally liable for something for which he or she is morally responsible.[132] Any such argument threatens to undermine the project of integrating the criminal law with moral philosophy.

Of course, any number of *practical* considerations conspire against punishment for mental acts. In particular, the difficulties in law enforcement loom so large as to be nearly insuperable. In the absence of an act, it is barely conceivable that evidence "beyond a reasonable doubt" could be obtained to prove that a defendant performed a given mental act for which liability was to be imposed. Confessions might provide the only reliable means of gaining such evidence.[133] Needless to say, such confessions would be exceedingly rare. Moreover, the potential for abuse would be enormous if the state were forced to rely on confessions in order to convict persons for a given offense.[134]

If these practical difficulties are so formidable, what is the advantage of enlarging the scope of criminal liability to include mental acts? I readily admit that little would be gained by this enlargement, and much could be lost. Nonetheless, there would be *some* benefits to this revision in criminal theory. Because most commentators categorically reject punishment for thoughts, including mental acts, I will in what follows concentrate on what can be said in favor of some such offenses, without rehearsing the familiar reasons against them.

I assume without argument that *harm* plays a crucial role in the justifiability of criminal offenses.[135] Paradigm cases of criminality are *consummate* or *choate* offenses; harm is caused on each occasion in which these offenses are committed. Every token of arson, theft, or rape is harmful to a victim.[136] But not all crimes are consummate. Some criminal offenses impermissibly increase the *risk* of harm – that is, they increase the likelihood that a subsequent harm will occur. Such crimes are *nonconsummate, inchoate,* or *anticipatory.* Attempt, conspiracy, solicitation, and possession are the most well-known examples of nonconsummate offenses. Because harm need not occur on each occasion on which a given mental act is performed, the imposition of criminal liability for mental acts would enlarge the scope of nonconsummate liability. Thus, the justifiability of punishing a person for a mental act must be assessed by whatever standards are used to justify the creation of nonconsummate offenses generally.[137] The task of justifying a nonconsummate offense gives rise to a somewhat different set of problems from those associated with the attempt to justify a consummate offense. But theorists should not presuppose without argument that no mental act can possibly satisfy whatever criteria justify the creation of a nonconsummate offense. In particular, the mental act of the foregoing prospective bank robber – which I will describe as a firm intention – might well qualify.[138] Such firm intentions impermissibly increase the risk of a subsequent harm.

Criminal liability for that class of mental acts I have called firm intentions need not constitute a whole new category of substantive offense. The most compelling basis for punishing a firm intention would extend the law of attempts beyond its present boundaries. Commentators are nearly unanimous in agreeing that liability for a criminal attempt, no less than liability for any other crime, must conform to the act requirement. But *what* act must be performed before liability can attach? This question gives rise to the various tests to decide when in the course of a criminal plan a person should become subject to punishment for an attempt.[139] Theorists have struggled to draw the elusive line between "mere preparation," when liability is premature, and genuine attempt, when liability first becomes appropriate.[140] Few theorists believe that liability must wait until the defendant has performed the "last act" before completing the intended crime. But how far prior to this final act is punishment deserved?

The Model Penal Code endeavors to answer this question by defining a criminal attempt as "an act or omission constituting a substantial step in the course of conduct planned to culminate in [a] crime."[141] The act requirement is preserved here. But those who drafted the code failed to provide an account of when a "step" toward attainment of a criminal objective is "substantial." The only guide is that a step is *not* substantial unless it is "strongly corroborative of the actor's purpose."[142] This comment suggests that the required act is important insofar as it provides *evidence* of criminal intent; the act has no significance independent of its evidentiary role. Hence it is plausible to suppose that liability is really imposed *for* the criminal intent. The failure to attach a nonevidentiary significance to the required act becomes important when one searches for a principled reason to withhold liability in those somewhat unusual instances in which reliable evidence of a firm intention is somehow gained despite the apparent absence of an act.

U.S. v. Still is one of many such cases.[143] Here the defendant was found wearing a disguise while parked in a van approximately 200 feet away from a bank. Following his arrest, Still volunteered: "You did a good job. You caught me five minutes before I was going to rob a bank. That's what I was putting the wig on for."[144] Despite this compelling evidence of criminal intent, Still's conviction for attempted bank robbery was reversed because he had failed to take a "substantial step" toward the attainment of his criminal objective. The court noted that Still had not made "either actual movement toward the bank or actions that are analytically similar to such movement."[145] Reasonable minds can differ about whether Still's "step" toward bank robbery was "substantial"; such cases are typically cited to raise the question of *what* act should be required to give rise to liability for attempts. But why is *this* the right question to ask? The more basic inquiry is whether it is sensible to insist on an act at all in these circumstances. Why is punishment unjustifiable until Still performed *whatever* action – such as a motion toward the bank – is alleged to be required?[146] Even if Still had made such a motion, no one would be inclined to say that punishment was imposed *for* his motion. Punishment would still be *for* his firm intention rather than *for* his act, with the latter providing evidence of the former. In this kind of example, the act requirement is more likely to frustrate than to promote justice.

Because there is no reason to doubt that Still had control over his firm criminal intention, substitution of the control requirement for the act requirement would remove the obstacle to his conviction.[147] There is much to recommend the extension of criminal liability for attempts that would follow from dispensing with the act requirement and allowing such defendants to be convicted. The rationale of nonconsummate liability in general and of the law of attempts in particular – to prevent harms *before* culpable persons succeed in bringing them about – provides no clear reason to insist that liability must await the performance of an act. When there is overwhelming evidence that a defendant firmly intends to commit a crime, why should punishment be undeserved simply because the act requirement is unsatisfied? I am unaware of a principled answer to this question. In such contexts, the implications of the control requirement – however radical they may appear to be – seem preferable to those of the act requirement.

Conclusion

I hope to have made progress in assessing whether criminal liability requires an act by clarifying the question itself. I have described some of the difficulties that arise in assessing this thesis and have discussed the role the act requirement has played in the larger project of integrating moral philosophy with the criminal law. The act requirement, even if applicable to criminal law, would not suffice to distinguish the conditions of moral and criminal responsibility. But if my attempts to clarify the question have been successful, I think it is relatively clear that criminal liability does *not* require an act. I have defended this conclusion while avoiding controversial metaphysical commitments about the nature of action.

The arguments that purport to establish the act requirement actually support the somewhat different requirement of control. Ultimately, the verdict on my proposal to substitute the control requirement for the act requirement depends on whether the implications of the former are preferable to those of the latter throughout the entire body of the substantive criminal law. I have contrasted the implications of the control requirement with those of the act requirement for two kinds of offenses: controlled status crimes and crimes of firm intention. In these contexts, at least, the control requirement has principled advantages over its counterpart and rival.

My thesis also describes directions for further research. Suppose I am correct that the substantive criminal law both requires and ought to require that persons be liable only for those states of affairs over which they possess the requisite degree of control. Suppose also that I am correct to explicate control in terms of what it is reasonable to expect from persons. If so, theorists should be encouraged to undertake the difficult task of deciding whether and under what circumstances persons lack the requisite degree of control and thus should be ineligible for punishment. I see little option but to approach these questions by drawing from moral philosophy. In any event, theorists who accept this invitation will help to decide the merits of the project of integrating moral philosophy with the criminal law. Perhaps reasons will emerge to hold persons criminally liable for states of affairs for which they lack moral responsibility. I will not hazard a prediction about how these complex issues will ultimately be decided. But I hope to have provided a powerful challenge to one thesis frequently invoked to differentiate the conditions of moral and criminal responsibility – the thesis that criminal liability requires an act.

Notes

1 See Alan Norrie, *Crime, Reason and History* (London: Weidenfeld and Nicolson, 1993).

2 See the discussions in R. A. Duff, "Principle and Contradiction in the Criminal Law," and John Gardner, "On the General Part of the Criminal Law" (this volume).

3 I offer no general account of the relationship between criminal responsibility and criminal liability, other than to assume that the former is a necessary condition for the latter.

4 Michael Moore, *Act and Crime* (Oxford: Clarendon Press, 1993).

5 Or an omission to act. *Model Penal Code,* Sec. 2.01(1), is typical. It stipulates: "A person is not guilty of an offense unless his liability is based on conduct that includes a voluntary act or the omission to perform an act of which he is physically capable."

6 Other explanations might be given. For example, commentators may disagree about whether criminal liability requires an act because they are uncertain about whether a given hardship imposed by law is an instance of *criminal* liability. If some hardships imposed by law did not require an act, but there were some controversy about whether these hardships involved criminal punishment, theorists would be expected to divide over the question of whether or not criminal liability requires an act. Indeed, the determination of which legal hardships impose criminal liability is notoriously difficult. See, for example, *Fleming v. Nestor,* 80 S.Ct. 1367 (1960), where the Court divided over the issue of whether a statute that terminated Social Security benefits because of prior membership in the Communist Party constituted punishment. More recently, see *Austin*

v. U.S., 113 S.Ct. 2801 (1993), for a discussion of the circumstances under which civil forfeiture might amount to punishment.

7 Throughout this chapter I use "acts" and "actions" interchangeably. Some philosophers distinguish acts from actions. See, for example, Eric D'Arcy, *Human Acts* (Oxford: Clarendon Press, 1963), 6–7.

8 Any number of anthologies on action theory are available. For a useful recent bibliography, see Jonathan Bennett, *The Act Itself* (Oxford: Clarendon Press, 1995).

9 "Usage within the relevant speech community is the ultimate test of the validity of analysis of a concept," even though "judges or legislatures may . . . stipulate or adopt . . . meanings . . . which fall short of philosophical standards of clarity." Nicola Lacey: "Contingency, Coherence, and Conceptualism" (this volume, p. 14).

10 See the reservations about the use of philosophical methodologies to solve social and political problems raised in Richard Posner's essay "What Are Philosophers Good For?" in his *Overcoming Law* (Cambridge, Mass.: Harvard University Press, 1995), 444–67.

11 Perhaps the most frequently cited objection to this project stresses that law has a special set of purposes or aims that limit the application of philosophical analyses. Consider, for example, the following remarks of Bernard Williams, expressed in the context of dismissing the relevance of the philosophy of action to issues in the criminal law:

> The best that one can do is to take some distinction or conclusion necessary to the criminal law and show that a theoretical account of it can be given that is at least not inconsistent with formulations motivated by the philosophy of action. It seems obvious, on reflection, that there must be areas about which this is true. The criminal law, after all, has special aims and purposes, and the requirements that it imposes on describing people's actions are unlikely to coincide throughout with distinctions that are motivated quite independently of those special purposes. . . . There is no reason to believe that the various distinctions we use will provide, *ready-made,* what the criminal law needs, without taking account of special requirements within the criminal law. (Williams: "The Actus Reus of Dr. Caligari," 142 *University of Pennsylvania Law Review* [1994], 1661, 1661–62.)

Williams does not describe the peculiar functions and objectives that allegedly motivate philosophers of action to formulate their analyses. Nor does he explicitly identify the "special aims, purposes and requirements" of the criminal law that are said to limit the relevance of philosophical analyses. But his claim that the criminal law *has* these special purposes and aims is familiar.

12 Rollin Perkins and Roland Boyce, *Criminal Law* (Mineola, N.Y.: Foundation Press, 3d ed., 1982), 830.

13 W. Hitchler, "The Physical Element of Crime," 39 *Dickenson Law Review* (1934), 96, 96.

14 One legal theorist has recently defended the claim that "the property of moral wrongness attaches to completed actions" rather than to "other possible objects" such as motivations and intentions. She is mistaken, however, if she believes that it is somehow incoherent, nonsensical, or otherwise misguided for moral philosophers to judge that

any states of affairs other than acts might be wrongful. See Heidi M. Hurd, "What in the World Is Wrong?" 5 *Journal of Contemporary Legal Issues* (1994), 157, 160.

15 Act-morality itself may have (at least) two further subdivisions. The first evaluates acts in order to guide conduct *ex ante;* it addresses the question: What act should one perform? The second subdivision evaluates acts in order to judge conduct *ex post;* it addresses the question: Is the act that one has performed right or wrong? The relationship between these two subdivisions of act-morality is complicated and contentious.

16 Some of these issues are explored in Stephen Hudson, *Human Character and Morality: Reflections from the History of Ideas* (Boston: Routledge & Kegan Paul, 1986).

17 As one commentator notes, "It is not only expedient but also desirable to avoid using the metaphysics of action as much as possible in the public realm. High metaphysics, including the metaphysics of action, is one area on which citizens in a democracy cannot agree." Samuel Freeman, "Criminal Liability and the Duty to Aid the Distressed," 142 *University of Pennsylvania Law Review* (1994), 1455, 1455.

18 The literature responding to Michael Moore's contributions confirms this suspicion. Significantly, most of Moore's critics have attacked his philosophical account of action – especially its metaphysical realism – and have said relatively little about whether criminal liability requires an act according to this conception. See the *Symposium on Act and Crime,* 142 *University of Pennsylvania Law Review* (1994), 1443–840.

19 Clarification of this thesis is essential in order to provide a non-question-begging assessment of whether criminal law accepts or rejects the act requirement. I do not seek to clarify this question for the express purpose of supporting the thesis. The best explication of this thesis may well indicate that criminal liability does not require an act after all. Some commentators, however, claim to prefer one analysis over another on the ground that it guarantees the truth of the act requirement. See, for example, Hyman Gross, *A Theory of Criminal Justice* (New York: Oxford University Press, 1979). Gross asks (at 133) "why we want to understand the concept of an act." He answers that "it is only acts that we regard as a proper basis for criminal liability." Gross actually goes so far as to *define* acts so that the act requirement is preserved. He writes (at 56): "An act consists of events or states of affairs for which a person might be responsible according to the principles of responsibility that guide such judgements; and so an act has taken place when such events occur or when such states of affairs exist." According to this methodology, the act requirement could not possibly be false; criminal liability requires an act *by definition.* This approach, however, simply begs the question in favor of the act requirement.

20 Some of these criticisms of Moore appear in Douglas Husak, "Book Review: The Relevance of the Concept of Action to the Criminal Law," 6 *Criminal Law Forum* (1995), 327.

21 Moore also describes the limitations of the project of integrating the criminal law with philosophy. These limitations are especially important in the context of his approach to double jeopardy. For a description of these limitations, see Michael Moore, "More on *Act and Crime,*" 142 *University of Pennsylvania Law Review* (1994), 1749, 1750–51.

22 (1933) 24 Cr.App.R. 74.

23 The "almost certainly" qualification is needed because nothing has yet been said about the relationship between the act and criminal liability that is necessary to satisfy the act requirement. Surely Larsonneur committed an act at some time or another. But the act

she committed does not bear the appropriate relationship to liability needed to satisfy the act requirement. For a pessimistic view that this "appropriate relationship" can be explicated, see Mark Kelman, *A Guide to Critical Legal Studies* (Cambridge, Mass.: Harvard University Press, 1987), 92–3.

24 I am not aware of any criminal theorist who explicitly adheres to this interpretation. For a possible exception, see Gross, *Op. Cit.* note 19.

25 Imagination is not needed to perform this thought-experiment. If *Larsonneur* counts as a counter-example to the act requirement construed as a contingent truth, it surely provides a counter-example to the act requirement construed as a necessary truth.

26 Exceptions need not be regarded as mistakes or aberrations if the act requirement is only *prima facie* and is subject to being overridden by considerations more stringent than those that militate in favor of the requirement of an act. This interpretation of the status of the act requirement is coherent and plausible. Few theorists, however, argue that apparent exceptions – such as *Larsonneur* – are justified by considerations more weighty than the act requirement.

27 One commentator describes *Larsonneur* as the "acme of strict injustice!" See Jerome Hall, *General Principles of Criminal Law* (Indianapolis: Bobbs-Merrill, 2d ed., 1947), 329, n. 14.

28 Moore, *Op. Cit.* note 4, 4. In fact, however, Moore's defense of the act requirement as a descriptive generalization is qualified. He does not really conclude that "there can be no criminal offence without the doing of a voluntary act" (at 4). He freely acknowledges that omissions, which are not reducible to acts, represent an important class of exceptions to the act requirement. He writes: "The most one can say of the Anglo-American criminal law's act requirement is that either an act or an omission is required for liability" (at 34). He is somewhat less candid, however, about a second class of exceptions he implicitly acknowledges. Moore grudgingly recognizes the existence of status crimes, such as "being a vagrant" or "being a drunkard" (at 19). See Part V *infra* for a more detailed discussion of status crimes.

29 *Id.,* 18.

30 *Id.,* 46–60.

31 *Id.,* 34.

32 In addition, I am unsure whether my proposal is consistent with the Model Penal Code, which states only that liability must be "based on conduct that includes a voluntary act." *Model Penal Code,* Sec. 2.01(1). This statute allows liability to be imposed when an involuntary act is somehow caused by the defendant's prior voluntary act. For a critical discussion of such situations, see Norrie, *Op. Cit.* note 1, 117–22.

33 No less an authority than Glanville Williams appears to express confusion on this issue. He writes: "If a man is punished for doing something when drunk that he would not have done when sober, is he not in plain truth punished for getting drunk?" This rhetorical question mistakenly suggests that punishment must be for any "but-for" cause of liability. See *Criminal Law: The General Part* (London: Stevens & Sons, 2d ed., 1961), 564.

34 For a contrasting view, see Michael Moore, "The Independent Moral Significance of Wrongdoing," 5 *Journal of Contemporary Legal Issues* (1994), 237. Moore argues (at 238) that "between the two, wrongdoing and culpability, wrongdoing thus is something

of the poor relation. For culpability is both independently necessary and independently sufficient as a basis for some punishment, whereas wrongdoing is neither."

35 I draw from the discussion of this ambiguity in George Fletcher, "What Is Punishment Imposed For?" 5 *Journal of Contemporary Legal Issues* (1994), 101.

36 Some commentators use "desert basis" to describe that for which liability is deserved. See George Sher, *Desert* (Princeton, N.J.: Princeton University Press, 1987), 7.

37 Moore, *Op. Cit.* note 4, 17.

38 Among those theorists Moore lists as having proposed that the act requirement admits of exceptions, see Douglas Husak, *Philosophy of Criminal Law* (Totowa, N.J.: Rowman & Littlefield, 1987), Chapter 4.

39 Moore, *Op. Cit.* note 4, 17.

40 *Id.*, 17–18.

41 *Id.*, 18.

42 *Id.*, 18–19.

43 *Id.*, 21.

44 *Id.*, 21.

45 *Id.*, 21.

46 *Id.*, 21.

47 *Id.*, 22.

48 *Id.*, 18.

49 *Id.*, 21 (emphasis added).

50 635 p. 2d 435 (1981).

51 1938 1 K.B. 506.

52 *Op. Cit.* Note 4, 19, n.5.

53 *Id.*, 19, n.5.

54 *Id.*, 19, n.5.

55 *Id.*, 19, n.5.

56 I cannot argue for a desert-based theory of punishment here. For an extended defense, see Andrew von Hirsch, *Past or Future Crimes?* (New Brunswick, N.J.: Rutgers University Press, 1985) and *Censure and Sanction* (Oxford: Clarendon Press, 1993).

57 Moore, *Op. Cit.* note 4, 48.

58 *Id.*, 49–50.

59 *Id.*, 49.

60 *Id.*, 49–50.

61 *Id.*, 51.

62 *Id.*, 51.

63 *Id.*, 51.

64 *Id.*, 53. Notice that in this (and in subsequent) quotation(s) Moore apparently construes the act requirement in terms of the "for" relation.

65 *Id.*, 54.

66 *Id.*, 53.

67 *Id.*, 51.

68 *Id.*, 53.

69 *Id.*, 53.

70 I can find no better locution than "states of affairs" to describe the diverse objects of

deserved punishment – that is, to represent the many possible things for which a person may be criminally liable.

71 David Richards, *The Moral Criticism of Law* (Encino, Calif.: Dickenson Publishing Co., 1977), 201.

72 Moore, *Op. Cit.* note 4, 59.

73 Moore subsequently admits that "inadvertent risk creation cannot be accommodated within the choice model of culpability." Nonetheless, he believes that this admission requires no "conce[ssion] to [his] critics that choice should be abandoned . . . as the touchstone of culpability." No concession is required because "choosing . . . to do a wrongful act is the dominant form of culpability." The culpability of the negligent defendant "pales before that of wrongdoers who choose to do their wrongful acts in a world they see clearly." See Michael Moore, "*Prima Facie* Moral Culpability," 76 *Boston University Law Review* (1996), 319, 328.

74 Moore, *Op. Cit.* note 34.

75 Theorists who defend this view are listed by Moore in *Id.,* 239–40.

76 *Id.,* 257.

77 I am not especially embarrassed about my failure to provide a thorough account of the concept of control. After all, theorists have yet to produce an adequate analysis of the concept of an act, despite having labored for centuries.

78 Control over a state of affairs provides *a reason* for holding a person responsible for it. Still, control cannot suffice for responsibility. For criticisms of the control requirement as sufficient for liability, see Christine Sistare, "In the Land of Omissions: An Opinionated Guide," 14 *Criminal Justice Ethics* (1995), 26.

79 See Parts V and VI *infra.*

80 For useful examples contrasting two senses of control, see John Fischer, "Responsibility, Control, and Omissions," 1 *Journal of Ethics* (1997), 45.

81 In particular, commentators have debated whether social and economic deprivation might preclude the degree of control required for criminal responsibility. See, for example, George Wright, *Does the Law Morally Bind the Poor?* (New York: New York University Press, 1996).

82 Ascriptivist accounts of action are exceptions to this generalization. According to ascriptivists, the determination of whether an agent has done x is partly or wholly a function of whether or not he is responsible for x. See P. J. Fitzgerald, "Voluntary and Involuntary Acts." in Anthony Guest, ed., *Oxford Essays in Jurisprudence* (London: Oxford University Press, 1961), 1.

83 See the intriguing discussion of the contrast between dichotomous and continuous functions in the criminal law in Paul Robinson and John Darley, *Justice, Liability and Blame* (Boulder, Col.: Westview Press, 1995), 208.

84 For a sophisticated treatment of some of these issues, see Stephen Morse, "Culpability and Control," 142 *University of Pennsylvania Law Review* (1994), 1587.

85 Jeffrie Murphy, "Involuntary Acts and Criminal Liability," in his *Retribution, Justice, and Therapy* (Dordrecht: D. Reidel, 1979), 116.

86 *Model Penal Code,* Sec. 2.01.

87 Reluctance to adopt an "irresistible impulse" test of insanity is one of the few contexts in which ambivalence and uncertainty about the need for a voluntary act have been expressed. This uncertainty is difficult to understand as a matter of principle. It is hard

to believe, for example, that a person might deserve punishment for a criminal act that is truly irresistible. On closer examination, the rationales for imposing liability in this situation tend to cite policy grounds. Impulses that are truly irresistible rarely exist and are all but impossible to distinguish from impulses that are merely not resisted. Almost no principled opposition has been raised against the claim that persons should not be punished for what they cannot control.

A second possible exception to the requirement of a voluntary act arises when liability is imposed for an involuntary act that is somehow caused by the defendant's prior voluntary act. For a defense of the charge that judges have tended to decide these cases by attempting to "have their cake and eat it," see Norrie, *Op. Cit.* note 1, 120.

88 The Model Penal Code does not provide a general definition of nonvoluntary action but, after listing several putative examples of nonvoluntary acts, includes a catch-all for any act "that is not a product of the effort or determination of the actor." See *Model Penal Code,* Sec. 2.01 (2) (d).

89 "The traditional view . . . takes willing or volition to be the key to voluntariness." Michael Corrado, "Is There An Act Requirement in the Criminal Law?" 142 *University of Pennsylvania Law Review* (1994), 1529, 1529.

90 Joel Feinberg, *Harm to Self* (Oxford: Oxford University Press, 1986), 117.

91 Norrie, *Op. Cit.* Note 1, 111.

92 My thesis is that such a requirement makes the act requirement superfluous and unnecessary. If a person exhibits sufficient control over a state of affairs to be responsible for it, why impose the additional requirement that the state of affairs be an *act*?

93 Additional examples could be described. Some aspects of the law of provocation might also be explained by reference to the control requirement rather than the act requirement. I do not discuss provocation, however, because its foundations are too controversial. See Jeremy Horder, *Provocation and Responsibility* (Oxford: Oxford University Press, 1992).

94 *Model Penal Code,* Sec. 2.09(1).

95 See, for example *U.S. v. Park,* 421 U.S. 658 (1975).

96 One commentator laments that contemporary theories of corporate liability are "trapped" in the "framework" of supposing that "criminal liability is concerned with individual defendants as authors of acts or omissions." Andrew Ashworth, *Principles of Criminal Law* (Oxford: Clarendon Press, 2d ed., 1995), 111.

97 Thus a defendant should not be vicariously liable if his or her stolen vehicle is parked illegally. See the discussion in Wayne LaFave and Austin Scott, *Substantive Criminal Law* (St. Paul, Minn.: West, 1986), 357–8. The authors also discuss a few cases in which liability was imposed even though the defendant had "no control" and "had done everything in his power to prevent the violation." According to the control requirement, such cases must be classified as mistakes.

98 The Court has indicated as much. See *U.S. v. Park,* 421 U.S. 658, 673 (1975).

99 See, most notably, *U.S. v. Moore,* 486 F.2d 1139 (1973).

100 For further discussion, see Douglas Husak, *Drugs and Rights* (Cambridge: Cambridge University Press, 1992).

101 Liability for these kinds of omissions is called *derivative liability* by George Fletcher, *Rethinking Criminal Law* (Boston: Little, Brown, 1978), 581.

102 Many strategies have been pursued to reconcile liability for omissions with the act

requirement. One theorist goes so far as to describe liability for omissions as an "illusion." See Gross, *Op. Cit.* note 19, 63.

103 Moore, *Op. Cit.* note 4, 56.

104 *Id.,* 59.

105 The claim that persons have control over their omissions is noncommittal about whether persons should be criminally responsible for their omissions per se and/or criminally responsible for the consequences their omissions bring about. The difference is important. According to the first interpretation, a "bad Samaritan" who fails to perform an act of easy rescue is responsible precisely for the failure to act – not for the death that he or she did not prevent. According to the second interpretation, the "bad Samaritan" is responsible for the death he or she did not prevent. He or she commits a kind of homicide by omission. Here I take no position on how this issue should be resolved.

106 Several other examples of non-acts might merit careful scrutiny. One commentator provides a useful inventory:

> The law finds us liable and penalizes us for various kinds of things. It may be for our *omissions*. . . . Or it may penalize us for what those in various ways *related* to us, for example as spouse, servant, employee, do or omit to do (i.e. vicarious liability). Or it may be because of some *happening,* for example when a piece of glass from the window of our building injures a passer-by, our unattended horse causes damage, or our lion attacks someone. Or it may be because of some *situation* we are in, as when we are in charge of a vehicle when unfit to drive or in possession of an article for use in a burglary, of offensive weapons, or of drugs, or are found in the country without permission. Or it may be because of what we *are.* (Alan White, *Grounds of Liability* [Oxford: Clarendon Press, 1985], 23)

107 Although Moore discusses "crimes of status" at some length, he neglects to explicitly define them. I construe a status crime as an offense that proscribes what a person is. Moore's account of status (which I do not believe he intends as a definition) is as follows: "A state differs from an act in two ways: (1) like all events, acts tend to be of short duration, while states can be quite long-lasting or even permanent; (2) human acts essentially involve the choice (or willing) of the actor in a way that states of that actor do not." Moore, *Op. Cit.* note 4, 19.

108 Moore admits that there are some statuses we can "help getting into" and "could easily get out of." *Id.,* 49.

109 There might be *some* differences nonetheless. For a discussion of the different jurisdictional issues that surround each kind of offense, see Fletcher, *Op. Cit.* note 101, 427–33.

110 Hence the comment: "Punishing an addict for using drugs convicts for addiction under a different name." *Powell v. Texas,* 392 U.S. 514, 548 (1968) (White, J., concurring).

111 *Larsonneur,* note 22.

112 Andrew Ashworth is among the few commentators who seem to have reached this conclusion. He writes: "It may be quite defensible to impose situational liability if the law is so phrased as to ensure that defendants are in control of their activities." Ashworth, *Op. Cit.* note 96, 105.

113 English law has created a number of offenses that impose what some commentators have called "situational liability." See the examples in P. R. Glazebrook, "Situational Liability," in P. R. Glazebrook, ed., *Reshaping the Criminal Law* (London: Stevens, 1978), 108.

114 *New Jersey Criminal Code Annotated,* 2C:34–1(1).

115 *Id.,* p. 554.

116 Of course, some tokens of this status-type may be beyond a defendant's control. A person should have a defense from liability if he or she lacked control over this status. Someone kept as an inmate in a house of prostitution against his or her will should be no more subject to liability than someone who committed an act of prostitution under duress.

117 At least, no reason arises from the arguments that theorists typically advance in favor of the act requirement. Arguments to decriminalize prostitution raise a host of considerations largely unrelated to the act and control requirements.

118 See *Op. Cit.* note 13.

119 Moore, *Op. Cit.* note 4, 19.

120 *Id.,* 19.

121 Herbert Packer, *The Limits of the Criminal Sanction* (Stanford, Calif.: Stanford University Press, 1968), 78.

122 Moore, *Op. Cit.* note 4, 34. See also "There is and should be an act requirement, although it is and should be subject to an exception in the case of certain omissions." *Id.,* 59.

123 *Id.,* 19.

124 Moore cites *Robinson v. California,* 370 U.S. 660 (1962) as authority for his general position on the unconstitutionality of status criminality. For a rejoinder to Moore's interpretation of *Robinson* and its implications for status criminality, see Husak, *Op. Cit.* note 38, 86–90 and 100–2.

125 See Glazebrook, *Op. Cit.* note 113.

126 See LaFave and Scott, *Op. Cit.* note 97, 279.

127 For a possible exception, see Williams, *Op. Cit.* note 33, 631: "Austin put forward the interesting view that in attempt the party is really punished for his intention, the act being required as evidence of a *firm* intention. There is much to be said for this."

128 According to one commentator, "there never was a time when . . . criminal liability could be rested upon mere intent as evidenced by an overt act rather than upon the overt act itself." Francis Sayre, "Criminal Attempts," 41 *Harvard Law Review* (1928), 821, 826.

129 In this context, recall John Stuart Mill's well-known defense of freedom of speech and his claims about the importance of rehearsing arguments against even those propositions known to be false.

130 But see Michael Stocker, "Responsibility, Especially for Beliefs," 91 *Mind* (1982), 398.

131 See the several examples provided in Joel Feinberg, *Harmless Wrongdoing* (New York: Oxford University Press, 1988). He writes (at 23): "We are all proud of the Anglo-American law for its traditional reluctance to punish evil thoughts, but legal commentators themselves, when explaining this reluctance, eagerly pass the whole subject off to the moralists, who have always attached great importance to it."

132 Laypersons are quite prepared to punish persons whose criminal intention is sufficiently settled or fixed. See Robinson and Darley, *Op. Cit.* note 83, 84.

133 At common law, there is some doubt about whether an uncorroborated confession of the accused in a criminal case is sufficient to support a conviction. See John Wigmore, *A Treatise on the Anglo-American System of Evidence* (Boston: Little, Brown, 2d ed., 1923), Secs. 2070–71.

134 It is noteworthy that the ascendancy of the act requirement in Anglo-American criminal theory coincided with misgivings about reliance on confessions. See Orville Snyder, *Criminal Justice* (New York: Prentice-Hall, 1953), 111.

135 For a sustained defense of this assumption, see Joel Feinberg, *Harm to Others* (New York: Oxford University Press, 1984).

136 Of course, the harmfulness of some of these tokens may be outweighed by a greater good, as when the offense is justified.

137 Many of these conditions are explored in Douglas Husak: "The Nature and Justifiability of Nonconsummate Offenses," 37 *Arizona Law Review* (1995), 151.

138 I offer no test to identify when an intention qualifies as firm. Clearly, however, the case in favor of criminal liability for mental acts becomes most plausible for those criminal intentions that have persisted over time.

139 These tests are discussed in LaFave and Scott, *Op. Cit.* note 97, 29–38.

140 "It is a legal commonplace that attempting to do an act and preparing to do it need differ in no way other than that identified by an actus reus test for attempt." Barbara Levenbook, "Prohibiting Attempts and Preparations," 49 *U. Missouri at Kansas City Law Review* (1980), 41, 50.

141 *Model Penal Code,* Sec. 5.01(1) (c).

142 *Id.,* Sec. 5.01(2).

143 850 F.2d 607 (9th Cir. 1988).

144 *Id.,* 608.

145 *Id.,* 610.

146 See George Fletcher: "On the Moral Irrelevance of Bodily Movements," 142 *University of Pennsylvania Law Review* (1994), 1443.

147 I am skeptical, however, that a crime of firm intention that dispensed with the need for an act could still be called an *attempt.*

3

'Simulacra of Morality'?

Beyond the Ideal/Actual Antinomies of Criminal Justice

ALAN NORRIE

> To grasp totality is to break with our ordinary notions of identity. . . . It is to see things *existentially constituted,* and permeated, *by their relations with others;* and to see our ordinary notion of identity as an abstraction not only from [its] existentially constitutive processes of formation (geo-histories), but also from [its] existentially constitutive inter-activity (internal relatedness). . . . When is a thing no longer a thing but something else? . . . [I]n the domain of totality we need to conceptualise *entity relationism.*
>
> (Bhaskar 1993: 125)

In recent years, Anglo-American jurisprudence has been marked by debates between those in the liberal tradition and those who take more critical and sceptical positions. These debates have sometimes been marked by acrimony. Recently, Michael Moore described 'those of a sceptical cast of mind' as 'gadflies' and as the 'stray dogs of the intellectual world' (Moore 1993a: 130). He felt able to 'put aside' one sceptical critique without consideration or formal citation. For sceptics, it is perhaps some consolation to keep Moore 'honest' (1993a: 130), but I hope to show not only that scepticism is defensible in itself but also that it is a means to a greater good. My substantive aim is to use a critical jurisprudential method to go beyond liberal thinking on issues of legal and moral responsibility, to transcend their limits, but to understand the attraction of such ideas and give them proper recognition within a critical framework. The time has, I believe, passed when liberals and critics should abuse each other, and this chapter is presented in a spirit of engagement and dialogue. There is much of value in liberal theory, both in its intellectual content and in its political significance, but there are also fundamental difficulties that have never been properly explored.

In talking of what is 'fundamental', I should say that I will not espouse the argument of 'fundamental contradictions' as developed ambivalently and ambiguously (Norrie 1997a) by the North American critics Moore failed to cite. I will, however, argue that liberal thinking about criminal justice is founded on historical antinomies, the most fundamental of which is that between the 'ideal' and the 'actual', and that a critical engagement with that antinomy and its variants helps one to understand quotidian conflicts in liberal thought about crime and punishment.[1]

Let me introduce what will follow through brief discussion of four quotations. In the first, Antony Duff identifies a relationship between individual agency, legal responsibility, and moral responsibility:

> [I]ntentional agency provides the paradigm of responsible agency. This is why intention is the central or paradigm determinant of moral culpability. . . . As with morality, so with law. (Duff 1990: 102)

It is a common theme in liberal criminal law theory and the political philosophy of punishment that individual responsibility is the proper basis for legitimate punishment because of a homology between legal practice and moral thought. As Michael Moore puts it, one theory of punishment 'demand[s] that legal liability track moral responsibility' (1993a: 154). The specific locus of this homology is the retributive theory of punishment that ties law and morality together, and this theory is a specific focus here.

We can, however, contrast this view with the philosophical argument of Alasdair MacIntyre, who considers that moral categories in modern western societies are inadequate precisely *because of* what moral-legal liberalism sees as the root of moral being:

> We possess indeed simulacra of morality, we continue to use many of the key expressions. But we have – very largely, if not entirely – lost our comprehension, both theoretical and practical, of morality. (MacIntyre 1985: 2)

For MacIntyre, the failure of modern morality is the result of the invention of a 'distinctively modern self', and what was invented was, precisely, 'the *individual*' (1985: 61). Part of my aim here is to apply this view to the specific, overlapping areas of criminal law theory and the philosophy of punishment, to consider whether the responsible subject within the criminal law and retributive theory is not better viewed as a 'simulacrum' of morality. I will ultimately argue that there is much to be said for a MacIntyre-style approach, but I will stop short of his conclusion in that I will argue for a *partial and contradictory nexus* between legal and moral thinking organised around the modern concept of the individual.

This brings me to my third quotation, from A. C. Ewing, who almost seventy years ago summed up the ambivalence that surrounds the sense of justice associated with the punishment of an individual for a crime:

> The ideas of desert, of 'justice' as a good-in-itself, and even of proportion between guilt and penalty, are too deeply rooted in our ethical thought to be dismissed lightly, however hard they may be to rationalise. (Ewing 1929: 45)

Ewing wrote at the end of a period of major revision of the classical retributive theory of punishment, when most of its precepts had been rejected. Philosophers in the first three decades of the twentieth century were convinced of the poverty of retributive justice. They thought it practically useless, backward-looking, and cruel, and they saw as the core weakness the idea of an ideal or abstract moral relationship of requital between the individual and the state. Ewing shared this view, yet like many liberal scholars since he acknowledged that there was something in the idea of retributive justice to maintain. He also admitted the difficulty in rationalising what he felt intuitively. Putting Ewing's view together with MacIntyre's, I aim to take up a MacIntyre-style critique of the liberal theory of punishment, in both its legal and philosophical manifestations. I want to expose to critical scrutiny the workings of the individualism at the core of both, but then, *beyond* such a critique, to explain and locate the continuing attraction of ideas of individual justice.

Beyond a MacIntyre-style critique, where should we go? At this point, my final quotation becomes relevant, but to explain why, I must first elaborate briefly upon my view of MacIntyre. I have endorsed thus far a critique after his 'style', because although I am in sympathy with his work and see many parallels to my own, it seems to me ultimately unsatisfactory. We share an engagement with and critique of modern individualism (see Norrie 1991, Norrie 1993b). We also share a conviction that a historical perspective is necessary to understand modern moral philosophy. For MacIntyre, it was the emergence of 'a largely new social setting' (1985: 61) in northern Europe in the seventeenth and eighteenth centuries that constituted the basis for modern individualism. From this point, however, our views diverge, for I would like to explore a more *ambivalent,* rather than negative, attitude to the moral idea of the individual, and this requires a more thorough exploration of *what it means to be an individual* in modern society than MacIntyre provides.

For this, I seek to marry themes in moral philosophy and social psychology through examining and interpreting the work of Rom Harré, who seeks a synthesis of moral, social, and psychological concerns. He writes of the complex location of the individual in modern society:

> [H]uman beings are poised between two 'domains' . . . , the personal . . . and the social. . . . What anybody does . . . can be fully explained only by reference to both . . . domains. This we call 'the dual control of action.' (Harré, Clarke, and de Carlo 1985: 21)

Harré seeks to explain modern individual subjectivity as existing between two domains, as both an *individual, psychological,* and a *collective, sociological* phenomenon. He thus offers a basis for exploring the nexus between history and society on the one hand and 'the individual' and individualism on the other. I referred previously to Ewing's sense of ambivalence about ideas of individual justice in law and philosophy. I will use Harré's social psychology to relate this ambivalence to the underlying *ambiguity in modern subjecthood,* based as it is between two dialectically related domains, the personal and the social. Of course, one might argue that *all* subjectivities, ancient and modern, are located between these two domains, but what is particularly significant about modern Western subjectivity, as represented in liberal understanding, is the insistence upon individual*ism:* individual autonomy and responsibility *to the exclusion of* the individual's actual location between the personal and the social. This is seen in liberal legal and philosophical models of crime and punishment associated with individualistic retributive ideas. A Harréan insistence on the double location of individual agency helps us to understand the *ambiguities* of modern individual agency and responsibility and hence the *ambivalence* expressed by Ewing towards a system of punishment based upon retributive ideas of justice.

This chapter has three main sections on the philosophy of punishment, criminal law theory, and social psychology. My argument in the first two sections will both reflect and evaluate the liberal understanding that criminal law theory and the philosophy of punishment are homologous, but this homology is seen in their mutual *failure* to reflect the real moral basis for judgments of culpability. Both discourses fail to locate individual responsibility where it should be located, between the two domains of the personal and the social. Both are structured by a primary antinomy between 'the ideal' and 'the actual' that establishes an artificial separation, a second antinomy, between 'the individual' and 'the social.' The falsity of this dichotomy undermines the logic of retributive and criminal law theory and renders them incoherent and unsustainable. Subjectivity, as represented in liberal criminal law and retributive philosophy, focuses on an 'ideal' conception of the individual to the exclusion of the 'actual' social and moral context in which individual agency occurs. Yet liberal accounts of justice are unable to maintain the division they themselves create between the 'ideal' and the 'actual', the 'individual' and the 'social', and this failure forces us to move beyond their terms.[2] The first and second sections thus drive us towards the third section, which elaborates upon an account of individual responsibility and justice based upon Harré's social psychology.

Before concluding this introduction, I should like to make two further comments. The first concerns my general standpoint, which is informed by the same critical approach I have developed in earlier works on criminal law, the philosophy of punishment and legal theory (Norrie 1991, 1993a, 1993b). Drawing on critical realism (see, e.g., Bhaskar 1979, Outhwaite 1987, Collier 1994), I argued for an approach to legal philosophy and doctrine that would combine an 'internal' commitment to 'taking law seriously' with an 'external' commitment to seeing law as a social, historically structured, contradictory phenomenon

(Norrie 1993b: xiii). I argued for a 'historical and sociological approach which [could] grasp the duality of law as a specific form of historically constituted sociality' (Norrie 1993a: 17). Such an approach is continued here, but I want to develop what has been implicit in my earlier work: an understanding of law's *dialectical* quality. In recent work (Norrie 1996a, 1996b, 1997b), I have followed Roy Bhaskar's exploration of the concept of dialectic from a critical realist standpoint (Bhaskar 1993), and my prefatory quotation reflects this approach. The crux of the constructionist method I will develop in the third part, as well as the critical arguments I generate from exploring Antony Duff's work, is that retributive concepts in law and philosophy rely on an *individualism* that can always be deconstructed to reveal an underlying *social individuality.* Such individuality is located *between* 'the individual' and 'the social' so that individualist retributive concepts always invoke and deny Bhaskar's dialectical question 'When is a thing no longer a thing but something else?' Such concepts rely on the possibility of 'our ordinary notion of identity' as complete and self-contained and are challenged by what we can call (following Bhaskar) social psychology's 'entity relationism' – that is, its identification of the individual as a being constituted within and by preexisting social relations.

The second point concerns the important role in what follows of Duff's work on the philosophy of punishment and the criminal law. Over the past fifteen years, Duff has brought a philosopher's sophistication to both areas. His account of the philosophy of punishment provides a powerful backdrop to his more detailed analysis of fault concepts in the criminal law. What is particularly significant, however, is the way in which he develops both a critique and a defence of punishment and criminal law from an approach that is broadly interpretive and communitarian. This gives him, in my view, a unique view of the problems in both discourses aligned with a commitment to their better explanation. He seeks new theoretical tools to perform an old theoretical task, the rationalisation of the liberal theory of punishment and criminal law. From my point of view, I do not think that the revised explanations he provides are successful, and this sediments a set of contradictions in his work. However, the conflicts between his philosophical method (interpretive and communitarian) and his moral goals (the rationalisation of punishment and law as social practices) are instructive, pointing beyond that which he seeks to defend. Duff's interpretive and communitarian method exposes problems in liberal theory in a critical way, while his proposed solutions tend to confirm their fundamental character. Thus I read Duff *sceptically* as a defender of liberal individualism, *symptomatically* as revealing liberal individualism's deepest problems, and *critically* as providing some of the theoretical means to go beyond it. I read Duff's work as being 'at the edge' of liberalism, still within the tradition but also pointing beyond it, and that is why I focus on it here.

The Ideal and the Actual in Retributive Philosophy

It is almost seventy years since Ewing wrote of the paradoxical nature of our relationship to ideas of justice and desert. On the one hand, modern western society finds it hard to deny ideas that are deeply rooted in its ethical thought. On the other hand, it finds it extremely difficult to explain them. Today, it seems that things are little better. Antony Duff (1996) has recently presented a wide-ranging review of the philosophy of punishment. He seeks a new position to move it beyond the old conflict between consequentialists and retributivists, but he concludes an impressive and wide-ranging essay by acknowledging a lack of confidence. He wonders whether the 'ideal conception of punishment' he offers represents a practical aspiration for modern criminal justice systems, and, even if it does, whether it is 'an ideal we should try to actualise' (Duff 1996: 88). Duff is persuaded of the moral value of a modified retributive philosophy, so he endorses ideas of desert and justice. Yet he wonders whether such a philosophy could or, in its most morally tenable form, should be applied in practice.

What lies behind Duff's ambivalence?[3] I want to interrogate the way he formulates his dilemma, that is, the idea of a relationship between an *ideal* theory of punishment and the *actualities* of social and political life with which it is contrasted. In taking this position, I will place Duff's formulation in the line of liberal theorists of punishment that begins with Kant. The basic problem, I shall argue, is the relationship between the ideal and the actual in the Kantian account, and all Kantian-derived accounts, of punishment. My argument will be that modern liberal accounts such as Duff's draw on this older tradition, and that this fundamentally undermines the effort to rationalise ideas of justice and desert. It may seem strange to argue this, because Kant and Hegel are normally recognised as the classical exponents of such ideas. I shall argue, however, that it is precisely the particularly Kantian beginnings of the liberal philosophy of punishment that are the problem and that Kant's writings represent a barrier that has not been overcome, even by philosophers such as Duff, whose work *ex facie* reveals no direct relationship. In examining the tradition of Kant (and, as an extension, Hegel), we will better understand the failure of modern accounts to deliver an analysis of the sense of justice.

The relationship between the ideal and the actual is examined as it affects conceptions of both the individual and the community in the philosophy of punishment. The Kantian tradition takes two ideas as central to the understanding of justice and desert: the idea of *individual responsibility* and, based on this idea, that of a *consensual community of judgment.* Problems within this tradition relate to the idealisation (or abstraction) of the categories of responsibility and judgment at the heart of the Kantian enterprise. I begin by looking at the ideal and the actual in classical liberal theory and then move to consider it under modern social conditions.

The 'Ideal' and the 'Actual' in Classical Liberal Theory

The central problem for the classical retributive theory of punishment was that it relied upon an ideal conception of the individual in order to do two things: to construct a conception of the *responsible moral subject,* whose punishment was justified because of his or her prior act, and to construct a conception of a *moral community* with agreed norms that would make judgment, condemnation, and punishment possible. This idea of community was itself based upon a prior conceptualisation of the responsible moral subject. The problem was that the ideal conception of the individual contrasted, and could not be reconciled, with the actuality of individual life in modern society. In dealing with classical retributivism, I focus primarily on Kant with regard to the responsible subject, and Hegel with regard to the moral community. As I have dealt with the detail of such theories at length elsewhere (Norrie 1991: chs. 3–5), I provide only a brief analysis here in order to locate my main focus in this section, Antony Duff's recent work on punishment under modern social conditions.

THE RESPONSIBLE SUBJECT IN KANT. The responsible subject was conceived of as an abstract individual responsible for his acts and worthy of punishment. Presented as a generic human subject, as 'the individual' without particular characteristics, this figure was seen as existing in a prior moral relation with the rest of humankind because of his rationality. This relationship justified the use of punishment as a response to wrongdoing. For Kant, punishment was a right of personhood (Kant 1965: 100), whereas, in Hegel's memorable formulation, the individual demanded his own punishment as a rational being (Hegel 1952: 70). But this abstract conception of the individual as worthy of respect in and through punishment was at odds with a more 'sociological' understanding of actual individual life that was repressed by the theory but that threatened nonetheless to disrupt it. The essential problem was the gap between the ideal image of the individual who stands up to be punished as a rational or consensual being and the empirical reality of crime and criminality as a social issue associated with poverty and attendant problems.

Kant produced a theory of law and punishment based upon a fundamental dichotomy between what he termed *Wille* and *Willkür* (Norrie 1991: 45–8), the result of which was an antinomous view of punishment. This involved a view of the ideal rational subject and the actual criminal as two *different people:*

> When . . . I enact a penal law against myself as a criminal it is the pure juridical legislative reason (*homo noumenon*) in me that submits myself to the penal law as a person capable of committing a crime, that is, as another person (*homo phaenomenon*) along with all the others in the civil union who submit themselves to this law. (Kant 1965: 105; for further discussion, see Norrie 1991: 55–9)

The resulting problem was that, at the level of the phenomenal (the actual level of crime and criminality), no rational justification of punishment was possible. There were no criteria for establishing the moral responsibility of the (nonrational) individual, the *homo phaenomenon* capable of committing a crime. It was only when Kant considered the individual in an entirely different light, as an ideal rational being, that a moral justification of his punishment as a rational person was possible. Kant's theory of punishment established both an individual form of guilt (the fault of the individual conceived as a rational being) and the moral character of wrongdoing (wrong as an offence against rational and universal – categorical – principles of right). However, both guilt and wrong were grounded on the noumenal will, which was a 'different' will from that of the person who actually commits the crime.

Kant produced an ideal theory of punishment, but one that as a result applied only to ideal persons. He sensed the problem. In a world governed by actual men rather than by moral principle, he wrote in a letter, guilt and wrongdoing lacked the moral certainty they would otherwise have. In the actual world, 'the necessity of punishments is only hypothetical' (Kant 1967: 199), not categorical. The backdrop to this problem, however, as revealed by his consideration of contemporaneous empirical issues, was *social.* This is illustrated in Kant's discussion of the punishment of a mother who kills her illegitimate child, or a soldier who kills a comrade in a duel. In such cases, the crimes are committed out of a nonrational 'moral' sense of shame that society has inculcated in the killer. The criminal acts according to social norms that conduce to immoral outcomes according to the ideal law. In such a 'barbaric and underdeveloped' moral condition, *society* 'is responsible for the fact that incentives of honour among the people do not accord (subjectively) with the standards that are (objectively) appropriate.' How can one blame the actor as an objectively rational (noumenal) being for his or her subjective (phenomenal) wrongdoing? The dissonance between ideal and actual is revealed so that ideal 'public legal justice as administered by the state is injustice from the point of view of the people' (Kant 1965: 107). Such an example reveals very clearly the difference between subjectivity understood as a noumenal and as a phenomenal matter.

Kant's division between the noumenal and the phenomenal was too radical. The noumenal remained ethereal in its abstraction, while the phenomenal remained prosaic and mute in its concreteness. Morally, the ideal could say nothing to the actual, while the actual could say nothing 'on its own behalf.' The logical upshot of Kant's dualism was a paradox. Kant acknowledged that the

> more legislation and government are brought into harmony with [moral laws] the rarer would punishments become, and it is therefore quite rational to maintain . . . that in a perfect state no punishments whatsoever would be required. (Kant 1965: 107)

To the extent that individuals were morally free, their punishment would be justified but unnecessary. To the extent, however, that they were governed by their immoral desires, their punishment would be necessary but unjustified. Punishment was justified where it was not needed, and needed where it was not justified.

THE MORAL COMMUNITY IN HEGEL. For Hegel, as for Kant, individual subjectivity and rationality were the basis not only for responsibility but also for moral community. From the form of the rational, responsible individual was deduced the existence and normative content of a moral community. For Kant, this community was understood according to the dictates of the categorical imperative. For Hegel, it was understood as a rational deduction from the concept of subjective right, which was then located in the ethical life of civil society. Kant's account was more abstract than Hegel's, but both held an idealised conception of moral community, in which consensual judgment on right and wrong was possible. The problem was that this idealised conception of consensual community was called into question by the social actualities of modern life.

We have already seen how Kant expresses the problem of 'false motives among the people' in terms of a 'subjective' falling short from an 'objective' moral standpoint. The problem could equally be diagnosed, however, as the product of conflicting views in the community of what is morally right. Kant's examples open up the possibility that there are conflicts in society as to what constitutes right and wrong. Such a possibility threatens to undermine the 'objective' moral side of the Kantian theory because it roots the experience of crime, law, and punishment in an actual, conflictual, social, and political context. That context may be suppressed by the theory's ideal conception of the moral community, but it remains – lurking, as it were – in the shadows.

Following Kant intellectually and historically, Hegel was much exercised by social problems that threatened to undermine the modern moral community. Of course, he portrayed such a community ideally as the realm in which individual rational activity could flourish. 'Civil society' was 'an association of members as self-subsistent individuals', while criminal justice in such a society was the 'reconciliation of the criminal with himself' and 'with the law known by him' (Hegel 1952: 141). However, at the edge of his theory, Hegel acknowledged that civil society had a different, darker dialectic that undermined the existence of moral community by exposing it to deep-seated structural conflict. The division of labour, Hegel wrote, leads to 'the dependence and distress of the class tied to [unskilled] work' and to an 'inability to feel and enjoy the broader freedoms and especially the intellectual benefits of civil society.' There develops in the moral community 'a large mass of people [which] falls below a certain subsistence level', and it becomes apparent that civil society is unable 'to check excessive poverty and the creation of a penurious rabble' (Hegel 1952: 147-8). In one passage, Hegel wrote that poverty leads to a 'loss of the sense of right and wrong' (1952: 150), but what was really lost was a *consen-*

sual view of right and wrong, the possibility of universal norms in a moral community:

> Against nature man can claim no right, but once society is established, poverty *immediately takes the form of a wrong done to one class by another.* The important question of how poverty is to be abolished is one of the most disturbing problems which agitate modern society. (Hegel 1952: 277–8; emphasis added)

The *sociological* dialectic described in these passages is at odds with the *rational* dialectic of the Philosophy of Right. It directly challenges the central values and norms, and therefore *the possibility,* of moral community. To turn this around, the possibility of consensual moral community was achieved only by denying fundamental social conflicts, and this was achieved through the ideal image of the rational individual.

The 'Ideal' and the 'Actual' under Modern Conditions

Antony Duff provides the most thoughtful engagement among retributive philosophers on the relationship between the theory of punishment and the conflictual conditions of modern society. While others evade the relationship, Duff faces it head on.[4] The results of this confrontation are analysed in what follows, but I begin by outlining Duff's position. Duff wishes to hold on to the moral dimension of punishment but to give it an end that goes beyond simple requital. Part of his awareness of the problem of crime as a social phenomenon emerges in his contention that it is not enough for punishment to restore an abstract sense of right. Punishment must have a further goal in the form of moral reform or rehabilitation, although not in the sense of producing better citizens by 'technical means.'[5] Punishment operates as moral dialogue or communication that may lead to repentance, reform, and the restoring of moral relationships in the community. It is this conception of punishment that he refers to as 'teleological communication.' In the process, there may be good social consequences, but these stem from the essentially moral dialogue that takes place between the offender and the community. Thus while Duff's theory reflects consequentialist concerns, these are built into a moral theory that can be described as 'enhanced retributivism.' Punishment seeks to communicate to the criminal the wrong she has done, and to get her repentance. The criminal is thus not just persuaded to refrain from further criminal activity but is restored by her repentance to membership of the moral community she has wronged. Crime involves an attack on social relationships of which the individual is a part. It is therefore an attack on herself as a moral being in a community. Punishment conduces to the restoration of the moral standing of the individual in the community, and to her own moral good.

The classical retributive theory of punishment sought to portray punishment as a matter of individual responsibility within a moral community and came into conflict with the 'actuality' of Western communities as places of structured social and moral conflict. Duff emphasises the role of moral community in educating the individual in the rights and wrongs of citizenship, giving his retributivism a teleological edge. The question remains whether this modified retributivism can avoid the problems of the ideal and the actual at the heart of the classical tradition, or just relocate them. I will argue that a tension runs through Duff's account concerning whether he is seeking a justification of punishment in a world like our own – that is, the 'actual' world of Western societies that are socially unequal and unjust – or whether he is seeking simply an 'ideal' justification of punishment. If the latter, why? I deal with these questions in terms of the way Duff accounts for issues of responsibility and community, though, given the emphasis in his theory, I will reverse the order of discussion employed previously with regard to the classical tradition.

THE MORAL COMMUNITY. Ostensibly, Duff draws a clear distinction between an 'ideal' justification of punishment and the 'actual' world to which it is applied. One cannot justify punishing those who have not 'flouted the values and damaged the bonds of a community to which they *genuinely* belong, one within which they are themselves treated as full members' (Duff 1996: 54; emphasis added). If we cannot say that offenders have typically 'wronged members of a *genuine* community . . . that respects and cares for them, and that thus has the *moral standing* to criticise them' (Duff 1996: 85; emphasis added), punishment is not justified.[6] Duff's conclusion is that his 'ideal' conception of punishment may not apply to the actual world in which we live (1996: 88).

This argument should, however, be compared with the seemingly contradictory view that criminals *do* typically share moral understanding with those who would punish them. Duff argues that we 'must surely see that many criminals know full well that they are doing wrong' (Duff 1996: 47), meaning moral (as opposed to legal) wrong. Yet if Duff's requirement of a genuine moral community for punishment to be justified is not met, it is not clear why many criminals *should* so know. They may recognise *legal* wrong, but that is something else. Perhaps Duff is arguing about 'ideal world' criminals, if such people could exist, but his examples seem very 'actual' and contemporary. He writes, for example, that few thieves 'would agree that it is morally permissible for others to steal from them, or claim some special moral privilege that makes it right for them to steal' (Duff 1996: 47). This is empirically questionable and, in the terms of Duff's moral account, beside the point. On that account, the morally justified punishment of wrongdoing depends on the existence of a genuine moral community. Moral culpability must then be linked to this, rather than a sense of what is universally justifiable in terms of 'do unto others as you would be done to' or a matter of special privilege. Were the criminal to consult Duff on the wrongfulness of her crime, as presumably she is entitled to do, she would surely ask if she belonged to a genuine moral community. If not, then on this theory, she would presumably be able to steal and to argue that she commits no moral wrong for which she could be legitimately punished.

Evaluating how thieves perceive their activities in the actual world would probably lead to variable, contextually determined conclusions. The problem for Duff is that many people are in fact ambivalent about the morality of theft, viewing it differently depending on the context. A moral view of stealing may be selective as between taking from a supermarket, a rich man, an old lady, or a child.[7] Nor is variability of judgment a problem just with less serious crimes. Duff claims that 'to suggest that an armed robber does not know that armed robbery is wrong' is to call into question his capacity 'as a responsible moral agent.' Yet there is ample criminological evidence to the contrary. The paradigmatic armed robber, the professional, sees armed robbery as a morally legitimate form of business. One can say this without in any way calling into question whether such a person is an irresponsible moral agent. In other situations, within the community that *he* recognises, he may act in quite moral ways (Hobbs 1994). What also of organised crime and criminal organisations such as the Mafia, which are, internally, held to maintain many of the features of moral communities? I suggest that Duff *must* call into question the armed robber's status as a responsible moral agent if he is to apply his ideal theory to the actual world of crime and criminals, but that he does so *illegitimately* as a way to evade the problems of moral conflict about crime in modern society.

Perhaps then, we should excise these passages as illegitimate extensions of an otherwise acceptable ideal theory, but we would then face an equally difficult question. What would be the point of such a theory? Duff argues that individuals may be justifiably punished only where they belong to a genuine moral community, by which he means a community which 'respects and cares for them.' But in a community in which the individual has *really* been respected and cared for, it is hard to see why such a person would knowingly commit a crime. A *genuine* moral community, wherein individuals were properly brought up in moral relationships, would surely be one in which breaches of those relationships would not knowingly be undertaken. A community that really had the moral standing to punish would be one in which, on Duff's account, punishment had become unnecessary. Here, Duff runs into a modern variant of the old Kantian paradox, and it is directly linked to the question of social justice. His ideal theory applies only in the ideal circumstances he depicts and not to the actual, socially unjust world in which punishment is needed. Duff imagines an ideal moral world, a genuine moral community wherein individuals would be respected, cared for, and morally well brought up. They would hardly commit crimes. This is contrasted with an actual world in which moral relations are poor and there is no genuine community. In that world punishment is needed, but it cannot be justified. The justification holds where the institution is unnecessary, but not where it is necessary.

How might Duff respond? One possible counter to this would be to argue along these lines. The ideal theory may not vindicate punishment in the here and now but may point the way forward to a better world. The ideal argument may have a critical and reforming thrust in that it may lead us to see the need for social reform (cf. Murphy 1979). But it is not clear why the critical argument should be expressed in terms of *punishment.* Would not a social critic be better occupied in the critique of political and economic institutions that lie at the *core* of inequality, rather than of an institution that is secondary and epiphenomenal? If the issue is human dignity, there are many more obvious ways in which modern society denies this to many of its members. More important, it is hard to see the value in elaborating a moral theory of an institution, punishment, that will be justifiable only at the very moment it ceases to exist. Perhaps an example might illuminate. What would happen if we compared 'a moral theory of punishment' with a 'moral theory of prostitution'? One could of course have a moral critique of both and trust that in an ideal world neither would be necessary. If we consider prostitution, however, would we want to advance an ideal theory of such a practice? If the answer to that question is 'no', why should we want to have an ideal theory of punishment?

THE RESPONSIBLE SUBJECT. Just as the persisting ideal/actual antinomy affects the right to punish in the modern community, so it affects the question of individual responsibility for crime. If the individual needs to be morally educated by punishment, and if moral relations in modern society do not give rise to genuine obligations, how can the criminal be blamed for his crime? We have already seen how Duff argues that the thief or the armed robber will still possess a moral relationship with the community that can be re-invoked through penal communication (Duff 1996: 47), yet this is at odds with his basic premise that modern societies lack the sense of genuine community which establishes the necessary moral relationship that is to be re-invoked.

Later, this problem leads Duff to a more fundamental issue when he defends the practice of the criminal law against 'radical critics.' The radical criticism is that law fails to attend to the individual's situation in attributing fault. It fails to consider 'the particular social factors and contexts that gave birth to that crime.' To allocate guilt or responsibility to the criminal is to locate fault in the wrong place, and we would 'do better and more justly to look instead at the context from which her action flowed' (Duff 1996: 74). Given Duff's own view (1996: 88) that modern society does not enjoy the moral relations that lead to just punishment, one might think he would support this argument in relation to criminal law. But given his overall aim of a vindication of punishment, one might wonder, to the contrary, if he will resist it, for the radical argument takes us away from the validity of punishment and therefore criminal law. It is the latter aim that wins out, but the result is an argument that Duff cannot ultimately sustain. Duff solves his dilemma by arguing for a theory of criminal responsibility as 'answerability' rather than 'culpability':

> All that [criminal justice] requires is a conception of individuals as agents who are (often) responsible for what they do: responsible in the sense that it is for them to answer for what they do to those who have the standing to call them to account. (Duff 1996: 74)

'Answerability' dissolves the radical objection, because even the radical would accept that any alternatives to law and punishment must include dialogue. But does Duff's argument genuinely reflect what happens in crime and punishment, or is it an evasion? Is answerability what criminal responsibility really involves? In a footnote, Duff acknowledges that there 'is a further question whether . . . holding people answerable for their actions should involve condemning or punishing them' (1996: 74). Is this further question not equally a question for the criminal law? Does not criminal justice, in addition to 'calling someone to answer' – that is, to 'give an account' – also call that person to answer in the crucial sense of convicting and punishing him for his culpable acts? In other words, 'responsibility' involves both being 'called to respond' (answerability) and being 'found responsible' (culpability). Duff hopes to evade the radical criticism of criminal law by a thin conception of responsibility – one that sidelines culpability – but I do not think he succeeds.

We will see later how Duff uses this argument in a parallel way in order to defend law's practice in his criminal law theory (Duff 1990), but it is worth noting at this stage the contradiction in his account. Although he argues there that holding someone responsible for her 'intentional action . . . is to hold her *answerable* for it: she may be asked to explain or to justify her action', so that 'to ascribe responsibility is not yet to blame the agent' (Duff 1990: 78), this argument is contradicted by Duff's own assertion in the same work that 'the concept of intention is in fact used, both in morality and in the law, to identify . . . different kinds . . . of *culpable responsibility*' (1990: 36, emphasis added). He writes that 'ascriptions of criminal liability ought to reflect justified ascriptions of culpably responsible agency' (1990: 103). Thus Duff's own argument reveals that 'responsibility' entails both answerability prior to blame and culpability. His own argument therefore defeats his claim to defend criminal justice by sidelining culpability in favour of answerability. Yet that same flawed claim, or one like it, is necessary if he is to defend Western criminal justice against the radical criticism that legitimacy is achieved only by an illicit decontextualisation.

Beyond Retributivism's Antinomies?

In this section, we have sought the sense of justice that seventy years ago Ewing both acknowledged as important and found hard to rationalise. That sense of justice has always been associated with the retributive theory of punishment, but, following MacIntyre, I have sought to show that the fundamental flaw in retributivism was its ideal individualist basis, and that this established antinomies between an 'ideal' conception of the individual and the 'actuality' of individual (criminal) lives in modern society. These antinomies were present at retributivism's beginning, and they remain in its most recent manifestations. I argue, to use the language of tax lawyers, that although they may be evaded, they cannot be avoided.

This accounts for Ewing's sense of unease, but it leaves us with the lingering question of why retributive ideas retain an attraction in modern society. Is it simply the play of ideological power, or perhaps 'false consciousness'? If not, where do we go from here? I will ultimately argue that if we are to give sense to the idea of individual justice, we need to move our discussion beyond those theories, classical and modern, that have their genesis in the Kantian tradition. To do this, we need to develop two things: a conception of community that is not based on the idea of consensus, and a conception of individual responsibility that is not abstract but is genuinely located within the context of social community. I will return to these ideas in the third section, but I will finish here by pointing to arguments in Duff's work that begin to show the way forward.

THE MORAL COMMUNITY. As regards the nature of community in modern society, Duff reflects on what he describes as two models of punishment, the liberal and the communitarian.[8] In his argument, the communitarian is more ambitious and for that reason perhaps less suited to modern social conditions. It depends 'on the existence of genuine communities to which both offender and victim belong, and with which the offender can be reconciled' (Duff 1996: 85). But this kind of reconciliatory justice is really possible and appropriate only 'between neighbours or friends (in a broad sense of that term) . . . : between people whose lives are structured by shared values and mutual concern.' Perhaps, then, a liberal theory of punishment is more appropriate. Such a theory, with its emphasis on the morally limited kinds of punishment such as formal censure or deterrence, is 'appropriate for strangers: for those who might have no genuinely common life together (who form no community), but who must work out a way of living next to each other (rather than truly together) that will allow them to pursue their own separate goods' (1996: 85).

As regards the nature of community, it seems to me that these two models, the liberal and the communitarian, are both inadequate. Neither can form a good basis for an adequate theory of punishment. Concerning the liberal model, it should first be noted that, *pace* Duff, even it does not deny the existence of community but rather establishes minimal conditions for it in a 'world of strangers.' If we accept this modification in Duff's description of the liberal model, it is still not the case that there is only a minimal common moral life or community in modern society. The model abstracts from modern realities. Nor, however, is the alternative view of the communitarian accurate, that there is (or ought to be) a homogeneous sense of community in society as a whole. What is required is a view of moral community and communities in which there is genuine agreement about certain things at certain times. Moral community (communities) exist(s), but it (they) is (are) shifting and limited, structurally fractured and conflictual. The example of theft, discussed previously, reveals the way in which moral agreement about wrongdoing can exist, but it is variable and contextually determined. There can be agreement about the wrongfulness of stealing from a child or from an old lady much more easily than about stealing from a supermarket or a corporation. My argument is that there is a middle position between Duff's two alternatives. The social context within which punishment occurs is one in which there are moral communities, so the liberal individualist model, in which only a minimal community is formed, is an inaccurate depiction of social reality. So too is the communitarian model if it assumes one common moral life. The modern community is a fragmented, structurally fractured society in which a variety of communities informed by variables of class, race, and gender compete and intersect. Any universal theory of moral community is therefore inadequate, and this is true for both the maximalist communitarian approach and the minimalist liberal approach. If we are going to talk seriously about our experience of justice in modern society, *we have to start on the basis of overlapping moral communities that are fractured and conflictual.*

THE RESPONSIBLE SUBJECT. What model of individual responsibility should we look for? Here, I find myself closer to Duff than in his models of moral community. We have already seen that he defends the idea of criminal law by arguing that it is concerned with responsibility only as answerability, of individuals who are 'responsible in the sense that it is for them to answer for what they do to those who have the standing to call them to account' (Duff 1996: 74). I have argued that this is not the most important thing that criminal law does, so that if Duff is going to defend criminal law, he will generate a contradictory analysis, but I am sympathetic to the thinking that lies behind his argument and that points the way beyond criminal law theory. Duff is arguing against abolitionists and others (including myself) who provide a 'radical critique' of the law's abstract individualism. Radical critics do not, Duff asserts, abandon 'any notion of responsible individual agency.' They talk instead of 'individual, socially situated agents', and they want to 'enhance the responsibility of individual members of the community for their own lives.' They still want to 'hold individual agents to be answerable, or call them to account, for their actions' (Duff 1996: 75).

Aside from the question as to whether Duff's account accurately reflects the way criminal law works, it seems to me there is some truth in what he says here about a critical account of individual responsibility. Individuals accounting for their agency *is* important, but what Duff misses, I believe, is the sense that responsibility in such a view is always something that is fundamentally shared *by* the individual *with* the community. Where it is morally relevant to hold the individual to account, it is also relevant to hold the community to account. Individual responsibility is always intermixed with social responsibility for wrongdoing, and it is this that distinguishes a critical account from any that is based on the liberal tradition. The latter, even in a modern revisionist account such as Duff's, always needs to seek a measure of separation in order to make judgment of the individual possible. If we are going to talk of individual responsibility, it is therefore necessary to establish a model of what it means to be a responsible agent *in* a community. I mean this in the deep sense that it ultimately becomes impossible to speak of responsible agency in a way that separates it from what happens in community. To talk of agency, subjectivity, or responsibility *is, apparently paradoxically, also to talk of what appears to deny it: the role of community in constituting agency, subjectivity, and responsibility.* This is a complex, synthetic, theoretical task that I begin to address in the third section through the social psychology of Rom Harré.

Before moving to social psychology, however, I want first to develop my critique to consider where criminal law theory stands in relation to retributive philosophy. I will argue that parallel problems and antinomies operate there. The ideal in criminal law takes the form of a theory of individual responsibility that is held to operate in abstraction from a field of 'substantive' moral and political issues that govern community life. When we have considered the nature of legal responsibility, we will further appreciate the need to move beyond a liberal way of understanding individual justice.

The Ideal and the Actual in Criminal Law Theory

Philosophers of punishment often identify close links between retributive theory and the criminal law. This is the homology expressed in Moore's demand that 'legal liability track moral responsibility' (Moore 1993a: 130) or in Duff's summatory 'As with morality so with law' (Duff 1990: 102). I too argue for a close parallel between retributivism, a philosophical morality, and legal theory, but I argue that it consists in an inability to capture fully the moral sense of justice and desert in modern society. In one sense, Moore and Duff are right. Law is homologous with morality, but it is *with a certain kind* of morality, the kind that MacIntyre calls 'simulacral.'[9]

The problem lies in the ideal representation of morality, through the forms of the abstract individual, that lies at the heart of concepts of subjective responsibility and community in law as in retributive philosophy. The legal account of individual responsibility focuses on an ideal conception of the individual and excludes the broader social and moral context within which individual agency occurs. My focus will be on the idea of a 'general part' in the criminal law and its typical components *mens rea, actus reus,* justification, and excuse. My argument will be that analysis of the 'general part' is central to a liberal account of the morality of the criminal law because of the central focus in that analysis on the nature of individual responsibility. However, I shall also argue that the conditions for responsibility within the 'general part' are essentially limited in order to suppress the broader social and moral context within which individual agency occurs. Just as retributive morality was based on an ideal conception of the individual that suppressed the social context of crime and criminality, so is legal morality, as understood within liberal theory. Thus what liberal theory sees as the basis for moral claims on behalf of law is here seen as a means of *excluding* moral issues. As with morality, so, indeed, with law.

The relationship between the ideal and the actual is examined in the contrast between the liberal conception of criminal law as possessing a general part of *mens rea, actus reus,* and 'subsidiary' features of justification and excuse and a historical understanding of how this 'legal architectonic' (Norrie 1996b) operates to suppress underlying moral conflicts and claims of right. The contrast between the law's ideal individualism and the actualities of modern social life is then explored as it impinges on and disrupts legal theory. If there is a mismatch between legal morality and broader moral issues with which the law must engage, one of the ways this would manifest itself would be the law's failure successfully to exclude the broader moral issues from its theory and practice. These do not go away simply because the law's 'architectonic of judgment' wishes it. Rather they return to haunt the law, cropping up at various points as problems for it. One function of criminal law theory, I argue, is to maintain the appearance of rationality of the law's categories of responsibility, in a game of inclusion and exclusion in the context of a contradictory social environment.

In the first part of this section, I outline law's architectonic of judgment, its 'morality of form' as understood by liberal theory. I counterpose a critical perspective, arguing that law's individualist morality represses as well as expresses moral concerns. In the second part, I examine one attempt to defend the rationality of law's architectonic by arguing for the centrality of intention to human responsibility and blameworthiness. Once again I choose Antony Duff's work because it seems to me to be sensitive to the problems caused by legal individualism, while wishing in innovative ways to defend a liberal account. Focusing on his analysis of the place of intention, my argument will be that Duff's attempt to defend legal individualism fails and that the failure indicates the artificiality of the suppression by law of moral issues. Legal categories of responsibility are constructed *against* moral judgments of responsibility, not in line with them, and this destabilises even the most sophisticated attempts to rationalise them. In the third section, I then use Duff's critical method to consider how one might move beyond the liberal positions he seeks to defend.

Law's Ideal-individualist 'Morality of Form'

In the orthodox view, criminal law contains a 'general part' of principles and rules that reflect a philosophical understanding of the relationship between the individual, the law, and the state. This liberal individualist understanding is elegantly expressed by Andrew Ashworth (1995), for example, in the idea of respect for individual autonomy, from which stems desert for punishment. Criminal law is, should, or can be reflective of the idea of individual choice, and penal sanction should follow only a freely chosen act. Retributive ideas of desert and justice, explored in the previous part of this chapter, are thus established at the core of criminal law theory. From these premises is born the subjective approach to criminal law principles, affirming the need for voluntariness, intention, foresight, knowledge, and belief concerning actions and their consequences. These constitute, in Ashworth's terminology, the 'positive fault requirements' that have to be established in order to prove an offence. Beyond these, there exist certain 'negative fault requirements' that operate to supplement and qualify judgments of responsibility that might otherwise be made on the basis of the positive requirements. Into this category there fall the various 'defences' – 'excuses' and (on some analyses)[10] 'justifications' – that may negate responsibility otherwise established on the basis of the positive criteria. The excuses and justifications operate as secondary and residual categories, permitted to override in limited circumstances the operation of the otherwise default logic that '*mens rea* plus *actus reus* equals crime.'

This picture of a general part consisting of principles concerning voluntary acts and mental elements, qualified by justificatory and excusatory defences and based upon principles of individual autonomy, presents the image of a society resting on individual autonomy and social cooperation under a universal rule of law. It seems to provide a relatively straightforward basis for organising the criminal law. What is really compelling, however, is the relationship it posits between legal and moral judgment. At one level it is an axiom of liberal theory that there is a division between law and morals, so that legal and moral justice are essentially different. Max Weber expressed this in terms of the distinction between law's formal rationality (decisions deduced from existing rules) and substantive rationality (decisions based upon substantive ethical ideas). Yet the separation of 'legal form' and 'moral content' does not mean that legal judgments of responsibility are lacking in moral significance. On the contrary, legal justice, though 'separated' from morals and politics, is regarded as morally and politically legitimate because it is based upon respect for individual autonomy in a community. Individual responsibility, as represented in the 'general part', is central to law's 'morality of form', based upon universal attributes of the individual and regarded as expressive of human freedom.

Opposed to this view of law's expression of freedom is the view that this 'morality of form' was a historical means of suppressing legitimate moral demands of oppositional communities in the period of the birth of the modern criminal law. I have argued this at length elsewhere (Norrie 1993b: esp. ch. 2, 37–40; Norrie 1996a) and so will be brief here. One can begin with two linked alternative discourses that historically threatened the idea of the responsible subject within the criminal law. The first is a discourse of need, the second a discourse of competing (counter-) right. The former states that a person broke the law because of acute personal or familial need. The latter claims that the breaking of the law was not wrong in the first place but entailed a legitimate moral counterclaim. The problems of need and counter-right were confronted by criminal lawyers from the late seventeenth through to the early nineteenth century when capitalism was developing and consolidating its hold upon social relations, and when the liberal ideology of individual subjectivity was first dominant. This set up a potential conflict because the ideology of individual subjectivity could not immediately rule out disruptive discourses of need and counter-right. The legal task at hand was to draw the boundaries of the legal subject-citizen in a way that 'respected' his or her liberty and freedom, but within the limits of the new evolving social and political order. Legal individualism was at the same time a means of freeing *and* suppressing moral subjectivities: recognising civil and political status, but *within* capitalist social, political, and economic relations.

One central tool in the lawyers' locker was the division of motive and intention. A modern conception of mentality conceived of the individual as a purposive actor acting in the context of his or her environment, reacting to the surrounding opportunities and constraints. This was represented as a modern subjectivity of intention and motive. Both could be taken as universal features of subjectivity. All people form intentions to act regardless of who they are, whence they come, what they experience; everyone experiences the force of desires and fears and is motivated by them to action. But motive could go further. It could contextualise the subject in his or her social and political environment. The poor and dispossessed could say that their motive was *need,* or could claim that they acted on *right.* Motive represented a threat to legal control and was therefore excised from legal subjectivity, from the juridical attributes of responsible citizenship. Abstract mental states of intention, recklessness, and agency were constructed as *the* moments of liberal legal subjectivity, to the exclusion of motive. Motive could open the door to broad moral arguments of excuse and justification. These had to be marginalised within law's architectonic if law was to present itself as impartial and just within a conflictual social environment.

A 'universal' definition of right and wrong, based on the idea of the abstract, ideal individual, was used as one means to legitimate terrible social need and the expropriation of existing communities within new relations of production. It was the political success of the industrial and mercantile middle classes in imposing their interests which ensured that legal reformers could express legal rules, which were the product of historically sharp social conflicts, in terms of consensus, good common sense, and opposition to anarchy. The rule of private property became the 'rule of law', so that attacks on the former could be condemned as attacks on a universal social good. Instrumental in this process was the creation of an abstract and formal definition of human subjectivity that would cut off reference to substantive moral argument. This ideal conception of human subjectivity was central both to the philosophy of the period (see previous part) and to the criminal law with its constrictive cognitive version of individual responsibility.

Legal formalism was thus a means of repressing as well as expressing moral claims; it cut both ways. Its legacy is seen throughout the criminal law in the ways in which concepts from the law's formal morality, such as intention, are asked to do moral work for which they are not equipped. In choking off alternative moral and political voices and social arrangements, legal formalism also constricted its own potential for moral judgment. I have analysed the consequences of this for law elsewhere (Norrie 1993b, esp. ch. 4; 1996a), but one illustration would be the English intention and murder cases where there is a gap between the legal-moral concepts mobilised to judge killings, and the moral quality of those killings. The legal-moral judgment of responsibility is based on intention to kill or cause grievous bodily harm (the *mens rea* of murder), yet the haphazard doctrinal progress from *Smith* ([1961] AC 290) through *Hyam* ([1974] QB 99) to *Moloney* ([1985] AC 905), *Hancock and Shankland* ([1986] 2 WLR 357) and *Nedrick* ([1986] 1 WLR 1025) suggests a deeper moral agenda that is unsatisfied by the law of intention. All these cases have hinged upon the definition of direct and indirect intention, but as Nicola Lacey, Celia Wells, and Dirk Meure argue, the legal categories of judgment operate inadequately in the place of fuller moral judgments:

> Although often obscured by the conceptual apparatus of the law with its use of mental elements as a means of delineation, a moral judgment is also being made. . . . [T]here is

> an ever more desperate search for a magic formula whereby the murderer can be distinguished from the manslaughterer through the use of the notion of intention. (Lacey, Wells, and Meure 1990: 268; cf Lacey 1993: 624–6, Norrie 1993b: 47–57)

Legal definitions of direct and indirect intention do not distinguish among actions that are substantially dissimilar from a moral point of view, but they are used in law's morality to distinguish the culpability of the murderer from that of the manslaughterer. The legal categories consequently have to be manipulated against their own logic to reflect the underlying moral quality of the killings in particular cases. A man who shoots his loved stepfather in a drunken race to load a gun after a family party (*Moloney*) is not morally the same as a woman who puts petrol through a letter box and kills two young girls in order to frighten a rival (*Hyam*), or two striking miners who drop a concrete block off a bridge in order to obstruct a motor convoy but kill a taxi driver (*Hancock and Shankland*). Yet all three are cases in which the law of indirect or oblique intention is the critical legal tool manipulated to produce both a legal *and* a 'behind the scenes' moral judgment of culpability. Because the tools of legal and moral judgment are dysphasic, this is not possible without substantial conceptual discomfort within the law. What is lacking in the legal-moral determination of responsibility is consideration of the different moral contexts and motivations that gave rise to these deaths. There is a moral decontextualisation at work, which historically the law's individualist morality of form brought about by *excluding* moral judgments.

At the most basic level of law's architectonic, this exclusion is seen in the problematic splitting of issues of responsibility into questions of *mens rea, actus reus,* and what are seen as residual, exceptional questions of justification and excuse. Treating issues of justification and excuse in this way is necessary because these categories potentially contain the moral and political issues the law wishes to ignore. The two alternative discourses of right and need discussed previously reflect the potential content of categories of justification (right) and excuse (need). As Lacey et al. remark, these 'residual' categories constantly threaten to subvert the central categories of *mens rea* and *actus reus* because the latter do not have the conceptual solidity to which the law pretends. As they say, 'the neat conceptual frame may be useful as a model, but on close inspection we find that its elements shade into one another in a way that ultimately defies the analytical clarity boasted and sought by doctrine' (Lacey, Wells, and Meure 1990: 40). The reason for this, I argue, is that the 'conceptual frame' of law's formal subjective morality was designed to exclude deeper moral and political contestations from the business of ruling. Law's morality of form is a means of conducting this business; its claims to reflect moral concerns, to rationality, and to coherence are its victims.

What is necessarily lacking in law is a synthetic judgment of the relationship between mental state, social and moral context, and criminal act, but the possibility of synthesising different aspects of responsibility and judgment was consciously suppressed historically by the prioritisation of cognitive states above matters of excuse and justification. The apparent neutrality of the criminal law's individualist concepts of responsibility was achieved at the cost of neutering the process of judgment.[11] This historical backdrop to legal practice cannot leave legal theory untouched. It leaves law a simulacrum, a pale and ambiguous doppelganger, of moral judgment. In the next section, I explore one way in which legal theory attempts to rationalise law's constantly failing logic.

Rationalising Law's Morality of Form

In the standard view, the structure of criminal law involves a 'general part' that applies *ceteris paribus* to the specific offences. The general part is composed of definitions of *actus reus* and *mens rea,* which occupy the central position (Smith 1989). While acts and intentions are central to the establishment of criminal responsibility, general defences incorporating ideas of justification and excuse may operate where *actus reus* and *mens rea* have been established to exonerate the accused according to the nature of the defence invoked. It is this conception of a general part in which *mens rea* is central to legal judgment, while defences of justification and excuse are regarded as secondary and exceptional, that I describe as the architectonic of legal judgment. It is presented in orthodox accounts as both moral and rational, if problematic in its detail. In this section, I explore one attempt, by Antony Duff, to explain law's conception of its general part. Duff argues that it is legitimate to defend a 'formal' account of law's morality based upon the primacy of intention as a culpable state, and to maintain a separation between intention and the broader normative issues that surround it. He defends in particular the paradigmatic centrality of intention to responsible agency as compared with matters of justification and excuse (Duff 1990: 100).

Duff's analysis is, however, ambivalent. On the one hand, intention in his account is central to both legal and moral responsibility, so that he seeks to rationalise the morality of form that legal judgment entails. On the other hand, because of the rigour of his exposition allied to an 'interpretivist' approach to judgment, Duff ends up by showing the irrational and morally repressive character of judgment within law's architectonic. I deal with this in relation to three aspects of Duff's work. The first concerns Duff's account of the relationship between intention, justification, and excuse; the second involves Duff's account of the nature of intentional agency; and the third relates to Duff's critique of what he describes as the orthodox consequentialist and dualist account of criminal responsibility. I deal with the first two of these in this subsection, the third in the final subsection. My argument will be that in all three areas, Duff's discussion reveals the impossibility of maintaining a separation of questions of intention (on which the responsibility of the abstract legal subject is founded) from the broader context of normative judgment (the moral issues at large in the community) that law attempts. The morality of form, with intention as its anchor concept, is shown to be irredeemably infected with, and unsustainable apart from, the broader moral context within which it operates but which it seeks to deny.

THE INDIVISIBILITY OF INTENTION, JUSTIFICATION, AND EXCUSE. According to Duff, intention is integral to human action, and intended and intentional agency form the central paradigms of responsible agency. This is true in both law and morality:

> The underlying assumption here is that criminal liability should, in principle, be ascribed in accordance with moral responsibility. A defendant should be criminally liable only for conduct for which she can properly be held morally responsible or culpable. . . . That is why *mens rea* should be required for criminal liability, and why intention should be the most serious kind of criminal fault. (Duff 1990: 103)

Duff recognises that a central question for any explanation of law's architectonic of judgment is why *mens rea* has 'pole position' ahead of questions of justification and excuse (1990: 99–100). There is *prima facie* the problem that *mens rea* may not be sufficient to establish criminal guilt, for an act may be intended yet be justified or excused. This raises the question of whether intended agency is truly the central question for criminal responsibility as contended, or whether matters of justification and excuse have overriding importance. As regards justification, Duff argues that this *prima facie* case can be countered:

> One who justifies her action is prepared to *answer* for it, by showing it to be right: the possibility of avoiding blame or criminal liability by justifying our intended or intentional actions, therefore, does not undermine the claim that intended and intentional actions are paradigms of responsible agency. (Duff 1990: 100)

As regards excuses, these operate with, not against, intentional agency, for they 'at least qualify, even if they do not wholly rebut, the ascription of intended or intentional agency' (1990: 100). Justification and excuse issues are therefore compatible with the centrality of intended and intentional agency to moral and legal culpability. The relationship is complementary rather than contradictory.

Let us explore these claims, dealing first with justification. Duff's analysis of justification and intention hinges upon his understanding of responsibility, which, as we saw (p. 114), is cast in terms of answering for one's actions:

> To act with the intention of bringing a result about is to make myself fully responsible for that result – I must be ready to answer for (to explain, to justify, to accept criticism

> for) my action of bringing it about; and I bring about intentionally those effects for which I am held responsible. (Duff 1990: 99)

Hart (1968: ch. 9) has shown, however, that there are a number of different meanings of the word 'responsibility', and although he does not identify Duff's conception of 'being called to respond' as one of them, it is doubtful whether this idea fits with either legal or moral notions of responsibility. What Duff, I think, needs is something like Hart's account of 'moral liability-responsibility.' For Hart too, there is substantial homology between legal and moral responsibility. Differences, he says, 'are due to substantive differences between the content of legal and moral rules and principles *rather than to any variation in meaning of responsibility*' (Hart 1968: 225–6, emphasis added). But Hart explains such responsibility not in terms of being 'called to respond' but in terms of being 'morally blameworthy, or morally obliged to make amends for the harm' (Hart 1968: 225). Duff's account by comparison appears to describe a preliminary situation prior to that of ascribing blame, in which the issue of blameworthiness has yet to be settled. To be 'called to answer' is, put simply, not the same as to 'have one's answers found wanting', and Duff seems to acknowledge as much in other passages where he describes 'culpable responsibility' in addition to answerability (Duff 1990: 36, 102–3).

Because the concept of responsibility-as-answerability does not settle the issue of responsibility-as-blameworthiness, it cannot settle the proper relationship between intention and justification with regard to culpability. John Gardner and Heike Jung have suggested (1991: 587) that Duff's account gives rise to a kind of *prima facie* culpability, but this is surely wrong. Even a *prima facie* culpability requires an appropriate, if provisional, allocation of matters of justification with intention, and this is not suggested in Duff's account. Once one recognises that answerability and culpability are both central to legal responsibility, Duff's sidelining of justification vis à vis intention becomes impossible. Yet this is Duff's chosen means of reconciling justification with intention.

As regards excuse, Duff examines the twin defences of duress and necessity, which present problems for his analysis of the centrality of intention. He argues that intentional actions are done for reasons, and that this means that intention is linked to rationality. Duress and necessity claims

> serve to rebut the presumption of rational competence which ascriptions of intentional agency normally involve. Duress or necessity should excuse if the pressure to which the agent is subjected is so severe that it impairs her capacity to grasp, to weigh or to act on good reasons for action – to realise that and why she should resist the pressure, or to carry through a resolution to resist it. (Duff 1990: 102)

Note first that this 'irrationalist' analysis (i.e., of the pressures that make rational intentionality impossible) is at odds with the standard analysis of the way in which duress and necessity operate in relation to intention. According to that approach, it may be perfectly rational to intend to commit an act under duress because of the threat that has been made (Norrie 1993b: 165).[12] There is no assumption that the agent cannot grasp, weigh, or act on good reasons for action. She may perfectly well realise why she should resist the pressure yet submit to the duress.

Duff's account, I think, recognises as much in that he introduces the idea of *good* reasons for action, but the significance of this goes against rather than for his argument. In introducing in effect a notion of morally substantive rational agency *into* his conception of intention, he reveals that it is not simply the issue of intention that grounds a notion of responsibility, but intention related to a particular, morally substantive context.[13] Thus duress as excuse forces Duff into a position on responsibility in which a substantive moral position is needed to supplement his analysis of intention. This, however, is a 'dangerous supplement' (Fitzpatrick 1991: 2)[14] because it reveals that the matter of normative content is a central and constitutive component of responsibility *alongside* the ability to form intentions and act intentionally. Intention and intentionality do not have the paradigmatic centrality to issues of responsibility that Duff claims.

To put this another way, duress and necessity are defences that operate to deny responsibility *notwithstanding* the existence of intended or intentional agency, and therefore they undermine the claim that intention and intentionality are the central moral features of judgment. It transpires, in these cases, that excuses invoke broader issues of normative judgment as the basis for settling matters of responsibility, and that questions of intention and intentionality are relevant only within this broader context. Although it is true that law's architectonic of judgment, of which Duff's analysis is a very good representation, focuses on intention and intentionality, the extreme cases of duress and necessity reveal that the normally hidden substratum of these categories is moral and political. Duress and necessity force this normative basis into the open, revealing that intention and intentionality are the primary categories of responsibility only so long as this deeper normative element remains hidden.

The legal conception of responsibility seeks to suppress the 'contextually synthetic' nature of judgment in favour of a morality of form, in which apparently neutral categories like intention are given primacy. Potentially threatening normative issues such as those of justification and excuse are portrayed as contained and secondary exceptions. Yet a sophisticated attempt to rationalise this position such as Duff's shows only the act of suppression and denial that goes into law's architectonic. Moving to Duff's conception of intention itself, we will see the continuing juridical need to suppress moral content (and contentiousness) in favour of a morality of form, and a vivid example of the logic of legal practice in this regard.

THE MORAL CONTEXT WITHIN INTENTIONAL AGENCY. Intention in Duff's account includes both 'direct' and 'oblique' forms. One either acts with the intention of bringing something about or one brings something about as a foreseen by-product or means to an end of one's actions. In the latter instance, one does not 'intend', but one still acts 'intentionally.' With regard to oblique intention, he considers whether we should ascribe responsibility with regard to all or only some unintended but foreseen consequences.[15] Duff observes that we cannot ascribe every foreseen consequence to an agent because there is a moral dimension involved: 'Ascriptions of intentional agency do not describe neutral facts: they express normative judgments of responsibility, in which we may disagree' (Duff 1990: 84).

This is effectively the point Duff denies in his defence of the paradigmatic centrality of intention over justification and excuse, and I have argued that this denial was a rationalisation of a legal practice that was historically narrowed to exclude competing moral claims. If he now argues to admit moral judgment into a central legal category, will this not open up the law to moral conflict? If it does, how does Duff see the law as dealing with this? Duff argues as follows. Normative judgments involve a potential conflict of view as to what an agent *ought* to recognise and take into account as a foreseen effect of action. If an examiner fails a student to the student's serious detriment, the examiner, Duff argues, is not responsible even where the consequences are foreseen, for it is part of the normative role of an examiner to judge a student on his or her performance and not on the consequences of that performance. Similarly, whether a doctor is criminally liable for aiding and abetting unlawful sexual intercourse by prescribing contraceptives to an underage girl depends upon how one views the role of the doctor. Morally, is a doctor's duty only to the patient, or to the patient and the law? If one adopts one or other normative view of the doctor's role, one will come up with a different conclusion to the question of whether the doctor intentionally aided and abetted the offence.

This issue of normativity has emerged in cases like *Steane* ([1947] KB 997) and *Ahlers* ([1915] 1KB 616). Both involved charges of intending to assist the enemy in time of war. In the former case, Steane was acquitted because he broadcast for the Germans under threat of death to his wife and children; in the latter, Ahlers, a German consul, was held not to have intended to assist the enemy by helping Germans to return home because he was only doing his duty as a consul. Both cases involve a normative judgment about the scope of what was intended, because to broadcast and to assist repatriation were both actions that *ceteris paribus* would be foreseen to have the effect of assisting the enemy.

Normative questions involve matters of moral and political judgment and raise centrally the question of what justifies a person in acting in a particular way. Duff's analysis of intentional agency, as I have said, undermines his account of intention and intentionality as the paradigms of responsible agency. Justification is a central and constitutive component of an intentionality-based judgment – part, as it were, of its 'molecular structure.' To extend the chemistry metaphor, judgment is like a compound rather than an aggregate of separate atomic elements, of intention, justification, and excuse. But this is what the law has to deny, as Duff generally denies it, and for the *historical* reasons given in the previous section. It is this denial that drives a wedge between legal and genuinely moral judgment. While Duff shows that oblique intention involves potential normative disagreement, he also notes that such disagreement is 'more typically found outside the law than within it':

> Outside the law our different normative standards (our different moral values, for instance) will generate conflicting criteria of responsibility, of relevance, and of intentional agency: but the law provides authoritative criteria which determine our legal responsibilities, the legal relevance of expected side-effects, and thus the scope (in law) of our intentional agency. (Duff 1990: 84)

An individual swimming naked in public view might have no oblique intention to indecently expose him- or herself and might insist on being entitled so to swim. Still the law may hold that the conduct is intentionally disgusting, and, no matter what the person thinks, he or she 'will not be heard to deny that [he or she] cause[s] it intentionally.' In such a circumstance the law forecloses the issue of normative disagreement by insisting that the oblique intention is present whatever the individual's own normative view. The issue of judgment is settled by the court according to its view of what is acceptable. The normative issue of what is justifiable is finessed by the law's unilateral declaration of what the 'authoritative criteria' are to be. As with the distinction between motive and intention, or the sidelining of justification and excuse, so in relation to intentionality we see the way in which matters of normative justification and judgment are suppressed within the law's base categories. Once that is done, and these categories have been 'secured' against moral infection, issues of justification and excuse are permitted as 'subsidiary' categories within law's architectonic. These are held to be subsidiary issues because law has made them so, driving a wedge between legal and genuinely moral judgment. Law does not run with morality; it cuts against it.

A good example of how law operates to deny moral issues of culpability is seen in Duff's discussion of *Steane.*[16] Taking this to be a case of intentional rather than intended assistance of the enemy, there arises on Duff's account a substantive normative question that is a source of potential moral conflict. There must be room, on *his* analysis, for moral dispute as to whether Steane's assisting the enemy was *normatively* intentional. Rather than arguing the case on moral terms, however, Duff does what I argue the law does. He finesses the potential normative disagreement by positing a consequentialist argument as to why Steane should not be allowed to claim his assistance was unintentional:

> If we deny that he intended to assist the enemy, because he intended to save his family, we must likewise deny that one who broadcasts for the enemy in order to earn money intends to assist the enemy: but it would be outrageous to acquit such a person of 'doing

acts likely to assist the enemy, with intent to assist the enemy.' Mr Steane's defence should have been duress, not lack of intent; his intention to assist the enemy was excused by the threats under which he acted. (Duff 1990: 93)

There is, however, a world of moral difference between Steane and a mercenary that should, on Duff's analysis of oblique intention, be reflected in his consideration as to whether Steane acted *intentionally*. This can be seen if we compare Duff's treatment of *Steane* with that of *Ahlers,* where he asserts the moral issue in line with his argument. Ahlers' *intention* 'was simply to do his legal duty as consul, which required him to help enemy aliens return home when war began' (Duff 1990: 93). The difference between Ahlers and Steane is that the former was not a 'private citizen', and his role and duties as a consul constitute a moral threshold over which the known side effect of assisting the enemy cannot pass. This is, however, no more than a normative judgment that the role and duties of a consul are somehow more valid than those of a husband and father. Those too should be considered on Duff's analysis as a potential moral threshold. They should not be finessed by a simple consequentialist argument. In *both* cases there can be moral disagreement on Duff's account, and in neither can the matter be avoided (though it can be evaded) by a consequentialist argument. In foreclosing on the moral question of intentionality in *Steane* and sidelining it to the excuse of duress, Duff illegitimately, in his own terms, does precisely what the law does in order to avoid contestable moral issues around its paradigm categories of intention and intentionality.

Beyond Law's Morality of Form?

Law's architectonic of judgment thus privileges an apparently de-normativised (or de-politicised, de-moralised) concept of intention and intentionality, relegating the 'difficult' moral and political issues to what is constructed as a subsidiary category of justification and excuse. There, in the back alleys of legal judgment, they become relatively unimportant 'exceptions to a rule' rather than what they really are: inherently constitutive elements of judgment that were historically sidelined by a particular legal order.

Exploring Duff's defence of legal idealism/individualism took us in two directions. On the one hand, we saw his inability to defend law's focus on intention to the exclusion of justification and excuse and his ultimate acknowledgment that in the final analysis, law's exclusion of broader normative issues is a matter of political fiat. Viewed in this way, Duff can be read *sceptically* insofar as he defends legal reasoning and *symptomatically* to reveal law's foundational conflicts. In this final section, I now want to consider how his work can be used *critically* to point the way beyond legal methodology and its ideal/individualist form (see p. 105).

From Duff's discussion of intention, we can see the inseparability in the moral judgment of individual agency of questions of intention, justification, and excuse. The 'substantive morality' questions cannot be separated from the 'formal morality' issues, as law seeks to do. Intention-derived conceptions of fault are insufficient by themselves; they must be supplemented in order to make judgment possible. Legal responsibility is too narrow to reflect the realities of moral judgment. What is needed is a synthetic engagement of the formal and the substantive, which I sought to identify, with a metaphor from chemistry, as a 'molecular' compounding of intention, justification, and excuse. The process of moral judgment cannot be divided up into separate 'atoms' of intention, justification, and excuse. This compounding of 'formal' and 'substantive' issues of responsibility is particularly seen in the most radical part of *Intention, Agency and Criminal Liability* where Duff sketches a critique of the individualism, dualism, and consequentialism at the heart of the criminal law's categories. I will conclude this part by considering how this argument leads us beyond law's morality of form.

Duff argues that orthodox legal theory entails a number of dualisms, the most important of which is the subjective/objective dichotomy within a consequentialist account of harm and blame. For the consequentialist, harm is defined 'objectively' according to principles of political utility, and separately from questions of fault that operate as a side constraint. Fault in turn stresses practical issues concerning subjective individual knowledge and control over the occurrence of harm, and it is for this reason that questions of intention are central to the consequentialist theory of criminal responsibility. Consequentialism therefore de-politicises or de-moralises the question of criminal harm by establishing the bounds of harm 'objectively' and by identifying subjective responsibility for harm in terms of apparently 'factual' categories of knowledge and control.

Duff's critique in his 'non-consequentialist' account of responsibility correctly points out that this separation of subjective and objective components misses the *synthetic* nature of the moral judgment of harm. Such a judgment attributes responsibility for murder, for example, in terms of the quality of the mental state that *combines with* a particular resultant death.

> Both the murder victim and the victim of natural causes suffer death: but the character of the harm that they suffer surely also depends on the way in which they die. One who tries to kill me . . . *attacks* my life and my most basic rights; and the harm which I suffer in being murdered . . . essentially involves this wrongful attack on me. . . . The 'harm' at which the law of murder is aimed is thus not just the *consequential* harm of death, but the harm which is *intrinsic* to an attack on another's life. (Duff 1990: 112–13)

Criminal law, with its separation of *mens rea* (fault) and *actus reus* (harm), reflects the dualist position that Duff regards as inadequate. His argument is that the essence of murder is not the consequence of death but the intrinsic harm in the attack on another's life. That intrinsic harm is paradigmatically present in a wilful killing and therefore paradigmatically present when there is an intention to kill. Duff still insists on the centrality of intention, but it is, in *this* part of his argument, a morally substantive conception that he invokes in his discussion of the intention to kill. It is not the factual issue of control over one's conduct that is important but the moral badness revealed by one's intention:

> Human actions are purposive: they are done for reasons, in order to bring something about; their direction and their basic structure is formed by the intentions with which their agents act. It is through the intentions with which I act that I engage in the world as an agent, and relate myself most closely to the actual and potential effects of my actions; and the central or fundamental kind of wrong-doing is to *direct* my actions towards evil – to *intend* and to *try* to do what is evil. (Duff 1990: 113)

Duff's emphasis on the intrinsic connection between the subjective and objective elements in murder opens the door to a recognition that there is an element of interpretation and normative evaluation in the establishment of *any* death as murder that goes beyond the combination of result and mental state, narrowly conceived in terms of intention. His interpretive analysis of judgment, with its unification of moral form and content, still makes intention a central part of the judgment of wrongdoing, but it at the same time de-centres it. It is the 'moral colour' of the intention that is now crucial, and on which the judgment is based. It is impossible to judge intention separately from the quality of the act that is being done. If we return to the example of Steane and the mercenary who both broadcast for the enemy, it is clear that Steane's (indirect) intention to assist the enemy in no way matches that of the mercenary. The moral colour of Steane's oblique intention is provided by his direct intention to save his family. Steane, quite simply, does not seek in moral terms 'to do what is evil,' whereas the mercenary does. The interpretive account, against Duff's own analysis of *Steane,* takes this into account in a way that the consequentialist cannot.

In making these points, I argue that Duff quite rightly takes us beyond the narrow understanding of judgment contained within the traditional legal–consequentialist view. However, so doing, he also takes us beyond the law's de-moralised architectonic of judgment. The radical and critical thrust of Duff's interpretivism takes us beyond legal individualism towards the need for a synthetic account of the judgment of agency within a moral community. Thus, the argument of this second part takes us to a similar conclusion as the first part. In examining the ideal individualism of retributive theory and legal responsibility, we see the need to move to a synthetic account of individual and community in order to understand the judgment of moral culpability.

Beyond the Ideal and the Actual: Social Constructionism, Individuals, and Communities

I have argued that the responsible subject in the philosophy of punishment and criminal law theory was presented as an 'ideal' individual removed from the actualities of modern social life. I suggested that the attempt to maintain the separation of the 'ideal' from an 'actual' remains the impossible aim of liberal thought. There is a historical development in both the philosophy of punishment and in the criminal law that points both to the need to maintain a separation and to the inability to do so. The 'ideal'/'actual' antinomy remains the fate of liberal political and legal theory not because, in the abstract, any idealism will establish a tension between itself and what actually exists, but because liberal thinking on punishment and responsibility started from a particular, historically created model of the individual that is repressive as well as expressive. I have focused in both parts on the work of Antony Duff to show how a communitarian and interpretive approach to responsibility in the philosophy of punishment and criminal law can be read sceptically and symptomatically to show the foundational character of the problems within liberal theory.

I have also, however, read Duff critically, in the spirit of arguing that the failures of liberal thinking could lead us beyond it towards a new approach to individual, context, and community, beyond the antinomies of the 'ideal' and the 'actual.' Questions of judgment and responsibility cannot be taken apart from the relationships between individuals because individuals cannot be judged apart from their communities. It is because liberalism fundamentally makes such a separation that its conceptions of judgment and responsibility prove inadequate, leading to the ambiguous and ambivalent position expressed by Ewing. There is at the same time a desire to maintain and a desire to discard models of justice based upon the liberal individual. They resonate but prove impossible to rationalise. The question that we now have to face is whether it is possible to conceive of a model of justice that reflects the position of the individual as a *responsible subject in a community.* Can we understand this resonance on a critical basis? Can we understand individual justice on the basis of our scepticism about the liberal theory? Can we use the scepticism adopted here as the basis for a critical reconstruction of the 'sense of justice'? Can we move beyond an ideal individualist understanding of criminal justice?

In the following section, I will describe one way forward through social constructionist psychology. I will argue that Rom Harré's work can take us beyond the antinomialism of liberal theory. I will begin by locating Harré's approach in the constructionist field, explaining its significance for our purposes here. I will then outline his account of personal identity and selfhood, which I will argue can be the basis for a conception of responsible subjectivity. But I will argue, against the grain of some of Harré's own comments, that the most important aspect of this account is its ultimate refusal to separate the personal from the social. The insistence that individuality lies 'between' these dialectically locked spheres allows us to understand the value of liberal accounts without endorsing the false separation they create.

Different Directions in Social Constructionist Psychology

Paralleling the antinomies of liberalism, there lies at the heart of social psychology an ongoing battle between those who are under some description 'individualists' or 'constructionists' (Robinson 1992). One dilemma at the heart of this debate is how to understand the concept of 'the individual' without becoming an 'individualist.' Constructionism portrays individuals as social beings in communities but runs two alternative risks. The first is that, revealing the centrality of context to individual being, it will find it impossible to give an adequate account of what an individual is. The second risk *per contra* is that, giving such an account, it will ultimately fall back into the individualism it sought to avoid. The dilemma thus described echoes the antinomies of liberalism engaged with previously. Hence, it is possible that any resolution of this dilemma will be relevant to our own concerns.

The dilemma is seen in a recent paper by Kenneth Gergen that also raises issues of punishment. Gergen's constructionism follows Alasdair MacIntyre in arguing that it is 'only persons within relationship who can sustain forms of moral action' (Gergen 1992: 16). Participating in a moral order is not a private but a public act, one that is inseparable from the social relationships within which one is embedded. Accordingly, moral language does not refer to 'mental events located within the minds of single individuals and directing their actions' (1992: 22). Morality is a social affair, and therefore Gergen argues that 'selves as intentional agents are thereby removed from the center of concern' (1992: 22). Human relatedness is the originary source of moral agency, so that relationships, interdependence, and community are focal to conceptions of the self.

I agree with Gergen's basic starting point concerning the centrality of community and social relatedness to the establishment of the self as a moral agent, but one may ask whether he goes too far in stating that selves are not (at least) one 'center of concern' for a constructionist account. Gergen discusses this question with regard to punishment, and a particular instance in Philadelphia in which a woman dressed in battle fatigues opened fire with an automatic weapon in a shopping mall. He argues with regard to punishment that attributions of responsibility, including retribution or recrimination, are 'secondary' and that what is more important is a 'concern with the organisation of relationships' (1992: 24). With regard to the gunwoman, he suggests that the traditional punishment focus on the woman's mental state should be replaced with a broader concern for the complicity of social groups and institutions that led to the shooting. Questions could be asked about the role of the police, who were aware of her condition, the firearms store where she got the weapon, and the mall owners for their lack of adequate protection.

These are valid 'relational' questions to ask, and they do indeed take us away from a concern with the responsibility of the individual. But, so doing, do we entirely rule out questions relating to the individual and, in the Philadelphia case, her responsibility for what she did? This is the question that James Lamiell asks of Gergen in a perceptive reply to his argument. Lamiell notes that there is an equivocation in Gergen's account between either removing *all* individual, retributive considerations from the judgment of conduct, or seeing them as relevant but 'secondary.' Is it not pertinent in the mall case to ask about the state of mind of the gunwoman? More generally, Lamiell points to Gergen's repeated use of the third person impersonal singular to carry his analysis. If he wishes to 'de-ontologise' the individual in favour of the community, how can he properly refer to the ways in which 'one learns' (Gergen 1992: 15) to behave within a social code? Does this sort of language not open the door to talk about individual moral agents even within a constructivist framework? Lamiell argues, convincingly in my view, that 'not even social constructivists can speak coherently about moral action without some way of referring to individual persons' (Lamiell 1992: 34).

Lamiell concludes that there is an important distinction to be drawn between discourses rooted in individual*ism* and discourses that recognise the significance of individual*ity,* and that the latter are consistent with social constructionism. For Lamiell, the aim ought to be a 'non-normative conception of human individuality' within a theoretical paradigm that recognises the irreducibly social nature of moral action but that at the same time 'preserves such key rationalistic concepts as persons, selves, and agency, without which moral discourse simply cannot proceed' (Lamiell 1992: 41). The question that this proposal raises, however, is whether this is not just a form of individual*ism* 'by other means.' If we are to preserve the key concepts of individualism, do we not preserve the underlying system? Lamiell notes that constructionism might end up 'reinstall[ing] the psychologically functioning individual as the centre of discourse' (1992: 32). The task for social constructionism is to find a way of talking about the individual, and 'key rationalistic concepts' associated with the individual, without becoming an individual*ist.* In a further response, Gergen writes that a relational approach 'concentrat[es] on *the between*' (Gergen 1992: 245, emphasis added) in the relationships between people. I believe this to be the important insight of social constructionism, but it needs to be coupled with a full understanding of how persons act. Human action lies between personal agency and social relationality. We need a sense of what it means to be a responsible person in a relational context.

In following through this debate in social constructionism, I hope that the parallels between the dilemma in that discipline and my own concern with moving beyond the 'ideal'/'actual' antinomy in criminal law and punishment are clear. In law, I am also concerned with recognising the significance of 'the individual' without becoming an individualist. In the following sections, I consider Rom Harré's work as a 'concentration on the between' and as a means of locating questions of individual responsibility in a nonliberal, non-individualistic way. This will involve taking issue with some of Harré's own formulations, but the core theoretical arguments of his constructionism represent a brilliant contribution to the problem outlined previously.[17] In the next section, I explain Harré's account, and in the two following sections I consider important issues that act as bridges from Harré to criminal justice. These concern the nature of what he calls 'psychological symbiosis' as an enduring social phenomenon, and the relevance of conditions of social conflict and inequality to his theory. Thereafter, I seek briefly to develop a position on individual, non-individualistic, justice utilising a Harréan perspective.

Harré's Social Constructionism

A brief introduction to Harré's understanding of personal being must focus on his explanation of the possibility of selfhood, and his concept of the self. For Harré, the mysterious entity known, but never successfully understood, as the 'self' within western philosophy is the key to understanding personal being. An approach to it locates Harré's starting point in Kant's attempt to explain the self as a transcendental, non-experienced entity. Against Kant's transcendental idealism, Harré proposes a transcendental *realist* position (on this terminology, see Bhaskar 1975, 1979) based upon the development of social constructionist psychology. The concept of the self is deductively necessary to human beings, but that necessity is given in the nature of modern society rather than as a philosophical *a priori.*

Harré's position can be explained by taking up the philosophical problem 'bequeathed' historically by Hume to Kant. For Hume, the self was no more than the sum of the individual's perceptions, and the self could have no existence beyond those perceptions. Kant met this sceptical objection to the existence of the self by arguing for a synthetic doctrine wherein mind supplies by transcendental deduction the unity that is applied to the undifferentiated continuum of experience. The self in this conception is the non-experienced theoretical foundation that makes experiencing possible. A non-empirical representation of mind *constitutes* that which is experienced as an expression of the unified experience of being. Harré refers to the self as an '*inexperienced* theoretical entity' (Harré 1983: 28) because for both himself and Kant, it is transcendental. However, although Harré endorses the Kantian positing of the self as something not given in experience, but as an *a priori* necessity *for* experience, Harré's own transcendental deduction of the self is derived from the nature and needs of human beings in a social world. Thus, against Kantian idealism, it is the great advance of social constructivist positions that they see that *social* predicates can serve in discussion of the transcendental conditions and forms of mind. . . . [To be a self] is to have accepted a special kind of theory in terms of which experiences are categorised as 'of myself' and 'not of myself', and actions are taken as 'mine' and 'not as mine', the central theoretical concept being that of an organising, experiencing and active self. . . . [And since the self's] aetiology begins for each of us with the *public* concept of a person, any metaphysical or noumenal self, pulsing away beyond all possible experience, is quite redundant. (Harré 1983: 99, emphasis added)

It is this starting point, the answering of a Kantian question in a radically un-Kantian way, that marks Harré out from the standard constructionist approach. For Harré, constructionism without a transcendental edge is reductionist because it fails to grasp both the duality *and* the synthetic unity of personal being. Collectivity or community must be understood in social constructionism as yielding a conception of individuality that can do personal being justice. Harré's route is through social constructionism, via a transcendental *realist* enquiry, to individual life. This involves a depiction of society as composed of 'primary' (social) and 'secondary' (personal) structures, and of individual life as made up of 'personality' and 'selfhood.' The components of individual life, although real and causally effective structures in themselves, are generated effects of the primary structure of social life.

THE PRIMARY AND SECONDARY STRUCTURES. The primary reality in Harré's account is the 'normative structure of social conversations', and it is from this *primary structure* that the *secondary structure* of personal being is formed. It is the social 'array of persons' engaged in normative conversations that brings into being social and psychological reality for individuals. People and their modes of talk and other forms of interchange are made by and for social orders, while at the same time social orders are composed of people in conversation and other interchanges. The primary *social* reality therefore engenders and necessitates a secondary *psychological* reality, that of human minds:

Each person, a mere location in the primary structure, is formed as a secondary structure, essentially as a semi-systematic cluster of sets of beliefs. The psychological secondary structure is a reflection of the primary structure, the array of persons and their conversation which is the primary reality of the society which brings them into being. (Harré 1983: 65)

PERSON AND SELF. There is a duality of structures, the primary and the secondary, from which personal being emerges. Personal being straddles, as it were, two spaces: the public/collective and the private/individual. The latter develops as a consequence of the former and is necessitated by it. To recall Gergen's phrase, personal being remains *in between* these two spaces, and this 'in betweenness' is reflected in the nature of the *secondary* structure – that is, in what it means to have personal being. In particular, there is a crucial distinction within the secondary structure between the *person* and the *self.* A *person* is a 'socially defined, publicly visible embodied being, endowed with all kinds of powers and capacities for public, meaningful action' (Harré 1983: 26). The concept supplies the empirical denotation of an actor or role bearer in a public-collective realm. The person internalises the role provided in a social space that is normative and discursive (cf Bhaskar 1979, Archer 1995). Social conversations supply scripts for what persons ought to do, and persons, as agents, seek to 'bring these off' as required by the spatio-temporally specific roles with which they are provided.

Now the person as role player is readily recognised within an orthodox social constructionist framework, as an internalisation of what in Harré's account is called the 'primary structure.' The *self,* however, is more distinctive. It is defined as 'the personal unity I take myself to be, my singular inner being' (Harré 1983: 26). It is a development out of what it means to be a person, a player of roles, but remains qualitatively different. The self emerges from the person but is more than the sum of the parts the person plays. The self could not exist apart from what is constructed as the roles of personhood in the public-collective social space, but it is at the same time more than what could be there constructed. Personality is a 'source analogue' for selfhood so that selfhood derives from personhood. But the self goes beyond the person in that it is a transcendentally established deduction of what is necessary to organise experience, agency, and biography in a world that posits the necessity of persons acting within a public-collective sphere. The self is analogised from what it means to be a person – that is, an agent or player of many roles – and involves the establishment of a synthetic unity of personal being. Selfhood lies beyond the sense of being a role player, although it emerges from it, seeking to organise many roles as the experience of one self: *e pluribus unum.*

To return to Kant, what western philosophy conceived of as a transhistorical conception of individual*ism* Harré explains as a historically specific 'experience' of individual being. In modern western societies, agents operate with and through theories of consciousness, agency, and biography that are conceived of as unified in a personal being focused in space and time. This is the raw material from which an 'inner' self can be fashioned:

> [The] concept of 'self' . . . is a theoretical concept whose source analogue is the socially defined and sustained concept of 'person' that is favoured in the society under study and is embodied in the grammatical forms of public speech appropriate to talk about persons. Our personal being is created by our coming to believe a theory of self based on our society's working conception of a person. (Harré 1983: 26)

Selves, then, are formed out of what they are not, *social* conversations, in a dual structure of social and individual being. Out of duality, a unified conception of individual mind becomes organised around particular points: of consciousness and experience, of action, of biography and autobiography. Selves are located historically and contingently in an array of persons, but they share a sense of their commonality as individual loci of a general experience: the experience of being a self. To put it another way, to be a self is to be a conscious and active being with a biography and autobiography. The unified self is a phenomenal reality of modernity and a construction out of social difference. From the public-collective sphere that is the primary structure of social life, a crucially important secondary structure of private/individual being is generated.

Thus the locus of individual*ity,* of the individual, unified, conscious agent that individual*ist* theories assume to be universal and presocial, is historically specific social conversations in a particular kind of public-collective primary structure. The private-individual self is the secondary structure generated by the primary public-collective social structure, but although it could not exist without the primary structure, it is not reducible to its effect or to an epiphenomenal status. To say this, however, is still not to characterise exactly the status of the self. What is its relationship to the role-playing person that is its source analogue in the public-collective sphere? To raise such a question is to ask about the level of autonomy, and therefore individual responsibility, that the self possesses. This question is the most important to ask of Harré in terms of the dilemma outlined in the previous section. If the self, the transcendental, non-experienced being behind the *personae* of the social, is complete, enjoying substantial autonomy, the liberal individualist model will effectively have been reinstated via social constructionism. If on the other hand the self remains located 'in between' the public-collective and private-individual spheres, it may be possible to explain the existence of selfhood, but on the basis of a new, non-individualist theory that renders ambiguous the question of individual responsibility. So just how autonomous is Harré's self?

Psychological Symbiosis and the Autonomy of the Self

The idea of the self as a unifying transcendental basis for experience, agency, and (auto)biography suggests the possibility of a point at which the self moves beyond the appropriation of what is available in the primary structure and achieves unique social being. This may lead to the conclusion that individuals can 'so to speak, take over their own development' (Harré 1983: 256–7). In some places, Harré argues that individuals gaining self-knowledge and self-mastery establish 'identity projects in the sense of work[ing] towards the achievement of uniqueness, both as a social being and as a personal being' (1983: 258-9). Once one has achieved a theory of oneself as the sort of being that can organise one's own experience and actions, together with the knowledge of how one has experienced and acted in the past, one can develop a conception of the typical patterns of experience and agency of which one is capable. Self-knowledge and self-mastery are organised at a deeper level by the self *for* the self, and are the key to self-development.

At one level, then, Harré appears to be reinstating the kind of individual autonomy that lies at the heart of liberal individualist models. How far he can go in this direction depends upon how he interprets the central idea of 'psychological symbiosis', the process whereby the secondary structure of individual being is developed out of the primary structure of social conversations. *Symbiosis* refers to the interactive process between two people, in the course of which the psychological attributes of one are supplemented by the other. The supplementee becomes a more complete and competent social and psychological being as a result. It 'is a supplementation by one person of another person's public display in order to satisfy the criteria of personhood with respect to psychological competencies and attributes in day-to-day use in a particular society' (Harré 1983: 105). Now the classical psychological symbiosis is the mother-child relationship, and it is clear that, in most cases, the power of this relationship wanes as the child reaches adulthood. So if psychological symbiosis is just the transfer of public-collective competencies in the development of the child into a private-individual being, one can see how the symbiotic, dyadic relationship will fall away as the self develops. This gives rise to a conception of personal being with substantial autonomy, because the child increasingly controls its environment:

> Thus we reach another necessary condition for personhood as we conceive it: it is that psychological growth, which involves the appropriation of powers by the junior member within a symbiotic dyad or triad, will be *permitted* to restructure the dyad so that 'locus of control' will have shifted to favour the junior partner. (Harré 1983: 266)

In this account, symbiosis falls away as the mature self takes charge:

> It follows that under certain conditions one's own personal being *can become one's own project. . . . As psychological symbiosis dissolves,* we take over the work of the dominant member of the dyad within which we were created, and that includes the people-making work. (Harré 1983: 258, emphasis added)

This representation of psychological symbiosis as something that dissolves because it is rooted in an important but passing relationship between parent and child leaves the self as the ultimate author of its own fortunes (the 'people-making work'). It goes without saying that this degree of autonomy would leave the self responsible in large part for its own fortunes and misfortunes, a conclusion that would not be irrelevant to an orthodox retributive version of criminal justice! Yet in writing these passages, Harré appears to overlook a broader sense of psychological symbiosis he had earlier outlined. In this broader approach, symbiosis is a generic, *always enduring,* social relation that transcends the parent-child dyad:

> I want to extend the idea of psychological symbiosis . . . [to] every case in which a group of people complete through public symbiotic activity, particularly in talking for each other, inadequate social and psychological beings. . . . Why do these practices exist? I

> believe that the answer can be found by reference to the requirements of moral orders, as they are defined and sustained in particular collectives. By a 'moral order' I understand a collectively maintained system of public criteria for holding persons in respect or contempt and the rituals for ratification of judgments in accordance with these criteria. (Harré 1983: 105–6)

This broader conception would mean that symbiosis and supplementation were permanent features of social and individual life, while childhood remained one specific, highly significant, form. Continuing symbiosis would be directly tied to processes of self-knowledge and self-mastery so that self-knowledge would always be mastery and knowledge in relation to a moral order, would indeed be 'coming to see oneself in relation to a moral order' (Harré 1983: 260). I believe it is essential to Harré's account of the duality of personality and selfhood, and of the primary and secondary structures, that this latter account of symbiotic supplementation prevail. His work is not relevant to childhood alone. Self-knowledge is always knowledge of the way one has acted and lived in social contexts that continue to make their claims upon the self. The dyadic relationship we outgrow with our parents is replaced by those we enter into with partners, children, police officers, and 'significant others.' People, living through their historical knowledge of how they acted across space and time, come to know themselves in lives 'embedded within structures of social relations that ramify beyond the capacity for current techniques of discovery' (Harré 1983). It is only if we retain this more general account of psychological symbiosis that we can understand the sense of control and *at the same time* lack of control that is part of being a self. As Harré puts it elsewhere, what psychology has to explain is

> the paradoxical nature of our sense of control over our own affairs. On the one hand we feel we know all the facts that impinge upon us, and we seem to be in control of the actions we perform. We experience ourselves in one sense as being all-knowing and all-controlling. But at the same time life does not go as we want, and we do not understand why. (Harré, Clarke, and de Carlo 1985: 24–5)

The black and white terms in which Harré expresses the dilemmatic sense of being and not being in control might more usually be experienced in shades of grey ('am I or am I not in control of this situation?' seems to be a frequent question one asks), yet the ambivalence we feel about our control over our own lives hinges on the polarity Harré describes. This ambivalence stems from the ambiguous character of selfhood as an *understanding of oneself as autonomous,* yet existing on an edge between the assertion of autonomy and the underlying social contexts of heteronomy that stem from the public-collective location of being. For Harré, this ambiguous sense of autonomy forces us to see the self as never 'self-made', never as 'the strategic controller of the system, but just the middle manager of the mind, . . . subject to more compelling and longer patterns of authority' (Harré, Clarke, and de Carlo 1985: 24–5). It is, I argue, crucial to hold onto this concept of the self as complete/incomplete, as positioned symbiotically between the 'individual' and the 'social', the 'private' and the 'public',[18] between the primary and the secondary structures. This account refuses to reduce the space of the self to an epiphenomenon of the social, but it must equally avoid the opposite conclusion that the self ultimately can 'break free' from the social, as the child can from the parent. What we discard when we leave the parent is recreated, albeit at a higher level, with partners, friends, and institutions that compose our adult lives. It is only if we maintain the sense of selfhood 'in between' the individual and the social that we can recognise the socially constructed character of selfhood, give due accord to the significance of the self and its cognitive and agentive powers, and avoid the trap of falling back into a liberal individualist account.

While its particular child-parent form wanes, symbiosis is never completed, so that the space of the self is an ambiguous and ambivalent one. It forms and reforms, evolves and revolves in a world that is also evolving and revolving. It is from this broader conception of symbiosis, and the critical space that it maintains for the play of the social within the individual, that I want to address the problems of the philosophy of punishment: problems of individual responsibility within a social and moral order. As might be expected, this ambivalent and ambiguous self will generate a theory of responsibility rather different from that of retributive or legal theory, in which the self is seen generally as in control. Before moving on, however, one additional element must be considered.

Social Conflict, Moral Order, and Psychological Symbiosis

The primary structure in modern western societies is a public-collective sphere that generates roles for social actors to perform, and these provide the 'source analogue' for a secondary structure, a private-individual sphere that enjoys a 'relative autonomy' from the primary structure. Personal being is an emergent and real property of social structure. The internal *dialectical* connection between the primary (social) structure and the secondary (individual) structure of the self stresses the importance of normative conversation in the 'array of persons' in the formation of personal being, without reducing the latter to the former. Personal being owes its character to social processes of psychological symbiosis that teach persons how to conduct themselves:

> The moral value of persons and their actions are publicly displayed [in a moral order]. It is realised in practices such as being deferential to someone or censuring someone, by trials, by punishments, by insults, by apologies and so on. Psychological supplementation of another may be required if a display of personal incompetence or deficit is routinely taken as a reason for unfavourable moral assessment. (Harré 1983: 106)

Pace his comments on the child-parent dyad, Harré makes it clear that psychological symbiosis is a process that involves key social and political institutions. This makes it important to be clear about the nature of such institutions and the nature of the moral orders that they instantiate. These can be described initially in what we might describe as 'formal' terms. Moral orders entail rituals for marking respect and contempt. They relate actions to actors in ways that permit judgments to be made about both. They involve 'actual and potential talk, in the course of which interpretations of and warrants for what is going on can be negotiated' (Harré 1983: 245). Moral orders simply are the normative conversations that constitute the primary structure of society. Going beyond this formal description, however, to the actuality of modern western moral orders, we need to think about the significance of structural social and economic conflicts on our understanding of moral orders. Harré makes the important point that western moral orders are stratified and differentiated so that 'the rights to make moral reproaches are very unevenly distributed and differ from context to context and situation to situation. . . . [They] are permitted only to those who in this or that collective have the right to perform them' (Harré 1983: 245).

They are also pluralistic and conflictual, as, to give Harré's example from Carol Gilligan (1982), between the moral orders of women (care) and men (control and achievement). This raises the question of how far a society with such a moral order can be coherent and stable, and, if not, what effect this has on the relationship between moral ordering and individual agency. What are the implications of inequitable structuring, social stratification, and conflict for the secondary structure of personal being, formed out of processes of psychological symbiosis with the primary structure? Such features raise questions about inequality and exploitation, and the way power is exercised *through processes of psychological symbiosis and supplementation.* Harré recognises the point without developing it when he suggests, continuing the passage last quoted, that psychological supplementation may be as much in the interests of the supplementer as the supplementee. Remembering that personal being is formed across a double space of the public-collective and the private-individual, if the public-collective sphere is conflictual and stratified, symbiotic processes will be attempts to supplement individuals in the ways of a conflictual and stratified society and will themselves be the focus of conflict. Conflicts and inequalities will inform the normative conversations that symbiotic processes seek to internalise in the person, and may be resisted by him or her. Processes of judgment will be processes of repression, exclusion, and containment, reflecting the views of the powerful. They will invoke resistance and evasion as well as achieving conformity. Where particular judgments of right and wrong are seen to occur in overall contexts of injustice, there will be scope for serious contestation and widespread ideological conflict. In this kind of disjunctive moral climate, ambiguities already inherent in the process of judging individuals, based upon the 'in betweenness' of individual being, will be enhanced.

Punishing Persons in a Conflictual Moral Order

We can begin considering the consequences of Harré's theory for punishment with his own very brief comment, which in fact endorses traditional accounts:

> Moral orders involve institutions with which, in a ceremonial and routine way, violations of the moral orders are dealt with. The modern court is the main institution of justice moralities. The system of justice exists not only to punish wrongdoers and to point the way for the virtuous, but to repair the damage done by that wrongdoing. (Harré 1983: 239)

Harré concludes that '[p]sychologically we must, I think, accept all three classic theories of punishment', the retributive, the utilitarian, and the reformative, but there seem to be two things wrong with this argument. The first concerns Harré's assumption that the system of justice punishes wrongdoing and points the way to virtue. As Harré himself acknowledges, psychological supplementation may be more in the interests of the supplementer than the supplementee, and rights to make moral reproaches 'are very unevenly distributed and differ from context to context and situation to situation' (Harré 1983: 245). Modern community arose out of and expresses fundamental moral conflict. Modern societies are structured by deep conflicts over social class, race, and gender, and this leaves society's 'normative conversations' plural, conflictual, and incomplete.[19] Harré may of course simply be using terms such as 'wrongdoing' and 'virtue' conventionally, but the point remains that these *must* be contested terms in modern society. In such a context, neither the 'maximalist' communitarian conception of a moral community nor the 'minimalist' liberal conception of peace terms for a world of strangers can establish a consensual moral vocabulary for wrongdoing and virtue (see pp. 115–16). We have to acknowledge the fractured and conflictual character of moral community, and this then leads to a question about its effect on psychological symbiosis.

If Harré wishes to endorse the classical theories of punishment, his account of psychological symbiosis must be compatible with retributivism. Yet it is hard to see how this can be so, unless we accept the truncated version of his theory that equates symbiosis with the parent–child dyad. As we saw, however, Harré wishes to extend this analysis to all relations in which agents seek to communicate moral viewpoints to one another. Such processes of supplementation assume the incompleteness of the person who is to be supplemented, making individual responsibility something that is constructed out of an interaction, not something that is already 'vested' in the person. Symbiosis bridges the primary and the secondary structures out of which individual life is constructed. It involves a relationship, not an essence, so the ideal and separate individual whom the retributivist would punish does not exist on the extended view of symbiosis Harré proposes. As I have already argued (p. 117), talk of agency, subjectivity, and responsibility involves paradoxically talking about what appears to deny such things, the role of communities. If social constructionism simply produces a view of viable adults who move beyond symbiotic relations, then there is no paradox, but if it produces a concentration on what lies *between* the individual and the social, then any individualistic doctrine such as retributivism or criminal law theory entails is going to be in trouble. As we saw at the beginning of this section, Gergen went too far if he denied the significance of individual agency, but Harré goes too far the other way if he denies the continuing effectiveness of social construction.

Does this mean that if we follow this reading of Harré, we must abandon entirely the sense of individual justice that has been the stock in trade of retributive conceptions? We need not, because Harré's key achievement is to give sense to the importance of what it means to be an individual without becoming an individual*ist*. The idea of the individual as a relation between personal and social being leaves us with a conception of individual justice – that is, a sense of the attachment of moral significance to individual agency, but one to which essential ambiguity and ambivalence must be attached. Recall Harré's perhaps overly black and white image of a person's sense of being and not being in control. When I act, I know who I am, and that my acts are attributable to me, but at the same time, I am an actor in time, place, and context, an actor in a primary structure of social being. This primary structure provides the roles that I play, the acts I perform, the sense of selfhood that lies behind the attempt to construct coherent personal being. But because of this duality, personal being is always being in relation to others. Illustrations of the ambivalence to which such duality gives rise are commonplace. Consider, for example, in a nonpunitive context the ways in which we judge what we regard as the reprehensible conduct of those we like with that of those we do not. In the latter case, we are likely to accuse, to insist on the wrongful agency of a 'bad' person, to condemn. In the former case, perhaps initial irritation with or anger at the bad act gives way to empathy, sorrow, explaining, and excusing. These are contradictory responses, yet I argue that both are in a sense appropriate. Each is evoked by one facet of individual being and agency. Condemnation is relevant for acts over which the individual has control, whereas empathy and excusing are relevant for acts over which the individual has not. The point, however, is that *both* standpoints are one-sided because each reflects only one aspect of an ambiguous phenomenon – that is, the individual operating between agency and context.

With regard to crime, consider our reaction to persons who committed criminal acts in earlier times and different places. In the United Kingdom in the

1970s, a climate of what was later labelled as corruption developed in local government. Council officials and local developers became involved in relationships that were too close and involved the acceptance of hospitality and gifts by officials. These 'gifts' were later seen as bribes, but at the time they could be seen as simple emollients or as examples of 'just the way things are done.' When these officials were eventually tried and convicted for accepting bribes, they were held to be responsible persons who had engaged in corrupt acts, yet for many at the time, it probably seemed rather normal activity within a particular culture. At the same time, is it not possible that, at the back of their minds, a part of them also knew that there was something wrong in what they were doing? The point is that individual subjectivity is not fixed with regard to a moral code but rather shifts between vocabularies of right and wrong that social contexts provide and agents mediate. Agents do things that can be interpreted in different and contradictory ways. We can either view the convicted councillor as a corrupt agent in control and operating with a conventional moral vocabulary of right and wrong, or as a 'victim of the times.' Most appropriately, we should see both sides of the question, but if we do, we recognise the ambiguity in our sense of individual responsibility and the ambivalence in judging that goes with it. We also recognise the need for a theory that can explain the sense of individual responsibility and irresponsibility that inheres in personal being.

The two-sided character of agency gives rise to ambivalence in how an audience judges conduct. Ultimately, ambivalence about judgment is 'resolved' according to the general social, political, and moral standpoint of the onlooker. How does the onlooker view the actions of the friend or enemy, the actions of the local government officer? Such questions involve general and particular aspects. A friend's actions are judged as responsible or irresponsible in part on the basis that one is judging a friend, that of local government officers in part on how one feels about such people. Consider for example the likely different judgments of one who believes that local government officers generally 'mean well and try to do their best in difficult circumstances' and one who sees them as a 'drain on local resources.' What comes out is a judgment about individual responsibility for an act, but this is context-driven because personal agency is context-emergent.

Thus far we have considered the ambiguity in being 'an individual.' We have still to consider the additional layers of ambiguity and ambivalence which stem from the fact that our judgments are rooted in the soil of deep-seated social inequalities and conflicts. In a world in which most processed crime is crime against property and most processed criminals come from the most disadvantaged sections of what Will Hutton has described as the '30/30/40' society (Hutton 1995), it is not surprising that ambiguities about responsibility and ambivalences about judgment are increased, and this can briefly be illustrated by considering the different accounts that *as a society* we give of these matters. Thus in Britain, we are torn between an 'ethic of excusing' (seeing individuals in context) and an 'ethic of blaming' (seeing individuals as responsible agents). One political party states that it wants to be 'tough on crime and tough on the causes of crime,' while the other says it wants to 'understand a little less and blame a little more.' The second of these expresses the ambiguity completely.

The first view is apparently more alluring because it seems to claim that a focus on individual responsibility is consistent and compatible with the recognition of the role of time, place, and context in the creation of criminal behaviour. Yet if it is believed that crime is a social problem associated with imbalances of wealth and opportunity, then there seems to be no moral licence to hold individuals morally accountable for their crimes. Of course, when a crime is committed, it is committed by individual agents, not by social structures, so individual agency plays its part. Individuals commit crimes, but the decision to 'get tough' on such agents involves a political judgment to affix responsibility on the individual as a means of dealing with 'the problem of crime.' To justify being 'tough on crime', there has to be a separation off from the 'causes of crime' in the 30/30/40 society. The two halves of the slogan remain antinomous, inconsistent with each other.

Individual agency is always ambiguous on a constructionist model. Our moral judgments are always therefore ambivalent. But they are doubly ambivalent when individuals whom we presume to hold morally responsible for their crimes are those who have the least opportunities to develop other career paths and life patterns than those for which they are blamed. In choosing to find such people responsible, to blame and to punish them, we recognise that they are agents, but conveniently we forget that agency exists 'in between.'

Criminal Responsibility in a Conflictual Moral Order

The consequences of a constructionist approach for justice within the criminal law are anticipated in the second section where I analysed law's cognitive capacity-based morality of form in terms of the architectonic of the general part, the English intention/murder cases, and in the light of Duff's interpretivist/anti-dualist approach. As with punishment, we can focus on the idea of the 'in between' and the effect of seeing individuals as responsible agents in moral communities. Law seeks to deny the double-sided character of human agency, producing a 'simulacral' morality that is in the same moment expressive and repressive. The result is a moral language that is never complete and that always requires supplementation with moral perspectives that lie beyond it. The isolation of the 'ideal' legal individual is never sufficient unto itself. Because individual responsibility lies between the personal and the social, any attempt to locate responsibility in one place, the unified legal subject, will be unsuccessful. Law will always have to look beyond the individual of its 'morality of form' in order properly to judge the wrongdoer. Moral judgment has a synthetic or 'molecular' structure because personal being also has such a structure. Law seeks to convert social individuality into an 'atomic' individualist form, and although law's morality may seek (historically, *must* seek) to deny this, it never can. The legal individual remains incomplete as a basis for valid moral judgment so that there is a need to go beyond the individual to substantive moral categories.

A paper by Jeremy Horder (Horder 1990) may finally illustrate what I have in mind and conclude this section. Horder considers recent English cases on mistake that involve the appropriate cognitive test to deny *mens rea:* should a mistake be reasonable, or must it only be honest? These cases cover mistakes as to consent in the law of rape (*DPP v Morgan* [1976] AC 182), and as to the need to defend oneself or another in the law of self-defence. These include both a mistake as to the need to defend a presumed innocent third party (*R v Gladstone Williams* [1987] 78 Cr App R 276) and as to the need of an on-duty policeman to protect himself with a gun (*Beckford v R* [1987] 3 All ER 425). Horder argues that the cognitive test in either its subjective or objective form stands in the place of a proper moral enquiry that would judge in a morally substantive way how a defendant as an 'ethically well-disposed agent' should act in different politico-moral contexts. What we should expect from rapists, altruistic defenders of others, and armed police officers varies, so that legal standards should vary. Judgment of negligent mistakes requires us to look at intentions or at matters of 'reasonableness' not in the abstract terms of the law but in the context of their moral 'colour.' From a legal point of view, the demand of consistency stipulates that all three situations should be treated the same, according to a simple cognitive test of foresight or foreseeability. Horder cogently argues that the background emotions of the rapist (lustful, self-seeking), the defender of another (altruistic), and the armed police officer (calm and restrained, not hot-headed) should lead to different cognitive tests in these different contexts. Where the emotions are morally bad or self-seeking, we should expect the higher threshold of reasonableness of a mistake, but not where they are good (*Gladstone Williams*). The legal test as to individual cognition requires supplementation by a moral judgment from within the normative community.

Of course, from a legal point of view, this opens the door to great uncertainty because, in a conflictual society, there are competing conceptions of what 'ethically well disposed agents' should do. Not one of the moral descriptions provided by Horder would go uncontested in our society. Yet proper moral judgments of wrongdoing have regard to such contested views. According to legal cognitivism, everything is to be resolved according to subjectivist principles, whereas an objectivist simply turns subjectivism upside down by employing the concept of the foresight of the reasonable person. What is significant, however, beyond cognitivism, is the moral quality of what is being done, and that requires a step outside the mental processes of the legal individual and into the social and moral world of which he or she is a part.

Just as in psychological symbiosis, society supplements individuals morally, so judgments within the law require substantive moral colouration if they are to reflect morality. Law's abstract individual needs to be judged not just according to the control of action but according to the moral context in which action occurs. Law strives to evade this conclusion, but it cannot ultimately escape the constructionist's insight that individual responsibility involves something more and something less than the responsibility of the 'individual.'

Conclusion

My argument has taken me from the philosophy of punishment to criminal law theory, and from both to social constructionist psychology. My contention has been that the philosophy of punishment and that of criminal law run up against the same problems, and that social constructionism offers a way of resolving them. It is these problems that undermine the attempts to rationalise 'popular' moral concepts such as desert, responsibility, and justice in political philosophy and law as noted by Ewing. Yet the grip these ideas have on popular consciousness surely suggests something that requires to be understood. In turning to social constructionism, I have sought to understand these concepts within a framework that at first sight appears hostile but that I argue permits us to reflect the ambiguity and ambivalence in and around them. Understanding the significance of traditional concepts of justice involves going beyond the liberal tradition in which individualist categories are traditionally employed and towards a social constructionist account. That account must, however, be sufficiently sophisticated to reflect the significance of individual agency.

The main argument of the chapter addresses the divisions between the 'ideal' and the 'actual' as they exist in the philosophy of punishment and the criminal law. These divisions relate to the character of the ideal individualism in liberal thinking as simultaneously a mode of exclusion and a mode of representation. Liberal theory typically recognises and develops the latter aspect and is blind to the former, and this blindness then becomes the root cause of many of its theoretical problems. The key figure of 'the individual', abstracted from a social and moral context that is conflictually structured, is an inadequate basis on which to rest a moral conception of justice. This conflict between the liberal conception of law and punishment and a broader sense of justice gives rise to the very opposing views of Duff and MacIntyre. This is seen in, on the one hand, Duff's equation of individual justice, law, and morality ('As with morality, so with law'), and on the other, MacIntyre's dismissal of liberal individualist forms as 'simulacra of morality.'

In the first section, I argued that the retributive tradition reflects an antinomial conception of the 'ideal' and the 'actual.' The antinomies of the classical account have not been resolved in a modern account such as Duff's, despite his recasting their terms into those of a teleological retributivism. Modern writers within the tradition must face the old problems with still inadequate intellectual tools, and the best of these end up explicitly recognising or implicitly revealing that there is no way forward for the moral account of punishment.

In the second section of the chapter, I argued that the ideal image of the individual as a responsible being lies at the heart of problems in criminal law theory too. The homology between legal and moral judgment that retributivists argue for is based upon their parallel espousal in the criminal law of an ideal rational and cognitive agent that cuts out essential moral and political information required to make proper moral judgments as to a person's responsibility. *Pace* the legal retributivists, moral judgments are in fact split off from legal judgments of wrongdoing and responsibility because the ideal legal subject is a way of suppressing moral issues at large in the community. The illustration of moral differences among killers led into a discussion of the motive/intention split in criminal law, and then into a consideration of Duff's argument about the isomorphy of legal and moral judgment.

Throughout the chapter, I have read Duff's work sceptically with regard to his revisions of traditional liberal approaches, symptomatically as revealing the problems attached to liberalism, and critically to show the need to move forward to a new constructionist basis for understanding the place of the individual with regard to matters of wrongdoing and responsibility. In this part, I argued that his re-rationalisation of a legal conception of subjectivity was undermined by the broader moral issues that remain 'at large' behind the legal individual, that 'infect' the legal architectonic, and that are in fact exposed by Duff's own theoretical standpoint – against the grain of his rationalising project. As in the philosophy of punishment, so indeed in the law. Ideal conceptions of responsible subjectivity are undermined by social and moral conflict behind the individualist categories.

In the third section of the chapter, I developed a social constructionist account of subjectivity as a route beyond these problems. Developing Harré's account of psychological symbiosis as a social phenomenon connecting the primary and secondary structures of moral life and individual being, I argued that the concept of individual justice has a phenomenal reality in the psychological construction of a 'self', but that there is no easy road from this individuated agent to the individualism of the law and the philosophy of punishment. To be a self means to be in a relation, which means that the self is always itself a relation. Selfhood is always more and less than the individual being in which it is instantiated, and this in part accounts for the ambiguities of individual responsibility and the ambivalences in moral judgment stemming therefrom. An additional set of problems develops from the structured and conflictual character of processed crime and criminality in societies that reveal gross disparities of wealth and opportunity. These can only increase the ambiguities of responsibility and ambivalences of judgment already described. Yet the Harréan account does provide a sense of individual selfhood and so is able to supply us with the means to rationalise the resonance concepts of individual justice possess while insisting on their intrinsically problematic character. Indeed this is the ultimate strength of this approach, for it gives sense to both the significance of and the ambivalence towards a concept of individual justice.

My argument then has been for a sense of individual justice that is real but that involves inherent ambiguity and ambivalence. Lurking behind the individual*ism* of legal theory and the philosophy of punishment lies an individual*ity* that liberalism exploits and to some extent defends without properly comprehending. Individual agents are always more and less than the individuals that liberalism sees and invokes. It is for this reason that the easy equation between legal and moral accounts of responsibility proves to be much more complex, conflictual, and fractured than liberal legal theorists imagine. Liberalism is always one-sided in its recognition of the individual in ideal, abstract, and universal terms. These effect an exclusion of social and political differences in favour of the dominance of a world of private property and social inequality.

It is this one-sidedness that MacIntyre picks up in his description of liberal individualism as giving rise to a morality that is only simulacral. Yet it must be remembered that liberalism's ideal individualism *represents* individuals *as well as* excludes them. There is a *double moment* at play in the juridicisation of the modern subject, so that if MacIntyre is read too absolutely, the representational side of liberal legalism and philosophy is in danger of being overlooked. As I wrote at the beginning, the time has gone by when liberals and their critics should throw stones at each other. A more helpful approach is one that recognises the foundational tensions beneath liberal thinking and the moral and political complexities to which these give rise. There are no easy answers to the moral and legal problems of modern societies, but it is certainly no answer to hope, as does MacIntyre at the end of *After Virtue,* that 'men and women of good will' will somewhere somehow re-create local moral communities (MacIntyre 1985: 263). If MacIntyre believes, as he writes there, that 'the barbarians are not waiting beyond the frontiers; they have already been governing us for some time', we would all do well to recognise that a barbarian in liberal garb is still preferable to one sporting his or her true colours. Social theory must be able to reflect the Janus-like character of liberal theory, its moral force as well as its weaknesses. But, consistently with the ambiguous character of the liberal phenomena explored here, and the ambivalence to which this gives rise, one would also have to say that many barbarous things are and have been done through and in the name of liberal ideas. Many such things occur in our penal systems today, and they do so in the name of criminal justice.

Notes

1 I use the word 'antinomy' throughout in a sense akin to Quine's, who defines it as a paradox that 'produces a self-contradiction by accepted ways of reasoning. It establishes that some tacit and trusted pattern of reasoning must be made explicit and henceforward be avoided or revised' (Honderich 1995: 40). This definition suggests the sense of antinomy as 'false dichotomy.' My argument is that liberal theories of law and punishment are caught within an 'ideal'/'actual' antinomy and its variant derivatives. This antinomy is emergent from the historical structure of modern western societies and is the theoretical expression of a set of sociopolitical practices – a 'praxiology' as I term it elsewhere (Norrie 1993b: 231–3). Liberal theories constantly have to engage with, to contain, to rationalise the antinomies at their roots. My quest is to find a non-antinomial account of criminal justice, the better to understand how it works, its strengths, its limits.

2 In critical analysis, one seeks to recognise that liberal categories are both real (practical, efficacious) and, because they instantiate false dichotomies, misleading. Discussing them therefore presents a dilemma of presentation. One can either treat them as they would be treated within liberal texts, as simply the concepts one uses, or treat them as categories that occupy a social space but that are ultimately inadequate to it. If the latter, one will be inclined to the inelegant use of scare quotes; if the former, one will not. When discussing such categories I have adopted both practices, depending on whether I am following through a discussion within liberal theory or wanting specifically to communicate my critical handling. On the underlying issues, see Bhaskar 1979, Outhwaite 1987, Sayer 1987.

3 This section draws upon the perspective and argument in Norrie 1991. My interest is in present-day accounts of the philosophy of punishment that I was not able to consider in the earlier work. For the reasons stated in the Introduction, however, I focus on Duff's work. This decision was overdetermined by considerations of space and time. A fuller analysis would consider other important theorists such as Michael Moore, Andrew von Hirsch, and Jeffrie Murphy (briefly commented on in footnote 4). It would also have developed an argument in my previous work concerning the historical diminution of the responsible individual from the classical to the modern liberal period (Norrie 1991: ch. 5 and see footnote 5 here). Because of these limitations, any general conclusions I draw must remain provisional.

4 Michael Moore's account (Moore 1987, 1993b) self-consciously pursues a justification based on the emotions rather than according to a 'general principle of justice' that would involve 'general ideas about reciprocal advantage in social relations' (Moore 1987: 183). This produces interesting views on punishment, but it does not avoid the need to locate emotional reactions in the context of broader issues of principle in a conflictual society.

Earlier, Moore (1985) had considered the role of social environment on crime, but only in the context of the free will/determinism (itself a false dichotomy: Norrie 1991, ch. 7) debate. Andrew von Hirsch confronts the issue by abandoning the theory in which it *is* an issue (the 'just deserts' theory) in favour of one in which it is marginal ('censure') (von Hirsch 1993: 7–14, 106–8). Jeffrie Murphy's doubts about Kantian retributivism are particularly related to the problem of social justice in his early work. His later exploration of an emotion-based approach points in the same direction as Moore but equally does not avoid the need to consider questions of punishment and political justice (Murphy 1979, 1987; Murphy and Hampton 1988).

5 In this regard, Duff's work on punishment and moral education is directly in the line established by neo-classical philosophers of punishment in the idealist tradition (Bradley, Bosanquet, Green, and McTaggart) and their realist critics in the first decades of the twentieth century (Rashdall and Ewing). This work has largely sunk below the horizon of modern discussion, but there is much in it that Duff's argument tracks. I have analysed the trajectory of this work elsewhere (Norrie 1991: ch. 5), arguing that its negotiation of the social problems that underlie crime led to a diminished conception of the moral subject of punishment. Something similar happens in Duff's conception of the responsible subject, I argue, though I have not had the space to develop the underlying connection suggested here.

6 Duff is primarily talking of systems of 'informal justice' as regards this latter quotation, but he makes it clear that the communicative conception of punishment also relies on the existence of genuine communities.

7 It is because of this issue that the question of what constitutes 'dishonesty' in the law of theft is such a difficult one for criminal lawyers. The problem is precisely the difficulty of achieving consensus in modern societies on whether it is wrong to steal (Williams 1983: 725–7; Norrie 1993b: 42–5).

8 Duff sees himself as a 'communitarian' when compared with the 'liberal' position he describes here. In my view the difference between these positions is one of degree rather than total opposition. Liberals of every persuasion are concerned with some sense of community, even if it is only a 'community of strangers', and it would take a radical communitarianism indeed to posit a community without some sense of the individual. It is because I do not see a full opposition between these terms that I would describe Duff as himself a liberal, though obviously not the 'classical liberal' he describes here.

9 My reservations about MacIntyre's approach are addressed in the Conclusion.

10 Ashworth in fact treats justifications separately from the negative fault requirements, though he notes the provisional character of his and others' schemata (*op. cit.*, 78–9).

11 One response to this problem is the pragmatic one that the real difficulty in the U.K. is the mandatory life sentence for murder. This ensures that the broader moral issues cannot be reflected in the court's judgment. On the ambiguous role of sentencing as a symbiotic yet contradictory mode of judgment to that provided by the categories of legal responsibility, see Norrie, 1993b: 45–6. My argument is that the non-availability of mitigation highlights the inadequacies of the categories of judgment within the criminal law. Their narrowness invokes a number of administrative escape routes where the conflict between legal and moral judgment is most heightened. These include prosecution decisions, 'perverse' jury verdicts, and, normally, sentencing.

12 For a developed analysis that incorporates the orthodox argument, see Duff 1993. If Duff

concedes that necessary behaviour may be rational, how can he maintain that rational-intentional agency is subverted by necessity, as his argument here requires?

13 If Duff himself argues, as he does in connection with the law of oblique intention, that legal categories import broader normative judgments, why is it revelatory to accuse him of doing so here? My analysis of Duff's work sees it as juxtaposing a task, the rationalisation of law's individualistic architectonic of judgment, with a method, which is interpretive and anti-dualist. These pull in different directions, so that end and means are at odds. Duff is at his least persuasive when he is directly defending law's forms of judgment (e.g., the centrality of intention) and most convincing when he is developing his interpretive standpoint to analyse cases. Defending law leads him in some places to deny the significance of broader moral issues to individual responsibility, for example in his discussion of responsibility-as-answerability as a means of maintaining the paradigmatic centrality of intention over justification and excuse. Interpretivism and anti-dualism lead him to argue *per contra* for their significance, in the process exposing the antinomies of legal analysis (see below, where I discuss how this happens with *Steane*).

14 I have made this argument previously with regard to Duff's analysis of recklessness (Norrie 1992). On the idea of a 'dangerous supplement', see Fitzpatrick 1991: 2: 'To supplement jurisprudence, then, could be just a matter of making sure that valuable things are kept on board. The supplement provides what is lacking. It serves to complement and complete that which is supplemented. . . . But, as Derrida has it, the supplement is also "dangerous." The supplement is not fully assimilable. It remains outside, challenging the completeness and the adequacy of that which is within.'

15 For an earlier discussion of oblique intention, which also explores its moral dimension, see Norrie 1989. An important paper in this area is Williams 1987.

16 *Steane* was in fact decided as an intention case, though for reasons that are not entirely clear.

17 For a recent interchange focused on the issue of responsibility, see Harré (1997) and Norrie (1997c).

18 Within this account, the liberal understanding of concepts such as the 'individual' or the 'private' is rejected in favour of a synthesised conception of personal being across the primary and secondary structures of personal agency and social relationality. Concepts such as the 'individual' denote a real entity, but liberalism understands it in terms that are misleading. To liberalism's individualism, I oppose constructionism's individuality, which recognises the relationality in being an individual.

19 For one attempt to deal with this from within liberalism, see Rawls (1985, 1987, 1989). A stringent critique is provided by Anne Barron (1993).

References

Archer, M. (1995). *Realist Social Theory: The Morphogenetic Approach.* Cambridge: Cambridge University Press.

Ashworth, A. (1995). *Principles of Criminal Law* (2nd ed.). Oxford: Oxford University Press.

Barron, A. (1993). 'The Illusions of the "I": Citizenship and the Politics of Identity', in A. Norrie (ed.), *Closure or Critique: New Directions in Legal Theory.* Edinburgh: Edinburgh University Press.

Bhaskar, R. (1975). *A Realist Theory of Science.* Leeds: Leeds Books.

Bhaskar, R. (1979). *The Possibility of Naturalism.* Brighton: Harvester.

Bhaskar, R. (1993). *Dialectic: The Pulse of Freedom.* London: Verso.

Collier, A. (1994). *Critical Realism.* London: Verso.

Duff, A. (1990). *Intention, Agency and Criminal Liability.* Oxford: Blackwell.

Duff, A. (1993). 'Choice, Character and Criminal Liability.' *Law and Philosophy* 345, 350–61.

Duff, A. (1996). 'Penal Communications: Recent Work in the Philosophy of Punishment', in M. Tonry (ed.), *Crime and Justice: A Review of Research.* Chicago: University of Chicago Press, 1–97.

Ewing, A. (1929). *The Morality of Punishment.* London: Kegan Paul.

Fitzpatrick, P. (1991). *Dangerous Supplements: Resistance and Renewal in Jurisprudence.* London: Pluto.

Gardner, J., and H. Jung (1991). 'Making Sense of Mens Rea: Antony Duff's Account.' *Oxford Journal of Legal Studies* 11, 559.

Gergen, K. (1992). 'Social Construction and Moral Action', in D. Robinson (ed.), *Social Discourse and Moral Judgment.* London: Academic Press, 9–27.

Gilligan, C. (1982). *In a Different Voice.* Cambridge, Mass.: Harvard University Press.

Harré, R. (1983). *Personal Being.* Oxford: Blackwell.

Harré, R., D. Clarke, and N. de Carlo (1985). *Motives and Mechanisms.* London: Methuen.

Harré, R. (1997). 'Pathological Autobiographies.' *Philosophy, Psychiatry & Psychology,* 4, 99–109.

Hart, H. (1968). *Punishment and Responsibility.* Oxford: Clarendon.

Hegel, G. (1952). *The Philosophy of Right.* Oxford: Oxford University Press.

Hobbs, D. (1994).'Professional and Organised Crime in Britain', in M. Maguire, R. Morgan, and R. Reiner (eds.), *The Oxford Handbook of Criminology.* Oxford: Oxford University Press, 441–68.

Honderich, T. (1995). *The Oxford Companion to Philosophy.* Oxford: Oxford University Press.

Horder, J. (1990). 'Cognition, Emotion and Criminal Culpability.' *Law Quarterly Review* 106, 469–86.

Hutton, W. (1995). *The State We're In.* London: Jonathan Cape.

Kant, I. (1965). *The Metaphysical Elements of Justice.* Indianapolis: Bobbs-Merrill.

Kant, I. (1967). *Philosophical Correspondence 1759–1799* (ed. A. Zweig). Chicago: University of Chicago Press.

Lacey, N. (1993). 'A Clear Concept of Intention: Elusive or Illusory?' *Modern Law Review* 56, 621.

Lacey, N., C. Wells, and D. Meure (1990). *Reconstructing Criminal Law.* London: Butterworths.

Lamiell, J. (1992). 'Persons, Selves and Agency', in D. Robinson (ed.), *Social Discourse and Moral Judgment.* London: Academic Press, 29–41.

MacIntyre, A. (1985). *After Virtue.* London: Duckworth.

Moore, M. (1985). 'Causation and the Excuses.' *California Law Review* 73, 1091–149.

Moore, M. (1987). 'The Moral Worth of Retribution', in F. Shoeman (ed.), *Character, Responsibility and the Emotions.* Cambridge: Cambridge University Press, 179.

Moore, M. (1993a). 'Foreseeing Harm Opaquely', in S. Shute, J. Gardner, and J. Horder, *Action and Value in Criminal Law.* Oxford: Clarendon, 125.

Moore, M. (1993b). 'Justifying Retributivism.' *Israeli Law Review* 27, 15–49.

Murphy, J. (1979). *Retribution, Justice and Therapy.* Dordrecht: Reidel.

Murphy, J. (1987). 'Does Kant Have a Theory of Punishment?' *Columbia Law Review* 87, 509.

Murphy, J., and J. Hampton (1988). *Forgiveness and Mercy.* Cambridge: Cambridge University Press.

Norrie, A. (1989). 'Oblique Intention and Legal Politics.' *Criminal Law Review* 793.

Norrie, A. (1991). *Law, Ideology and Punishment.* Dordrecht: Kluwer.

Norrie, A. (1992). 'Subjectivism, Objectivism and the Limits of Criminal Recklessness.' *Oxford Journal of Legal Studies* 12, 45.

Norrie, A. (1993a). 'Closure and Critique: Antinomy in Modern Theory', in A. Norrie (ed.), *Closure or Critique: New Directions in Legal Theory.* Edinburgh: Edinburgh University Press, 1–21.

Norrie, A. (1993b). *Crime, Reason and History.* London: Butterworths.

Norrie, A. (1996a). 'The Limits of Justice: Finding Fault in the Criminal Law.' *Modern Law Review* 59, 540–56.

Norrie, A. (1996b). 'From Law to Popular Justice: Beyond Antinomialism.' *Social and Legal Studies* 5, 383–404.

Norrie, A. (1997a). 'Critical Legal Studies' in D. N. MacCormick and B. Brown (eds.), *The Philosophy of Law.* Routledge Encyclopedia of Philosophy. London: Routledge.

Norrie, A. (1997b). 'Law's Relationality', in R. Bergalli and D. Melossi, *The Emergence of Law Through Economy Politics and Culture* Onati: Onati papers, 41–58.

Norrie, A. (1997c). 'Comment on "Pathological Autobiographies"' *Philosophy, Psychiatry & Psychology,* 4, 115–18.

Outhwaite, W. (1987). *New Philosophies of Social Science.* London: Macmillan.

Rawls, J. (1985). 'Justice as Fairness: Political not Metaphysical.' *Philosophy and Public Affairs* 14, 219.

Rawls, J. (1987). 'The Idea of an Overlapping Consensus.' *Oxford Journal of Legal Studies* 7, 1–25.

Rawls, J. (1989). 'The Domain of the Political and an Overlapping Consensus.' *New York University Law Review* 64, 233–55.

Robinson, D. (ed.). (1992). *Social Discourse and Moral Judgment.* London: Academic Press.

Sayer, D. (1987). *The Violence of Abstraction.* Oxford: Blackwell.

Smith, J. C. (1989). *Justification and Excuse in the Criminal Law.* London: Sweet and Maxwell.

von Hirsch, A. (1976). *Doing Justice: The Choice of Punishment.* New York: Hill & Wang.

von Hirsch, A. (1985). *Past or Future Crimes.* Manchester: Manchester University Press.

von Hirsch, A. (1993). *Censure and Sanctions.* Oxford: Oxford University Press.

Williams, G. (1983). *Textbook of Criminal Law.* London: Stevens.

Williams, G. (1987). 'Oblique Intention.' *Cambridge Law Journal* 46, 417.

4

Principle and Contradiction in the Criminal Law

Motives and Criminal Liability

ANTONY DUFF

In *Crime, Reason and History* (1993), Alan Norrie aimed to show that 'criminal law is neither rational nor principled' (p. 9). Whilst not 'wholly irrational', it cannot claim to be '(in principle) rational and just' (p. 14), because 'irrationality and "unprinciple" are as much a part of [it] as their opposites' (p. 57). We cannot hope to achieve 'a rational principled criminal law', because legal reasoning is 'necessarily contradictory' (p. 11). Thus, whilst Norrie eschews the 'simple negation' of the 'trashing' practised by some proponents of Critical Legal Studies (p. xiii; see Kelman 1981, 1984) and insists that we must recognise the 'positive' aspects of this contradictory system (see pp. 31–2, 132, 223–5), he shares their aim of undermining the criminal law's claims to principled rationality by exposing the contradictions that infect it.[1]

Two years earlier, Andrew Ashworth published *Principles of Criminal Law* (1991).[2] Nothing in the book suggests that he intended its title to be ironic. Ashworth 'does not argue that English criminal law is grounded in a stable set of established doctrines', because its development is influenced by 'a disparate group' of 'sometimes conflicting' arguments and assumptions. But he does hope to identify, and subject to rational appraisal, 'the principles and policies which appear to play a significant part' in the criminal law: Are they 'soundly based', suitable to 'the proper aims, forms and limits of the criminal sanction in modern Western societies'; or are there 'other principles and policies which would be more appropriate' (p. v)? He thus seems to believe that English criminal law (to some degree) is, and (to a greater degree) could and should become, a matter of principle – and so of reason, insofar as principles are purportedly rational.

We might then expect to find significant differences in the ways in which each book approaches the law. Norrie will expose inconsistencies, failures of reason, and lacks of principle, whereas Ashworth will display the law as coherently structured by rational principles. Now there are such differences – notably, the prominence of the idea of 'contradiction' in Norrie's book. What is striking, however, is the extent of the similarities between the books. Ashworth, like Norrie, portrays the law as a locus of conflicting principles and policies.

Indeed, one central conflict that he identifies, between 'the principle of individual autonomy' (1995: 26–8, 83) and 'the policy of social defence' (1995: 64–5, 75–6), closely resembles one central 'contradiction' that Norrie identifies, between the law's 'liberal individualism', which emphasises individual responsibility, and 'the social control needs of the state' (1993: 57). Ashworth notes that such conflicting principles and policies are 'sometimes invoked selectively', whilst their role might not be 'openly avowed' in courts' and commentators' arguments (1995: v); he is ready to criticise judicial reasoning as unprincipled or irrational, and to point out inconsistencies in the law; and he admits that there may be no determinate 'right answers' to some of the conflicts he identifies.

So is Ashworth just wrong or naïvely over-optimistic to believe that English criminal law is, or could become, a matter of principle and reason? Or is Norrie just wrong, or over-pessimistic, to believe that it is not and cannot be? Or are they perhaps applying different conceptions of what it is for a system of law to be 'principled' or 'rational' – one of which might be more appropriate than the other?

We can tackle this general question only by examining some of the purportedly rational principles that supposedly structure the law, and some of the 'contradictions' that, 'critical' theorists argue, undermine such pretensions to principled rationality.[3]

I will examine one such principle: the principle that 'motive' is irrelevant to criminal liability. I will argue (in section 3) that this doctrine can, once properly understood, be defended against Norrie's charges of 'contradiction', as can the 'abstraction' of individual agents from their concrete contexts which it involves (see section 4). I will also argue, however (in section 5), that Norrie's critique does point us towards some fundamental problems for our criminal law: problems that concern not its *internal* rationality or consistency but its *preconditions.* Before embarking on this argument, however, we should note (in sections 1 and 2) some general points about what it is for a practice to be 'principled' and 'rational', or 'contradictory.'

1. Principles and Reason

Norrie focuses his critique on various aspects of the 'general part' of the criminal law – on those general principles that are supposedly applicable to most, if not to all, specific crimes.

The 'general part' of a system of criminal law could be expected to include certain general principles of liability – the principle, for example, that criminal liability normally requires a 'voluntary' act or omission (see Williams 1961: 1; Moore 1993: 17–43; Model Penal Code s.2.01(1); 1989 Draft Code cl.16); and that it generally also requires some specified type of 'fault' (see Model Penal

Code s.2.02(1); 1989 Draft Code cl.20(1)). We could also expect it to include explications of any key concepts figuring in its principles that lack a sufficiently clear extra-legal meaning, or are to bear a technical legal meaning: explications, for example, of the concept of a 'voluntary act' (see 1989 Draft Code cls.15-16; Model Penal Code ss.1.13, 2.01(2)), and of the central 'fault' concepts (see Model Penal Code ss.1.13, 2.02(2); 1989 Draft Code cl.18).[4]

These principles and explications might be given statutory formulation (see Model Penal Code, Part I; 1989 Draft Code, Part I). But they need not take this form. A common law system can be structured by general principles, which may be made explicit by its courts or be discernible as implicit in the courts' practice and arguments: The fact that English criminal law is not yet codified does not show that it lacks a general part. Even codified systems of law are likely to include general principles that do not figure in the statutory code. For example, the principle that no one should profit from his own wrong (see Dworkin 1978: 23) seems to be part of English and American criminal law but does not figure explicitly in the Model Penal Code, while the mere fact that neither the Model Penal Code nor the 1989 Draft Code explicitly includes the principle that motive is irrelevant to liability does not show that principle not to be part of American and English criminal law.

There is of course plenty of room for controversy not only about what principles should figure in the general part of the criminal law, or about their interpretation (see, e.g., Husak's critique of the 'act requirement': 1987, ch. 4, and in this volume), but about how extensive the general part should be. How far should the law aim to define all or at least most specific crimes in terms of a common structure of concepts and principles specified in the general part; how far should it, instead, define specific crimes in terms peculiar to their own character (see Gardner and Jung 1991, Gardner 1994, and Gardner [this volume])? I will not discuss such controversies here; my concern is with the question of what makes a general part (and the system of which it is the general part) 'principled' and 'rational.'

Principles

Legal principles figure in the law not merely as descriptions of what is done but as normative principles. So the legal theorist who seeks to identify the principles by which a particular legal system is structured seeks to identify not just certain regularities in the behaviour of the system's actors, but normative principles by which their actions are guided (see Hart 1961: 54–9); to sustain a claim that the system includes a particular principle, she must show that that principle does indeed guide its practitioners' activities.

The principles that structure a legal system will often be made explicit in its code, if it has one, and by its practitioners: Those practitioners (legislators, judges, lawyers) will often be called on to justify what they do or say; in doing so, they will articulate the principles that they think rationalise what they do or say. The explicit articulation of a principle by a system's practitioners is, however, neither a necessary nor a sufficient condition for that principle's being a part of that system. It is not necessary, because a theorist might be able to show that the system is implicitly rather than explicitly structured by that principle; that certain features of that system are best explained (nonpejoratively rationalised) in terms of that principle. It is not sufficient, because some explicitly avowed principles might turn out on closer examination to be merely (pejoratively) rationalisations of actions actually motivated by different considerations; and because the theorist might be able to argue that practitioners have misunderstood their own principles.

(Thus when Husak argues that we should replace the supposed 'act requirement' in criminal law, the principle that criminal liability must be for an 'act', by a 'control requirement', that agents should be criminally liable only for states of affairs over which they had control [see Husak 1987, ch. 4; Husak (this volume)], his claim is not merely [although it is partly] that the law *should* be structured by a 'control requirement' rather than by an 'act requirement'; it is also that we can make better sense of central aspects of existing American and English law if we interpret them as embodying a 'control requirement' rather than the 'act requirement.' We might not be persuaded by either his interpretive or his normative claims [see my 1996a: 243–5, 311–20], but his interpretive argument is not refuted by the mere fact that legal practitioners and theorists orthodoxly take the law to be structured by the 'act requirement.')

Nor, indeed, is it either necessary or sufficient for a theorist who claims that a legal system includes a certain principle to show that its actors' conduct uniformly accords with that principle. It is not sufficient, because she must show that their conduct does not merely coincide with but is guided by that principle – that the practitioners act as they do *because* they recognise that principle (perhaps implicitly or inarticulately) as an authoritative guide to conduct. It is not necessary, because whilst a lack of fit between conduct and principle requires explanation if it is not to undermine the claim that the system includes that principle, such explanations might be available. In particular, deviations might be explained as errors in the system's own terms – errors that (the theorist must be able to claim) the system's actors would themselves recognise if they saw the matter clearly; or as cases in which a principle is qualified by an exception-clause or is overridden by some conflicting principle. I will return to this latter kind of case shortly.

Rationality

What is it for a practice, such as a legal system, to be 'rational' and 'principled'? Or (which will be a better way to express our question), what do we mean when we call a practice 'rational' and 'principled'?

One thing we mean, of course, is that the practice is structured by principles which do, to a significant extent, explain and justify (rationalise) its practitioners' actions. One question, which I will not pursue here, then concerns the way in which principles must be connected to the actions that they are to justify. Are those actions shown to be rational, as justified by those principles, only if there is available a strictly deductive route from some principle to the conclusion that the action is right? Does the absence of such a deductive justification undermine the law's claim to be 'rational'?[5] Or should we recognise that such a deductive model of justification is inappropriate to practical (including legal) reasoning (see Alexy 1989, MacCormick 1978, though both still show some tendency to see deductive justification as the ideal of a rational system)?

Another thing that we mean is that the principles themselves are rational: They are not simply arbitrary stipulations but reasonable principles by which that practice is appropriately structured. This is not to say that the theorist who aims to explicate the principles of a particular practice must herself accept those principles (if she is not a member of that practice, that might not be an issue) or think that the practice *should* embody them. But to understand the principles and their implications, the theorist must understand the values or purposes that they reflect; and to portray the practice as rational, the theorist must be able to show how it is reasonable for such a practice to be structured by those principles. A further question, which again I will not pursue here, then concerns the justification of principles. Must any rational justification of principles derive them from a set of *a priori* first principles, themselves wholly free from historical contingency? Or does the failure of that rationalist dream show, not that practical principles cannot be rationally justified, but that this is not the appropriate model of justification?[6]

I mention these two questions about the rationality of practices partly to set them aside for my present purposes, but also to remind us of a general point about the controversies between those who deny and those who insist that the criminal law is or could be 'rational' or 'principled.' Just as philosophical sceptics who deny that we can claim (strictly speaking) to know what we naïvely think that we know judge our knowledge claims against purported standards or criteria of knowledge, so critical theorists who deny the rationality of the law judge it against certain purported standards or criteria of rationality. One way to meet that sceptical challenge is to try to show that our ordinary knowledge claims can satisfy their criteria; one way to meet the critical theorist's challenge is, similarly, to try to show that the law and its modes of reasoning can satisfy the criteria that she applies.

Another way to respond to philosophical sceptics, however, is to argue that they misunderstand the concepts of knowledge and doubt and thus misportray the kind of freedom from doubt that the mode of knowledge under attack requires; or that they misapply to that mode of knowledge conceptions of certainty that properly belong to quite other modes of thought.[7] Similarly, another response to critical legal theorists is to argue that they judge (and condemn) the law by inappropriate standards of rationality (standards that, admittedly, they might have drawn from some of the law's own defenders); and that once we recognise what it is for such a practice or mode of practical reasoning to be rational, we will also see that the law can meet the appropriate standards. This general point will be important when we come to discuss what it is for a practice or a system of reasoning to be 'contradictory.'

First, however, I must say a little more about what is involved in seeing a practice as 'principled' and 'rational.'

'Rational Reconstruction'

To claim that some practice is principled and rational is not to claim that it is perfectly rational, nor that its rational structure is easily discerned, by its practitioners or by theorists. Any human practice will predictably be in various ways rationally lacking. Its agents will not always be motivated purely by a regard for its principles; they will sometimes misinterpret or flout those principles. Even if there is apparent agreement about which principles structure the practice, there might be uncertainty or disagreement about their precise meaning or implications, about their justification, and about how conflicts between them should be resolved. Any practice that has a history (any human practice) will also change; so at any given time we can expect to find a number of inconsistencies that reflect the slow, partial process of change (see Krygier 1987). But the imperfections, irrationalities, and disagreements that we will predictably find need not rebut a claim that the practice is 'rational' and 'principled.'

What then does such a claim involve? It is partly the claim that those principles that the theorist identifies do play a substantial role in the practice: Its practitioners respect them and try (with some success) to follow them; they are not merely a theorist's invention, or mere window-dressing for actions actually motivated by other, less respectable considerations (though they will doubtless be sometimes so motivated). It is also the claim that we can treat the practice, and its actors, as aspiring (fallibly, i.e. humanly) to principled rationality; that it is worth taking the practice seriously and criticising aspects of it in its own terms – in terms of the principles by which it purports to be structured.

Sometimes the point of such a critical appraisal is to expose a sham for what it is. By showing how radically a practice flouts the values to which it purportedly aspires, we show that those purported aspirations are merely purported, that what we are offered is in the pejorative sense mere rationalisation; this opens the way to a different explanation of the practice (see Kelman 1984: 293). But in other cases, if we can respect the practice and its agents as being seriously (although fallibly) committed to its avowed principles and aspirations (principles that we can respect even if we do not share them), we can properly engage *with* those agents in the enterprise of trying to make rational sense of, and so to improve, their practice; whereas the 'trasher', like a good postmodernist, merely plays the game of pretending to engage in such an enterprise.

So we can properly see a practice as 'rational' and 'principled' although, in one sense, 'irrationality and "unprinciple" are as much a part of [it] as their opposites' (Norrie 1993: 57); even though decisions and actions within the practice are as often (in terms of its own purported principles) irrational or unprincipled as they are rational and principled, we can still properly treat and criticise it as a practice that aspires to principled rationality. But so to treat it is also to deny that 'irrationality and "unprinciple" are' in another sense, 'as much a part of [it] as their opposites': for they now figure as *defective* aspects of the practice.

All of which is partly to say that the enterprise of explicating the principles, the rational structure, of an existing system of law has to be one of 'rational reconstruction' (see MacCormick 1990). In arguing that a certain structure of principles makes best sense of a practice, we will usually be arguing not that it already consistently and unequivocally displays that structure but that it would *come* to make best sense if it were thus structured.[8]

To engage seriously in this enterprise of rational explanation, criticism, and reconstruction requires a degree of faith: in the rational aspirations of the practice's actors (in their willingness to attend to rational criticisms); and in the power of 'reason' (of rational inquiry and argument) to show us how we should act and motivate us to act appropriately. This is why our question should be what we mean in calling a practice 'rational' and 'principled': What matters is not just the extent to which (as judged from some detached standpoint) a practice satisfies the appropriate criteria of rationality, but the extent to which it is possible and worthwhile to *treat* it as rational. The critical theorists' claim is perhaps that any such hope is unjustified. To sustain that claim, however, they must show not merely that our existing law suffers various, even serious, lacks of reason and principle, but also that it lacks the resources (and its agents lack the commitment) to remedy such defects. That is, of course, just what they claim to show: in particular that the law is beset by irresoluble 'contradictions.'

2. Conflict and Contradiction

Norrie argues that the criminal law is 'necessarily contradictory' (1993: 11), but what is it for a practice to be contradictory? The term is clearly pejorative: It picks out some defect of reason. But what kind of defect does it point to?

Conflict and Contradiction outside the Law

In the simplest case, two propositions are contradictory if they cannot both be true – if the truth of one entails the falsity of the other. Thus, the propositions 'p' and 'not-p' are straightforwardly contradictory; so is a pair of propositions, if one entails 'p' and the other entails 'not-p.' A set of propositions or a theory is thus internally contradictory if it includes propositions of the form 'p' and 'not-p', or propositions that severally entail 'p' and 'not-p.' Assertions and theories that aim at truth are rationally defective if they assert or include contradictory propositions: for they cannot be true. Indeed, contradiction is a *fatal* defect in an assertion or a theory that aims at truth. One cannot admit the contradiction and yet insist that the assertion or the theory is acceptable as it stands: One might hope that further inquiry will remove the contradiction, by disproving one of the contradictory propositions; but if the contradiction cannot be eliminated, the assertion or theory must be rejected as fatally flawed.

These remarks apply most obviously to non-normative propositions or theories: for instance, to empirical claims or theories about how the world is. Some argue that they also apply in normative contexts. A person who believes of the same action both that it is wrong and that it is right (obligatory or permissible) contradicts herself; a normative theory that includes two principles one of which prohibits a certain action whilst the other requires it is contradictory; and that contradiction marks a defect of reason in that person's beliefs or in that theory. Someone might, of course, accept two principles that, as so far articulated, are contradictory: Perhaps he believes both that one should never lie and that one should always save life if one can easily do so, but finds himself in a situation in which he can save a life only by lying.[9] In finding that these principles contradict each other, however, this person finds a defect in his set of moral beliefs and must revise those beliefs, by abandoning or making an exception to one principle, so as to render them consistent (see Hare 1952, 1963); and in so doing, the person comes to recognise, or decide, that one action is the unqualifiedly right thing to do.

Now something like this does often happen, when we face apparent moral conflicts: cases in which two moral principles that we accept seem to require each of two incompatible actions, or to require and to prohibit the same action. When we consider the situation and the principles more carefully, we come to see how we should dissolve the apparent conflict. However, there are at least two different ways in which such dissolution can be achieved.

First, we might arrive at a fuller, more precise articulation of one or both of the apparently conflicting principles: a more precise '*determinatio*' (see Finnis 1987: 146–7; MacCormick 1990: 548–9) of the value which that principle expresses. Thus one way to come to see that it is right to lie to the would-be murderer to save the intended victim's life would be to come to see honesty as something that we owe to others – but not to someone who intends to use our truth telling as a means to do great evil. Or someone who holds that it is wrong to kill, except that one may (or must) kill unjust aggressors to save their victims' lives, might believe that what is absolutely wrong is deliberately killing an *innocent;* and killing an unjust aggressor to save a victim's life is wholly consistent with that belief (and might be required by it, if the value it expresses is that of respect for innocent human life). In such cases we do not so much resolve an actual conflict as dissolve an apparent conflict: We realise that the relevant values, once properly understood, are not in real conflict.

Second, however, there are other cases in which (unless we are implausible moral monists who believe in just one fundamental moral value) we face a genuine conflict between two moral principles; but in which that conflict is readily resolved in favour of one of them. A doctor's promise to take her child to the theatre is obviously overridden by the sudden arrival in her casualty unit of a large number of accident victims who could not get the emergency treatment they need if she finished her shift at the specified time: Clearly, she and we might say, she should stay on duty despite her promise to her child. We cannot believe that her promise breaking is sanctioned by the very value which underpins the principle that one should keep one's promises: but that principle is here clearly overridden by the more stringent demands of her professional duty.

Even in such cases, in which a conflict is readily resolved, the situation might be significantly disanalogous to one in which we resolve the conflict between two contradictory beliefs by qualifying or abandoning one of them. Though the doctor is rightly certain that she must break her promise, the thought that she should have kept it retains some force: She has let the child down, even if she can hope that he will come to recognise that she was right to do so; there is a moral remainder (see Williams 1973, Melden 1970). If there is such a moral remainder, if the value that is admittedly overridden still bears significantly on the situation, there might be room to talk of 'contradiction': the contradiction between her duty to her child and her duty as a doctor. Even if we would talk in such terms, however, this would not be to point out a rational deficiency in the doctor's perception of her situation or in her decision. For not only can we agree that she did what was in that situation the right thing to do; we might criticise her if she *failed* to recognise the force of both those conflicting demands.

Can all conflicts be thus straightforwardly resolved, however? Discussions of this question usually focus on various dramatically tragic examples in which, some have argued, there is no unequivocal 'right answer' as to what the agent should do. More precisely, one or both of two claims might be made about such cases. First, that even if it is clear (to the agent, to the observer, to any morally sensitive person) what the agent must do, in doing it she still does a serious wrong, whose moral character as a wrong is not negated by its tragic necessity. Second, that although the agent must act (for in such cases inaction is not a morally untainted option), we cannot say with unequivocal certainty that one action is 'the right thing' to do. The agent herself might act with anguished and irremediable uncertainty; or, even if the agent becomes clear about what she must do, neither the agent nor others might think that *anyone* in such a situation must act thus; whilst observers might properly think that it is not for them to criticise the agent's decision, or even reach a view about what she ought to do (see Winch 1972; Gaita 1991: ch. 5).

In such cases there is more room to talk of 'contradiction': the irresoluble contradiction the agent faces between two irreconcilable moral demands. But to talk thus is still not to identify a rational deficiency in the agent's moral perception of her situation, or in her decision. For if we believe, as those who argue that such tragic dilemmas occur insist, that the moral world *is* one of irreconcilably conflicting values (see, e.g., Nagel 1979), we would rather count it a defect in the agent's moral perception if she did *not* recognise that conflict, or thought it could be easily resolved.

If we are to get clear about the critical theorist's charge that the law is 'contradictory', however, we need other kinds of example: not ones, like those typically discussed in the literature on moral dilemmas, in which an agent faces a one-off conflict in a particular situation, but ones in which the agent faces a *persisting* conflict, through a significant stretch of his life. Here is one such example.

A university teacher might be committed both to teaching and to research. These two commitments can, to some extent, be consistent with each other; each should indeed sustain the other. But (at least in contemporary British universities) they will also, persistently, conflict: The demands of each are, if taken seriously, practically unlimited; one must constantly be sacrificed or compromised for the sake of the other. Individuals, or groups, might achieve reasonably stable compromises between these demands, but such compromises will be prone to persistent, irremediable destabilisation: The demands will intrude on each other; the compromises will be undermined; the teacher will often feel, not that she is living by a consistent set of commitments which she has successfully reconciled, but that she is having to make continual *ad hoc* compromises and sacrifices.

We (and the teacher) might talk of 'contradiction' here: The demands of teaching and of research are sometimes 'contradictory' in that they cannot both be satisfied to the extent that, taken separately, they demand. We might think too that there is no unique 'right answer' to this contradiction – neither in general, for every academic, nor in the particular case. There are plenty of wrong answers: ways of dividing one's time and attention that allow insufficient weight to one demand. But the most we can say is that there is a fairly wide range of possible compromises which are 'reasonable.' We would surely not, however, regard this kind of 'contradiction' as marking any defect, any lack of reason or principle, in the teacher's conception of her work or in the way she structures her working life – though we might see it as reflecting defects in the external conditions under which she works. We might, indeed, think that a *failure* to face that 'contradiction' would mark a lack in her relationship to the values that bear on her work: that any university teacher (in a system like our own) *should* face such a conflict.

Perhaps, however, this example does not involve the kind of deep and rationality-threatening conflict that critical theorists claim to identify in the criminal law. Four features might be relevant to this point. First, the values that conflict are nonetheless closely connected to each other: Both express the teacher's commitment to her subject. Second, the conflict between them is, in a sense, contingent rather than intrinsic: Neither value itself involves the positive rejection or repudiation of the other; they conflict just because each of them makes practically unlimited demands on her attention. Third, she is herself aware of the conflict as irresoluble: She does not suppose that she is doing or could do full justice to either of the values. Fourth, we can not only respect (I assume) both of those conflicting values; even if we do not share them, we can understand how a person could be committed to them both.

In other cases, lacking some or all of these features, we may be more inclined to talk not just of an agent who must face conflicting or contradictory demands, but of someone whose very life or activity is contradictory; in talking thus we will be talking about a serious deficiency (a lack of integrity or consistency, perhaps also a lack of reason or rationality) in that life or activity. These cases come closer to the kind of contradiction that critical theorists discern in the criminal law. Consider two further examples.

First, someone might confront irreconcilably conflicting demands that are not connected in the way that those facing the academic in my original example were: He faces, for instance, a conflict between the demands of a worthwhile job and the urgent needs of his parents, whom only he can help. He might, like the academic, be able to reach some uneasy compromise between them, but he might recognise that he cannot hope to do adequate (or even tolerably inadequate) justice to both of them. In the latter case, he might be able (although at some moral cost) to escape from the conflict by abandoning either his job or his parents, but he might feel unable to do this; and sympathetic observers might not be able to say that he is misguided or wrong to feel this. He faces a deeper contradiction than did the academic: He feels his life, and himself, to be deeply riven by this conflict; or perhaps he will try (and to some extent manage) to conceal it from himself by pretending that he can do justice to both demands.

Second, someone might face (or profess to face; we might now see reason to doubt his professions) a conflict between two values that seem so intrinsically inimical to each other, and one of which is so utterly corrupted, that we cannot understand how one person could be drawn by them both. Imagine another academic, a philosopher working in and professing commitment to a tradition in which philosophical inquiry is understood as a cooperative search for truth; a tradition that insists on the importance of freedom of thought, and of mutual respect between colleagues (whether teachers or students), as fellow inquirers. But he is also the faithful servant of a regime that seeks to stifle any dissident thought (by propaganda, imprisonment, torture): He produces propaganda for the regime, and denounces to the police colleagues and students who express dissident ideas.[10]

He might not see any deep conflict between these two aspects of his life: Perhaps he avoids thinking about the relationship between them; or he offers an interpretation of them which portrays them as consistent; or he portrays what he admits to be occasional conflicts between them as requiring only a compromise between two contingently conflicting demands. We would probably reject such reconciliatory interpretations, however, and insist that his life is radically contradictory. Either he is radically at odds with himself (for how could someone be genuinely committed both to philosophy and to this regime?) or his actions contradict his words (for how could anyone who believes what he professes to believe also do what he does?).

This is no doubt partly because we condemn one of the values to which he professes to be committed – but it is also, I think, because each directly repudiates the other. Insofar as he faithfully serves the regime, he must see his students and colleagues as dangerous subjects who must be watched and controlled; who are dangerous just because of their commitment to the kind of philosophising to which he is purportedly also committed; and with whom he therefore cannot engage, with mutual respect, as collaborators in a rational inquiry subject to the discipline of truth. Insofar as he is committed to philosophy, however, he must see his colleagues and students in just that light that his commitment to the regime forbids. But how could a person be genuinely committed to (let alone hope to find an honest compromise between the conflicting demands of) two kinds of value which so directly repudiate each other?

These examples bring us closer to the kind of 'contradiction' that critical theorists think infects the criminal law, and to which we must now turn.

Contradiction in the Criminal Law

There are simple ways in which a legal system could be defective because contradictory – for example, if the law explicitly prohibited and required the same action, and provided no resources to resolve that conflict. However, that is not the kind of contradiction which critical theorists claim to identify.

Kelman suggests that critical theorists aim to portray 'liberal' thought as

> a system of thought that is simultaneously beset by internal *contradiction* (not by 'competing concerns' artfully balanced until a wise equilibrium is reached, but by irreducible, irremediable, irresolvable conflict) and by systematic *repression* of the presence of these contradictions;[11]

and a 'contradiction' is 'a set of paired rhetorical arguments that both resolve cases in opposite, incompatible ways and correspond to distinct visions of human nature and human fulfillment' (1987: 3).

So what makes the criminal law 'contradictory' is not merely the fact that it includes conflicting principles or policies that taken severally would generate different, incompatible legal doctrines and rules. It is that the law provides no resources for reconciling such conflicts, or for achieving any rational compromise: Those conflicts are deep and irresoluble, reflecting as they do a conflict between 'distinct visions of human nature.' Conflict are of course settled, in one way or another, by legislatures and courts; and the law might achieve a relatively stable practice for a time, by regularly giving priority to one of the conflicting values (see, e.g., Kelman 1987: 4, 13, 258). But we must distinguish 'settled *practices*' from '*settled justificatory schemes*' (Kelman 1987: 13). Such 'settled practices' as the law achieves are not rationally well founded and are anyway fragile and liable to collapse; the competing values that the law attempts to silence are never wholly silenced, but are always liable to irrupt and destabilise (see Norrie 1993: 40; Kelman 1987: 86–7).

(To say that the law cannot rationally resolve such conflicts is not necessarily to say that courts never have *reasons* for preferring one value or principle to the other, that their decisions are always a-rational. Critical theorists may argue that courts have political reasons, to do with the preservation of a certain social order, for their contradictory practices and decisions – indeed, that the law's contradictory character is functionally efficient in serving certain [class] interests [see, e.g., Hunt 1986: 35–6; Lacey 1993: 637–42; but contrast Kelman 1987: 260–2]. Critical theorists can still, however, portray the law as arbitrary and unreasoned: for their claim is that no reasons, *of a kind that would be legitimate in terms of the law's ideology,* are available to resolve its conflicts. The law presents itself as a coherent system of principles and policies that suffice by themselves to determine rational decisions in particular cases. But it is no such thing: In the terms in which it presents itself, it is contradictory; its courts' decisions lack adequately rational legal grounds. To understand the courts' decisions, we must look beneath the surface rhetoric of the law, to the political motives which actually drive it.)

Thus, as the discussion in the previous subsection reminded us, the criminal law is not shown to be in any rationally defective way 'contradictory' merely by showing that it includes principles and policies which conflict with each other, and that we cannot suppose there to be a 'right answer' (discernible by rational deliberation) to all such conflicts. My original example of the academic involved both these features: but we would not for that reason count her life or thought as (in a pejorative sense) contradictory.[12] It must also be shown that those conflicting values are so profoundly opposed to each other that no tolerable compromise can be found between them – as was true, in different ways, of my other two earlier examples. To see whether that is true, however, we must look carefully at the meaning and implications of those values.

Consider, then, one basic 'tension' that Norrie identifies in the criminal law: between the law's 'liberal individualism', which emphasises individual responsibility, and 'the social control needs of the state' (1993: 57).[13] This tension would certainly be genuine and deep if these two concerns reflected 'distinct visions of human nature' (Kelman 1987: 3) – if, for instance, whilst the law's liberal individualism portrays citizens as autonomous and responsible agents to whom respect is due, a concern for 'social control' portrays them as a set of (actually or potentially) recalcitrant subjects who must be controlled by whatever means might be economically effective. One might then say that there is a 'contradiction' in the law: These two conceptions of the law's citizens/subjects contradict each other in that they straightforwardly deny each other; but how could two such profoundly opposed views co-exist in a coherent and integrated system?

One might even then try to resolve the conflict by some suitable ordering of the conflicting concerns. For instance, following Hart, one might suggest that just as the 'justifying aim' of punishment is the prevention of crime (an aim that would itself sanction measures that flout the demands of individual justice), the 'justifying aim' of the criminal law is social control – the prevention of socially harmful or disruptive kinds of behaviour. But our pursuit of that consequentialist aim is subject to certain side constraints set by the demands of justice: we must pursue it only by means that are consistent with the citizens' standing as autonomous and responsible agents (see Hart 1968).

One objection to such an attempt to resolve the conflict between the consequentialist aim of control and nonconsequentialist demands of justice is that that resolution is inherently unstable (see, e.g., Lacey 1988: 46–56; Morison 1988). For once we admit (see, e.g., Hart 1968: 20, 24–5, 33–4) that we might sometimes have to compromise the demands of individual justice for the sake of effective control or crime prevention, and thus that the demands of justice cannot be *absolute* constraints, we also admit that these two disparate values always make conflicting demands, between which no stable compromise is possible. Another objection is that no practice whose justifying aim is understood simply as 'prevention', or as 'control' – an aim that does not itself embody a respectful conception of citizens as autonomous and responsible agents – can genuinely respect them as such, even if our pursuit of that aim is subject to negative side constraints of justice (see Duff 1986: 178–86).

We might then admit that this is a genuine, irresoluble conflict (or contradiction), but argue that it is one which the criminal law should indeed recognise: both concerns make a proper claim on us (on the law), although we cannot consistently satisfy both. The question then would be whether any tolerable compromise between them could be achieved. One might instead, however, seek to resolve this conflict by arguing that we should see the 'justifying aim' of the law, not as 'control', but as something like 'subjecting human conduct to the governance of rules' (Fuller 1969: 122): the notion of 'control' is then itself understood in a way that respects the moral standing of those whose conduct is to be 'controlled' (see Duff 1986: ch. 3). A due respect for individual autonomy and responsibility is now built into the very aims of the law, so that measures which fail to accord such respect are not (as on Hart's account) measures that might achieve the law's aims (although at unacceptable moral cost) but measures that cannot achieve its proper aims at all (compare Duff 1996a: 199–201). Conflicts between the demands of individual justice and social control would not then vanish: but they would not be as profound as those who talk of 'contradiction' argue they are.

To put more flesh on these bare bones, I will discuss one aspect of our criminal law that, Norrie argues, exposes its (necessarily) 'contradictory' nature: the orthodox slogan that motive (as distinct from intention) is irrelevant to criminal liability.

3. Intention and Motive

The doctrine that motive is irrelevant to criminal liability appears (according to doctrinal theorists) to be 'as firmly established . . . as any rule can be' (Norrie 1993: 37)[14]: but, Norrie argues, this is one context in which we can see the fundamentally contradictory character of the criminal law (see also Norrie [this volume]: 120–3).

The orthodox doctrine can be expressed by saying that intention is normally a sufficient condition of criminal liability. Proof that the defendant carried out an intention to do something that the law defines as a crime normally suffices to convict that defendant of that crime – whatever his motive for acting thus. But can we provide any coherent account of why motives should be irrelevant to liability; and of why they sometimes nonetheless appear to be relevant?

It might seem that any discussion of the role of 'motive' in the criminal law should begin with a definition of that concept; and, in particular, that anyone concerned to defend the orthodox doctrine of the irrelevance of motive to liability must offer a definition which can clearly distinguish (legally relevant) 'intention' from (legally irrelevant) 'motive.' In fact, for reasons that will appear shortly, a thorough account of the concept of motive is not necessary: but I should say a little here.[15]

A motive is, trivially, what motivates an agent (or, as when the detective asks who had a motive for the murder, what could motivate an agent). Often, what is cited as my motive for doing *X* will simply be my further intention in doing *X: D*'s motive for a theft might be to get money to pay off his debts. In other cases, what we cite as a motive is not an intention but some underlying emotion, concern, or commitment by which an agent is moved: love, fear, greed, and commitment to a cause can all be motives. But even in these cases motives are connected to intention: to be motivated by fear, for example, is to form and act upon certain appropriate intentions, most obviously an intention to escape what one fears; to be motivated by commitment to a cause is to form and act on intentions to do with its furtherance. So even motive-explanations that do not explicitly cite intentions still make implicit reference to the intentions with which an agent thus motivated acts, and set those intentions in the larger context of concerns and commitments from which they flow.

The legally relevant distinction between motive and intention is (as we will see shortly) given in and by the law itself. But we must first identify the various contradictions that Norrie argues infect this aspect of the criminal law.

The Contradictions

First, the law claims to be based on 'individual justice through the operation of a fault requirement.' But in excluding motives, it 'ignores a normal mental element in human conduct in its attribution of fault' (Norrie 1993: 37); ignoring significant moral differences between agents who act with the same legally defined intention, it becomes a very 'blunt instrument for the allocation of fault' (40; see 45–6).

Second, the law cannot completely 'suppress' motive; despite its official exclusion, it 'persistently irrupts within legal discourse' (40). This irruption might be overt, as with such defences as duress (see ch. 8) and self-defence: The agent's motive for acting in a way that is normally criminal can exempt her from liability. But it is sometimes covert: Courts can acquit defendants with whose motives they sympathise, by redescribing their intentions in terms of their motives to make it appear that they did not act with the appropriate criminal intention (41, 55–7).[16] The official doctrine that motives are irrelevant to liability is thus contradicted by their relevance in some cases. Furthermore, the discretion that courts sometimes allow themselves in identifying a defendant's 'intention' shows that they are not in fact applying determinate legal rules to particular cases (as the ideology of the 'rule of law' claims). The distinction between 'intention' and 'motive' provides no determinate or rational basis for their judgments; it rather functions, indeterminately and arbitrarily, to express logically prior judgments of culpability.

Third, once 'motive' is allowed to be relevant in some cases, the courts have no good (doctrinally relevant) reason not to allow it to be relevant in many other cases. If the motive of one who acts under what the courts recognise as exculpatory duress is allowed to exempt him from liability, why should not the motive of someone who steals from need, or the socially contextualised motives of rioters, exempt them from liability (see 38, 39)?

Fourth, motive is allowed to be relevant in sentencing. In thus abandoning the issue to the effectively unconstrained discretion of sentencers, however, the law contradicts the liberal ideology of the 'rule of law': '[h]aving insisted upon a strict legal code so as to protect the liberty of the individual, it transpires that at the end of the day, the individual's liberty is dependent not upon the rule of law at all but on a group of men operating with a wide discretion at the sentencing stage' (46).

Such contradictions reflect two deeper tensions that infect the criminal law: 'between an abstract individualism of legal categories and the concrete reality of individuals' lives within a conflictual society' and 'between the law's liberal individualism and the social control needs of the state' (57). In officially declaring motives to be irrelevant, the law reflects that 'abstract individualism' which abstracts individual agents from those concrete contexts which give rise to their crimes; while in sometimes (and inconsistently) making motives relevant, it recognises that individual justice makes such concrete contexts crucially relevant to liability. The principles of liberal individualism require attention to defendants' motives, as being relevant to the culpability of their conduct: but if the law allowed motives to exculpate too often, it would cease to be an effective means of social control.

These 'contradictions' can of course be explained – they are not merely intellectual aberrations – but their explanation will refer to factors external to the ideology in terms of which the law claims to make sense. The law's official exclusion of motive reflects its role as an instrument of social control, imposed by one class on another. If the law were to attend, for instance, to the poverty that drives a person to theft, or to the social and economic frustrations that motivated a riot, it would have to question whether agents motivated by such factors ought to be held criminally liable. To raise such questions seriously, however, would threaten the law's efficacy in performing its crucial function: 'the protection of private property and particular social interests' (40).

This is a good example of a critical exposure of contradictions. An official legal doctrine is shown to contradict another principle or value that the law purports to embody. That official doctrine is then shown not to be applied consistently: Even if it is embodied in *relatively* stable practices, the contrary value sometimes 'irrupts.' Nor, it is argued, do courts have any doctrinally sanctioned reason to exclude or limit its irruptions. This specific contradiction is then shown to reflect deeper contradictions in the law's underlying principles and goals; and those contradictions are shown to serve further political purposes, which are not part of the law's official ideology.

Two Quick Responses

We should note two quick responses to Norrie's argument. Neither is in itself satisfactory, but the second points us in the right direction.

The first response is that the slogan that motive is irrelevant to liability is simply false (see, e.g., Husak 1989, Sistare 1987): on any plausible interpretation of the concept of 'motive', motives *are* (more often than Norrie notes) relevant to criminal liability. Thus, to offer just three examples, if my motive for picking up a dropped wallet is to return it to its owner, my action is not a theft; if it is to keep the wallet, my action is theft. If my motive for damaging another's property is to protect my own property, I might avoid a conviction for criminal damage (Criminal Damage Act 1971 s.5(2)(b)). If my motive for carrying what counts in law as an offensive weapon is to defend myself against a threatened, imminent attack, I might avoid conviction for carrying an offensive weapon; but if my motive for carrying an otherwise innocent article is to use it to commit an assault, I am guilty of that offence (Prevention of Crime Act 1953 s.1).[17] Rather than saying that motive is formally excluded by the law but 'persistently irrupts' within it (Norrie 1993: 40), as if the law tries unsuccessfully to exclude motives, we should realise that liability often does depend on the defendant's motives; the slogan that motive is irrelevant should be rejected as an example of practitioners' (and theorists') failure to understand the principles that actually structure their practice.

This response is too quick: partly because there is, as we shall see, more to the orthodox doctrine than it allows; but also because it does not meet Norrie's challenge. We would still need to ask why so many commentators should have persisted in what is, on this view, such an obvious mistake; and whether the law provides any principled or rational distinction between those motives that can be relevant to criminal liability and those that are not – to which Norrie will reply that it does not.

The second quick response is so to define 'motive' that it is a definitional truth that anything which counts as a 'motive' is irrelevant to criminal liability, thus making the orthodox doctrine true by definition.[18] Thus, if a particular motivating factor is relevant to criminal liability, we count it as a matter of 'intention' rather than of 'motive'; whilst if some motivating factor is irrelevant to liability, we call it a matter of 'motive.' If what motivates *D* to kill *V* is a desire to spare *V* (at *V*'s own request) further terminal suffering, this is a matter of 'motive': for under current English law, such a motivation is irrelevant to liability for murder. But if what motivates *D* is instead a concern to protect himself against *V*'s murderous attack (in what he thinks is the only possible way), this is a matter of 'intention': for such motivation is legally relevant.

It is tempting to dismiss this second response as an example of a lamentable 'tendency among commentators to advance principles that are initially defended as important substantive insights, but become embellished as vacuous tautologies' (Husak 1989: 6). But that would be too hasty: by portraying the orthodox doctrine as a definitional truth *about the task of adjudication,* we can see it as embodying a substantive doctrine about the 'rule of law', and the distinction between the tasks of legislatation and of adjudication. To avoid the appearance of triviality, we might better express the doctrine as holding not that 'motive' is irrelevant to criminal liability, but that '*further* motive' is irrelevant to liability; and as a doctrine that applies to courts, not to legislatures.

The legislature defines crimes, by defining kinds of action that must count as criminal. Those definitions might include motivational factors, as identifying features of the relevant kind of action, as in the examples given previously. So too, were the law to define certain species of euthanasia as noncriminal, or as a lesser species of criminal homicide, it might define the relevant kinds of killing by reference to the defendant's motives: was she motivated by a desire to spare the 'victim' further terminal suffering? Or were the law to define assaults motivated by racial hatred as aggravated assaults, rather than leaving such motivation to be relevant only at the stage of sentencing, it would make a racist attacker's motives relevant to his liability. Nothing in the orthodox doctrine as thus interpreted forbids legislatures to define crimes in this way; and, in deciding how particular crimes should be defined, legislatures will be asking what kinds of motive should make what kind of difference to criminal liability.[19]

Once the legislature has defined crimes, it is for the courts to apply those definitions to determine defendants' criminal liability; and in doing so, they should attend only to the issue of whether the defendant's actions matched the law's definition of a crime.[20] They will thus often have to attend to questions about what motivated the defendant, because such motivational questions will often be relevant to her liability: but they must *not* attend to motivational factors that are not declared relevant by the law. A court might sympathise with and respect a defendant's motive for killing her terminally ill partner at his request, and might think that the law ought to be so reformed as to exculpate such killings: But until the legislature changes the law, that motive is (i.e., should be) irrelevant to the question of whether she should be convicted of murder. Once it is proved that the defendant did an action that the law defines as a crime, he must be convicted, whatever his further motive for acting thus; whilst if that is not proved, he must be acquitted, however immoral or despicable were his further motives.[21]

Even if this response does not trivialize the orthodox doctrine, however, it is still too quick. For we still need some *justificatory* account of this division of labour between legislatures and courts; we must still ask whether there is a principled distinction between those kinds of motive that legislatures can properly make relevant to criminal liability (for some kinds of crime), and those that they should not make relevant; nor does this response (any more than did the first) justify the relevance of motive to sentencing.

Verdict and Sentence

We can begin with sentencing. As Norrie insists, if punishment is to be justified by the offender's culpability, his motive can make a significant difference to the penal fate he deserves: for it can make a significant difference to his culpability. The crucial question, however, is how (and how far) the criminal process should be so structured as to give practical recognition to this.

There are two distinct problems here. Both reflect tensions in the law; but neither reveals a lack of rationality, principle, or consistency that should count as 'contradiction.'

One issue concerns the proper division of labour between verdict and sentencing (which may also be a division of labour between judge and jury). How far should the law seek to capture all the relevant features of an offender's action at the stage of conviction, in a formal verdict on his conduct (how precisely should offences be defined and distinguished); and how far should some of these be left to be dealt with in sentencing?

Various considerations could be adduced on either side; nor need we suppose that there is a uniquely 'right answer' to this question (see Ashworth 1995: 86-90). There is a principled presumption in favour of making verdicts, and therefore the definitions of distinct crimes, as precise as possible: a presumption founded on the importance of 'fair labelling', and on the demand that factors which will affect a defendant's sentence should, as far as possible, be proved publicly in court. But that presumption cannot be absolute: A practicable system of law must operate with general categories of crime, within which there will be relevant differences between individual instances. In defining crimes, the law must therefore attempt to balance these conflicting considerations; and if it achieves some reasonable (which need not be the only reasonable) resolution, which defines morally significant categories of crime, its rationality and consistency are not threatened by the mere fact that there will also be relevant differences between individual cases within any one category. This issue can be problematic for legislatures[22]: But once we recognise that the doctrine of the irrelevance of motives applies to courts, not to legislatures, it does not threaten that doctrine or show it to be in contradiction with other aspects of the law.

The other issue concerns the sentencing process itself. There is a tension between two conceptions of 'doing justice' in sentencing (see Duff 1996b: 61–6). On the one hand, sentencers should try to do individual justice – to determine the sentence appropriate to the individual offender and her particular offence: This demands a wide discretion in sentencing, so that sentencers can be sensitive to the particularities of each case – including the offender's motives. On the other hand, however, justice demands that like cases be treated alike: that different courts be reasonably consistent in sentencing decisions. But the wider the discretion we allow to sentencers, the greater the danger of inconsistency (apart from the questions of how far we can trust sentencers to do individual justice, and of how far the courts should be allowed to take the intrusive interest in the offender's character and situation which doing individual justice seems to require). Thus we also have reason to constrain sentencers' discretion: perhaps to specify in advance, through strict sentencing rules, a limited range of possible sentences for each offence, and of mitigating or aggravating factors that can justify making the sentence harsher or more lenient.

This tension is an instance of Kelman's conflict between 'rules' and 'standards' (1981: 598–600, 652–62; 1987: 15–63). MacCormick responds that this 'contradiction' in fact involves nothing more dramatic than a 'spectrum' of rules, 'ranging from the most tightly drawn and determinate of rules to particularly open-textured standard-stipulating rules'; a lawmaker's task is 'to find the most appropriate degree of determinacy in a given context' (1990: 545–6). Now we do indeed face here a spectrum of relative (in)determinacies, whose poles are at one end a set of wholly non-discretionary rules specifying the precise sentence for each category of offender, and at the other a rule simply requiring courts to impose on individual offenders the particular sentences that they deserve: but there is still a real problem. This is partly because it is not clear that we can talk of *the* 'most appropriate degree of determinacy' here: as if for any system there will always be a precise degree of discretion that should appropriately be left to the courts. It is also because (as I noted previously) we are pushed in opposing directions along this spectrum: We have good reasons both to allow courts more discretion than they now have, and to constrain them further. We may be able to find some tolerable compromise between these conflicting concerns, but we cannot claim to have wholly resolved that conflict.

But if we think that both sets of conflicting considerations are significant; that any tolerable penal system must attend both to the demand for individual justice, and to the need to constrain judicial discretion: it is not clear that a system which finds an admittedly uncomfortable compromise between them is therefore 'contradictory' – especially since both sets of considerations reflect a concern for the rights of individual defendants, who would (we fear) be unjustly treated both by a wholly discretionary system of sentencing, and by one allowing judges no sentencing discretion at all (see pp. 166–7 above).

The critic might claim that a system of law like our own cannot hope to find even a tolerable compromise here. Any sentencing system that was to provide even minimally adequate protection against the excesses of judicial discretion would be so rigid that it would also do serious injustice to individual defendants, by subjecting them to its crudely general categories; but any relaxation of that rigidity, to allow something more like individual justice to be done, would open the door to intolerable disparities and injustice. How far such a pessimistic conclusion is justified depends on the possibility and acceptability of the kind of 'abstraction' that is involved in any non-discretionary system of sentencing guidelines; I return to this issue later (section 4).

Particular Controversies about Motives

Legislatures, I argued, can properly attend to motives: They can so define particular crimes that the agent's motives are relevant to whether or for what he is to be criminally liable. Sometimes motives play an inculpatory role: An agent's criminal motive for carrying an otherwise innocent article can make him guilty of a crime (Criminal Damage Act 1971, s. 3; Prevention of Crime Act 1953, s.1). Sometimes they play an exculpatory role: The defendant can avoid liability by arguing that he was motivated in some way recognised as non-culpable either in the definition of the particular crime (as when he claims 'lawful excuse' for damaging another's property; Criminal Damage Act 1971, s.5) or by a general defence (as when he claims to have been motivated by a fear of threatened violence that the law recognises as constituting exculpatory duress).

There are, of course, controversies about the exculpatory or inculpatory relevance of particular kinds of motive to criminal liability. There are controversies about the law's treatment of motives currently recognised as relevant: for instance, about the defence of duress (whether it should be available against a charge of murder or attempted murder; whether only threats of death or serious injury should count: see Smith and Hogan 1996: 237-45) and about the partial defence of provocation (under what conditions killings motivated by extreme, reasonably provoked anger should be partly excused: see Horder 1992). There are also controversies about whether particular motives should be given a statutory relevance that they do not now have. For instance, should the fact that a killing was motivated by concern to spare the victim further, terminal suffering (and was committed at the victim's own request) entitle the killer to an acquittal, or to conviction of a lesser crime than murder? Should the fact that an attack was motivated by racial hatred make the attacker guilty of a more serious crime?

Such controversies typically involve two kinds of argument. One concerns the difference that the relevant motive makes to the moral character of the action, or to its agent's culpability. Is a killing motivated by compassion for a terminally ill victim (and carried out at her own request) morally justified, in which case it should *prima facie* be legally permitted; or wholly or partially excusable; or at least so different in its moral character from other deliberate killings that it should be formally recognised as a distinct and lesser kind of homicide? Is an attack motivated by racial hatred so different, in its wrongful character, from other kinds of assault that it should be formally defined as a distinct, more serious crime? These arguments focus on the action or its agent: not just on whether such action, thus motivated, is to some degree justifiable or excusable, but also on whether its wrongfulness (if it is still wrong) is sufficiently distinct from that of otherwise motivated actions falling within the same general category to justify defining it as a distinct crime.[23]

The second kind of argument concerns the practicability, and the likely effects, of trying to give those sorts of moral consideration which underpin the first kind of argument formal recognition in the law. For instance, could the proposed new law be expected to make a significant difference to people's behaviour, or to have a suitable declaratory significance? Can it be so formulated that courts could be expected to apply it with tolerable consistency? How easy will it be, within the constraints of the (justified) rules of evidence and procedure, to prove or disprove matters that the new law would make relevant? How much danger is there that innocents will be mistakenly convicted, or that guilty agents will secure acquittals by spurious appeals to a new defence? These arguments have to do with the law as an institutional practice, subject to various practical constraints. But some of them also involve a concern for the law's relationship to individual citizens – that the law should not require courts to pry too far into the 'private' realm of thoughts and feelings in order to establish legal guilt or innocence.[24]

There are tensions between these two kinds of argument: We might see good reasons of the second kind not to give formal legal recognition to motivational factors that make a significant difference to the moral character of an action. Such tensions might be related to the conflicts that Norrie identifies, between 'an abstract individualism of legal categories and the concrete reality of individuals' lives', and between 'the law's liberal individualism and the social control needs of the state' (1993: 57). For they reflect tensions between the law's need, as a public institution, to deal in general, easily recognised categories of conduct, and a concern to do justice to the moral character of individual actions; and also between that latter concern and a concern that the law be effective in dissuading criminal conduct. But this is not yet to say that those tensions are so radical that no tolerable compromise can be found (admittedly, at some moral cost), or that we should talk of 'contradictions.'

A critical theorist might again argue that no tolerable compromise is possible: The kind of abstraction involved in providing practically efficacious definitions of crimes will also inevitably (in societies like ours) so seriously distort, or fail to recognise, the moral character of particular defendants' actions that the law cannot but fail to do anything like justice to individual defendants. Such particular controversies, however, about the proper scope of motive-based crime definitions are not really the critical theorists' central concern. Their central argument is, rather, that once the law recognises the kinds of motive-based defence that our law already recognises, in accordance with its concern for individual responsibility, it has no good reason to deny more radical extensions to such defences: but such extensions would utterly undermine its role as an instrument of social control, and are for that reason (a reason not sanctioned by the law's official ideology) rejected. We can understand this argument by examining two kinds of case that Norrie discusses.

Politically Motivated Crimes

The first kind of case is that in which the defendant seeks 'to argue the moral or political rights and wrongs of his action in the courtroom' (Norrie 1993: 41). By denying the relevance of the moral or political motives that led someone to do what the law counts as a crime, by an 'ideological process of decontextualisation' that abstracts action and immediate intention from underlying motive, the law silences 'opposing political and ideological reasons that individuals would give for their actions if they could' (171). Indeed, the law silences those reasons even when it is itself so formulated that they appear relevant: as when the Law Lords held, in *Chandler,* that defendants who planned an anti-nuclear demonstration at an air force station could not argue that their 'purpose' was not 'prejudicial to the safety or interests of the state', because it was for 'the state', not for individual citizens, to determine where its safety and interests lay (*Chandler v DPP* [1964] A.C. 763; Offical Secrets Act 1911 s.1 (1); see Norrie 1993: 41–2). But in refusing to attend to such motives the law contradicts its professed concern with individual responsibility.

For almost any reader, Norrie could cite cases of politically or morally motivated crime that would arouse respect or sympathy, and might tempt us to feel that the defendant should not be convicted or punished – cases, for instance, in which the defendant breaks what we agree is an unjust law, or commits a relatively minor crime for some admirable motive. His argument is not, however, that the law should be so reformed that it allows such defendants to secure acquittals. It is, rather, that such cases expose the contradiction at the heart of systems of law like our own. The ideology of fault-based criminal liability and individual responsibility by which the law is supposed to be structured requires that the law acquit such defendants: but, as an instrument of social control, the law cannot be allowed to do so. What is not yet clear, however, is *why* that ideology requires their acquittal.

Those who believe that the law should 'be based upon individual justice through the operation of a fault requirement' (Norrie 1993: 37) are surely not committed to believing that a defendant should be acquitted just so long as *he* believes that his action was justified – that, for instance, a racist attacker should be acquitted if he believed he was justified in thus defending white territory against black 'intrusion.' Some of Norrie's comments on recklessness do seem to reflect the belief that a properly 'subjective' test of criminal liability (of the kind that liberals supposedly favour) can condemn someone's conduct only by appealing to values that he shares (1993: 74–7), which might suggest that in his view a liberal respect for individual responsibility must involve judging anyone's conduct only on the basis of his own values. But nothing in legal 'subjectivism', nor in liberal ideology, entails this.

Subjectivists argue that agents must 'be judged on the facts as they believed them to be' (Cross 1975: 540; see Ashworth 1987, 8–13): but the normative standards by which they must be judged are those provided by the law, or by the 'reasonable person', even when those differ from the defendant's own standards. I might think it reasonable to take what I recognise as a significant risk of damaging another's property: but if, by the standards of 'reasonable' people, that risk is an unreasonable one, subjectivists will consistently hold that I can be condemned as reckless.[25] I might think it morally justifiable to vandalise the car of someone who 'steals' my parking place: but it does not follow that I have a 'lawful excuse' for damaging her property.

Liberals do typically attach importance to respect for 'private'conscience; the law ought not to force a citizen to act against her conscience (see, for instance, Abortion Act 1967, s.4). But, though it is difficult to specify the range of issues that should count as matters of 'conscience', and the range of conscientiously held moral views that should thus be respected, a respect for conscience does not involve holding that citizens should be legally required to act only in ways that they themselves see as right, or should be legally condemned only for acting in ways that they themselves see as wrong. A liberal system of law, like any system of law, claims to declare authoritative standards of conduct – to specify norms that citizens should obey and by which their conduct will be judged.[26]

It is also true that on a plausible conception of responsibility (which connects responsibility with answerability), to hold an agent culpably responsible for an action is to assume that he could have seen its wrongness for himself. Our judgment must therefore appeal to values that the agent can understand and could come to share, even if he does not now share them; and those values must therefore be so connected to his existing values that there is an intelligible route by which he could come to accept our judgment for himself. But Norrie does not suggest that this requirement is not satisfied: that those who offer 'opposing political and ideological reasons' for their actions cannot understand the values they oppose.

Does Norrie think that a consistent (liberal) respect for individual responsibility would require us to allow a defendant to argue in court that her action was justified, and gain an acquittal if she can persuade the court to accept or respect her argument, whether or not it is consistent with what the law had until then been taken to be? The *Chandler* defendants would then have been entitled to acquittals if they could persuade the court that 'the safety or interests of the state' would be best served by nuclear disarmament (or that nuclear disarmament was right independently of its implications for the safety or interests of the state) and that their protest was justified as a means of pursuing that end. So too, if the jurors who acquitted in *Pottle and Randle* did so because they believed that the defendants were right to help the Russian spy George Blake to escape from prison, they would have been doing their legal duty, whereas as the law now stands they were clearly nullifying the law.[27] On this account, a racist attacker would also be entitled to an acquittal if he could persuade a jury that his violence was justified in order to keep black families out of a 'white' area.

It is true that if the law is to be a rational enterprise that treats its citizens as responsible agents, such 'opposing political and ideological reasons' must be heard: There must be space for dissenters to try to persuade others of their opposing values, and thus to change the law. We could also imagine a legal system in which the courts provided part of this space: in which courts had not only to apply the law, but to justify it to the defendant, to attend to any opposing view he wanted to offer, and to acquit him if persuaded by that view. In such a system, a criminal trial would be more closely analogous to moral criticism (see Duff 1986: 47–54, 135–9). For if I criticise another's conduct, I must be ready to listen to her justification of what she did, even if it appeals to values other than those on which my criticism is based, and be willing to be persuaded by her that I was wrong. It is also, however, quite consistent with the demand that citizens be respected as responsible agents to support a system which, like ours, maintains a clearer division of labour between courts and legislature.

Such a division of labour, according to which law is made for a community by its elected legislature and is applied by its courts, reflects a familiar conception of representative democracy, and the 'rule of law' values of consistency and certainty. It is not for unelected (and so not democratically answerable) judges or juries to make the law from scratch; to approach each case as if the rightness or wrongness of the defendant's alleged conduct was an entirely open question. It is, rather, for the community's elected representatives to specify general criteria of rightness and wrongness; and it is in that legislative forum, not in the courts, that dissenters must find a hearing for their alternative 'view of the just social order' (see Norrie 1993: 45). Furthermore, if courts did have so extensive a power to accept justifications offered by defendants, the law would then become radically uncertain and inconsistent.[28]

(This is not to argue that civil disobedience, even under a just legal system, can never be *morally* justified. One could consistently believe that some types of civil disobedience are morally justified, but also that they should nonetheless be punished, because the courts should not be given general discretion to decide which [if any] acts of disobedience are really justified. Note too that on accounts of punishment which insist that if punishment is to respect individual autonomy it must consist essentially in a rational communication of censure, a civil disobedient's punishment is [like any offender's] justified only if it leaves her genuinely free to maintain her view that she was right in what she did [see Duff 1996b: 50, 54].)

Norrie might reply that this division of labour between courts and legislature is indeed central to the ideology of our criminal law; but that, given the character of our legislative processes, it amounts not to the provision of a separate forum in which 'opposing political and ideological reasons' could be heard, but to silencing them. Our criminal law is the result of a 'long political and social process of . . . imposing one definition of lawful and unlawful conduct on a resisting populace.' It reflects, not the agreed values of 'a consensual society', but 'intense social conflict': a conflict that was forcibly won (not rationally resolved) by those with the power to impose their own political views. The law's formal exclusion of motive is one aspect of its function as *excluding* 'competing moral and political views', to *impose* 'one particular, but contestable, moral view of the just social order' (1993: 45).

The law does indeed, in virtue of its character as law, 'impose' one 'contestable moral view of the just social order', and thus also 'excludes' others. It declares certain kinds of conduct to be wrong or required, certain justifications to be available or unavailable; it claims authority for those declarations as being binding even on those citizens who dissent from their content. But that is so far to say simply that the law is law; and that in a society in which there are conflicting views about issues that fall within the proper scope of the law, it must 'impose' (i.e., give legally authoritative status to) one view and 'exclude' others. However, this is certainly not an adequate reply to Norrie, because his remarks raise two further important issues about the line of argument sketched here.

First, it clearly matters how the 'counter-claims' that the law 'excludes' are 'defeated' – in particular, how far they are defeated through a political process in which they receive a fair hearing, or defeated because never properly heard. A legal system that refuses dissident defendants an opportunity to argue their political views in the courtroom, while still claiming to treat them as responsible citizens of a democracy, depends for its legitimacy on there being another, political forum in which those arguments can be made and heard. For the court must be able to say to a defendant that *this* is not the forum in which her dissent is to be heard – and that she has an obligation to obey the existing law until she can reform it in the appropriate forum (see Duff 1986: 136–9). But if no such genuine forum is available to her, that claim loses its legitimating force.

This raises a range of questions in political philosophy, about the structures and procedures of a properly democratic society. What kinds of institution and legislative process must exist if a society is to count as democratic – as a society in which all citizens have proper access to fora in which they can secure a fair hearing for their views? I will not embark on these questions here. All we need note now is that insofar as such democratic structures do not exist, an essential precondition for the justice of not allowing defendants 'to argue the moral or political rights and wrongs of [their] action in the courtroom' is lacking. This does not mean that the law would then be 'contradictory'; it is to say that an important precondition of its legitimacy would be lacking (see section 5).

The second issue concerns consensus and conflict. If the law is to claim to impose obligations on the citizens, rather than merely oblige them to obey its demands by the threat of punishment, it must claim to offer them good reasons to *accept* its demands.[29] In the case of the criminal law, those reasons will sometimes refer to the law's content: Most obviously in relation to *mala in se* on whose wrongfulness there is general consensus, the law claims to prohibit wrongful conduct because it is wrong; and that is a reason it offers the citizens for accepting its demands. But those reasons must also refer to the procedures through which law is made: The claim must be that the citizens should accept the law because it results from some appropriate legislative procedure. This reason is obviously relevant to *mala prohibita,* or to issues on which there is no such consensus: The claim must be that citizens should accept the law even when they do not, independently of its status as law, agree with its content, because it results from an appropriate process. But such procedural issues are also relevant to what are generally agreed to be *mala in se:* If the law is to have a proper claim on the citizens' obedience, it must be able to claim not just that the conduct it prohibits is wrong, but also that it has been properly made a *criminal* wrong.

Now the mere fact that a citizen does not accept, or see herself as legitimately bound by, the content of the law or the procedures by which it came to be law, the fact that there is conflict, rather than complete consensus, on such a matter, does not undermine the law's claim to obligate her. But if she is denied any real voice or standing in the procedures by which the law is formed, that claim is undermined. What the law must claim, in claiming to obligate her, is that this law is *her* law as a member of the society: that she should accept it as her own. In societies that do not even purport to be democratic, the claim might simply be that she should accept the law as properly declared by higher authority. In purportedly democratic societies, however, it can be said to be her law only if she had (or could have had, had she chosen) a suitable role in its formulation. If she is denied any such role, the courts cannot legitimately say that it is her law, which binds her and which she ought to accept.

We thus face again the question of the preconditions of the legitimacy of the law in a supposedly democratic society. But we should note here a further way in which such preconditions may be involved in the legal process: when, given the availability of a motive-based defence, the 'moral rights and wrongs' of a defendant's action will to some extent be argued in court.

A court's judgment that a motive-based defence does or does not succeed must depend on a value judgment. For example, was the threat under which the defendant acted so serious that even a 'reasonable' person, one with an appropriate respect for the law and a proper degree of courage, would not have resisted it (see Duff 1993: 350–61)? Did the defendant's motive for damaging another's property, or for carrying an offensive weapon, constitute a 'reasonable' or 'lawful' excuse (see text at note 17)? These value judgments are constrained by the law: Statutes and common-law doctrines set limits on the kinds of motive that could provide a defence, and the kinds of context in which they can do so.[30] But within such constraints there is a value judgment for the court to make, and so also an argument about values for the defendant to offer. Now a court's judgment cannot claim to be legally authoritative if it amounts merely to saying something like '*I* [as judge or juror] do not think this excuse is reasonable.' If it is to have authority, as a legal judgment on the defendant's conduct, it must be justifiably expressible as '*We* [the society to which this defendant belongs, and by whose values she is bound] do not regard this excuse as reasonable'; so we must ask what is required if courts' judgments are to claim such authority.

Ideally, we might say, the judgment would be one with which any citizen would (come to) agree: For the law aspires to be the law of the community – to embody values in which the community agrees, and to apply them in ways that the community will see as appropriate. We must then recognise that such an ideal is far from being actualised: that courts often cannot claim to be expressing or applying what are in that ideal sense the values of the whole community. That does not show, by itself, that their judgments lack authority: For they could still claim that those who disagree are *wrong;* and that members of a democratic community should also be ready, for the sake of the rule of law, to accept some judgments with which they disagree. The question will be, however: What conditions should be satisfied for such claims to be acceptable? I return to this later; but we should first look at another kind of case that Norrie discusses.

Crimes Motivated by Need

This is the example of crime, in particular property crime, motivated by 'acute personal need.' Norrie suggests that the denial of the relevance of such motivation to criminal liability flows historically from the ruling classes' need to sustain the 'rule of private property' against the demands of the poor (1993: 39–40).

An impoverished single parent steals clothes from a supermarket for her children. She is convicted of theft: She clearly intended to deprive the clothes' owner of them permanently; her appropriation of the clothes (hiding them in her bag) was, as she surely realised, 'dishonest', by 'ordinary standards' (Theft Act 1968, ss. 1–2; *Ghosh* [1982] 2 All ER 689); her motive is not one that the law recognises as providing a defence – any sympathy the court has for her plight or motives is relevant only at the sentencing stage. But, critical theorists argue, by thus abstracting her action from its concrete social context, the law contradicts its pretensions to do individual justice.

Now many people would no doubt feel rightly uneasy at her trial, conviction, and punishment, however light that punishment. We should, however, distinguish different grounds for such an uneasiness.

First, it might be argued that her theft was *justified* as a matter of necessity.[31] Second, it might be argued that though her theft was not justified, it should be *excused,* because of 'duress of circumstances' or 'economic duress' (see, e.g., Hudson 1995: 71). Both these arguments appeal to existing legal doctrines. They claim that the principles embodied in those doctrines require such a defendant to be exempt from liability: either because she rationally chose the clearly lesser of two unavoidable evils, or because the pressures on her were such that we cannot honestly say that she freely broke a law which she had the capacity and a fair opportunity to obey.

Critical theorists like Norrie, however, do not seek to persuade us that such already recognised defences should be extended to cover such cases; they are not in the business of such (relatively) modest legal reforms. Rather, they note how courts actually resist any such extension of the defence of 'necessity'; explain that they are bound to do so, given the law's function of 'protect[ing] private property and particular social interests' (Norrie 1993: 40); and argue that the law's function as a 'State instrumentality' thus contradicts its purported concern to do 'justice to individuals by punishing them only for their voluntary acts' (Norrie 1993: 169).[32]

Two arguments might be used against allowing such extensions to the necessity defence; the question will be whether they are consistent with the law's structuring principles. First, that the state makes adequate welfare provisions for the needy[33]: When such provisions exist, citizens should seek assistance from them, and will not be allowed to invade the property rights of others to meet their own needs.[34] This argument need not involve the judgment, by the court, that those welfare provisions are adequate; judges might well think them inadequate. The argument is again one about the proper division of responsibility between courts and government: It is for the government to decide what level of welfare provision is adequate.[35]

The second argument appeals to the effects, or implications, of allowing such a defence. As Lord Denning notoriously said (in a case concerning homeless squatters), 'If homelessness were once admitted as a defence to trespass, no-one's house could be safe. Necessity would open a door which no man could shut. . . . The plea would be an excuse for all sorts of wrongdoing.'[36]

On one reading this argument appeals to the *implications* of allowing such a defence in the instant case: that to do this would commit the courts to allowing it in so many cases that no one's property would be secure. On another reading (suggested by Lord Denning's reference to 'all sorts of wrongdoing'), it concerns the predictable *effects* of allowing such a defence in a particular, sympathy-arousing case: that this would 'open a door' to too many *spurious* appeals to such a defence, which prosecutors would find it hard to disprove; it would encourage people to invade others' property without adequate excuse.

It might seem that, on either reading, this argument plays into the critic's hands. For on either reading a defendant who might well (considered by herself) have a defence that the law ought to accept is to be convicted because to acquit her would have damaging and (in the court's eyes) unacceptable consequences for social order and the protection of private property. But this is to admit that there are defendants whose economic deprivation is such that they ought not in justice to be convicted, but who must be convicted if the law is to be an effective instrument of social control: which implies that the demands of individual justice come into irresoluble contradiction with those of 'political utility' (see Norrie 1993: 169).

Now the first argument is anyway sufficient by itself, in terms of the law's internal logic, to justify the defendant's conviction in my example: in which case such examples reveal no contradiction in the law, or its ideology. However, even if courts need (or think they need) to rely on the second argument as well, it does not have to be interpreted in a way that allows the critical theorist to cry 'contradiction.' It invites such a cry if the interests that are to be defended are those of people *other* than the defendant, of classes *other* than her own; which is indeed how critical theorists interpret the argument. But we could instead read it as a version of 'Suppose everyone did that?' Suppose that anyone could get away with theft, or trespassing on other legally recognised rights, by offering such a defence (get away with it legally, or by a spurious appeal to such a defence): You, the defendant, would not regard that as acceptable (for your own interests could then also be injured); so you must be convicted. That is, the social order that the law is to defend, and that it can defend (so this argument claims) only by rejecting such a defence, is one that benefits the defendant herself; the interests to be protected include her own interests (for instance, in whatever property she has, or could hope to have in the future).

As thus interpreted, the argument does still recognise a tension between the demands of individual justice in this particular case, and the demands of the preservation of 'social order.' What is being said to the defendant, however, is not that she must be convicted to protect the interests of *others* (interests in which she herself has no share), but that the law must demand that she refrain from theft, even in her unfortunate situation, for the sake of a social order in which *she* has a significant stake.

I do not suggest that this argument should satisfy us. It does, however, meet the charge of contradiction; so we must look elsewhere for the grounds for our appropriate unease at her conviction.

Both arguments discussed so far presuppose that this defendant is bound by the law. She has an obligation to obey the law, and can properly be called to account for (to justify or excuse, or accept condemnation for) her conduct by the courts: The question is whether she should be able to avoid conviction by justifying or excusing her conduct. If she is bound by the law, however, the grounds on which the courts would, predictably, convict her seem persuasive. But could it be argued instead that she is not bound by the law, or is not bound as stringently as others who are not thus disadvantaged (see, e.g., Hudson 1995: 68–9)?

Suppose we see her situation (her poverty; the lack of any other means of maintaining any minimally adequate standard of living) as a result not of her own culpable failings, but of serious, persisting injustices that she has suffered: the systematic injustices of economic and political structures that deny her (and many others) any fair share in the substantial political and economic benefits that others enjoy, or a fair opportunity to share in them; which deny her the support, or access to the resources, necessary to lead a tolerable life, by the standards current in our society; which offer her only wholly inadequate welfare provisions. This would be to see the needs that motivated her theft as the result of serious injustices that she has suffered – not, perhaps, directly at the hands of the criminal law (though the law would perpetuate those injustices if it convicted her), but at the hands of the society whose law it is. How then could we still insist that she has that stringent obligation to obey the law which supposedly lies on all citizens of this society?

In its strongest version such an argument claims that she has no moral obligation to obey the law as such, because an essential precondition of that obligation is lacking. The law has no justified claim on her obedience, because it can properly claim to bind only those who are genuinely treated as members of the society whose law it is (or, on a different model, those who have a fair share in the benefits of the society, and thus an obligation to accept those burdens involved in obeying the law). Someone who is denied the respect, the benefits and opportunities, that should be accorded to members of the society cannot be bound by its laws.

Weaker versions of the argument are available – for example, that such a person's general obligation to obey the law is weakened, but not totally negated, by the injustices she suffers (a weakened obligation being one that is more easily overridden, for instance by her family's need); or that, while she still has some general obligation to obey most of the law (which helps maintain the social order that benefits her as well as others), she has no, or a weaker, obligation to obey any laws that are directly implicated in the injustices she suffers. On the latter view, she would not have an obligation (or so strong an obligation) to obey whatever laws are directly involved in inflicting injustice on her (the laws defining and penalising social security fraud, for instance); or laws that help sustain the unjust structures under which she suffers, or that she must break in order to secure a tolerable life (most obviously, the law of theft).

(Note that on any version of this argument, the focus is not on the moral rightness or wrongness of her actions viewed independently of the criminal law, nor on their excusability: We need not believe that her theft was morally justified, or excusable. What matters is, rather, the claim that she is not bound by, and should therefore not be judged, convicted, or punished by, the law.)

Any adequate examination of this argument would require thorough discussion of the conditions under which the citizen has any kind of moral obligation to obey the law (see Finnis 1980: 354, 359–61, on the different possible sources of such an obligation); of the implications of the non-satisfaction of such conditions (see Finnis 1980: ch. 12); of whether one can talk of degrees of (stringency of) obligation to obey the law; of how far we can talk of obligations to obey some but not all of the law. In relation to the first of these tasks, we can distinguish a minimalist from a more ambitious account of the preconditions of obligation. On the minimalist view (see, e.g., Davis 1989), a citizen has an obligation to obey the law so long as she is better off under it than she would be if there were no law at all – a condition that is probably satisfied for all members of our own societies. On a more ambitious view, more than this is required – at least the partial, if not the complete, satisfaction of much more stringent demands that flow either from values internal to the very idea of law (for instance, the demand that the law treat those bound by it as rational and responsible agents; see Duff 1986: ch. 3) or from independent conceptions of justice: To the extent that such more stringent demands are not met, the obligation to obey (all or some of) the law is weakened or, in the end, negated.

I will not pursue such arguments here; my interest is in another (though related) argument. What should worry us about the conviction and punishment of the impoverished shoplifter is not, I suggest, the question of whether from some detached standpoint she can be said to have an obligation to obey the law. It is whether we, and the courts that act in our name, have the moral standing to judge her. (By 'we', I mean all those, including likely readers of this book, who do not suffer the kinds of economic and political injustice that she, I am supposing, suffers; those who are not excluded, as she is excluded, from the substantial social and economic benefits, or from participation in the political life, of the society.)

Can we, or the courts that act in our name, honestly say to her, as the law must be able to say to those it claims to bind, something like: 'As a member of this community, sharing in its life and goods, you have an obligation to obey these laws: laws which are your laws; which serve the common good of this community, and thus your good as one of its members'? Can we, or the courts, honestly say to her, as we must be able to say if we are to claim the moral standing to call her to account as a member of the community to which we and she belong, that we have collectively shown her the respect and concern which fellow membership of a community involves, so that we can now hold her to be answerable to us?

(This argument is distinct from the previous one, about whether such a defendant has any obligation to obey the law, if the question of whether she has any such obligation is distinct from the question of whether her fellow citizens have the standing to call her legally to account for her actions; if those questions are not distinct [and I suspect they may not be], it is another way of expressing the argument about her obligation to obey the law.)

We can reach this same point by looking at the idea of 'abstraction' – another target for 'critical' theorists (see Hudson 1987, 1993, as well as Norrie 1993, *passim*); and at the related idea of 'normal' conditions, and 'normal' agents.

4. 'Abstraction' and Normality

The law's 'abstract individualism', Norrie argues, abstracts the individual agent from the concrete social context that gave rise to his crime – and by reference to which we must, if we are to do individual justice, understand and judge his conduct. The criminal trial thus consists, not in a real attempt to judge a defendant's conduct in its appropriate and concrete particularity, but in an artificial process that is focused selectively upon one aspect of his conduct: the aspect that relates to the law's abstract definitions of crimes.

This is not to say that 'abstraction' as such is objectionable: We must hope that judges will ignore – abstract the defendant from – those aspects of his character and situation that are irrelevant to his criminal liability. The objection is rather that the abstraction which is intrinsic to the criminal process is a serious distortion, in terms of the law's supposed concern with individual justice and culpability, because it excludes factors that should be relevant to a well-founded judgment of culpability. Similarly, critics of the 'just deserts' model of sentencing, when it is used as the basis for strict sentencing rules that sharply constrain judicial discretion, argue that a sentencing process cannot do justice to individual defendants if it attends only to the factors that the sentencing rules allow to be relevant (see, e.g., Hudson 1987; Norrie 1991, 1993: ch. 10; Carlen 1989; Morris and Tonry 1990: ch. 4; contrast von Hirsch 1992, 1993).

Our criminal process does clearly involve the kind of 'abstraction' to which these critics object. The law defines certain kinds of conduct as being normally criminal, when done by a normal agent in a normal situation, regardless of the particularities of the agent or her situation (including her motives); it recognises only a limited range of conditions, of the agent or her situation, that count as sufficiently 'abnormal' to exempt her from liability for doing a normally criminal act. A 'normal' agent (who does not satisfy any of the strict legal criteria of non-responsibility, such as infancy or insanity) who acts in a way defined as being normally criminal is guilty of a crime, unless she can cite some recognised abnormal factor that constitutes a defence – a general defence, such as duress; or one that figures in the definition of the particular crime (such as having a 'lawful excuse' for damaging another's property). Within the broadly defined bounds of normality of agents and their situations, the law disregards individual particularities.

Some abstraction of this kind, some such idea of 'normality', is not, perhaps, a necessary feature of criminal law as such: One could imagine systems whose courts engaged in much more particularised and context-sensitive judgments on defendants' actions, unconstrained by general rules determining what kinds of action they must hold to be right or wrong, justified or excusable (see text at note 38). But it is a necessary feature of a system like ours, which provides general definitions of offences and defences that its courts must then apply; and whose courts are not to pry too deeply into the private realm of its citizens' lives (see text at note 24). The courts of such a system must be able to judge defendants and their actions under general categories of normally criminal conduct, and to judge them as being for the most part normal agents in normal situations.

The concept of 'normality' obviously has a strong normative dimension here. A 'normal' agent is one who can properly be expected to understand and respect the law, and to be guided by the reasons for action that the law provides. A 'normal' situation is one in which such normal agents can properly be expected to refrain from kinds of conduct that the law defines as criminal. A type of action is 'normally' criminal if it is of a kind that can properly be held to be wrong in normal situations, and that other citizens should be able to expect not to suffer while they go about their normal lives. But 'normality' also has an important statistical dimension. Most (adult) agents must be 'normal'; and the 'abnormal' situations, in which a normal agent could avoid liability for a normally criminal action, need to be statistically unusual. For only then can the law operate practicably as a system of rules or norms that ordinary citizens can be expected to understand and obey (and expect others to obey), and that courts can be expected to understand and apply.

The applicability of these three related notions of 'normality' – normal agents, normal situations, normally criminal actions – is thus a precondition of the practicability *and* the justice of a system of law like our own. If the law is to be effective in its declaratory, action-guiding, and adjudicative-punitive roles; and if its practical efficacy is to be consistent with the demands of justice, in that it treats citizens with a predictable consistency that does not unduly ignore relevant differences between them: It must be able to define certain kinds of action as normally (i.e., except in statistically and normatively abnormal situations) wrong – either as *mala in se,* whose wrongness citizens can be expected to recognise independently of the law; or as *mala prohibita,* which are justifiably prohibited for the sake of some common good. These must be kinds of conduct that (statistically and normatively) normal citizens could reasonably be required to refrain from in (statistically and normatively) normal situations: kinds of conduct that they could normally be properly condemned for committing, and from which other citizens should normally be able to expect to be safe.

This requires there to be a citizen body most of whose members, whatever the differences may be in their individual characters or capacities, are able, and willing, to grasp the reasons for action that the law offers, and to guide their conduct by those reasons. It requires too that we can talk, without undue distortion, of the 'normal' lives of such citizens: Whatever the differences in their economic, social, or political standing, in their power and resources, or in the ways of life they want or are able to lead, we can talk of the normal conditions of their lives, in which those kinds of conduct defined by the law as (normally) criminal are indeed wrong. We must be able to say, for example, that under normal circumstances it is wrong to kill or injure another person, or to deprive her of her property without her consent, or to drive at a speed faster than that which the law defines as safe.

Those normal circumstances will of course include circumstances in which people might be strongly tempted to engage in such conduct, and we realise that some people will (through no fault of their own) be more liable to such temptations than others. Someone who is relatively poor will be more tempted to steal the food or clothes that others can simply buy; someone who is homeless will be more tempted to break into a house to find shelter than will those who have homes of their own; nor need the concerns (for food or shelter for oneself and one's family) and circumstances (poverty or homelessness) that generate such temptation reflect any fault in those thus tempted to do what the law prohibits. There are, more generally, various kinds of fear or pressure to which people are subject that might motivate criminal conduct – including, for instance, 'fear of economic ills, fear of displeasing others' (Williams 1961: 751).[37] The law will, however, insist of many such pressures and fears that they are features of 'normal' life which normal citizens should be expected to resist, or to deal with other than by breaking the law.

Such an insistence involves various presuppositions that help to distinguish such 'normal' pressures from the 'abnormal' pressures that can ground such defences as duress or necessity: We should note two here. First, there are presuppositions about the kinds of burden that normal citizens, with a 'reasonable' regard for the law and the values it expresses, should be prepared to accept rather than break the law. Second, there are presuppositions about the availability of adequate and legally sanctioned remedies for the kinds of harm by which citizens may (normally) be threatened: about, for example, the availability of adequate social services for the poor and the homeless, and of adequate legal protections for employees.

Against such a background, of the 'normal' conditions of social life, the kinds of pressure or threat that are parts of that normal life (and the kinds of support on which any citizen can draw to meet those pressures and threats), such defences as duress and necessity will quite properly be available only when some abnormal pressure or threat irrupts into a citizen's normal life. There will be room for controversy about the precise scope of such defences: But they will not have that kind of open-ended character which critical theorists think that their logic requires, since they are precisely concerned to deal with *abnormal* situations. The courts will no doubt say to an impoverished thief, or to the homeless squatter, that they were not faced with the kind of sudden emergency threatening life or safety, for which no lawful remedy is available, which might drive a normal person with a reasonable regard for the law to break the law; their situation was not that abnormal – others are poor, others lose their homes; and the state makes reasonable provision to help them through the social services.

If these three connected notions of normality are applicable, if these presuppositions are satisfied, we can hope to justify the kind of 'abstraction' that the criminal law involves. In thus abstracting agents and their actions from their specific contexts, the law is of course a very 'blunt instrument for the allocation of fault' (Norrie 1993: 40), and excludes from the courts consideration of moral and political questions that citizens will rightly want to argue. But it can still claim that its allocations of fault are (roughly) just; and that there are other appropriate fora in which those questions can be argued. Furthermore, as Norrie insists (1993: 223–5), such abstraction also serves to *protect* individual citizens against the otherwise over-intrusive power of the state. For if the scope of the criminal law is limited (and nothing I have said argues against the view that it should be much more restricted than it now is), and if courts are not to delve too deeply into defendants' further motives, then citizens will normally be able to avoid the coercive attentions of the law, and of those who want to improve their moral condition.

We can see the force of this last point by noting the dangers of oppression and injustice involved in the kinds of 'informal justice' that some radical theorists favour. A system of local, informal, and community-based courts might aim to do more context-sensitive, more particularised, and thus more appropriate justice to individual members of the community: Rather than judging them under crude, general categories of criminality, ignoring the particular concrete contexts from which their actions flowed, such courts could aim to achieve an appropriate understanding of, and judgment on, their actions in all their concrete particularity. But such courts, unconstrained by the abstractions that characterise our own legal process, could easily become instruments for the serious oppression of 'deviants.'[38]

The success of such a rationale for the 'abstractions' that our criminal law involves, however, depends upon the extent to which the presuppositions I have noted are satisfied: which brings us back to my suggestion at the end of the last section, that critical scrutiny should focus, not on the alleged internal contradictions of the law, but on the extent to which the preconditions for its legitimacy are satisfied.

For, the critic can argue, even if the notion of normal life and normal conditions does not require anything approaching equality of political or economic power or resources; even if one can argue that in a society in which such power or resources are unequally distributed, all are still equally bound by the law: Some kinds of radical, persistent inequality must undermine this notion of normality – and the legal structures that presuppose it. Can we (and again the question arises of who 'we' are) honestly say to the impoverished single parent, or to the homeless person, that they are full members of the community, whose common good the law serves; that their suffering is an aspect of that normal life which we all share, and which they are expected to deal with within the law; that the welfare state anyway makes adequate provision for them; that they are therefore obligated to obey the law which protects them as it protects all citizens?

The point is not that poverty, or homelessness, or the kinds of condition that might provoke riots (see Norrie 1993: 38, 170–1), should be recognised as 'abnormal' conditions that (like the kinds of condition that can now ground defences of duress and necessity) can render some kinds of normally criminal conduct legally justifiable or excusable: Those conditions are all too normal for too many people. The claim is rather that the persistence of such conditions, the failure of the state (and of those who benefit from its economic and political structure) to take such conditions seriously, make it questionable whether those suffering under such conditions are truly obligated to obey the law that they break; or whether 'we' have the moral standing to judge or condemn them.

But how powerful are these arguments? What implications do they have, for the law or for our relationship to it?

5. Preconditions, not Contradictions

I have argued that critical theorists who claim to identify 'contradictions' within the criminal law, and so to expose it as lacking in rationality and principle, have missed their target. If we attend to the law's internal structure, we find conflicts of value: conflicts to which there might be no 'right answers' in that different people, arguing within the framework of the law's values and aims, can reasonably find different ways of dealing with them. There is also (and unsurprisingly) controversy about the content of the law, about what values should structure it, about how we should interpret the values or principles that we agree should structure it: controversies that might be in fact and in principle rationally irresoluble, in that we may not be able either to hope that they will be in fact be resolved by agreement, or to claim that they would be resolved if only everyone thought them through carefully and rationally. The activities of courts and legislatures (like those of any human institution) often also reveal failures of reason or principle: decisions that cannot be justified in terms of the values on which they supposedly depend, and that we might reasonably suspect to be motivated (not, perhaps, consciously) by concerns that are not legitimated by the law's own principles.

All of this is only to say, however, that the criminal law is a human practice, not an abstract system of thought, such as a system of formal logic (see section 2). That is to say, first, that we must not judge the law by criteria of rationality or of consistency that are appropriate only to other modes of thought. As Aristotle argued, we should not expect more precision than our subject matter permits (*Nicomachean Ethics,* 10941b11–14): We should not expect the practice to rest upon a set of principles (themselves justified in some *a priori* way that frees them from any possibility of controversy) from which we can derive, in a formally watertight way, determinate answers to every problem. Second, it is to say that to claim that a system is 'rational' or 'principled' is not just (or primarily) to comment on its actual achievements, since one can consistently admit that it is in practice riddled with confusion and uncertainty: It is rather to to comment on its genuine aspirations; and to express confidence in the point of treating it, and its practitioners, in accordance with those aspirations.

It might seem so far that I am simply reasserting that 'liberal' faith which critical theorists claim to undermine, that possibility of the 'rational reconstruction' of the criminal law which 'liberal' theorists, like MacCormick and Dworkin, purvey. However, first, I am not keen to engage in debate about whether my position is 'liberal': There is sufficient confusion among both liberals and their critics about what 'liberalism' amounts to (see Dworkin 1986: 440–1); and even if many theorists of 'rational reconstruction' should count as 'liberals', that is not to say that the practice which they seek to reconstruct must be interpreted in liberal terms (indeed, I have appealed to certain communitarian ideas and values). Second, I have argued that there is room (and a need) for a radically critical approach to the criminal law – but one focused on its preconditions rather than on its internal (lack of) logic. For, I have argued, the criminal law, as a supposedly principled enterprise that seeks to articulate and enforce certain essential duties of citizenship, depends on two crucial, related preconditions: that it can claim to be binding on all those to whom it is applied; and that it (its officials and those in whose name those officials speak) can claim the moral standing to apply the law to all those on whom it is supposedly binding.

One could express these preconditions in liberal terms, perhaps as concerning the normative plausibility of a social contract whose terms the courts are to apply. Can one plausibly see all those whom the law purports to bind as parties to a social contract whose terms are tolerably fair (or not intolerably unfair)? Can those by whom or in whose name the contract's punitive clauses are applied plausibly claim to have done their (quasi-contractual) duties by those against whom those clauses are applied? Or one could express them in more communitarian terms, as concerning the existence of a genuine community whose laws the courts can apply to those who are its members. Can it be plausibly said that all those who are judged by the criminal law are full members of the community, bound by the laws that serve its and their common good? Can the courts, and those in whose name they speak, claim to have treated those who are judged as full members of the community?

I suggested that it is at least not clear whether such preconditions are satisfied in our own societies: but that even if they are not, this would not show (as critical theorists argue) that the law is internally 'contradictory.' It would show that the law was 'contradictory' (in a way related to that argued by critical theorists) *if* it could be argued that, in terms of its own internal values and structure, the law should recognise the failure of such preconditions as grounds for acquitting a defendant for whom they were not satisfied: But such an argument is not plausible.

The argument would need to be that a legal system committed, as ours is meant to be, to a respect for individual responsibility (to doing 'individual justice through the operation of a fault requirement' [Norrie 1993: 37]) must therefore be committed to making the satisfaction of the kinds of precondition that I have noted a condition of criminal liability – that the law should recognise, and the courts adjudicate, a formal defence like 'lack of obligation to obey the law', or a claim that the court lacks the standing to judge the defendant. Critical theorists could then argue that to allow such a defence would undermine the law's function as a mode of 'social control' (particularly since such control is most needed in relation to the kinds of people who would be likely to claim such a defence): In a society as permeated as ours by systematic injustice, courts could not serve their role as 'State instrumentalities' if they recognised such a defence, although consistency would require them to do so.

However, on the account I have sketched, the courts can properly say that it is not their responsibility to judge the extent to which such preconditions are satisfied, any more than it is their responsibility to allow defendants 'to argue the moral or political rights and wrongs' of their action in the courtroom (Norrie 1993: 41; see pp. 179–82 above) or to judge the adequacy of the state's welfare provisions; there are (courts must assume there to be) other fora in which such moral and political issues are to be argued. This is not to say that those who administer the legal system can just close their eyes to such questions: As citizens, and as moral agents, they must indeed ask themselves whether they are administering a just and legitimate system of law. Rather, it is to say that such questions should be understood as questions about whether they can properly serve this system – not as questions *within* their official activities.

That is why my argument that it is at least doubtful whether the law's preconditions (preconditions that reflect values internal to the law itself) are satisfied is distinct from a critical theorist's claim that the law is internally 'contradictory.' The law might well be internally as principled and coherent as one could expect a human institution to be; and I argued that in dealing with the relevance of motives to criminal liability it is. But its legitimacy, its authority, in relation to some of those whom it claims to obligate might still be questioned, on the ground that its preconditions are not satisfied.[39]

It might still seem that my disagreement with critical theorists is trivial: We agree both that something is radically amiss with the law, and (perhaps) roughly about what it is; we disagree only about whether the fault lines lie within the law itself or between the law and its preconditions. But, even if I am as pessimistic as they are about the principled viability of a system of law like our own, the difference between us matters. For, first, it matters that critical theorists aim at the right target: partly because if they do not, it is too easy for opponents to answer them by showing (as I have shown in one context) that the law *is* internally principled, and rational. Second, even if (as they and I agree) any changes of the kind that would be needed to render the law adequately justified cannot begin with the law (they must begin with the conditions that undermine the law's claim to legitimate authority), there remains the question of how far the law can be seen as a (potential) instrument for good. If it is contradictory, the answer must surely be 'Not far' (though we have noted that Norrie, unlike other critical theorists, insists on the positive values of liberal law); if it is not contradictory, we might have more hope for it.

However, though I have raised some questions about the extent to which the law's preconditions are satisfied, I have not offered determinate answers to those questions, nor indeed any account of just how stringent those preconditions should be taken to be.

As far as the obligation to obey the law is concerned, I distinguished minimalist from more ambitious accounts of its preconditions (see p. 188 above). On a minimalist view it need only be shown that anyone who is supposedly obligated by the law benefits from its existence, in that she is better off than she would be were there no law at all; such a condition appears more than adequately satisfied in our own societies. This is not to say that, on such a view, there is nothing seriously wrong with the law. Minimalists can admit that the law bears more harshly, and unjustly, on some groups than on others; that those economic, political, and social structures that it helps sustain treat some groups unjustly; that such groups have little or no effective power to make their voices heard, within the courts or within the political process. But it is to argue that, because the law still gives even such disadvantaged groups substantial benefits, they have an obligation to obey it. That minimal condition is, however, surely too modest: The stringent obligation to obey the law, which is to justify punishing those who flout it, should surely be founded on something more than this. The question then, however, is: how much more?

As far as the courts', or 'our', moral standing to judge defendants is concerned, I suggested that the question is not whether from some detached standpoint their actions are justifiable or excusable. Nor is the question whether we can be sure that we would not act as this defendant acted had we been in her situation: We can sometimes justifiably condemn a person for doing what we admit we would probably have done in her situation.[40] Nor is it relevant (even if it is true) that others, no less disadvantaged than this defendant, resisted the temptation to break the law. Rather, the question is who, if anyone, has the moral standing to make such a judgment on her: Do we have the kind of relationship to her, within the political and legal structures under which we live, that allows us (or the courts that speak for us) to judge her?

Here again we can distinguish a minimalist from a more ambitious answer to the question. On a minimalist view the most that is needed to give us such moral standing is that we have not (directly or maliciously) denied her such rights or benefits as the law assigns her (assuming that the law itself satisfies the minimalist conditions of legitimacy). On a more ambitious view, we must (collectively or institutionally, if not individually or personally) have treated her as a member of the community in a richer sense than this: We must have treated her as a full and respected participant in our common life. For insofar as that condition is not satisfied, we might think that a proper response to her offence is not condemnation and punishment (however punishment is understood) but rather a serious attempt to help her to secure that proper standing in the community which she has been denied (and whose denial helped to create the situation in which she offended).

But how far (if at all) beyond the minimalist conditions should we move? How far must a more ambitious set of preconditions be satisfied before we can think that we are justified in enforcing, or in consenting to the enforcement of, the criminal law against those who are in various ways seriously, unjustly disadvantaged? Here we reach a point at which we can speak only personally. We can point out the various kinds of serious injustice that raise the question of whether the law's preconditions are adequately satisfied; and we might hope to persuade others that such injustices do raise this question. Any answer to it, however, involves a balancing of admitted and serious injustices against what must also be recognised as significant benefits (including benefits of justice) in which even the most severely disadvantaged do to some extent share – a balancing that we must each do for ourselves.

Nor can we expect to be able to offer one general answer to this question: to be able to say, of the law as a whole, that its preconditions either are or are not satisfied in relation to all citizens. Different offenders will be differently situated in relation to such preconditions. Those who must wonder whether they have the standing to judge offenders will themselves be related in significantly different ways to the law, to those underlying structures that provide (or fail to provide) its preconditions, and to different offenders; consider the difference, for instance, between a harsh employer who condemns his workers for petty pilfering, and an impoverished person burgled by someone who is no worse off. And different kinds of crime will raise the question in different ways and with differing degrees of urgency. The kind of theft I described in section 3, or social security frauds committed by desperate people suffering under inadequate welfare provisions, raise the question clearly and urgently, as do the kinds of vandalism or riotous violence that we can see as the product of serious social deprivation and injustice: But other kinds of crime (brutal rapes, maliciously violent attacks on defenceless victims) do not raise it in the same way.

My aim in this chapter, has not, however, been to answer the questions that, I have argued, must be raised about the preconditions of the law's legitimacy. It has, rather, been to show that the critical theorists' charges of 'contradiction' are misdirected; but that they do point us towards these serious questions.[41]

Notes

1 Though Norrie focusses, as I will also focus, on the modern English criminal law (and though his emphasis on the need for a historical understanding of law suggests that he would not want to claim that *any* system of criminal law will be necessarily contradictory), his arguments suggest that he would at least expect to identify similar contradictions in any modern capitalist system. It is worth noting too that in his chapter in this volume he prefers to talk of 'antinomies' rather than of 'contradictions': but I will focus on his use of the idea of 'contradiction' in *Crime, Reason and History.*

2 A second expanded edition was published in 1995; page references are to the second edition.

3 The scare quotes round 'critical' (which I will not tediously repeat hereafter) are meant to remind us that, while the notion of a 'critical' inquiry has a particular meaning in the Critical Legal Studies movement, proponents of that movement are not the only theorists who engage in a critical study of law; see Finnis 1987: 145.

4 For a useful classification of the elements of the general part see Gardner in this volume (pp. 207–9).

5 See, for example, Norrie 1993: 232 on 'undercut[ting]' the 'rationality' of law as 'a sys-

tem of logically derived rules' that enable conclusions to be reached 'in a formally rational way'; also Kelman 1981: 591 and 1987: 11 on whether legal decisions can be 'deduced' or 'derived.'

6 Compare Finnis's charge (1987: 160) that critical theorists may be 'disappointed methodological absolutist[s].'

7 For discussions of this kind of response to philosophical scepticism see Stroud 1984; Williams 1996.

8 This weakens the positivist distinction between 'analytical' and 'censorial' jurisprudence: Claims about what the law 'is' will not be sharply distinguishable from claims about what it 'ought to be.' But there is still a distinction between a 'rational reconstruction' that aims to make a practice more principled or rational in its own terms, and an attempt to transform a practice into the theorist's own favoured image. We can understand practices whose values we do not share, and suggest ways in which they could be reformed so that they would more adequately express those values. So there is still a distinction between claims about what a system of law 'is' or 'ought to be', in terms of the values internal to it; and claims about what it 'ought to be' in terms of other values to which the theorist herself is committed.

9 As in the example that famously worried Kant (1797): A friend being chased by a would-be assassin hides in my house; the assassin comes and asks me if my friend is there; and I know that a refusal to answer would result in his searching the house and finding my friend.

10 I owe this example to Alan Norrie.

11 Contrast Dworkin 1986: 268–71, 275–5, on the distinction between 'competition' and 'contradiction' between principles.

12 Compare Finnis 1987, MacCormick 1990, for the argument that, even if in hard cases there is no 'right answer', only a set of 'reasonable' answers, the law still sets rational constraints on the courts and their reasoning, because some answers would be certainly *unreasonable.* Critical theorists might respond that any choice between two equally 'reasonable' decisions is still 'arbitrary'; and that courts will reach different answers – which thus renders the law, as a whole, contradictory. But first, we must distinguish *arbitrary* choices from choices that reflect an agent's weighing of the conflicting reasons (even when she recognises that others might reasonably weigh them differently). And, second, consistency is itself one value that the courts recognise, and that can help to guide their decisions.

13 I will not be very much concerned with 'liberalism' in what follows. Although 'liberalism' is a broad enough term, and although 'liberal' ideas have played a large role in the historical development of our legal institutions, it is not obvious to me that the features of the criminal law that Norrie connects to 'liberalism' must be so interpreted. In particular, one does not need to be a 'liberal' to think individual responsibility important for the criminal law; or if that is taken to be a criterion of 'liberalism', 'liberalism' is an even broader church than one might have thought.

14 See, for example, Hall 1960: 88 (quoted by Husak 1989: 3); LaFave and Scott 1986: 227–31; Williams 1961: 48–50, 748–50, and 1983: 75–6; Smith and Hogan 1996: 81–3.

15 For useful discussions of the meaning of 'motive' in relation to the criminal law, see Husak 1989, Sistare 1987.

16 See also Lacey, Wells, and Meure 1990: 32 ('[D]octrinal insistence on the irrelevance of

motive can be at once maintained and bypassed by conceptualising motive as an aspect of intent where this is thought by judges or commentators to achieve the "right" result'); also Kelman 1981: 667.

17 See further Ashworth 1995: 138–9; Smith 1989: 45–61.

18 See, for example, Smith and Hogan 1996: 81–3; Williams 1961: 48–9; for criticism see Husak 1989: 5–6; Lacey, Wells, and Meure 1990: 32.

19 But see further footnote 24.

20 For present purposes we can take a crime's definition to include the absence of any of the general defences that preclude liability.

21 The points made in the last two paragraphs apply, most obviously, to systems in which crimes are defined by statute. But they also apply to common-law systems, in which many crimes are defined by judicial tradition rather than by statute, insofar as those systems respect a doctrine of precedent: The orthodox doctrine then holds that in determining liability, the courts must not attend to motivating factors that authoritative precedents do not make relevant.

22 See further pp. 177–9 below.

23 See Gardner 1994 for a good example of this latter kind of argument.

24 Arguments that appeal in this way to the idea of a 'private' realm are, of course, most familiar in liberal thought: But even those who argue from a more communitarian perspective can see good reasons to insist that the state should leave its citizens an extensive sphere of protected privacy (see Duff 1996a: 200–2, 310–17). Note too that such considerations also give the doctrine that motives should be irrelevant to criminal liability *some* relevance to the legislator's task as warning legislators not to require the law to take too intrusive an interest in agents' deeper motives.

25 I do not intend to defend the orthodox subjectivist account of recklessness, which I have criticised elsewhere (see Duff 1990: ch. 7): My point is only that subjectivists need not judge the agent by her own standards of 'reasonableness' in risk taking. Nor am I assuming that the 'facts' can always be clearly distinguished from those normative standards by which we judge the agent's conduct: I assume only that in legal contexts we can draw a distinction that allows the subjectivist's view to be coherently articulated.

26 I leave aside here the argument offered by other critical theorists, that 'liberals' espouse a radical value subjectivism which precludes condemning anyone for an action that he thinks is justified (Kelman 1987: 64–85; in response see Dworkin 1986: 440–1).

27 *Pottle & Randle* ([1991] *The Times* 27 June, p. 1) was one famous case in which the jury apparently ignored the law to acquit defendants with whom it sympathised; see also *Ponting* [1985] *The Times* 12 February, p. 1.

28 Hence the Law Lords' claim in *Chandler* that it is for the 'state' to determine where its safety and interests lie. Such an account of the division of labour between legislature and courts assumes that there is a distinction between making and applying law: But some such distinction can be drawn, even if there is a fairly large and shady border area in which applying and interpreting shade into developing and making; even if there are many 'hard cases', there are many easy cases (*pace* Kelman 1981: 662–9).

29 See Duff 1986, ch. 3, developing Hart 1961: 80–1.

30 Compare the Model Penal Code formulations of justificatory defences (section 3). *Kronlid, Needham, Wilson and Zelter* (see *The Guardian* 31 July 1996, 1) is interesting here. The defendants had damaged a fighter plane that was to be sold to the Indonesian gov-

ernment. They argued that they had 'lawful excuse' to damage it, because they were using reasonable force to prevent the commission of the crime of genocide, in which the plane would have been used by the Indonesian government (see Criminal Damage Act 1971 s.1; on the use of 'reasonable force' to prevent crime, see Criminal Law Act 1967 s.3, Smith & Hogan 1996: 259–70). The judge allowed them to argue this defence; they were acquitted. Had they been convicted after not being allowed to argue this defence, and appealed, the Court of Appeal might have rejected the appeal on grounds similar to those argued in *Chandler:* It is for the 'state', as represented by the government of the day, to decide what exports to allow or prohibit; their case for prohibiting such exports should be pursued in another available forum. But they could argue that other, legitimate means of preventing these exports had been tried and had failed; this was the only way in which they could try to prevent what the law recognises as a crime.

31 Sometimes it might be argued that a justified appropriation was not 'dishonest' (see Smith 1989: 50–2), but this case would rather need to be portrayed as one of justified dishonesty.

32 See Williams 1983: 144 for 'State instrumentality'; and Norrie 1993: ch. 8 on duress and necessity, 113–22 on 'voluntariness.'

33 See Smith 1989: 50; compare Hale 1736: 54, cited in Norrie 1993: 156.

34 This is, it will be argued, the crucial difference between this case and that of the lost mountaineer who takes food from a hut in order to stay alive (see Smith 1989: 51; and footnote 31 here): The state welfare provisions are not meant to cover such an 'abnormal' situation. But see further section 4.

35 Thus a court might believe that excluding certain categories of asylum seeker from welfare provisions would be inhuman (see the Court of Appeal's comments in *B* [1996] *The Guardian* 22 June, p. 3): but if that exclusion is duly approved by Parliament, it does not have the authority to overturn it (see Asylum and Immigration Act 1996).

36 *London Borough of Southwark v Williams* [1971] 2 All E.R. 175, 179: quoted in Norrie 1993: 161; Smith and Hogan 1996: 253.

37 Williams suggests that such fears do not 'differ in kind' from that 'fear of violence' which can found a defence of duress. Norrie takes this to indicate that the law is inconsistent in allowing only very limited kinds of threat to found a defence of duress (1993: 166, 170): My argument is that the law can consistently distinguish those 'abnormal' threats that could ground such a defence from those kinds of fear which are an aspect of 'normal' life.

38 On 'informal justice', see especially Abel 1982, Cain 1985, Matthews 1988, Hulsman 1991; also Duff 1996b: 83–7. For cautionary comments related to those made here see Christie 1981: 109–16.

39 Compare Murphy 1979: 103, on theories as being 'formally correct (i.e., coherent, or true for some possible world) but materially incorrect (i.e., inapplicable to the actual world in which we live).'

40 See Lord Coleridge, in *Dudley and Stephens:* we 'are often compelled to set up standards that we cannot reach ourselves, and to lay down rules which we could not ourselves satisfy'; [1881] 14 QBD 273, 288. Norrie criticises Lord Coleridge (1993: 157–8) for replacing the 'morality of equals', which would show compassion for their plight, by 'an absolutist, authoritarian moral tone demanding self-sacrifice in the name of principle': But, whilst it is of course all too easy to condemn, as from on high, those who give in to

terrible pressure, we can sometimes appropriately judge of others, as we hope we would of ourselves, that they did terrible wrong, although under terrible circumstances.

41 Grateful thanks, for helpful discussions and comments, to the other contributors to this volume, and to Sandra Marshall. Thanks also to the participants in a Legal Theory Workshop in Toronto, where I presented parts of this chapter – and in particular to David Dyzenhaus and Arthur Ripstein, who showed me that I need (at least) to develop further and in more detail the argument in section 5 that the courts should not be expected to deal with the question of whether the preconditions that I identify are satisfied; regrettably, I have not been able to embark on that development here.

References

Abel, R. (ed.) (1982). *The Politics of Informal Justice.* New York: Academic Press.

Alexy, R. (1989). *A Theory of Legal Argumentation* (translated by R. Adler & D. N. MacCormick). Oxford: Oxford University Press.

Ashworth, A. J. (1987). 'Belief, Intent and Criminal Liability', in J. Eekelaar & J. Bell (eds.), *Oxford Essays in Jurisprudence,* 3rd Series. Oxford: Oxford University Press, 1–31.

(1995). *Principles of Criminal Law* (2nd ed.). Oxford: Oxford University Press.

Cain, M. (1985). 'Beyond Informal Justice', 9 *Contemporary Crises* 335–73.

Carlen, P. (1989). 'Crime, Inequality and Sentencing', in P. Carlen & D. Cook (eds.), *Paying for Crime.* Milton Keynes: Open University Press, 8–28.

Christie, N. (1981). *Limits to Pain.* London: Martin Robertson.

Cross, R. (1975). 'Centenary Reflections on Prince's Case', 81 *Law Quarterly Review* 205–22.

Davis, M. (1989). 'The Relative Independence of Punishment Theory', 7 *Law and Philosophy,* 321–50.

Duff, R. A. (1986). *Trials and Punishments.* Cambridge: Cambridge University Press.

(1990). *Intention, Agency and Criminal Liability.* Oxford: Blackwell.

(1993). 'Choice, Character, and Criminal Liability', 12 *Law and Philosophy* 345–83.

(1996a). *Criminal Attempts.* Oxford: Oxford University Press.

(1996b). 'Penal Communications: Recent Work in the Philosophy of Punishment', 20 *Crime and Justice* 1–97.

Dworkin, R. M. (1978). *Taking Rights Seriously.* London: Duckworth.

(1986). *Law's Empire.* London: Fontana.

Finnis, J. (1980). *Natural Law and Natural Rights.* Oxford: Oxford University Press.

(1987). 'On "The Critical Legal Studies Movement"', in J. Eekelaar and J. Bell (eds.), *Oxford Essays in Jurisprudence,* 3rd Series. Oxford: Oxford University Press, 145–65.

Fuller, L. (1969). *The Morality of Law* (2nd ed.). New Haven, Conn.: Yale University Press.

Gaita, R. (1991). *Good and Evil: An Absolute Conception.* London: Macmillan.

Gardner, J. (1994). 'Rationality and the Rule of Law in Offences against the Person', 53 *Cambridge Law Journal* 502–23.

Gardner, J., & Jung, H. (1991). 'Making Sense of Mens Rea', 11 *Oxford Journal of Legal Studies* 559–88.

Hale, Sir M. (1736). *Pleas of the Crown.*

Hall, J. (1960), *General Principles of Criminal Law* (2nd ed.). New York: Bobbs-Merrill.

Hare, R. M. (1952). *The Language of Morals.* Oxford: Oxford University Press.

(1963). *Freedom and Reason.* Oxford: Oxford University Press.
Hart, H. L. A. (1961). *The Concept of Law.* Oxford: Oxford University Press.
(1968). *Punishment and Responsibility.* Oxford: Oxford University Press.
Horder, J. C. N. (1992). *Provocation and Responsibility.* Oxford: Oxford University Press.
Hudson, B. (1987). *Justice Through Punishment.* London: Macmillan.
(1993). *Penal Policy and Social Justice.* London: Macmillan.
(1995). 'Beyond Proportionate Punishment', 22 *Crime, Law and Social Change* 59–78.
Hulsman, L. (1991). 'The Abolitionist Case: Alternative Crime Policies', 25 *Israel Law Review* 681–709.
Hunt, A. (1986). 'The Theory of Critical Legal Studies', 6 *Oxford Journal of Legal Studies* 1–45.
Husak, D. (1987). *Philosophy of Criminal Law.* Totowa, N.J.: Rowman & Littlefield.
(1989). 'Motive and Criminal Liability', 8 *Criminal Justice Ethics* 3–14.
Kant, I. (1797). 'On a Supposed Right to Tell Lies from Benevolent Motives'; translated by T. K. Abbott, in *Kant's Critique of Practical Reason and Other Works.* London: Longmans, Green & Co., 1889, 361–6.
Kelman, M. (1981). 'Interpretive Construction in the Substantive Criminal Law', 33 *Stanford Law Review* 591–673.
(1984). 'Trashing', 36 *Stanford Law Review* 293–348.
(1987). *A Guide to Critical Legal Studies.* Cambridge, Mass.: Harvard University Press.
Krygier, M. (1987). 'Critical Legal Studies and Social Theory – A Response to Alan Hunt', 7 *Oxford Journal of Legal Studies* 26–39.
Lacey, N. (1988). *State Punishment.* London: Routledge.
(1993). 'A Clear Concept of Intention: Elusive or Illusory?', 56 *Modern Law Review* 621–42.
Lacey, N., Wells, C., & Meure, D. (1990). *Reconstructing Criminal Law.* London: Weidenfeld & Nicolson.
Lafave, W. R., & Scott, A. W. (1986). *Criminal Law* (2nd ed.). St. Paul, Minn.: West.
MacCormick, D. N. (1978). *Legal Reasoning and Legal Theory.* Oxford: Oxford University Press.
(1990). 'Reconstruction after Deconstruction: A Response to CLS', 10 *Oxford Journal of Legal Studies* 539–58.
Matthews, R. (ed.) (1988). *Informal Justice.* London: Sage.
Melden, A. I. (1970). *Rights and Right Conduct.* Oxford: Blackwell.
Moore, M. S. (1993). *Act and Crime.* Oxford: Oxford University Press.
Morison, J. (1988). 'Hart's Excuses: Problems with a Compromise Theory of Punishment', in P. Leith & P. Ingrams (eds.), *The Jurisprudence of Orthodoxy.* London: Routledge, 117–46.
Morris, N., & Tonry, M. (1991). *Between Prison and Probation.* New York: Oxford University Press.
Murphy, J. G. (1979). 'Marxism and Retribution', in his *Retribution, Justice and Therapy.* Dordrecht: D. Reidel, 93–115.
Nagel, T. (1979). 'The Fragmentation of Value', in his *Mortal Questions.* Cambridge: Cambridge University Press, 128–41.
Norrie, A. W. (1991). *Law, Ideology and Punishment.* Dordrecht: Kluwer.
(1993). *Crime, Reason and History.* London: Weidenfeld & Nicolson.

Sistare, C. (1987). 'Agent Motives and the Criminal Law', 13 *Social Theory and Practice* 303–26.

Smith, J. C. (1989). *Justification and Excuse in the Criminal Law.* London: Stevens.

Smith, J. C., & Hogan, B. (1996). *Criminal Law* (8th ed.). London: Butterworths.

Stroud, B. (1984). *The Significance of Philosophical Scepticism.* Oxford: Oxford University Press.

Von Hirsch, A. (1992). Proportionality in the Philosophy of Punishment', 16 *Crime and Justice* 55–98.

(1993). *Censure and Sanctions.* Oxford: Oxford University Press.

Williams, B. (1973). 'Ethical Consistency', in his *Problems of the Self.* Cambridge: Cambridge University Press, 166–86.

Williams, G. (1961). *Criminal Law: The General Part* (2nd ed.). London: Stevens.

(1983). *Textbook of Criminal Law* (2nd ed.). London: Stevens.

Williams, M. (1996). *Unnatural Doubts.* Princeton, N.J.: Princeton University Press.

Winch, P. (1972). 'The Universalizability of Moral Judgments', in his *Ethics and Action.* London: Routledge, 151–70.

5

On the General Part of the Criminal Law

JOHN GARDNER

1. The Idea of the General Part

It was, I think, Glanville Williams who first envisaged the formal division of English criminal law into a 'special part' and a 'general part'.[1] He explicitly borrowed the distinction from continental legal systems, many of which carry it on the face of their criminal codes.[2] Although Williams did not state it consistently, it seems that the distinction is supposed to be drawn along the following lines: The special part supplies the details of particular criminal offences and arranges them into families. The general part, meanwhile, is made up of doctrines that cross the boundaries between (some or all of) these different families of criminal offences. One source of problems in the application of this distinction is readily apparent. It comes of the idea of a 'family' of offences. You may well ask: When does the application of a certain doctrine across a number of offences turn those offences into a 'family', such that the doctrine in question belongs to the special part rather than to the general part? And don't some 'families' of offences (such as 'sexual offences', 'offences of specific intent', and 'inchoate offences') overlap, so that some doctrines unavoidably spill over from one family to another and mutate in the process from special-part doctrines into general-part doctrines? These are certainly challenging questions. I hope that the argument which follows will help us to make progress towards some answers. But one thing that the questions already bring to light by themselves is that the distinction between the general part and the special part is bound to have some grey areas, in which convention and convenience may well be the only points of reference.

It does not follow, however, that the whole distinction should be written off as a distinction of convenience, devoid of any deeper significance. It seems to me that, on the contrary, different attitudes to the general part, and different views about the role it ought to play in the law, can reflect profound philosophical divergences. Many of the leading academic criminal lawyers of our age – Williams himself is a notable example – have been unabashed enthusiasts for the general part, typically pressing for more doctrines to be more conscientiously and more consistently applied, other things being equal, to an ever-wider range of criminal offences.[3] This academic enthusiasm was at an early stage injected into, and continues to infect, the Law Commission's work on criminal law codification, which aims to set out the largest number of criminal laws with the smallest amount of doctrinal variation among them.[4] Of course, it is crucial for all of these enthusiasts that the doctrines in question be sound ones. Nobody, to the best of my knowledge, commends the generalisation of what he or she believes to be an unsound doctrine just for generalisation's sake. But so long as doctrines are sound, their generality is regarded as a further boon. The common assumption seems to be that a substantial dose of generality is needed to displace what Williams calls 'the ramshackle creations' of English criminal law's history.[5] To modernise our criminal law, the thinking goes, we must tame its unruly special part by subjecting it to the disciplined governance of a more expansive, more exacting, and indeed more general general part. Only thus can we move closer to the ideal of 'a rational and principled criminal law', to borrow the oft-cited words of J. C. Smith and Brian Hogan.[6] And who could be against such a move?

One obvious philosophical issue raised here is whether the last question is rightly framed as a rhetorical one. I believe that it is. To my way of thinking it is analytically true that the criminal law should be rational and principled. Criminal law is a human institution that can be reformed and altered (whether *ad hoc* or systematically) by human hand. It is therefore precisely the kind of thing that answers to (practical) reasons and to (practical) principles. I do not mean that every doctrine of the criminal law is already supported by reasons and principles, let alone by good reasons and sound principles. I mean only that it can always be asked, perhaps without much hope of a convincing answer, but at least without making a category mistake: 'Why should we enact or retain a criminal law like this? For what reason? On what principle?' That is the only test that needs to be satisfied to show that the criminal law is capable, in theory, of being rational and principled.[7] Moreover, it is built into the very ideas of the rational and the principled that anything which is, in theory, capable of having these qualities ought to have them, the former unconditionally and the latter *ceteris paribus*.[8] This has the implication that anyone who commends their absence in such a setting has necessarily misunderstood them. If one accepts this, it follows that the ambition to have a more rational and principled criminal law cannot be open to doubt.

Thus, in engaging with the widespread enthusiasm for the general part identified here, our attention has to shift away from the demand for rationality and principle *per se* and onto the supposed connection between rationality and principle on the one hand and generality on the other. Here we encounter further, and I think more troublesome, philosophical issues. They concern the resources of reason and the power of principles, and the extent to which we should expect these to conspire in exerting a largely homogenising, rather than diversifying, pressure on legal doctrines. It must be admitted that many people nowadays, and not only the writers of criminal law textbooks, expect reason to be allied with principle in the cause of tidiness and uniformity. We even have a fashionable word – 'rationalisation' – which conveys the common assumption that tidiness and reason go hand in hand. When some institution or practice or organisation is being 'rationalised', idiosyncrasies and incongruities are the target. Loose ends are to be tied up. I think the implication here that rationality abhors loose ends is false and moreover can be explained in a way that shows what is false about it. The explanation is not, however, a straightforward one, and only a crude sketch-map can be given over the following pages. It forces us to confront a variety of intimidating problems about the components of a good life, the nature of morality and moral agency, and the concept of responsibility. Before that, it involves us in isolating and diagnosing the cause of a mistaken view about the proportion of rationality's work that is done by principles. One major dimension of rationality, namely its non-instrumental dimension, is wrongly but understandably viewed by many as the exclusive domain of principles. In ways that I hope will become clear, this dimension of rationality looms large in the justification of criminal laws, and thus the error makes a notably striking impact here. The implications, however, go much wider and deeper. In ways I can only hint at, they bear on our whole conception of ourselves and our relationship with and role in the world we inhabit.

2. A Preliminary Classification

The general part, as I explained it, is made up of 'doctrines.' But doctrines come in more than one form and perform more than one function. A more refined understanding of the idea of the general part can be achieved by dividing its doctrines into three groups.

1. The *auxiliary* general part, with which we will not be much concerned in the pages that follow, provides for the automatic or semi-automatic creation of various parasitic modes of criminal liability. When a certain activity is criminalised, the auxiliary general part can transform certain other activities logically connected with that activity into crimes as well, and in many legal systems it does so by default. The main doctrines of the auxiliary general part in English criminal law are those dealing with inchoate forms of liability, and those governing secondary participation in crime. With few exceptions, if ϕing is a crime known to English law, then, by operation of law, so is attempting to ϕ, inciting others to ϕ, or conspiring to ϕ, as well as aiding, abetting, counselling, or procuring ϕing by others. Although it need not be so, in England the doctrinal content of the auxiliary general part remains more or less constant for any given ϕ. But notice that the auxiliary general part, by its very nature, remains silent on the subject of how the crime of ϕing itself may be constructed,

organised, delimited, or characterised, save, of course, that for the auxiliary general part to operate on it, ϕing must be the kind of thing that can be attempted, incited, counselled, and so on.[9]

2. There is no such silence on the part of the *supervisory* general part, which contains guiding principles for the creation, interpretation, and application of new criminal laws. There may of course be principles in the supervisory general part that govern the workings of the auxiliary general part, but the supervisory general part has a wider sphere of influence, being capable of governing the creation, interpretation, and application of non-auxiliary crimes as well – that is, capable of bearing on the criminalisation of ϕing itself. The supervisory general part may also bear on the provision of criminal defences. The applicable principles may be mandatory, advisory, or even permissive. They may apply to judges, or to legislatures, or to both. Familiar examples in English law include the *Woolmington* principle that the burden of proof is on the prosecution,[10] as well as our rather narrow version of the *nullum crimen sine lege* principle, by which express words are needed to create a new statutory criminal offence. Also included is the oft-cited principle that *actus non facit reum nisi mens sit rea.* Some would say that the latter is too often dishonoured in English law to be counted as an authentic example. But that depends not only on what it means but also on how general it is supposed to be. The supervisory general part, like the rest of the general part, may be more or less general. It is possible that in English law the *actus non facit reum* principle crosses the boundaries between some families of criminal offences but not between all and thus is not necessarily being dishonoured on every occasion on which a crime is created that is devoid of *mens rea* elements. So long as it applies across at least some families of crimes, and on condition that it provides a principle by which, in the eyes of the criminal law itself, particular acts of criminalisation or decriminalisation may be judged, the doctrine nevertheless belongs to the supervisory general part.
3. I identified the doctrines of the supervisory general part as 'principles' to distinguish them from the doctrines of the *definitional* general part, which also governs the creation, interpretation, and application of new criminal laws, whether auxiliary or otherwise. Principles are standards at a relatively high level of abstraction, which leave the question of *how* they are to be complied with open: In theory there is more than one way to do their bidding.[11] This openness is, correspondingly, the hallmark of the supervisory general part. But the doctrines of the definitional general part are not open in the same way. They are doctrines that specify how crimes (and defences to crime) are to be defined. They provide the detailed linguistic and conceptual apparatus of the law. This does not mean that they are always mandatory doctrines; like those of the supervisory general part, the doctrines of the definitional general part may equally be advisory or permissive. Nor does it mean that the doctrines of the definitional general part are typically of less general application than those of the supervisory general part; they may, like any other general-part doctrine, vary enormously in point of generality. It means only that they set down the *hows* rather than the *whys* of criminalisation and decriminalisation. The question of whether the words 'intention' and 'recklessness' (and their cognates) should bear standard meanings across different families of offences is a question about whether they should be adopted into the definitional general part. So is the question of whether these terms, or the con-

cepts identified by them, should be *used* more generally in English criminal law – for example, as the recommended or even the prescribed way of fulfilling the otherwise open demands of *actus non facit reum nisi mens sit rea.* This last example draws attention to one consequence of the fact that the supervisory general part is more abstract than the definitional general part. Doctrines in the supervisory general part can help to justify doctrines in the definitional general part, but not vice versa.[12] That remains true even if, as seems to me quite likely, the distinction is one of degree – that is, even if some principles are more principled than others.

3. Between Principle and Policy

Lawyers sometimes contrast arguments of principle with arguments of policy. The contrast was famously put to philosophical use in Ronald Dworkin's early writings. Arguments of principle for legal rules, he argued, were the legitimate province of judges, whereas arguments of policy were properly available only to legislatures.[13] Few follow Dworkin in putting the distinction to this particular use. That judges too may resort to (at least some) policy considerations is widely agreed, and not only among judges themselves. But many have nevertheless taken their cue from Dworkin in making the principle/policy distinction pivotal to their arguments about the justification of legal rules. Take, for example, Andrew Ashworth's characteristically trenchant remarks about the retention of some rules of constructive liability in English criminal law:

> Whether this is properly described as a policy or a principle is open to debate. Some of its adherents take no trouble to develop a principled argument, whereas others argue that the decision that is morally most significant is the decision to cause harm intentionally to another: once a person has crossed this moral threshold, there is good reason to impose liability for whatever consequences ensue. However, even those who accept this moral foundation appear not to apply it generally throughout the criminal law. It seems to be reserved, presumably for policy reasons, to cases where a person intentionally inflicts physical harm on another.[14]

One feature of this passage is particularly worthy of note. The principle/policy distinction is portrayed by Ashworth not only as exclusive[15] but also as exhaustive. Any argument for or against maintaining a rule of criminal liability falls to be interpreted either as an argument of principle or as an argument of policy or as a mixture of the two. This contrasts dramatically with Dworkin's repeated warnings that the principle/policy distinction should not be conceived of as exhaustive: 'These two sorts of argument do not exhaust political argument';[16] there are 'principles, policies, and other sorts of standards.'[17] Ashworth's departure from Dworkin's position on this point may reflect a supposition that principles and policies are the only argumentative tools available in the justification of criminal laws, even if other argumentative tools are available elsewhere in the affairs of the state, or elsewhere in life; but Ashworth does not explain why this should be so. And in the absence of such an explanation, unfortunately, his construction of the principle/policy distinction as exhaustive is apt to beg the question in favour of a particular account of the relationship between the supervisory general part and the definitional general part, and of the relationship, consequently, between the general part and the special part.

That is so because this construction artificially narrows the range of rational resources that lie at our disposal in justifying relatively localised variations in the definitions of criminal offences and defences. Arguments of principle, as I said earlier, are arguments conducted at a relatively high level of abstraction. This means that, as Ashworth rightly observes, they have a built-in tendency towards generalisation. If the law does not in fact allow them to apply as generally as, by virtue of their high level of abstraction, they apparently ought to, we want to know the reason why. Here is where, in Ashworth's thinking, arguments of policy come in. For they do not share the relatively high level of abstraction, and the consequent built-in tendency towards generalisation, that is the essence of an argument of principle. They can therefore restrict the power of arguments of principle to standardise the definitions of particular offences and defences. They can rationally account for local variations. Does this mean that an argument of policy is simply an argument that is conducted at a relatively low level of abstraction, and therefore with less of a tendency towards generalisation than an argument of principle? We could certainly stipulate such a definition, but it misses a key nuance of the word 'policy' that Dworkin, Ashworth, and most other users of the contrast evidently wish to retain and exploit. It neglects to draw attention to the fact that a policy argument is by its nature an *instrumental* argument. A policy argument is, in Ashworth's terms, a 'pragmatic' argument 'about what is expedient',[18] or, in Dworkin's terms, 'sets out a goal to be reached, generally an improvement in some economic, political, or social feature of the community.'[19] Here we can immediately see why Dworkin warned against regarding the principle/policy distinction as exhaustive. If it is regarded as exhaustive, considerations that are neither instrumental nor at a relatively high level of abstraction mysteriously drop out of the picture. Not being instrumental, they are not policy considerations. Not being at a relatively high level of abstraction, they are not principles either. In the context of the criminal law, the elimination of this class of considerations pushes one into a position where the special localised features in the definitions of particular criminal offences and defences have to be defended instrumentally or not at all. This summarily deprives the special part of the criminal law of a whole range of rational resources for its own defence. The general part enjoys a correspondingly summary boost in its doctrinal significance. In particular, it becomes more likely that the definitional general part will enjoy an enhanced role in shaping the criminal law. For if there are fewer localised considerations to provide a rational basis for the nonstandard definition of particular offences and defences, then the justificatory route from the supervisory general part to the definitional general part is less prone to be complicated or obstructed by such localised considerations, and the cause of definitional standardisation is thereby artificially enhanced.

4. Actions and Their Consequences

To bear out this accusation of artificial enhancement, we do of course need to arm ourselves with a clearer explanation of the distinction between instrumental and non-instrumental considerations, so that we can at least envisage what a localised non-instrumental consideration might look like. The core idea is obvious enough: instrumental considerations point to the consequences of our actions (or, in this context, of their criminalisation or decriminalisation) while non-instrumental considerations are concerned with the qualities of the actions themselves. But to get this distinction across more thoroughly, I want to explain it in terms of a slightly different, although related, distinction. This is the distinction between action-reasons and outcome-reasons.

Among the various reasons people may have for and against acting, some focus on the performance of certain actions, and others focus on certain things happening (or tending to happen) when and because we act.[20] Friends have some reasons to tell the truth to one another through thick and thin – that is, whatever may come to pass in consequence of their doing so. On the other hand, friends also have some reasons to perform actions – that is to say, any actions – that will reduce the risk of their friends' coming to grief. One familiar dilemma of friendship, then, is the dilemma of the protective lie: Should I lie to my friend (contrary to one rational dictate of friendship) if telling the truth will leave my friend exposed to extra dangers or difficulties (contrary to another)? We have all encountered the conflict in some form. But notice that this is a conflict not only between different reasons but also between reasons of different types. The first is an action-reason, that is a reason why a certain action (namely lying) should not be performed, whatever might happen as a consequence. The second is an outcome-reason, that is a reason why *any* action should be performed (be it lying, smiling, commanding, catching the bus, doing a handstand, or whatever) just so long as it has the tendency to prevent certain things from happening (namely, to prevent dangers or difficulties' befalling a friend).

This distinction is sometimes forgotten or neglected, not least because some actions are logically, as well as causally, related to things that happen. Take the action of killing, for example. This is partly constituted by someone's dying. It means that we may overlook the difference between the action-reason not to kill and the outcome-reason not to do anything that has someone's dying as a consequence. That is particularly a risk if we take a reductive view of causation, according to which all causal connections are alike. Such a view means that we can no longer see the fundamental causal difference between 'killing' and 'doing something – *any*thing – that has someone's death as a consequence.'[21] Thus the action-reason and outcome-reason are run together. Sometimes students and teachers of criminal law slip into this collapse when they explain the law of homicide. They give its common-law *actus reus* as 'doing something, the consequence of which is death within a year and a day' instead of 'killing, the death occurring within a year and a day.'[22] Fortunately the criminal law itself does not make the same mistake. Procuring another to kill is, as English criminal law recognises, an action that has someone's death as its consequence.[23] Yet, as English criminal law also recognises, procuring another to kill is not itself an action of killing. Thus procuring another to kill grounds secondary, not primary, liability for murder or manslaughter – that is to say, liability as an accomplice rather than liability as a principal. Of course we may say, even as lawyers, that procuring a killing was *tantamount* to killing, or that it was killing *in effect,* or that the secondary participant *as good as* killed the victim.[24] Fair enough – so long as one takes the italicised qualifications seriously. What the qualifications invite us to do is to remember that there are outcome-reasons as well as action-reasons at stake in a homicide case, and that these bring the various modes of homicide closer together even as the action-reasons prise them apart. The principal in murder acted against one action-reason (the reason not to kill) while the accomplice acted against a different action-reason (the reason not to procure a killing). But both acted against one and the same outcome-reason (the reason not to do anything in consequence of which someone will die). What needs to be remembered, although it is rarely at stake in the law, is that in theory the action-reasons could exist without the outcome-reasons, or vice versa. Here, for example, is an intelligible (I do not mean to suggest sound) view about Hitler's demise. During the war, there was for most people no reason not to perform actions – actions in general – that would have made Hitler's death more likely, or even inevitable. Hitler's death would not as such have been a matter of regret, but of pure celebration. But there were still reasons not to kill him or to procure his killing by another. Even without any loss in the outcome, there would still have been *prima facie* wrongs in performing various possible actions with that outcome. Perhaps, indeed, *every* feasible action with that outcome was coincidentally countermanded by an action-reason not to perform it. But even in that case, the massed ranks of action-reasons against various death-dealing actions are not to be mistaken for one overarching outcome-reason against actions with, or tending towards, fatal consequences. For the former focus on what is done, and the latter on what happens; and that remains a line etched in logic even when, as is often the case, what is done is logically related to what happens.[25]

Now it cannot be stressed often enough that the distinction between outcome-reasons and action-reasons does not exactly correspond to the distinction between instrumental and non-instrumental considerations. All non-instrumental reasons are action-reasons, but the opposite is not true. That is because actions may be among the consequences of other actions. The example of procuring a killing is a case in point. This action of procuring a killing has not only a death among its consequences but also, obviously, a killing. Thus even if we are considering the purely instrumental case for prohibiting this kind of complicity, action-reasons as well as outcome-reasons may figure in the argument. In framing such a prohibition, we may want there to be not only fewer deaths in the world but also fewer killings. It follows that, on the definition of a policy argument as a specifically instrumental kind of argument, action-reasons as well as outcome-reasons may figure in policy arguments. Thus my challenge to Ashworth's use of the principle/policy distinction is not that it fails to accommodate the possibility of action-reasons that are of local significance only to certain corners of the criminal law, such as reasons not to kill, or reasons not to deceive. My challenge is rather the familiar one faced by those strict consequentialists who are flexible enough to grant the possible existence of action-reasons.[26] If action-reasons are rationally relevant when they figure instrumentally, then why are they not rationally relevant when they figure non-instrumentally? If the fact that performing action ϕ now will bring about three more actions ϕ later can give you three good reasons for performing or not performing action ϕ now, why can't it give you four? If my lie will have as its consequence three further lies, and there are action-reasons not to lie, then why count the three instrumental action-reasons and not the fourth non-instrumental one? Of course Ashworth does not face the challenge in this simple form, because he, unlike the strict consequentialist, does allow the fourth action-reason to count. He allows it to count under the heading of principle. But that is only on the condition that it is an action-reason operating at a relatively high level of abstraction. And this only goes to compound and deepen the puzzle faced by strict consequentialists. Why should action-reasons have to sneak into the criminalisation argument *either* instrumentally, under the heading of policy, *or* abstractly, under the heading of principle? Why not otherwise?

5. Moral Agency as a Matter of Principle

One possible answer is that the set of action-reasons left over when one subtracts reasons of principle and reasons of policy is an empty set, because action-reasons are always reasons of principle. That this answer is so tempting reflects a complicated set of contemporary assumptions about the role of action-reasons in practical thought. One widespread assumption, starkly presented in the work of Hume and influentially worked out by his utilitarian successors, is that human well-being is a fundamentally passive affair. A life going well is a life in which predominantly good things happen, in which, for example, we have pleasant feelings and experiences, we are materially prosperous, our wishes come true, things go as we want them to, and so on. Except insofar as actions make or tend to make such good things happen to us, we are led to suppose, they have no special role in our (or anybody else's) well-being. This assumption tends to predispose us to be more sceptical about action-reasons than we are about outcome-reasons. For we can instantly see where (at least some) outcome-reasons acquire their rational force. Nobody could doubt that, other things being equal, it is better to have a better life and therefore rational to want and pursue one. Of course people differ in their views about which happenings, exactly, *make* for a better life: Some accounts are more objective (i.e., desire- and belief-independent) than others, some more pluralistic than others, some more materialistic or hedonistic than others, and so on. People also differ in their views about which reasons of well-being apply to whom: Some hold agent-neutral views according to which each of us is rationally concerned with the well-being of all indiscriminately, whereas others hold more or less agent-relative views according to which each of us is rationally concerned with the well-being only of some people, or of some more than others, or indeed only of ourselves. But whether one is subjectively or objectively inclined, pluralistically or monistically inclined, materialistically or hedonistically or spiritually inclined, agent-neutrally or agent-relatively inclined, it is an easy matter to combine the prevailing passive view of well-being with the tautologous proposition that well-being is worthwhile to make the existence of outcome-reasons very easily digestible, even among sceptical moderns like ourselves.

The payoff, however, is that action-reasons are, for many of us, harder to stomach. They demand fuller explanation. For, *ex hypothesi,* they cannot take their rational force from the importance of human well-being. And what is there, for human beings with a humanistic outlook, but human well-being? What comes to the rescue here is a thought with Christian roots, most influentially adapted into secular thinking by Kant. This is the thought that moral considerations are considerations in a different key from considerations of well-being – that moral considerations offer us flourishing in another dimension, respecting our higher or more perfect nature as human beings. They transcend our mundane, day-to-day preoccupation with being better off, calling us away from what Kant called our merely 'prudential' concerns. Here we find an alternative dimension for action-reasons to inhabit. But the need to provide a fuller explanation of action-reasons does not go away merely because we have found some logical space for them. Indeed, it escalates into a demand for a fuller explanation of morality itself. What is it for? Why should anyone care about it? What gives it rational force?[27] Against the backdrop of such hostile interrogation, the pressure to systematise morality is hard to resist. And without a supreme legislator to give morality a law-like, source-based systematisation, humantistically minded people feel constrained to provide it with a content-based systematisation instead. Each time a putative moral reason is cited, someone is bound to ask 'and why is *that* a reason?' Denying themselves a resort to the word of God, the reason's advocates feel compelled to climb to a higher level of abstraction and generality to provide a justification. As we show how each of morality's apparently diverse dictates is in fact an application of a more general moral doctrine, and that in turn an application of a yet more general doctrine, we gradually move towards systematisation of the whole of morality on the foundation of an ever-more restricted set of highly abstract principles. If action-reasons inhabit only this moral domain, then they too are hostage to this strongly felt need for content-based systematisation. Accordingly, we come to expect every action-reason to be a reason of principle – that is, to operate at, or at any rate to be a straightforward application of a further action-reason that operates at, a relatively high level of abstraction and generality.

This is, of course, a fairly rough-and-ready sketch of a huge body of thought. People differ widely on the details, as well as the terminology. But even my simplified and impressionistic explanation brings an important conundrum to the surface. When I first introduced principles into the discussion, I connected their abstractness, not only with generality but also with *openness.* I said that a principle, being relatively abstract, by its nature leaves more or less open the question of how it is to be complied with. When I introduced the distinction between action-reasons and outcome-reasons, meanwhile, I stressed that action-reasons are reasons for or against certain actions, whereas outcome-reasons are reasons for or against actions only in virtue of those actions making, or tending to make, certain things happen. One of the implications of this second contrast, you may say, is that action-reasons, unlike outcome-reasons, cannot be open. They are action-reasons precisely by virtue of the fact that they *do* dictate how – that is, by which action – they are to be complied with. This suggests that my sketch of contemporary assumptions about practical thinking must be a *reductio ad absurdam,* for it seems to commit some people to believing that considerations that cannot by their nature be open (action-reasons) are considerations that are by their nature open (reasons of principle). But I do not mean my sketch to be a *reductio,* because there is a way out of the conundrum. It involves adopting a restrictive view of moral agency, according to which the various apparently diverse specific actions that people perform (such as admitting the truth, firing a rifle into the air, laughing at jokes, going for an early night, or overthrowing the government) count, morally speaking, as mere instances of more general actions (such as treating people as equals, betraying oneself, using someone as a means, acting with integrity). Our repertoire of possible actions may be large, the argument goes, but our repertoire of possible *moral* actions is dramatically narrower. Many different actions are, in moral perspective, very much alike. Morally, they vary only in a limited number of dimensions. The effect is that an action-reason's built-in specificity, in combination with the thesis that all action-reasons are moral reasons, turns into a built-in generality instead. For the specific actions that action-reasons refer to are now, by their nature, actions described in moral terms, and thus described in terms of a restricted range of morally salient common features, and thus described at a higher level of abstraction, and endowed with a corresponding degree of openness.

This indeed was Kant's own solution to the conundrum I identified. He adopted a restrictive view of moral agency according to which the various otherwise diverse actions we perform are morally salient and hence fall within the bounds of our moral agency, only insofar as they are actions of compliance with, or violation of, the ultimate moral principle that he labelled 'the Categorical Imperative.' In this way apparently localised action-reasons (e.g., reasons in favour of keeping promises, or against lying, or for and against conscientious objection) are transformed into mere instantiations of one large and highly abstract action-reason. As one attempts to provide a rational basis for the apparently localised action-reasons, one moves through higher and higher levels of abstraction until one arrives at a principle of action that can be rejected only on pain of self-contradiction. One can then brush aside further 'why' questions with confidence. Here one has reached, says Kant, the Categorical Imperative, a principle that entails its own rational force. To its content and implications we will return in just a moment. The key point for now is that the Kantian way of rehabilitating action-reasons by carrying them up through the levels of abstraction is one to which many writers and thinkers nowadays exhibit a strong allegiance, even if unconsciously. It has the implication that action-reasons are not as localised as they may seem. In fact, so far as this way of defending them is concerned, they are all reasons of principle. This provides an intelligible and sympathetic basis for Ashworth's treatment of the principle/policy classification as an exhaustive classification of the criminal law's argumentative resources. On this account, Ashworth has artificially deprived the special part of no rational resources at all. Any non-instrumental reasons that could conceivably help to justify doctrines in the special part must, in the end, be capable of abstraction and generalisation, gravitating in the process from the justificatory apparatus of the special part to that of the general part instead. This not only expands the doctrinal content of the supervisory general part but at the same time effects a wholesale reduction in the range of localised countervailing considerations that might lie in wait, ready to exercise their disruptive force, on the justificatory route from the supervisory general part to the definitional general part. The account just sketched thus exerts a doubly expansive pressure upon the doctrines of the definitional general part.

6. Principled Moral Agency Turned in upon Itself

The Categorical Imperative was variously formulated by Kant. In its most famous formulation, it requires that one always act on a maxim through which one could at the same time will that it should become a universal law, that is a suitable maxim for all other rational beings as well as oneself.[28] The basic idea is that one's own will, to qualify as rational, could not claim a sovereignty that it would deny to other rational wills. Kant thought that this requirement could put an end to successive challenges to the validity of some action-reasons, because, as I already mentioned, shunning it was in his view self-contradictory. Whenever we act, we arrogate to our wills absolute authority. If one grants authority to the will, is it not inconsistent to deny authority to the will in general, irrespective of the accident of whose will it happens to be? I will not dwell on the well-rehearsed argument that this kind of inconsistency is moral rather than logical inconsistency and thus does not establish so much as presuppose the validity of at least some moral action-reasons.[29] Instead of focussing on Kant's undoing, I want to stress the ways in which his Categorical Imperative qualifies as a philosophical triumph. For here we will find the source of its tremendous influence on modern intellectualising about normative problems, including the problems of the criminal law and its organisation.

Kant's master-stroke was to focus all moral attention on the rational quality of an agent's will. Whenever we act, our will is implicated.[30] For the will is none other than the faculty that translates reasons into actions. It follows that an ultimate moral principle governing the operations of the will is a principle by which *every* action may be tested and judged. Accordingly, no human actions occupy an entirely morality-free zone; everywhere we go, morality goes with us. By the same token, a focus on the will provides an ideal way of factoring out, for moral purposes, the rich diversity of possible human actions. I already mentioned the restrictive view of moral agency, according to which the various apparently diverse particular actions that people perform are, morally speaking, mere instances of more general actions. Moving the golf ball with one's foot is a mere instance of cheating, cheating is a mere instance of breaking trust, breaking trust is a mere instance of failing to respect others, and so on. Now Kant's focus on the will takes us, in a sense, to the most general action of all. For him, everything worthwhile we do is, morally speaking, just an instance of our willing something correctly, because the Categorical Imperative binds only the will. The inevitable role of the will in action is the morally salient qualification that all actions have in common and in virtue of which, and to the extent of which, they are moral actions. Thus, although our agency may go further, our moral agency begins and ends with our wills. And this in turn allows for a sharp contrast between the moral realm and the realm of well-being or prudence. The realm of well-being is out there in the world, dense with fortuity and contingency. The moral realm, on the other hand, is within us, insulated from all that fortuity and contingency. The idea is not, as the banal determinist parodies it, that the will is uninfluenced and unaffected by the world beyond. Of course, as Kant appreciated, there is contingency and fortuity in the will one happens to have, as well as the predicaments one faces, and the use to which one puts one's will in those predicaments. That is not the point. The point is just that the contribution of the will is *logically* independent of what happens, – that is, it can be *specified* independently of it. Thus by the time questions of what happens arise, questions of what we did are, for moral purposes, over and done with. There is, morally speaking, no action of saving a life, where that implies success – that is, someone's staying alive. Morally speaking, one can but try to save, trying being the most that the Categorical Imperative, with its concentration on the will, can require. It follows that Kantian action-reasons are logically independent of, and not merely logically distinct from, outcome-reasons. To hold otherwise, thinks Kant, would be to muddy the water between morality on the one hand and well-being or prudence on the other; and this would undermine the original premiss, which was used to make the search for action-reasons intelligible in the first place, that morality offers us flourishing in a different dimension from the dimension of well-being, respecting our higher or more perfect nature as human beings and calling us away from our mundane prudential concerns. Our well-being is 'heteronomously' outside us, but our morality is 'autonomously' within us, and although often enough the twain shall enjoy a chance encounter, never the twain shall be forced together by logical interdependence.

This is the basis of Kant's well-known opposition to the possibility of what has come to be known as 'moral luck', which was, in spite of more recent attempts to turn it into a more sweeping campaign,[31] an opposition only to the possibility of moral luck *in the way our actions turn out,* that is to the possibility of a logical dependence of moral action upon its outcome. Even when it is correctly read subject to this limitation, there are, I should stress, certain profound difficulties in transposing the argument directly into the criminal law context. One of these is that Kant's doctrine of legality does not exactly replicate, even though it builds on and is consistent with, his doctrine of morality. Kant required that possession of a rational will and compliance with the Categorical Imperative be *sufficient* to stay on the right side of the law. He never held that such a will should be *necessary* for legal fidelity, as it is for moral flourishing.[32] Thus it would be perfectly possible to draft a criminal law that would be violated only on a certain eventuality's being realised without deviating from Kant's views on moral luck, so long as one could *also* avoid violating it by rational will alone. That would allow much constructive liability through the Kantian net, given that constructive liability is often triggered by actions that fall within the sovereignty of the will. For instance, constructive manslaughter liability in English law is triggered by intentional perpetration of an unlawful and dangerous act, the unlawfulness of which does not derive merely from the negligent manner of its performance; one can therefore avoid being a constructive manslaughterer by avoiding all unlawful and dangerous acts. There is also the important point that the Categorical Imperative is a principle of *right* action, whereas the principles governing the criminal law obviously have to be principles of *wrong* action. It would be a mistake to assume comprehensive symmetry between right and wrong, between good and evil, between positive action-reasons and negative ones. On one very credible interpretation, Kant's restrictive doctrine of moral agency applies only to the positive side. Whether or not one does the right thing depends on the rationality of one's will. But one may do the wrong thing either by facing one's will towards irrationality or by failing to face it towards rationality. There is one way to do right, but there are at least two ways to do wrong. It would follow from this interpretation that unthinking as well as deliberate wrongdoing could pass through the Kantian net, both in law and in morality. But these detailed interpretative problems need not detain us here.[33] The key point for our purposes is that the broadly Kantian view of moral considerations as lying autonomously within us, and thus of morality as binding on the will, and thus of moral agency as an agency of trying rather than succeeding, has exerted a profound influence on our contemporary intellectual culture.[34] It is not the technical working out, but the thrust of the Kantian doctrine – the co-extensiveness of moral agency and the power of the will – that has caught on. This forges a very direct connection between the view that all action-reasons are reasons of principle and the view that all action-reasons are reasons for or against trying rather than reasons for or against succeeding. It is no coincidence, accordingly, that those who are enthusiasts for the general part of the criminal law tend also to be, like Ashworth and the English Law Commission, *prima facie* antagonists towards criminal liability that depends on luck in the way things turn out.[35] They can see how such liability might be defended on instrumental, or policy, grounds, for example by referring to the damaging public disquiet that comes of failure to mark a death or injury, even if fortuitous, in the ways crimes are defined and administered. But for them it cannot successfully be defended non-instrumentally, unless as a matter of principle, because all non-instrumental reasons are action-reasons, all action-reasons are moral reasons, and all moral reasons are reasons of principle. And what is more, it cannot successfully be defended even as a matter of principle, because all moral reasons are reasons for or against trying rather than reasons for or against succeeding, and so morality cannot yield action-reasons that are violated or complied with depending on the luck of how the action in question turns out. And if morality cannot yield them, then there cannot be such action-reasons, because (by the earlier premiss) all action-reasons are moral reasons.

7. An Alternative Starting Point: Active Well-being

You may suspect that, by switching attention from the question of the general part's scope and significance to the question of its content, these last remarks represented a gratuitous digression from the topic of this chapter. But the digression was, in fact, far from gratuitous. My challenge to the view that all action-reasons are reasons of principle, and hence to the view that the general part has a monopoly on non-instrumental justification, is intimately connected with a challenge to the view that all action-reasons are reasons for or against trying, irrespective of success. The challenge begins at the very first step down the Kantian road. Kant's account of morality, you will recall, was forged against the backdrop of a view of human well-being that his philosophical adversaries had brought to prominence, namely the view that well-being is a passive condition, a matter of what happens to us. Kant did not challenge this view of well-being. Rather he accepted it under the heading of 'prudence', while seeking to depose it as a be-all-and-end-all by showing that there is more to life than well-being. We may agree with Kant that there is more to life than well-being. But this does not mean that we should follow him in granting his adversaries' view that well-being is a passive condition. There is an alternative, and broadly Aristotelian, view according to which human well-being is an active condition.[36] In the formulation I will adopt here, which I believe captures the main Aristotelian themes, our well-being consists in the wholehearted and successful pursuit of worthwhile activities.[37]

Whereas the Humean view of well-being demoted actions to a secondary role, as mere vehicles for making things happen, the Aristotelian view does just the reverse. It demotes what happens to us to a secondary role in our well-being by determining the importance of what happens to us largely in terms of the contribution it makes (whether instrumentally or constitutively) to our success in pursuing worthwhile activities. The illusion that what happens is paramount for well-being then has an obvious source in the requirement of *success*. Because our success often depends, not only instrumentally but sometimes also constitutively, on what happens to us, this requirement misleads us into supposing that what happens to us is the key to our well-being. But once we remember the earlier point that many actions are partly constituted by the way they turn out, we can see that the key thing was not what happened as such, but what happened *qua* necessary constituent of a successful activity. It was not that one ended up on top of a mountain that made the contribution to one's well-being. It was the fact that one climbed the mountain all the way to the top. Nor was the value of climbing the mountain to the top ultimately owed to something further that happened when one did, for example that one's desire to get to the top was satisfied, or that one was pleased to be there.[38] Climbing the mountain to the top was what ultimately mattered. That one desired to climb the mountain, and therefore had a satisfied desire when one got there, and was pleased to be there, testifies to the wholeheartedness of one's engagement in the climbing enterprise, which is a matter of no little importance. But otherwise one's desire to climb the mountain is but a pale reflection of the fact that climbing the mountain was independently worthwhile, and that succeeding in climbing it (assuming one climbed it wholeheartedly) accordingly contributed to one's well-being. That one's desire was satisfied by successfully and wholeheartedly performing a worthwhile activity shows only that one's desire was rational. There was, first and foremost, an action-reason to climb to the top, and that was the very reason which made it rational to want to do it. So far as one's well-being is concerned, then, the attendant outcome-reasons – that is, the raw pleasures and personal satisfactions of being on top of the world – turn out to be of largely derivative significance.

Again this is a crude thumbnail sketch of a complex tradition of thought. By way of elaboration, I will confine myself to commenting on just a few aspects that are of significance for the criminal law. First, the focus is on 'activities.' Working as a novelist or an engineer, going on a protest march or to church, doing up one's own house or doing over someone else's, sharing a flat or having an affair, going on a picnic or a pub crawl, playing on a football team or in an orchestra – all are examples of activities. An activity is simply a recognisable complex, or scheme, of actions (a category that, for these purposes, includes omissions). Larger-scale activities are also recognisable complexes, or schemes, of smaller-scale activities. Going on holiday is a complex or scheme of travelling, relaxing, engaging in recreational pursuits, adapting to different customs and cultures, leaving work behind, and so on. Each of these (often overlapping) sub-activities breaks down into various actions – for example, swimming in the sea, catching the train, eating shellfish, lying in the sun, climbing the ramparts, sizing up the local talent, turning off the mobile phone, and so on. Not all of those who go on holiday engage in all of the constituent smaller-scale activities, and not all of those who engage in the smaller-scale constituent activities act exactly alike. It is true of most activities that there is more than one way to engage in them, although some, like driving a car and dancing an eightsome reel, are physically constrained or rule-bound to such an extent that engaging in them does entail engagement in a highly standardised pattern of specific actions. The distinction between an individual action and an activity is not always clear-cut, but modern criminal law tends, for various rule-of-law reasons,[39] to regulate individual actions (having incestuous sexual intercourse,[40] making an abusive telephone call, failing to provide an adequate safety barrier on scaffolding[41]) while remaining relatively blind to the activities that they go to make up (having an incestuous relationship, pursuing a campaign of intimidation, running a cowboy operation). Occasionally, however, the criminal law regulates activities as such (membership of a proscribed organisation, living off immoral earnings), and sometimes it regulates individual actions only on the condition that they form part of a certain activity or range of activities (putting incorrect prices on display in a shop, accepting bribes in a public office). As these examples illustrate, the relationship between the value or disvalue of activities and the value or disvalue of their component parts can be very varied. Sometimes what makes the activity worthwhile (or worthless or base, as the case may be) is the combined worth (or unworth) of the actions that go to make it up. On other occasions, conversely, actions take their value or disvalue from the fact that they form part of a certain activity. Often, as activities like stalking and pimping illustrate, it is a two-way street. The actions of stalkers and pimps are some of them independently evil, some of them independently innocuous, and some of them in between. The innocuous actions are tainted with evil when and because they are part-and-parcel of the activity, which is in turn tainted with the evil of the independently evil actions that form part of it. The activity bequeaths evil to some of its component actions while it inherits evil from others and sometimes, indeed, bequeaths evil to and inherits evil from one and the same action.

This brings us to the second, and more troublesome, issue that calls for elaboration. I have just been speaking of the independent value and disvalue, even the independent *evil,* of actions and activities. You may protest at my apparently conclusory use of the word 'independent.' If human well-being consists in the successful and willing pursuit of worthwhile activities, we presumably need to know what makes these activities worthwhile apart from the contribution that successful and wholehearted pursuit of them makes to our well-being. If no such independent account of the value of activities can be given, then this Aristotelian account of well-being surely falls down the same hole as the Kantian account of morality in that it presupposes the existence of the very action-reasons it purports to defend. But that conclusion is premature. In the first place, I did not assume that all value, even as it bears on well-being, is to be counted in terms of well-being itself. There may be other kinds of value, and hence other families of reasons, in the world. Aside from the question of how our lives are going – the question of our well-being – there is also the key question of how we rate as people: the question of our virtues and skills. To some extent, once we embrace the active account of well-being, the question of how we rate as people is answered by asking how well our lives are going and then shifting into a more personal idiom by asking which aspects of our lives reflect upon us personally (the issue of our *responsibility* for what we do). Assessment of our lives therefore comes (logically) first, and assessment of us as people comes second. This may lead you to think that issues of virtue and skill will tend to be derivative or shadow issues in moral philosophy. But in fact it is, philosophically, a true chicken-and-egg situation. For our lives are going well, on the active account of well-being, if we are engaging in worthwhile activities, and one of the things that make activities worthwhile, and independently so, is the virtue and skill that, successfully engaged in, they demand of us. Different activities call for different virtues and different skills, lending the activities different intrinsic worth. These virtues and skills do not, however, owe their value only to considerations of well-being. Being good at golf contributes to one's well-being if one likes golf and plays it. That is true because golf is a worthwhile pursuit, and that in turn is true partly thanks to the valuable element of skill involved in playing it well. The value of the skill does not, however, stem purely from the contribution that playing golf well – that is, playing it with skill – makes to one's well-being. That would get us into a truly vicious circle. On the contrary, although it strikes me that the value of skills and virtues, or of some skills and virtues, does owe something to the well-being they bring into the world, it seems likely that the fundamental issues about the value of virtues and skills cannot be resolved by reference to an account of well-being alone. We still face the somewhat Kantian challenge of divining a further and complementary source of value separate from the value of human well-being. The difference is that, unlike Kant, we would now be looking not for two self-contained points of view – the 'moral' and the 'prudential', the higher form of flourishing and the lower – but rather for two families of considerations that constantly refer us back and forth to one another. In particular we are looking for value, as I said, that bears fundamentally on our well-being even though it is not the value of well-being itself.

The mind-boggling challenge of explaining this value cannot be taken up here. Suffice it to say that the value which our virtues and skills bring to our worthwhile activities is by its very nature intrinsic, or constitutive, value. Many activities, however, are also instrumentally good or bad. And when we come to the question of instrumental value, happily, there is no vicious circularity in tracing the value of worthwhile activities to the value of well-being itself. This kind of value can therefore serve to illustrate the main point.

Take being an aid worker in a war zone. True, it is an example of an activity with positive value, but on this score most of the lessons can be applied *mutatis mutandis* in the case of worthless or base activities, such as being a torturer or a child molester or a sender of hate mail or a wife beater, as well. The value of being an aid worker in a war zone comes primarily of the service it does to the well-being of the victims of war. Their well-being may in turn lie in the valuable work they are able to do with success and enthusiasm when returned to health and vitality, and that work may in turn be valuable because of the way it ultimately serves the well-being of yet further groups of people, for example by promoting reconciliation or building railways. Alternatively, the well-being of those people helped by aid workers may simply lie in the life of prayer or scholarship to which they can return, or the restoration of home and garden to which they can attend, without further consequences for the well-being of third parties. All of this is well-being instrumentally served by aid workers: The well-being of those aided, or others, is augmented as a consequence of the aid work. So surely none of it entails that the activity of being an aid worker is intrinsically worthwhile, that is that there are action-reasons to be an aid worker as such? Given the instrumentality of one's contribution to the well-being of the victims of war, isn't it rationally beside the point whether one makes one's contribution to the victims of war by being an aid worker or by some other route, such as sending donations or lobbying government, just so long as the contributions make the same impact on the beneficiaries, net of cost and effort? The answer is a resounding 'no' so far as one's own well-being is concerned. For well-being, actively conceived, consists in the successful and wholehearted pursuit of worthwhile activities, and however the activities may *come* to be worthwhile, one's well-being is constituted by one's successful and wholehearted pursuit of them *qua* activities. Thus if well-being is worth wanting and having, as we have all along assumed it to be, one has reasons to engage wholeheartedly and successfully in the relevant activities as such (e.g., action-reasons to be a successful aid worker, action-reasons to be a successful lobbyist, or whatever) *as well as* reasons to do whatever will have the consequences that these activities may have or tend to have. Those consequences, in turn, may be happenings or further actions. Insofar as they are consequences for well-being, on the active account of well-being they will be further actions (e.g., actions of restarting businesses, going fishing with one's children, or reconstructing villages). The mere fact that these too will contribute to well-being because they too are worthwhile activities successfully and wholeheartedly engaged in, and that their value too may come, in some measure, from instrumental contributions they make to someone's well-being further down the line, shows no damagingly infinite regress. We have no cause to want our manifold stock of action-reasons ultimately to be traceable to outcome-reasons, or indeed to more abstract action-reasons, unless we are *prima facie* sceptical about action-reasons. And we have no reason to be *prima facie* sceptical about action-reasons unless we tilted the odds against them at the outset by adopting a passive, Humean account of well-being.

8. The Standards of Success

But haven't we just done exactly what we purported to avoid, and traced all our newly uncovered action-reasons to one highly abstract action-reason, turning all action-reasons back into reasons of principle in the process? If all Kantian action-reasons are straightforward applications of his principle of dutiful trying, the Categorical Imperative, aren't ours straightforward applications of an alternative principle of wholehearted success? That brings us to the third and in some ways most important point about the active account of well-being. What counts as success varies from activity to activity, depending on the internal standards of the activity itself. Notice that Kant's Categorical Imperative is open, but not fundamentally incomplete. It specifies not only that one should try but also, admittedly at a high level of abstraction, what one should try to do:

One should try to do what can, at the same time, be willed as a universal law.[42] But the principle that (to live well) one should succeed willingly in worthwhile activities is radically incomplete. It does not specify, even at a high level of abstraction, which actions one should perform. Rather it refers one to the standards of the activities themselves for guidance on this point. The guidance of these internal standards need not be in any respect uniform. There need be no common themes uniting what a successful priest does with what a successful politician does, or linking either of these to what a successful grandparent or a successful lover does. Not only need there be no common themes; what is more, there may be inconsistent themes. Success in body building may mean disabling oneself from meeting some of the constituent standards for successful ballet dancing, so that one cannot, even conceivably, enjoy both successes in the same period of one's life. Success in environmental campaigning may, likewise, mean opposing some of the constituent standards of success as a stockbroker, so that success in the latter means failure in the former. The fact that the internal standards of these activities are not only different but also conflicting does not entail that one of the activities is good and the other bad (although that may coincidentally be the case). It entails only that none of the actions in question are dictated by any harmonising principle of wholehearted success, analogous to the Kantian Categorical Imperative, which purports to set the same standard for all activities.

That the active account of well-being does not elevate everything to a matter of principle is also illustrated by the ease with which Kantian standards can themselves be incorporated piecemeal into it, and their appeal re-explained in the process. In some activities, putting in the right kind of effort might itself be a secondary form of success. The consolation prize at school sports days is not meant ironically; the dedicated loser is not an outright failure by the internal standards of school sports days, even though, quite possibly, he or she is an outright failure by the internal standards of the individual competitive sports involved. Some teachers believe, similarly, that diligence should be rewarded even when it does not combine with talent and skill to produce excellent schoolwork. They hope to redefine the internal standards of success at school, at least in part, to give some localised credence to Kantian values. Perhaps, when school work tests only a very narrow range of talents and skills, these teachers have a point, because their attitude militates against crude and damaging rankings of pupils at a time when their lives may be forever blighted by official assessment. In my view, however, such cases should be regarded as deviant cases; in relatively few activities can trying alone count as a form of success, let alone as unqualified success. But be that as it may, the very possibility that trying might *sometimes* count as succeeding helps to bring out the point that there is no unifying principle of success, of which apparently localised action-reasons to succeed are applications. Accordingly, there is no

Aristotelian counterpart to Kant's Categorical Imperative. Each success in a worthwhile activity is a success in its own relatively localised terms. It is a success, the quality of which cannot properly be explained in abstraction from the activity in question and its menu of constituent actions. Thus the active account of well-being has no particular tendency to turn action-reasons into reasons of principle. Of course there may be some activities that are decidedly principled and that therefore set, predominantly, relatively abstract internal standards of success. Dworkin wrongly supposed judging to be an example; better examples might be those of working as a priest or a human rights campaigner, in which fields of work hypocrisy is often held to be the greatest vice of all. But there are no grounds for supposing that all activities are like this, so that the only worthwhile activities in the world (or the very best ones) are highly principled activities. Accordingly there are no grounds for those who accept the active account of well-being to assume that all action-reasons will be reasons of principle. In turn, those who adopt the active account of well-being into the criminal law are liberated from the assumption that reasons which are not reasons of principle must always be reasons of policy instead. They need not fear that a non-instrumental argument will always tend to favour generality, inflating the general part at the expense of the special part. For, on the active account of well-being, a non-instrumental argument could be at a very high, or equally at a very low, level of abstraction. Accordingly, it could be an argument of very general, or equally of very local, application.

9. Success by Design, Failure by Mistake

Only in deviant cases, I suggested, will trying be a logically sufficient condition of success in our activities. But is it a logically necessary condition? Some would say that it has to be, on the ground that trying is a necessary condition of all action, and of course the success we are talking about is success in action. Whatever we do, it is said, we do by trying to do something.[43] This is not a view I share: There are things, to my mind, that we do without trying, and by that I mean not only without trying to do those things but without trying to do *anything*. I give great credence to the idiomatic usage which tells us that some people succeed in what they do effortlessly, 'without even trying.' But I do agree that, barring exceptional cases on the borderline between what we do and what happens to us, it is true that whatever we do we do by doing something *intentionally*.[44] That is the real way in which the will enters into every action; it converts reasons into actions through the medium of intentions, which may or may not necessitate trying. And this certainly does point to a possible area of common ground between the Aristotelian account of well-being and the Kantian Categorical Imperative. Could it be that wholehearted success in worthwhile activities, like compliance with the Categorical Imperative, is by its very nature intentional on the part of the agent? The answer, subject to a couple of caveats, is affirmative.

Let me begin with the caveats. First, the requirement of intention should not be confused with the requirement of wholeheartedness. Criminal lawyers, at least, should find it easy to appreciate the difference between the two. A mercy killing need be no less intentional than a grudge killing, but the latter can be wholehearted where the former, by its nature, cannot. Conversely, the killing of passengers by blowing up an aircraft for cargo insurance need be no less wholehearted than the killing of passengers by blowing up an aircraft for life insurance, but the latter is intentional killing and the former is killing as a side effect, or incident, of destroying property.[45] Lawyers will recognise the 'cargo bomber' case as one to which judges and commentators sometimes stretch the legal definition of 'intention.'[46] We can already begin to see one of the reasons why they might do this: They regard the lack of intention as somehow compensated by the presence of wholeheartedness when they are rating the heinousness of the crime, and they manipulate the legal definition of 'intention' to reflect this. Perhaps this is even a morally legitimate manoeuvre in a clay-footed institutional system like the law. But we should nevertheless take care, in the less institutional context of a philosophical discussion, not to confuse the requirement of wholeheartedness with the requirement of intention. The requirement of intention actually comes, not of the wholeheartedness requirement, but rather of the *success* requirement. One is not succeeding, in the relevant sense, if one has no relevant intentions. And what are the relevant intentions? That takes us to the next caveat. The suggestion that success in our activities has to be intentional success may conjure up an image of a person both unpleasantly ambitious and oddly self-conscious. Unpleasantly ambitious, because intent upon success. Oddly self-conscious, because continuously aware of the nature of his or her activity and of the standards of success it sets. This image is doubly distorted. Contrary to the impression of excessive ambition, what the requirement of success demands in the way of intention is not an intention to succeed but an intention to engage in the activities in which, happily, one does succeed. The point is that, by the nature of success, one can succeed only in activities that one meant to engage in. Meanwhile, contrary to the impression of excessive self-consciousness, success does not require that one intend to engage in one's activities *under that description.* One must merely intend to engage in the actions that constitute the activity. And even these one need not engage in self-consciously, that is under a particular description.[47] A successful film critic must be good at the interpretation of films. But she need not conceive of herself as either as a 'film critic' or as performing acts of 'interpretation.' Indeed, she need not be aware of the practices, or even possess the concepts, of 'film criticism' and 'interpretation.' All she does, she may say, is tell people what is good or bad about films. That suffices so far as the relevant intention is concerned. For all that is needed to meet the requirement of intentional success is that a person intend, under some description, to perform the actions that go to make up the activity in which she succeeds. This final formulation makes it clear, in case you envisaged the Aristotelian and Kantian doctrines enjoying a total rapprochement regarding the centrality of the will, that on the Aristotelian side one's success may be a chance in a million, even a miracle, without foreclosing the evaluative significance of that success. The element of chance, on the Aristotelian view, lies in the realisation of the outcomes that are constituents of the activities and actions in which one succeeded and that make one's activities and actions successful. It does not lie in the performance of the actions or the pursuit of the activities themselves, which, I repeat, always has to be intentional.

It is, however, no coincidence that both the Kantian and Aristotelian doctrines do give intention a central role in their ideals of human flourishing. The central role of intention in human flourishing is dictated by some of the most fundamental features of practical rationality, ecumenically recognised across diverse philosophical traditions. These features cannot be investigated here.[48] As I already hinted in connection with the Categorical Imperative, however, these features do leave us with some important scope for asymmetry between the good life and the bad life, between the case of flourishing and the case of downfall. Good need not mirror bad, right need not mirror wrong, positive value need not mirror negative. That becomes particularly apparent when we look at the structure of the active account of well-being. On this account, there are more ways of going wrong in life than there are ways of going right, more ways of detracting from one's well-being than ways of augmenting it. One augments one's well-being only to the extent that one succeeds wholeheartedly in worthwhile activities. One may detract from one's well-being, on the other hand, in three quite different dimensions: *either* by failing in worthwhile activities, *or* by engaging in worthwhile activities halfheartedly or reluctantly, *or* by engaging in worthless or base activities. In the latter dimension, moreover, success and wholeheartedness both serve to make things worse, not better. If you are a gangland hitman, then other things being equal it is better to be both a failed and a reluctant one. If you are the kind of hitman who prides himself on never missing, that only goes to show that you are leading, other things being equal, a sad life of compound debasement: debased first by the baseness of your activity, second by your success in it, and third by the perverse pride you take in this success, which testifies to your wholeheartedness in pursuing it.[49] But if being a hitman were a worthy occupation, it would be *lack* of success or *lack* of pride that would do the damage. This means that intention can have only a rather fragmented or patchy role in people's downfall compared with the role that it has in their flourishing. Where they engage in worthless or base activities, success only makes things worse, and because intention is a component of success, intention forms part of what makes things worse in such cases, even though it does not by itself make things worse. But people's downfall often lies in failure at worthwhile activities rather than success in base ones, and there is, in general, no necessary connection between intention and failure. I say 'in general' here because sometimes, of course, failure consists in the performance of certain actions, the *omission* of which is a constituent of success at a certain activity. People fail as parents when they discriminate systematically between their children, fail as people of honour when they break their promises, fail as barristers when they turn down unappetising clients for that reason, and so on. Some such 'actions of failure' happen to be definitionally intentional, such as deceits and manipulations, whereas others, such as denigrations and breaches of promise and killings, do not have this feature. Where an action of failure is definitionally intentional, then that obviously introduces a requirement of intention into failure. But otherwise the issue of whether one failed does not depend on one's having the intention to do whatever constituted one's failure. One failed, for example, if one's actions simply did not turn out as they needed to to make the activity successful (e.g., if one never got anywhere near the top of the mountain one was trying to climb). One also failed in an activity if, for example, one failed to perform a certain action that is crucial to success in that activity (e.g., if one were a film critic who never actually bothered to watch a film), or failed to perform enough of the menu of possible constituent actions for one's actions to add up to the activity (e.g., if one went on holiday but, with or without realising it, spent the whole time working). Equally, one failed in an activity if one performed the constituent actions, but not intentionally under any description (e.g., if one were a shot-putter who won a competition only when one let the shot slip clumsily out of one's hand in mid-air). Where the cause of one's downfall in a given activity (generally or on a particular occasion) is failure in that activity, the last example makes clear, not intention but *lack* of intention may sometimes be the hallmark of one's failure. It shows that once we switch attention from those who are augmenting their well-being to those who are detracting from it, on the active view of well-being intentional agency quickly becomes just one of several modes of human agency that may do the detracting. At this point intention loses consistent evaluative significance.

10. Success and Failure in Criminal Law

Many are familiar with the principle that *harmless* activities should not be proscribed by law.[50] Some regard this as a more liberal alternative to the principle that *worthwhile* activities should not be proscribed by law, which they fear brings excessively moralistic considerations to bear on the scope of legislation and adjudication. My own view is that both principles bind the state under modern liberal conditions, so that, as a rule, activities should not be banned (or for that matter made so costly or difficult as to be wiped out in practice) unless they are *both* harmful *and* base or worthless. Troublesome cases for criminalisation then include not only virtually harmless activities (like the use of some recreational drugs, simple trespass on open land, and loitering) where invoking the law is using a sledgehammer to crack a nut, but also those (like boxing, some disruptive trespassing, and possession of firearms) that may have seriously harmful effects but nevertheless have notable redeeming value, either constitutively or instrumentally. The question of what exactly should be criminalised lies beyond the scope of the present enquiry. But the view that, as a rule, we should not be prevented by the state from engaging in worthwhile activities has implications not only for *what* should be criminalised but also for *how* things should be criminalised. If the law should normally target worthless or base activities rather than worthwhile ones, then the paradigm criminal is not a failure in his or her activities but on the contrary a success. For in the case of worthless or base activities, according to the explanation in the previous section, it is better to fail than to succeed, even though the opposite holds in the case of worthwhile activities. It follows (so long as we grant the modest assumption that the more heinous the crime, the closer to the paradigm the criminal comes) that the paradigm criminal is the successful criminal rather than the failed one. Much the same line of argument makes the paradigm criminal a wholehearted one rather than a halfhearted or reluctant one. This does not mean that the criminalisation of the halfhearted or the failed criminal is objectionable, even *prima facie.* It means only that the successful and wholehearted criminal is the key case relative to which the situation of the failed or halfhearted criminal falls to be assessed and determined.[51] Notice that this necessarily brings intention, as well as wholeheartedness, to the centre of the criminal law's attentions. Success, in worthless or base activities as much as worthwhile ones, depends on the intention to engage, under some description, in the actions that add up to one's success. It does not follow from this that intentional crime is *ceteris paribus* worse than unintentional crime. That would not necessarily hold where the crime in question lies in the zone of failure beyond the paradigm. All that follows is that the paradigm criminal is one who intends, under some description albeit not necessarily the law's description, his or her criminal actions.

This thesis, that crime is paradigmatically both intentional and successful, has been thoroughly and sensitively defended elsewhere by Antony Duff.[52] Although many of Duff's arguments could be interpreted as reflecting a broadly Aristotelian account of the good life, I am not clear whether he would agree with me in regarding the fact that crime is paradigmatically intentional as a payoff of the fact that crime is paradigmatically successful. What I am clear about, however, is that Duff's views and mine part company just as soon as we leave the paradigm behind us. For Duff, as for many criminal law textbook writers, the modes of criminality appear to spread outwards from the paradigm of intentional criminality in concentric circles, like the ripples from a stone that lands in the water. Beyond intention there is a band of recklessness, and then a band of negligence.[53] My own view is that, once we go beyond the paradigm of intention (touching on the way some genuinely borderline cases between the intended and the unintended), the mentalities of crime quickly fragment and lack any intelligible general ordering.[54] There are a number of reasons for this. The first is a consequence of the active account of well-being itself. When we leave the paradigm of success, our attention turns to failure. And there are, as I explained previously, many ways of failing in one's activities, whether they are worthwhile or otherwise. Some ways of failing involve intention to do the very actions that seal one's fate. Other ways of failing are ways of failing precisely for the absence of intention, for the fact that they are blunders. Some, I should add, require knowledge, or inkling, of what is going on, for example where one's failure consists in actions of betrayal or complicity. A great deal turns here on the peculiarities of the specific actions going to make up specific activities, because different actions have different mental elements built into their definitional fabric (and some have none at all). That is compounded by the second consideration, which has a more institutional character. As I already mentioned, there are rule-of-law reasons why the law by and large regulates individual actions rather than whole activities. One important payoff of this is that an action that may form part of a base activity or equally a worthwhile one is sometimes subject to criminalisation. Possessing drugs and possessing firearms are obvious examples; animal vivisection is a more controversial case. In these cases the law may try to use a licensing system to do the differentiation. But failing this – for example, in dealing with insider trading or certain forms of harassment – it must often add a variety of complex riders and provisos to the definitions of crimes, typically including specialised mental elements, to try and ensure that the worthwhile activity in question is not pulled down with its worthless or base counterpart. Apart from looking to the manner of performance, or focusing on certain distinctive ulterior intentions, the criminal law may attempt to isolate a certain kind of attitude or outlook that it thinks typifies the base activity but that is missing from the worthwhile one. Words like 'dishonesty', 'recklessness', 'negligence', and 'malice' have all played such a role in the law. It is a relatively localised role, once again, because needless to say such words connote attitudes and outlooks that typify different groups of base activities.

The matter is complicated yet further by the fact that, sometimes, the criminal law deliberately targets what it takes to be worthwhile activities, aiming to institutionalise clear standards of success and failure where the internal standards are in doubt or come to be widely disregarded. This is one way (among many) to demarcate the elusive category known as 'regulatory' crime: Regulatory crime, in this sense, is crime consisting of failure in (supposedly) worthwhile activities rather than success or failure in (supposedly) worthless or base ones. Examples might include driving without due care and attention and failing to display fire exit notices in a public building. Notice that regulatory criminalisation, in this sense, need not violate the principle that worthwhile activities should not be banned or effectively ruled out by law. Regulatory criminalisation complies with that principle on condition that the risk of failure in the activity in question, and consequent criminal conviction, does not *de jure* or *de facto* foreclose successful engagement in it.[55] Nevertheless, the consequence of the fact that regulatory crime in this sense is directed at failure in worthwhile activities rather than success in worthless or base ones is that the paradigm of intentional criminality is subverted. Because the paradigm of intentional criminality comes of the paradigm of successful criminality, where the focus is instead on failure the automatic centrality of intention is lost. We could say that regulatory crime forms its own alternative paradigm in which intention is, in general, neither here nor there. That is just one of several reasons why, as I have said, we should not regard the paradigm of intentional and successful criminality as imposing any general ordering, whether supervisory or definitional, upon the various mentalities of crime that lie beyond it.

11. Well-being and Moral Agency in Criminal Law

I have been assuming, in the last couple of sections, that the emphases and distinctions introduced by the active account of well-being are bound to go to the heart of the criminal law's structure. But even if you are attracted by the active account of well-being, you may doubt whether the criminal law should be much affected by it. After all, the nonprincipled, non-instrumental considerations that the active account of well-being introduces into our thinking are based on the well-being *of the agent him- or herself.* What I do is of the essence for my well-being, what you do is of the essence for your well-being, and so on. Correspondingly, what a scoundrel does is of the essence for his or her well-being: Being a scoundrel, this person is *ceteris paribus* badly off, leading a rotten life. But why should the criminal law, in regulating the activities of scoundrels, give tuppence for their well-being? To put the challenge less rhetorically: Given that they relate to the well-being of the offender, shouldn't we expect the nonprincipled, non-instrumental considerations generated by the active account of well-being to make only a rather trivial difference to the relationship between the supervisory general part and the definitional general part, and between the general part and the special part? Shouldn't we still expect all the *major* work to be done by Ashworth's principles and policies? Even if we grant that in the definitions of criminal offences the law should not be completely oblivious to considerations of the offender's well-being, presumably it should not give these considerations more weight than they have in comparison with the interests of others who are affected by criminality, particularly the actual and potential victims of crime. And frankly, in comparison with those interests, the way in which offending detracts from the offender's well-being may strike one as trifling. *A fortiori* if one thinks, as I myself earlier proposed, that the very legitimacy of a modern system of criminal law turns on its contribution to the objective of harm prevention.

In meeting this challenge, the first thing to point out is that the broadly Kantian approach favoured by Ashworth and many others is open to a closely related objection. After all, it avowedly delimits criminal offences according to the limits of the offender's moral agency. If something falls beyond the scope of moral agency, then (at any rate in the absence of forceful policy arguments) it should not figure in the definition of a crime. One might ask: Why grant the offender's moral agency such an extravagant role, allowing it to set the basic structure of criminal offences, when what we are trying to do in a legitimate system of criminal law is, apparently, to protect people from harm? Kant himself fixed the answer to this by elevating all moral considerations to a mandatory status *a priori.* The Categorical Imperative is, as its name suggests, an *imperative,* so that at least some countervailing considerations are eliminated from consideration, irrespective of their relative weight, whenever it is invoked. To add to the overuse of Dworkin's famous metaphor, the Imperative works as a trump card over at least some policy arguments.[56] Because the Categorical Imperative binds not only the individual agent but also the state, the state too is duty-bound to treat people as moral agents, to respect them as the bearers of potentially rational wills even when it might be useful not to; and that protection extends, of course, to alleged criminal offenders. Now of course this approach fails if there can be purely advisory moral considerations as well as mandatory ones, something that strikes me as highly probable as soon as we pull ourselves away from strict Kantian dogmatics. Nevertheless, there is an alternative and more ecumenical basis for the idea that the lawmaker is duty-bound to treat us as moral agents, even as he or she strives to protect other people from harm. It comes of the fact that a legal system by its very nature claims moral authority over its subjects. For this claim of moral authority to be borne out, legal rules must be of a kind that moral agents could in principle understand and, in their capacity as moral agents, come to accept or reject as guides to their actions. This lends support to the contention that, morally speaking, even a criminal wrong that is not a moral wrong should be defined in such a way that both committing it and avoiding committing it could, in principle, be actions of moral agents *qua* moral agents. Thus treating people as moral agents becomes mandatory for the lawgiver even when it might be (*pace* Kant) advisory for the rest of us, who do not normally claim moral authority. It means that the lawgiver's legitimate ambition of preventing harm must be pursued only in ways that are compatible with the moral agency of potential offenders, and at least some instrumental ('policy') benefits of ignoring that constraint must, however regrettably, be sidelined. An offender's moral agency therefore appears to take centre stage, as a *constraint* on criminalisation, even though (let us suppose) the main *point* of legitimate criminalisation is not to respect the moral agency of offenders but to protect their victims from harm.[57]

Now much the same train of thought can still be followed after we embrace the active account of well-being. We can still insist, and on the same grounds, that the criminal law should not simply sacrifice respect for our moral agency on the altar of harm prevention. The only significant difference is that the active account of well-being has its account of moral agency built into it, rather than elevating moral agency to a separate dimension or sphere of reasoning, with separate foundations, serving as an external constraint on the pursuit of well-being. It serves instead as a built-in constraint. Remember that the Kantian idea of morality as a higher or more perfect mode of flourishing, operating as a self-contained system, came into (secular) currency against a backdrop of acquiescence in the passive Humean view of well-being subsequently popularised by utilitarianism. With that passive view abandoned, the motivation to think of morality as a self-contained system instantly evaporates. There is no remaining objection to holding that some considerations of well-being may be moral considerations as well. Thus there is no objection to holding that my well-being and my moral flourishing may be, at least on some occasions, but two sides of the same coin. We may decide that the action-reasons to give to charity or to be a good parent or friend, action-reasons that arise directly from the active nature of well-being, are also moral reasons. We may take the same view, at the other extreme, for action-reasons against being a scoundrel or a pimp or a bigot. And we are at liberty, correspondingly, to determine the scope of moral agency by considering the range of actions that add up to success in such activities and that therefore constitute their contribution to, or detraction from, our well-being.

Things are made difficult here by the diversity of uses to which we put the word 'moral.' We sometimes label considerations 'moral' in contrast to 'legal' or 'institutional', to mean that the considerations in question do not take their force from the say-so of any authority; or in contrast to 'political', to mean that the considerations are matters for personal conscience rather than public resolution; or in contrast to 'pragmatic' to mean that the considerations are not considerations of short-term instrumental gain; or in contrast to 'self-interested' to indicate that considerations stem from the interests of a wider range of people than just the person who acts on them, or in contrast to 'aesthetic' to mean that the considerations bear primarily on action rather than primarily on appreciation, and so on. Once we are liberated from the Kantian idea of morality as a self-contained system, it is no longer a matter of great philosophical importance which of these various usages we adopt, so long as we make our meaning plain by context. The only important thing for our purposes, because we based the importance of the law's respect for moral agency upon the law's claim to moral authority, is that there should be consistency in the use of the word 'moral' on both sides of this equation, so that the demand for moral agency picks up the *point* of the law's claim to moral authority. I believe this condition is met if we regard the word 'moral' as simply indicating, in this context, the *fundamentality* of the considerations in question. The law's claim to moral authority is a claim to speak authoritatively even to the most basic aspects of our lives and identities. Our moral agency, meanwhile, is the agency that fixes our most elemental relations with the world around us. And by this standard, any attempt to forge a wholesale division between our well-being and our moral agency obviously has to be an artificial one. For if one thing is certain it is that considerations of well-being, which depend on *wholehearted* as well as successful engagement in our own pursuits, go right to the core of our lives and identities. It follows that the actions which add up to our success in our activities, from the most worthwhile to the most base, are *by that token* actions that fall within the scope of our moral agency in the relevant sense. Again I do not rule out that there might be other actions that belong to our moral agency on other grounds, relating to other fundamental groups of considerations. Therefore I do not rule out that one could, in theory, address someone as a moral agent without attending to that tranche of his or her moral agency that is organised around his or her well-being. But that is not what is at issue here. The objection under consideration now comes from those who say that the deterioration of the offender's well-being that criminality entails cannot be the criminal law's overriding concern when put alongside the well-being of victims and others affected by his or her crimes, especially once we have conceded the discipline of the 'harm principle.' I have just explained, in outline, how it can, on the contrary, come to be a matter of major concern for a criminal law that cares about the offender's moral agency. That the criminal law should care about the offender's moral agency is common ground between the Aristotelian model of criminal law sketched here and the traditional Humean/Kantian model offered by Ashworth and others. The main difference lies in the fact that, on my account, moral agency does not stop at the will but extends out into the world beyond it. Killing, which is partly constituted by a death, is an action; so is turning right, which is partly constituted by ending up facing right. Both are, moreover, actions within the scope of our moral agency. I have now explained why. It is because our well-being turns on our success in worthwhile activities. Assuming always that our well-being is a matter of moral significance, our moral agency extends straightforwardly into those actions that go to make up that success; and success, as I have been at great pains to emphasise, is very rarely a matter of will alone.

This remains true, to my mind, whether the activities in question are principled or not. If the criminal law should treat us as moral agents, then that affects the ungeneralisable, unprincipled dimensions of our moral agency neither less nor more than the generalisable, principled dimensions. And whereas the Kantian view of moral agency turns the whole of moral agency into a matter of principle, the Aristotelian account stresses the role of particular actions in the successful pursuit of diverse morally significant activities. Our moral agency simply extends as far as those actions extend. The Aristotelian account therefore does little to inflate, and indeed much to deflate, the role that has traditionally been carved out for the definitional general part of the criminal law. For it yields considerations that, being at a low level of abstraction and generality, are not at home in the principled justificatory apparatus of the supervisory general part, and yet that, being non-instrumental considerations of moral agency, are not policy considerations either. If we accept that the framers of criminal laws are duty-bound to treat us as moral agents because of the moral authority that they claim over us, this third family of considerations is capable of explaining and justifying a great deal of otherwise bewildering diversity in the way in which criminal offences are conceived, organised, articulated, and interpreted.

12. The Role of Responsibility

The law as whole is bound to address us as moral agents. But the criminal law has a special feature not shared by private law, which may lead us to underestimate the role of active well-being in disrupting the dictates of its general part. The criminal law gets personal. To be convicted of a crime is to be criticised, or even sometimes condemned, as a person. Now I already granted that the evaluation of people and evaluation of their lives occupy distinct, although closely interrelated, evaluative dimensions. One may fail in one's worthwhile pursuits (i.e., in aspects of one's life) because of one's weaknesses and limitations (i.e., aspects of oneself), and the 'because' in this proposition may fall to be read constitutively or causally depending on the internal standards of the pursuit in question. But one may also fail for reasons independent of any of one's weaknesses or limitations or for that matter succeed in spite of one's weaknesses and limitations. Notably, as I explained, one may succeed or fail because of how one's actions turn out. The criminal law, it might be thought, dramatically parts company with the active account of well-being in situations like this. For in cases where the quality of a life – that is, success or failure in worthwhile or base activities – is not a function of the quality of the person living it, the criminal law's interest must surely follow the person, not the life. Under such conditions, whether he or she succeeds or fails, and at what, is surely quite beside the point, and the active account of well-being therefore drops out of the picture.

This argument certainly points us in the right direction for a more complete understanding of the relationship between criminal law and the rest of the law. But in its enthusiasm it overshoots the mark. It is true that the criminal law, unlike other areas of law, does not evaluate aspects of our lives irrespective of how we come out of them personally. But nor, going to the other extreme, does it evaluate us as people irrespective of how our lives are going. It is not an inquisition into our virtues and skills as such any more than it is an inquisition into our quality of life as such. Its mode of evaluation represents a *tertium quid* between these two possibilities, focussing on us as agents whose actions, as well as adding up to the story of our lives, are capable of reflecting on us personally. This *tertium quid* is not an artificial one designed by the law itself. On the contrary, it figures equally in moral thinking under the familiar heading of 'blameworthiness', or 'culpability.' The distinctive point about a question of blameworthiness is that it synthesises attention to what we do with attention to who we are. It does not ask (simply) whether we are worthy or unworthy people, nor (simply) whether we did worthwhile or worthless things. It asks whether what we did both testifies and contributes to who we are. That is a difficult two-way relationship which calls for a great deal of elaboration. For our purposes it is adequate, and I hope accessible, to say that a judgment of (moral) blameworthiness requires a judgment of (moral) agency to be supplemented with an account of (moral) responsibility. In determining whether someone is to blame, we must ask first whether that person did anything wrong, and second whether he or she was responsible for doing it. The order of inquiry here is of the essence. The question of whether we are responsible does not arise until the question of what we are supposed to have done is answered.[58] This is closely reflected in the very grammar of 'responsibility.' In the relevant sense, I cannot be responsible *tout court.* I must be responsible *for* some action or actions of mine.[59] It is true that very often we ask, rather sweepingly, 'Was she responsible *for her actions* at the time?' or even 'Was she a responsible agent?' We do not isolate the *particular* action or actions in question. But this only goes to show that being responsible for what we do is, to a large extent, a continuing rather than a fleeting predicament. That is because many of the conditions of responsibility in the relevant sense are status conditions (that we were not infants, that we were not seriously mentally ill, that we were not brainwashed, etc.). I would go so far as to say that being responsible for what we do is our default condition, which falls into doubt only when our status as rational creatures is called into question. This does not make the question of what exactly we did redundant, or even subsidiary to the question of whether we were responsible for doing it. On the contrary the question of our responsibility for what we did can intelligibly arise only when the question of what we did has been answered. A demarcation of one's (moral) agency, to put it tersely, is always logically prior to a demarcation of one's (moral) responsibility. And only both together can add up to (moral) blameworthiness. To the extent that the criminal law trades in blameworthiness, then, it can never put on one side the questions of moral agency that are answered, at least in part, by the active account of well-being. Like the rest of the law it is bound by the principle that, in claiming moral authority over us, it must speak to us as moral agents. When it comes to the point of judgment, correspondingly, it must begin with questions about what the defendant is supposed to have done, before it can raise the vexed question of the defendant's responsibility for doing it. It cannot dispense with attention to our moral agency and move straight to the question of our moral responsibility. The more personal dimension of evaluation cannot be arrived at without going through the more impersonal dimension of evaluation, represented by the concerns of the active account of well-being, on the way.

What is the practical payoff of approaching the enquiry in this order? Take, once again, a passage of Ashworth's dealing with the controversy over constructive liability:

> If E committed a battery upon V, from which a reasonable person would have foreseen the risk of some harm (albeit not serious harm), and death resulted, a manslaughter conviction would follow [in English law]. Subjectivists would argue that this is contrary to principle. E intended only a fairly minor battery, and it is unfair to impose the 'manslaughter' label when the unlucky result was unforeseen and unforeseeable. . . . Whether or not a satisfactory analytical distinction can be drawn between what E tried to achieve (the assault) and what actually resulted (the death), it would be wrong to blame E morally or legally for the result, in view of the absence of culpability in relation to such a serious outcome.[60]

Everything turns here on Ashworth's extremely restrictive view of moral agency, a super-Kantian doctrine according to which what we do is, morally speaking, that and only that which we will. Our moral agency accordingly extends to none of the further things that we also do, perhaps quite accidentally, *by* willing what we will. Morally speaking, all E did was hit V, so that some extra outcome-oriented doctrine needs to be dragged in to bump her liability up artificially from assault to manslaughter. But this is not how English law approaches constructive manslaughter – and nor should it, by the lights of the broadly Aristotelian view of moral agency outlined here. Constructive manslaughter, in English law, is not acting dangerously with fatal consequences. It is killing by acting dangerously. That makes all the difference in the world. The key action in the *actus reus,* which brings with it the threat of primary rather than secondary liability for homicide, is that of killing, and the Aristotelian doctrine of moral agency allows that this could still count as a morally significant action even when unintended and hence fall within the scope of E's moral agency. Now, it is only once that action has been identified as falling within the scope of moral agency that the further question of moral responsibility arises. But Ashworth has already, by this stage, begged the question against our asking: Was E morally responsible for her actions when she killed? For on his analysis killing was not something that, morally speaking, E ever did. All she ever did, morally speaking, was assault. Thus we are now restricted to the question: Was E morally responsible for her actions when she assaulted? And *that* question naturally makes a manslaughter conviction seem like a grotesque result. It does so, however, by stacking the cards at the very outset, before questions of responsibility even arise. If we accept such a restricted account of moral agency, the possible objects of moral responsibility are narrowed down in advance to a small set of actions that pass the tough super-Kantian test. Thus all the hard work now has to be done by moderate defenders of constructive liability, who face the uphill struggle of showing why (on policy grounds) liability should be upgraded from assault to manslaughter, rather than the downhill slope of showing why, in view of the fact that the killing was accidental, the liability should be manslaughter rather than murder (intended killing being the paradigm). If the latter is the argumentative route that defenders of constructive liability envisage – and it is certainly the route that I would advocate – then they do not tend, as Ashworth alleges, 'to adopt an unduly narrow view of moral responsibility.'[61] Rather, they tend to share in a less restricted and more flexible view of moral agency, perhaps along the lines of the account outlined here, which can include agency going beyond the will's domain. They may then proceed to supplement this with any of a wide range of broader or narrower accounts of moral responsibility. But their account of moral responsibility (be it broad or narrow) must always play second fiddle, as it must for Ashworth too, to their view of moral agency. Before we can ask whether E was morally responsible for the killing of V, we must be prepared to acknowledge that killing V is, morally speaking, one of things that E did. If we will not acknowledge that, as Ashworth will not, then we are not adopting an account of moral responsibility such that E is not morally responsible for the killing. On the contrary, on such a view, because the killing is not on the agenda, the question of E's moral responsibility for it simply does not arise.

13. Having It Both Ways on Autonomy?

Throughout all this I have stood by the principle that the criminal law, like the rest of the law, should treat us as moral agents. According to the Kantian doctrine, the law treats us as moral agents if it treats us as *autonomous* agents. For Kantian morality, as I explained, conceives of our agency as logically independent of the heteronomous world beyond, a matter of our wills and our wills alone. I have rejected this doctrine of autonomous moral agency. But you may complain that I have been trying to have it both ways on the significance of autonomy. For I have invoked in passing a number of familiar principles – notably Mill's famous 'harm principle' and the principles of 'the rule of law' –

which are fundamentally autonomy-based principles. They are principles of law making and law application that are needed if the lawmaker or law applier is to respect and protect the autonomy of those who are subject to the law. If I conceive of people as autonomous agents for the purposes of these principles, am I not bound, at the same time, to conceive of them as autonomous agents for the purpose of the principle that the criminal law should respect the moral agency of those subject to it? Am I not bound, in other words, to concede the key Kantian point that moral agency is autonomous agency?

The key to dissolving this apparent inconsistency is to understand that people can be autonomous in a number of different, and only indirectly related, senses. What Kant had in mind was a condition that, in a Kantian vein, we could label *moral* autonomy. The morally autonomous agent is master of, rather than slave to, her own desires and inclinations. Not only can she grasp and apply reasons for action towards which she has no prior affective leaning, she can also act, as appropriate, on such reasons and rebuild her affective leanings, as appropriate, in the light of them. It means that she has both the power of reason and the power of will. Of course she may fail to use these powers, on occasions or habitually. Kant sometimes spoke as if failure to use these powers was to be equated with failure to have them – that is, as if someone who allowed his inclinations to lead him into error and never exercised his powers of reason or will was in the same predicament of heteronomy as the person who never enjoyed such powers in the first place. Neither had entered the Kingdom of Ends, the distinctively moral domain. One consequence of this was an occasional hint, in Kant's writings, that the only morally autonomous agents were good ones, that moral agency in wrongdoing was a contradiction in terms. This was not Kant's considered view. His considered view was that autonomous agency was located in the capacity rather than in its exercise. His error, meanwhile, was to treat this capacity as a condition of moral agency rather than as a condition of moral responsibility. Or rather, we should perhaps say, to make moral responsibility itself a condition of moral agency. The effect of this was to balance the whole edifice of morality upon the single pivot of the rational will. Once we are liberated from this error, we are liberated too from the famous anxieties about moral autonomy that it creates. In particular, we are liberated from the thought that the moral world, with its emphasis upon the autonomy of the agent, is hermetically sealed against contingency and never interacts with the natural world of causality. For now there is moral agency beyond the will, even out of the will's control. That is because the question of whether such and such an action was autonomously performed, so that its agent was morally responsible for performing it, does not also serve to dictate what the action in question *was*. It does not, as Kant assumed it would, turn all moral agency into the agency of the rational will alone. It therefore casts no doubt on the soundness, or the relevance, of the active account of well-being.

So much for *moral* autonomy, a capacity that is a condition of moral responsibility and should be reflected in the criminal law to the extent that the criminal law asserts the moral responsibility of those whom it judges. Such autonomy can be contrasted with *personal* autonomy, a particular ideal of human well-being that has come to prominence in the Western post-industrialised cultures of today. The ideal of personal autonomy is an ideal of a life shaped substantially by the successive choices of the person leading it. It is the ideal of a life that could have been otherwise, if the person leading it had made it so. Moral autonomy is neither a necessary nor a sufficient condition of personal autonomy. It is not sufficient, because one's personal autonomy depends not only on one's powers of reason and will but also directly on one's environment. One's personal autonomy depends, in particular, on the variety and number of alternative valuable actions and activities that are open to one at each turn and the extent to which one is free from the will of others in selecting from among these alternatives. On the other hand, moral autonomy is not strictly necessary for personal autonomy because the specific powers of reason and will it requires – that is, powers over one's inclinations and desires – are not inevitably implicated in pursuing a life of one's own choosing. One may be fortunate enough to face alternatives all of which suit one's inclinations and none of which requires any self-control. One need not encounter reasons except as they already figure in one's desires, and one may never have need to shape one's desires. Actually this last point needs to be qualified. A life led so wantonly, although it can be personally autonomous to some degree, cannot be a life of full personal autonomy. There is, for example, some personal autonomy available to people with very serious learning disabilities, who may lack sufficient control over their reason and will to be morally autonomous. They may be stuck in a never-ending infancy, and yet we rightly care about honouring their wishes, where we can, about how they are cared for, so as to give them some taste of personal autonomy, some small authorship of some small part of their own lives. But it can never be a life of full personal autonomy that they lead, because the fact of their lacking moral autonomy puts a narrow *a priori* limit on the range of options to which they can realistically have access. This shows that there can be connections between being morally autonomous and being personally autonomous. Nevertheless, the point remains that, even here, the connection between moral autonomy and personal autonomy is an indirect one. One feature that causes confusion between them is that fact that coercion necessarily violates them both. People who are coerced are those whose power over their own will is bypassed; their will is annexed to the will of another. This both eliminates or diminishes their moral responsibility for what they do and detracts from their well-being by violating their independent existence as moral agents. This local convergence has led some, including some neo-Kantians, to neglect the distinction between personal autonomy and moral autonomy across the board. The collapse can work in two contrasting directions. On the one hand, our moral responsibility is sometimes taken to depend on the history of our lives and the alternative lives we might have led. A thief is not morally responsible for what he does if he had a tough time of it with few opportunities and narrow horizons. The responsibility becomes society's instead; the thief was merely a casualty. This drops personal autonomy into the role of moral autonomy, turning an ideal of well-being into a condition of moral responsibility. On the other hand, whether our lives are our own, and we are well off leading them, is sometimes taken to depend only on the freedom of our rational wills. A sane adult with little opportunity and narrow horizons is therefore as well off as the principles of freedom demand so long as she is not coerced or subjected to one of a small range of related usurpations. This puts moral autonomy into the role of personal autonomy, inflating a mere condition of moral responsibility into an ideal of well-being. We may like to think of these as the left-wing liberal and the right-wing liberal confusions respectively. But both are equally confusions.[62]

The liberal legal principles that I have endorsed in passing, such as the harm principle and the principles of the rule of law, take their special force in Western post-industrialised cultures from the importance of personal autonomy in those cultures. We who live under the conditions of modernity can thrive only if we lead autonomous lives. This is the key ideal of human well-being for our age. Like all other ideals of well-being it has often been reconstructed as a passive ideal. In the eyes of some it takes its force from the prosperity it brings to cultures in which it dominates, from the fact that by choosing for ourselves we are more likely to have the experiences we want, from the fact that it has an egalitarian distributive side to it, and so on. But all of this is putting the cart before the horse. To the extent that it matters, under modern conditions, whether we are prosperous, equally resourced, or have the experiences we want, that is primarily because it matters for our personal autonomy. Personal autonomy itself is an intensely active ideal, demanding not a wide variety of experiences, sensations, possessions, and so on but a wide choice of worthwhile actions and activities, complete with their diverse internal standards of success and failure. The value of having money, comfort, entertainment, security, and so on lies in the service these things do to our having a range of valuable pursuits to choose from and from our choosing some over others and pursuing them successfully. In the autonomous life, the passive serves the active, not vice versa. That is equally true of other familiar valid ideals of well-being, such as the classical ideal of personal honour, and the Marxian ideal of self-realisation through labour. The validity of all of these ideals as ideals of human well-being turns on the fact that they are active ideals. The governmental and legal principles that they generate are correspondingly active in their orientation. I do not mean that they are principles of active government. They may or may not be. I mean only that the principles of government under these ideals are to be given, other things being equal, an interpretation that emphasises their relationship to action. The harm principle is a good example. It has sometimes been passively conceived, so that a 'harm', in the relevant sense, is something that happens to one's body or mind, or an unwelcome experience. But a harm, in the sense required by the liberal harm principle, is none of these. It is an attenuation of capacity or opportunity for action, reducing the range of alternative actions and activities that are available to the person who is harmed. Sometimes the reason for the loss of capacity or opportunity is that one was in pain, or lost a leg, or was shocked into submission. But be that as it may, it is the loss of capacity or opportunity, and not the pain or lost limb or shock in itself, that constitutes the harm. That is, perhaps, where the active quality of the ideal of personal autonomy shows its face most strikingly in the principles that govern the making and administration of the law.

The same active dimension also shows up in the principles of the rule of law. The value of personal autonomy turns respect for the rule of law into an obligation, rather than just a counsel of prudence, for modern governments. For respect for the rule of law ensures that, so far as possible, people will be able to predict their collisions with the law in order to be able to steer their lives around it. In the criminal law, the rule of law militates in favour of clear and certain offence definitions, good publicity, and conformity between announced rule and adjudicative standard. The same considerations also militate in favour of devices that allow those who are about to cross the threshold into criminality to be put on notice that they are doing so. This can be achieved in many ways, for example by placing warning notices, requiring an oral warning to be given by some official, setting up specialised training for those (e.g., drivers) whose specialised activities may put them constantly on the verge of criminality, and so on. In the absence of such devices one may achieve roughly the same effect by including an element of 'subjective' *mens rea* in one's offence definition. Such an element means that, assuming one knows the law itself, one also knows that a violation of it is now a possibility, because such knowledge is built into the very definition of the crime. This is a strong argument for making many everyday criminal offences into offences of subjective *mens rea;* indeed, it provides one of the key contemporary arguments for the principle *actus non facit reum nisi mens sit rea.* Here we have in our sights the most dramatic source of confusion, for contemporary criminal lawyers, about the role of considerations of autonomy in the criminal law. For many, requirements of subjective *mens rea* are responsibility requirements. Their connection with autonomy, on this view, comes of the fact that responsible agents are autonomous agents. But responsible agents, as I explained previously, are in fact merely *morally* autonomous agents. They are agents who have the power of reason and the power of will, whether or not they used it. No consideration of moral autonomy supports any requirement of subjective *mens rea* in the criminal law. In fact *mens rea* elements in crimes, subjective or otherwise, have nothing much to do with questions of responsibility. What does not follow is that the general principle of subjective *mens rea* in the criminal law should be abandoned. For as I just explained, such a principle is supported, quite differently and quite generally, by considerations of *personal* autonomy, which give rise to an obligation of respect for the rule of law. Because the ideal of personal autonomy is an ideal of active well-being, this reminds us that the active nature of well-being does not militate automatically against generality in the criminal law.

And yet the generality of the requirement of subjective *mens rea* that has just been established is in three crucial respects more limited than some enthusiasts for the general part have wanted it to be. In the first place, there are alternative ways to secure that people will realise when they are about to do something that has been criminalised quite apart from insisting on such realisation as an element of the crime itself. The law may make use of on-the-spot warnings, licencing systems, and many other devices instead. Second, the requirement of subjective *mens rea* introduced by the obligation to respect the rule of law is a requirement that does not necessarily extend to every element of an *actus reus*. So long as the law builds in an element of subjective *mens rea* at the point where people enter the realm of criminality, it matters very much less from the rule-of-law perspective that they may then commit a variety of different crimes with that same *mens rea,* some more serious than others. They were, after all, put on warning that this could happen by the fact that the law to that effect was correctly promulgated, publicised, and so on. Finally, the requirement of subjective *mens rea* defended in rule-of-law terms can be met in a wide variety of ways in the definitions of offences. It is a doctrine of the supervisory general part that need not give rise to any corresponding doctrine in the definitional general part. The law may meet its standards using a wide variety of terminological and conceptual frameworks depending on the particular crime and its structure. The law meets its standards whenever it makes the crime a crime of intentional agency, which is (for other reasons) the paradigm of criminality. The law also meets its standards by insisting on the *mens rea* elements that are built into particular *actus rei,* such as possession, conspiracy, or deception. The law may equally meet its standards in a wide variety of other ways, using a wide range of different *mens rea* words and *mens rea* concepts. Thus the definitional implications of *actus non facit reum nisi mens sit rea,* even given this 'subjectivist' interpretation, may well be found, and if I have been right about everything else ought to be found, in the special part of the criminal law rather than the general part.

14. The General Part in Its Place

The remarks towards the end of the preceding section may come as a disappointment. They make the conclusions of this essay seem less radical than some readers may have expected. For whereas I undertook to call into question the traditional view of the general part's centrality to a rational and principled criminal law, I may seem in fact to have spent a great deal of time reaffirming it. Here are just some of the traditional general-part doctrines that have come out of the discussion not only conserved, but indeed defended:

- The doctrine that intended criminality is the central case of criminality. This was defended subject to the caveats that (a) there is a competing paradigm in the domain of 'regulatory' crime and (b) there are no general implications of the doctrine for the ranking or ordering of *mens rea* elements other than intention.
- The doctrine that *actus non facit reum nisi mens sit rea.* This was defended in its classic 'subjectivist' reading, but on the understanding that it does not require an element of *mens rea* as to every element of the *actus reus* (i.e., that it does not entail the 'correspondence principle'), and subject to the caveat that it may be displaced by alternative methods of alerting people to the risk of their own impending criminality.
- The doctrine that unsuccessful criminal attempts (and unsuccessful incitements, etc.) are less heinous, *ceteris paribus,* than completed crimes.
- The doctrine that secondary participation in crime, or complicity, can be kept rationally distinct from participation as a principal even though it is not necessarily less heinous, even *ceteris paribus,* than participation as a principal.
- The doctrine that moral responsibility is a condition of criminal liability, so as to exclude young children and some seriously mentally ill people from the criminal law's ambit even when they do commit criminal wrongs.

The list could go on. What it shows is that my main quarrel has not been with the traditional textbook exposition of the supervisory or the auxiliary general part. Of course I have doubted the philosophical foundations upon which many writers have based their arguments for supervisory doctrines such as 'subjectivism' and the centrality of intention, or auxiliary doctrines about inchoate and secondary offending. I have tried to turn the tide against the unholy alliance between Kantian-inspired views of moral agency and utilitarian, outcome-oriented ideals of well-being, an alliance that has tended to dominate the modern discussion, in this field as in so many others.[63] In places this certainly leads me to tone down or circumscribe traditional claims about the supervisory and the auxiliary general part, as the various caveats and provisos in the foregoing list illustrate. But these caveats and provisos in the supervisory and auxiliary general part were not the main point of the exercise. The main point of the exercise was to show that the doctrines of the supervisory general part do not exert the pressure towards uniformity in the definitional general part that is sometimes expected of them. For they are open to alternative means of compliance within the definitional structure of particular crimes, and the rationality of those means does not depend, as some have thought, on whether one can show 'policy', or instrumental, reasons for departing from some idealised definitional norm dictated by 'principle' alone. On the contrary, much definitional diversity can be attributed to considerations that are neither considerations of principle nor considerations of policy. They are reasons that structure our moral agency and hence constrain the criminal law non-instrumentally, but that owe their force to no overarching moral consideration along the lines of the Categorical Imperative. It means that the supposition that a 'rational and principled' criminal law must tend towards definitional uniformity is ill founded. The definition of a particular offence (or defence) may, so far as this argument takes us, be rational (i.e., supported by valid reasons) and principled (i.e., conform to the sound principles of the supervisory general part) without showing any significant similarities to other offence or defence definitions, even in the same family of offences, and let alone beyond it.

The cautionary words 'so far as this argument takes us' should, of course, be taken seriously. In this chapter I considered only arguments for relative definitional uniformity that were themselves of a non-instrumental character – that is, those that did not rely on the alleged good consequences of having a criminal law with relative definitional uniformity. Some have said that a criminal law with many different words and concepts haphazardly arranged across its terrain has serious implications for clarity, certainty, and other rule-of-law values. For example, if the word 'reckless' is used in one statute and the word 'malicious' in another, and the two are held to have slightly different nuances, then whatever the rationality of each definition taken on its own, the juxtaposition of the two will lead to confusion and difficulty on the part of those who are at the law's sharp end. Thus the retreat from definitional generality that I licence also commits me to licencing a violation of the rule-of-law standards that I myself have endorsed. No doubt there is some force in this argument. But I believe its force has been seriously exaggerated. The exaggeration comes of an assumption that the law has only one sharp end, at which everybody's rule-of-law interests are aligned. In reality, however, what causes confusion and difficulty in the *administration* of the law (what lawyers think of as the law's sharp end) can be the very same thing that makes the law vivid and accessible to people outside the courtroom, on the way back from the pub or driving on the motorway or carrying the takings to the bank. A distinction is needed between the *textual* clarity that aids the law's administrators (legally trained or otherwise) and the *moral* clarity that aids people going about their ordinary lives.[64] Of course both clarities are important; excessive fragmentation in the criminal law can no doubt lead to errors in charging, trying, and convicting, all of which are deeply disquieting. Nevertheless, sometimes what looks like technicality or inconsistency or even absurdity when we sit in the measured, relatively deliberative ambience of the courtroom or the interview room is, deep down, the whole point of the law. Jeremy Horder has brought this out excellently by drawing our attention to the wide range of vivid *actus rei* – maiming, blinding, disfiguring, and so on – that were found in the original text of the Offences Against the Person Act 1861.[65] All are different actions, with different intrinsic features, which do not owe their wrongness, so far as I can see, to any unifying principle. But be that as it may, so far as the instrumental value of retaining such particular *actus rei* is concerned, their moral vividness is both their blessing and their curse. Blessing, because the crimes convey themselves very dramatically to those who are about to commit them, mapping onto bloodcurdling images in the public imagination. Curse, on the other hand, because the fine lines between these various *actus rei,* and the complex definitional puzzles they consequently pose, lead to trouble in directing juries and advising magistrates or police officers. I cannot go into the consequences of this tension here. Suffice it to say that in my view the instrumental case for relative definitional uniformity depends on the resolution of this tension in favour of eliminating the curse even if at the expense of the blessing, something that, for me at any rate, turns the priorities of the rule of law on their head, putting ease of administration ahead of public accessibility. That, however, is irrelevant to the argument that was conducted here. For what I aimed to show here was not that relative definitional uniformity has no benefits, or that its benefits do not outweigh its hazards. All I aimed to show was that those who call for a trend towards definitional uniformity cannot pretend thereby to be speaking the uniquely authentic voice of a rational and principled criminal law.

15. 'Families' of Offences

There is, however, one final promissory note to be honoured, and one final twist in the story. In the previous section, as in the first, I mentioned the idea of a 'family' of offences. I took it for granted that this would be read in the way that academic criminal lawyers customarily read it, as referring to criminal offences gathered together according to the harm that was done, or more broadly the interest that was affected, by the crime. Thus 'homicide crimes' make up a family of crimes defined in terms of their fatal consequences, 'crimes of property deprivation' make up another family including theft and fraud and other offences covered in England by the Theft Acts, and along the same lines we have 'public order offences', 'sexual offences', and so on. I have no real objection to this way of dividing the law into manageable chunks for convenient exposition. But my argument pointed to an alternative possible way of conceiving the limits of a 'family' of crimes. Crimes belong to the same family, on this account, when they are committed by the performance of the same action or actions. This criterion may, of course, have some piecemeal indirect connections with the more familiar harm-based criterion. Because murder and manslaughter both involve an action of killing, they also both have fatal consequences; they are united both in action and in harm. But we may argue that 'causing death by dangerous driving' does not involve killing even though it has fatal consequences and so, by this account, should not be regarded as belonging to the same family as murder and manslaughter.[66] Similarly, we may say that theft is not part of the same family as fraud or deception offences in English Law, because the former is a crime of appropriation and the latter are crimes of obtaining,[67] while the crime in section 20 of the Offences Against the Person Act 1861 belongs to a different family from the crime in section 47 of the same Act, because in spite of their related harm elements they are committed by logically unrelated actions (inflicting harm or wounding in the former case, assaulting in the latter).[68] And so forth. Naturally this leaves open the possibility of overlapping families of crimes, because many crimes are committed by more than one action, either alternatively or cumulatively. The section 20 offence just mentioned has two alternative actions by which it can be committed ('inflicting grievous bodily harm' and 'wounding'), whereas the offence in section 15 of the Theft Act 1968 has two actions that are cumulatively required for its commission ('obtaining' and 'deception', the former performed by means of the latter). Such examples show that the action-based criterion for families of crimes does not create hermetic seals around doctrines applicable to particular crimes and does not foreclose judicial cross-fertilisation of definitional doctrine through analogical reasoning. But then the arguments of this chapter were not meant to foreclose definitional cross-fertilisation but merely to counter the textbook *idealisation* of such cross-fertilisation, as something to be undertaken wholesale and aimed at minimising definitional variety. The fact that the action-based criterion of a family of offences can create an occasional pressure for localised blurring of familial boundaries is nothing especially to be afraid of. It merely reflects the fact that judges, unlike legislatures, have to use law to make law and sometimes, *faute de mieux,* have to use the law relating to one criminal offence to develop the law relating to another. Other things being equal, these should be offences with some family ties, and if the criterion of a family is action-based rather than harm-based, that in turn means crimes that are committed by the performance of the same, or logically related, actions, rather than crimes involving the same, or logically related, harms.

To defend fully the move to an action-based criterion of a family of crimes, we would have to take the argument of this chapter at least one step further. I have argued only that the localised action-reasons that are generated by the active account of well-being can serve to disrupt the justificatory path from the supervisory general part to the definitional general part, so that definitional variety, to be justifiable, need not be justifiable on policy grounds alone. This argument grants the assumption that the generality of the supervisory general part sets the default condition, so that the problem is always to justify definitional variety. The next step would be to argue that this assumption is misguided – that by default each criminal offence's definition falls to be justified on its own merits, so that definitional diversity is the law's default condition.

On this argument the localised action-reasons I emphasised in this chapter are very much the starting point. We need to begin by asking which particular actions are wrongful and only then ask whether some supervisory or other general-part doctrines should constrain or inform our attempts to criminalise them. I believe that we should take this further step and concentrate our interpretative and reforming efforts first and foremost on the job of justifying each crime on its merits, rather than justifying each crime relative to some other crime. Obviously I cannot argue the point here, but I can gesture towards the argument that would be needed by saying that it depends on the claim that the active account of well-being introduces a horde of new rational incommensurabilities on the back of its appeal to localised action-reasons. Such incommensurabilities interfere with the process of justifying the definition of one crime as a variation of another and hence throw us back much more often on the justification of our offence definitions taken one at a time. We are left, of course, with small families of crimes within which commensurability holds and within which relativised sorts of justification remain available. Within these families each variation from the norm does need to be justified, and uniformity is the default. But beyond these families variety is the default, and uniformity is what needs to be justified. The methodology of the special part should not, in other words, be carried over automatically into the general part, so that the 'rationalisation' of the criminal law, the tying up of its loose ends, becomes our ambition across the board. Of course, one side effect of this argument would be to make each special-part doctrine itself more special, that is to carve up the terrain of the criminal law into smaller families than we are used to. This chapter did not establish, however, that we should embrace this or any other of the more dramatic conclusions ventured in this paragraph. I did not do the work that would be needed in order to understand the structure of the special part of the criminal law, nor to show that beyond this special part fragmentation rather than uniformity is the criminal law's rational default condition.[69] I defended only the following more modest claim: that even if uniformity were the criminal law's default condition, so that each variation in its doctrines does need to be supported by reasons, the existence of action-reasons that are neither considerations of policy nor considerations of principle means that we should not expect to end up with the relatively expansive, relatively exacting, and relatively uniform definitional general part so beloved of textbook writers and codifiers in the modern English idiom.

Notes

1 *Criminal Law: The General Part* (Stevens, London 1953).

2 Ibid, v.

3 Some classic remarks lamenting the definitional variety of the criminal law: Williams,

Textbook of Criminal Law (2nd ed., Stevens, London 1983), 73 and 934; J. C. Smith and Brian Hogan, *Criminal Law* (8th ed., Butterworths, London 1996), 71 and 76 (also in previous editions); Andrew Ashworth, *Principles of Criminal Law* (1st ed., Clarendon Press, Oxford 1991), 281 and 358.

4 See, for example, Law Commission, *Criminal Law: A Criminal Code for England and Wales* (Law Com. No. 177, HMSO, London 1989), esp. vol. 1, paras. 2.8–2.9.

5 Williams, *Textbook of Criminal Law* (see note 3), 17.

6 Smith and Hogan, *Criminal Law* (4th ed., Butterworths, London 1983), v.

7 Contrast Alan Norrie, *Crime, Reason and History* (Weidenfeld, London 1993), 11, where a different test is used, according to which the theoretical inevitability of pervasive conflict among reasons and principles casts doubt upon the criminal law's theoretical capacity to be rational and principled. I agree with Norrie about the theoretical inevitability of pervasive rational conflict. But I think that this inevitability makes it theoretically easier, not theoretically harder, for the criminal law to be rational and principled. Where there is a conflict between two reasons (or two principles) which cannot be resolved by any further reasons (or principles), that makes it rational (or principled, as the case may be) to follow *either* of them, not neither of them. Both alternatives are acceptable. So the range of rational (and/or principled) ways forward is increased.

8 The difference in the qualifications here stems from the fact that all (valid) principles are reasons, but not all (valid) reasons are principles. This means that there can be rational alternatives to being principled, whereas there are no principled (or rational) alternatives to being rational.

9 Thus the operation of the auxiliary general part tends to be obstructed or confused by, for example, crimes of possession, where the *actus reus* is not strictly an action or activity but a state of affairs with a subsidiary active dimension. See Smith and Hogan, *Criminal Law* (see note 3), 325–6.

10 *Woolmington v. DPP* [1935] AC 462.

11 Joseph Raz, 'Legal Principles and the Limits of Law', *Yale Law Journal* 81 (1972), 823 at 837; Neil MacCormick, *Legal Reasoning and Legal Theory* (Clarendon Press, Oxford 1977), 259ff.

12 Raz, 'Legal Principles and the Limits of Law' (see previous note) at 838.

13 Dworkin, 'Hard Cases' in his *Taking Rights Seriously* (Duckworth, London 1977), 81ff.

14 Ashworth, *Principles of Criminal Law* (2nd ed., Clarendon Press, Oxford 1995), 85–6. For a similar invocation of 'principle and policy', see the report *Criminal Law: Codification of the Criminal Law. A Report to the Law Commission* (Law Com. No. 143, HMSO, London 1985), para 1.8.

15 I will not dwell here on the issue of the distinction's exclusivity, although for myself I cannot see any sensible way of avoiding the conclusion that something like 'serving the greatest happiness of the greatest number' counts as both a policy and a principle. Compare Neil MacCormick's critique of Dworkin's distinction in *Legal Reasoning and Legal Theory* (see note 11) at 259ff.

16 'Hard Cases' (see note 13), 82–3.

17 'The Model of Rules I' in *Taking Rights Seriously* (see note 13), 14 at 22.

18 *Principles of Criminal Law* (see note 14), 58 and 92.

19 'The Model of Rules I' in *Taking Rights Seriously* (see note 13), at 22.

20 Derek Parfit, *Reasons and Persons* (Clarendon Press, Oxford 1985), 104. Parfit speaks of

'aims' rather than reasons, but because whatever we aim at is regarded by us as a reason, Parfit's distinction can also be adapted to provide a classification of types of reasons. See also Joseph Raz, *The Morality of Freedom* (Clarendon Press, Oxford 1986), 145–6, which is the source of my terminology.

21 On the viability of this distinction, see, for example, David Lewis's valuable note on 'Insensitive Causation' in his *Philosophical Papers II* (Clarendon Press, Oxford 1986), at 184-6, or (better still) Jennifer Hornsby's discussion of causal transitive verbs in her *Actions* (Routledge & Kegan Paul, London 1980), at 124–32.

22 See, for example, Glanville Williams, *Textbook of Criminal Law* (see note 3), 378.

23 *Attorney-General's Reference (No. 1 of 1975)* [1975] QB 773; *Attorney-General* v. *Able* [1984] QB 795.

24 That is surely what the Accessories and Abbettors Act 1861 is getting at in section 8: 'Whosoever shall aid, abet, counsel or procure the commission of any indictable offence . . . shall be liable to be tried, indicted and punished as a principal offender.' We may interpret: Accomplices are not principals, but they are to be treated as principals because they are principals *in effect.*

25 Some things (e.g., what we often call 'reflex reactions', such as blinking as something flies into one's face or laughing spontaneously at a good joke) lie on the borderline between what we do and what happens to us, so the line etched in logic is not a perfectly sharp one.

26 Parfit is a consequentialist who accepts the possibility of action-reasons (*Reasons and Persons* [see note 20], 112–13); likewise Amartya Sen ('Rights and Agency', *Philosophy and Public Affairs* 11 [1982], 3). Both maintain the apparent strictness of their consequentialism, and answer the challenge posed here, by treating the fact that I ϕed as a consequence of my ϕing, so that non-instrumental action-reasons cast an instrumental shadow and can therefore be counted instrumentally. This achieves the right result but dodges the issue of practical rationality's non-instrumental aspect.

27 Thus the extensive literature that asks whether there are further (nonmoral, usually self-interested) reasons for being moral, a superior but still profoundly misguided example of which is David Gauthier's 'Morality and Advantage' in J. Raz (ed.), *Practical Reasoning* (Oxford University Press, Oxford 1978), 185. A natural riposte to the 'Why should I be moral?' of Gauthier and his fellow Hobbesians is 'Why should I be self-interested?', which (somewhat skittishly) puts the ball back in their court.

28 Kant, *Groundwork of the Metaphysic of Morals* (trans H. J. Paton, Harper & Row, New York 1964), 88.

29 For a sympathetic reconstruction of Kant's idea of consistency, see Onora O'Neill, 'Consistency in Action', in N. Potter and M. Timmons (eds.), *Universality and Morality* (Reidel, Dordrecht 1985), 159.

30 Again we need to be aware of the exceptional cases on the borderline between what we do and what happens to us, some of which we classify as 'involuntary actions' – that is, actions without the involvement of the will (see note 25).

31 I am thinking primarily of Thomas Nagel's 'Moral Luck', *Proceedings of the Aristotelian Society Supplementary Volume* 50 (1976), 137, in which Kant's objection to the possibility of moral luck in the way our actions turn out is progressively broadened out to confront other kinds of moral luck until '[t]he area of genuine agency . . . seems to shrink . . . to an extensionless point' (146).

32 It would have been perverse to hold it necessary, because those who already have a rational will are *ipso facto* those who have the least need of the law's guidance on what to do. Compare, however, John Finnis, *Natural Law and Natural Rights* (Clarendon Press, Oxford 1980), 231–2, where the role of the law in specifying *how* to do what the rational will directs us to do is emphasised.

33 I have given more detailed attention to them in 'The Purity and Priority of Private Law', *University of Toronto Law Journal* 46 (1996), 459.

34 I stress *intellectual* culture. There is little evidence that the idea has caught on in public culture at large, although there is evidence of some confusion over the issue.

35 Ashworth, 'Taking the Consequences', in Stephen Shute, John Gardner, and Jeremy Horder (eds.), *Action and Value in Criminal Law* (Clarendon Press, Oxford 1993), 107; Law Commission, *Legislating the Criminal Code: Involuntary Manslaughter* (Law Com. No. 237, HMSO, London 1996), 37ff.

36 Of many works exploring this point, a good starting point is John Ackrill, 'Aristotle on *Eudaimonia', Proceedings of the British Academy* 60 (1974), 339.

37 The formulation comes from Joseph Raz, 'Duties of Well-Being' in his *Ethics in the Public Domain* (Clarendon Press, Oxford 1994), 3, and its elements are also defended in Raz's book *The Morality of Freedom* (see note 20). Among many others who have defended an (at least partly) active view of well-being are Robert Nozick in *Anarchy, State, and Utopia* (Basic Books, New York 1974), 42–5; Bernard Williams in his debate with J.J.C. Smart published as *Utilitarianism: For and Against* (Cambridge University Press, Cambridge 1973), 108ff; and Elizabeth Anderson in *Value in Ethics and Economics* (Harvard University Press, Cambridge, Mass. 1993), 22–6.

38 It may be owed, of course, to further things one *did* there, for example sampling the view, taking photographs, hang-gliding, resuscitating an unconscious mountaineer. That would obviously allow being at the top of the mountain to contribute to one's well-being independently of how one got there, without switching attention away from what one did.

39 I say a little more about rule-of-law reasons in section 13 below.

40 Sexual intercourse is, of course, an activity to most of us; but to the law it is an action forming part of that activity, namely an action of penetration: See *Kaitamaki* v. *R* [1984] 2 All ER 435.

41 The example is chosen to make clear that actions, for present purposes, include omissions. Of course one of the implications of taking an active view of well-being is that actions and omissions with the same consequences may nevertheless differ in value. However, in keeping with the arguments to be developed here I doubt whether there is any *systematic* difference in value between actions and omissions, such that if one has a choice between doing some harm and failing to prevent the same harm, then other things being equal there is always, or normally, or depending on what is being held equal, a *prima facie* reason to choose the latter. A valuable discussion is A. P. Simester, 'Why Omissions are Special', *Legal Theory* 1 (1995), 311.

42 This is why, for all he defends a highly restricted view of moral agency, Kant presupposes a more diverse account of agency in general. For moral agency to consist in trying to do things, there must be other things one can do apart from trying. Otherwise the Categorical Imperative would involve a real infinite regress: You must try to try to try . . . and so on.

43 For example, Jennifer Hornsby, *Actions* (see note 21), 33–45.

44 Which Hornsby treats as equivalent to the 'trying' criterion; see her essay 'On What's Intentionally Done' in *Action and Value in Criminal Law* (see note 35), 55 at 58.

45 The example originates from Glanville Williams, *The Mental Element in Crime* (Magnes Press, Jerusalem 1965), 34–5.

46 Memorably Lord Hailsham in *Hyam* [1975] AC 55 at 74.

47 Some treat the locution 'under a description' as a licence to be reductivists about agency, holding that all we 'really' do is try (or will, or move) and the other things we say we do (e.g., eat, paint the house, play squash, torture animals) are just so many 'descriptions' of our tryings (or willings or movings). The *locus classicus* is Donald Davidson, 'Agency', in his *Essays on Actions and Events* (Clarendon Press, Oxford 1980), 43 at 58–9. Rarely has a philosophical claim been so influential and yet so palpably self-undermining. A (valid) description of an action is a description of it in terms of some or all of its constituents. Because reductivists about action strip out all the distinguishing constituents of our diverse actions, they leave nothing in terms of which validly to 'describe' that diversity. Kant's reductivism about moral agency obviously has a lot to answer for here, because it proved to be an inspiration for countless misguided attempts to make human agency, in general, into a contingency-free zone, even though it was only a doctrine of *moral* agency.

48 I have investigated them, or at least some of them, in my paper 'Justifications and Reasons' in A.T.H. Smith and A. P. Simester (eds.), *Harm and Culpability* (Clarendon Press, Oxford 1996), 103. In particular I have attempted to explain the basis of the asymmetry between right and wrong that I reintroduce here.

49 There is a complication here that arises out of the role of skill in well-being. Skills are partly a *means* to success in worthwhile activities and partly a *source* of worthwhileness in their own right. Thus the fact that one has and uses a skill does something for one's well-being even if one uses it for base ends. Nevertheless, one's success in these base ends detracts from one's well-being. We could say that, in such situations, skill gives with one hand and takes away with the other. Hence one (of several) way in which we can be 'admirably immoral'. On which, see, for example, Michael Slote, *Goods and Virtues* (Clarendon Press, Oxford 1983), 77ff.

50 The 'harm principle' first defended by J. S. Mill in 'On Liberty', in the collection of Mill's work *Three Essays* (Oxford University Press, Oxford 1975), 5 at 15.

51 On this method of analysis, which is fundamental for every concept with both institutional and evaluative dimensions, including the concept of law itself, see John Finnis, *Natural Law and Natural Rights* (see note 32), 6ff.

52 In his *Intention, Agency and Criminal Liability* (Blackwell, Oxford 1990), 111–15 (intended crime as paradigm) and 184–92 (successful crime as paradigm). Although these two passages have similarities, their interrelation is not brought out.

53 The picture comes across in *Intention, Agency and Criminal Liability* at 139 (on the recklessness band) and 156–7 (on the negligence band). I am indebted to Antony Duff for suggesting the image of 'concentric circles' to describe it. The image is complicated somewhat by the fact that Duff sometimes identifies two competing paradigms or central cases, involving two different concepts of intention (e.g., at 114), roughly equivalent to what others have called 'direct' and 'oblique' intention. This complication is not relevant to the present discussion, save that I should say that my own references to intention in this chapter are to direct intention only.

54 Here I attempt to bear out an objection Heike Jung and I raised in 'Making Sense of Mens Rea: Antony Duff's Account', *Oxford Journal of Legal Studies* 11 (1991), 559.

55 One important factor to bear in mind here is that some activities, for example friendship, are regulation-sensitive, meaning that they are destroyed by being officially regulated. I have discussed this problem in 'Private Activites and Personal Autonomy: At the Margins of Anti-Discrimination Law' in Bob Hepple and Erika Szyszczak (eds.), *Discrimination: The Limits of Law* (Mansell, London 1992), 148.

56 Dworkin, 'Rights as Trumps' in Jeremy Waldron (ed.), *Theories of Rights* (Oxford University Press, Oxford 1984), 153.

57 This is, of course, the essence of H.L.A. Hart's famous differentiation between the general justifying aim of criminal law and the distributive constraints on its enforcement against particular people; see his 'Prolegomenon to the Principles of Punishment' in Hart, *Punishment and Responsibility* (Clarendon Press, Oxford 1968), 1 at 8–13. (I should add that I do not accept what I granted for the sake of argument in the text, namely that the prevention of harm is a legitimate criminal law's main justifying aim. I accept only that its legitimacy turns on its contribution to this aim.)

58 There are notoriously many senses of the word 'responsible'. In one sense, sometimes known as the 'causal' sense, the question is whether I am responsible for such things as deaths, explosions, and misunderstandings – that is, for certain things that happen. Often (although not always) this question spawns the further questions of whether the deaths, explosions, and misunderstandings were consequences of my actions, and if so in what way, for example did I actually kill or did I just prompt or inspire a killing? This 'causal' sense is not the sense of 'responsible' I am invoking here. In the sense invoked here I can be responsible only for my actions, not for things that happen. On this and many other distinctions in the language of responsibility, a good starting point is H.L.A. Hart's 'Varieties of Responsibility', *Law Quarterly Review* 83 (1967), 346.

59 Many have discussed the conditions of responsibility. On the no less important but widely neglected question of the *parameters* of responsibility (i.e., the 'to' and 'for' elements), see Joel Feinberg's 'Responsibility *Tout Court*' and 'Responsibility for the Future', both in *Philosophy Research Archives* 14 (1988), 73 and 93 respectively. Feinberg's essays also help to develop some of Hart's suggestions about the various different senses of 'responsible.'

60 Ashworth, 'Taking the Consequences' (see note 35), at 118.

61 *Principles of Criminal Law* (see note 14), at 86.

62 I regard the central 'antinomy' of Alan Norrie's contribution to this volume ('"Simulacra of Morality"? Beyond the Ideal/Actual Antinomies of Criminal Justice', above page 101) as an instance of what I am calling the 'left-wing' confusion. Shamefully, many people living in broadly liberal societies such as ours suffer a paucity of options that leaves them a long way from the liberal ideal of personal autonomy. Nobody should pretend or deem otherwise. But in convicting these people of crimes on the same basis as other people the criminal law does not pretend or deem that they are more personally autonomous than they are. It does not assume that the 'actual' lives up to the 'ideal.' It asserts only that those convicted of crimes are *morally* autonomous and therefore morally responsible for their actions, which by and large they most certainly are. To deny this responsibility would be to compound the dehumanisation inflicted on these people by their appalling social conditions. That is because responsible agency is a condition of self-respect, with-

out which nobody can thrive. If the consequence of being held responsible (viz. criminal punishment) seems to be no less dehumanising, and no less of a threat to self-respect, than the denial of responsibility would have been, then the answer is not to deny the responsibility but to reform the structures and institutions of criminal punishment, and/or to use it more parsimoniously. And this is exactly what liberal-minded criminologists and penal reform campaigners have bravely struggled to achieve, against the bloodlust of populist government, throughout the modern age.

63 For explicit endorsement, see Nicola Lacey, *State Punishment: Political Principles and Community Values* (Routledge, London 1988), 103–5, picked up by Andrew Ashworth in the first edition of *Principles of Criminal Law* (see note 3), 24: 'The significance of welfare is that it is not a qualification or exception to the principle of autonomy but a rival.' The claim was toned down in Ashworth's second edition (see note 14) at 28–9, but its spirit still pervades the book.

64 The distinction was introduced in my 'Rationality and the Rule of Law in Offences Against the Person', *Cambridge Law Journal* 53 (1994), 502 at 512ff, where the points that follow were explored in more detail.

65 Horder, 'Rethinking Non-Fatal Offences Against the Person', *Oxford Journal of Legal Studies* 14 (1994), 335.

66 This depends, of course, on where the action of 'causing death' fits into the contrast between 'killing' and 'doing something with fatal consequences.' In the passages cited in note 21, Lewis and Hornsby seem to take contrasting positions on this point.

67 Cf. Peter Glazebrook, 'Thief or Swindler: Who Cares?', *Cambridge Law Journal* 50 (1991), 389, where a harm-oriented understanding of theft and obtaining by deception leads to a claim that any difference between them must be morally insignificant.

68 I discussed the last example in 'Rationality and the Rule of Law in Offences Against the Person' (see note 64), at 507ff.

69 A conclusion that would put me very much in sympathy with the fragmenting or destabilising thrust of Alan Norrie's argument in his *Crime, Reason and History* (see note 7), although simultaneously opposed to his interpretation of that argument as a challenge to the criminal law's claim to be rational and principled. For the record, that is indeed my position.

Index

Bare bibliographical citations, and self-citations, have not been indexed.